Trailblazer

Last Minute Guide

CHEMISTRY

for

CBSE XII

Archana Sharma

M.K. Sharma
(Co-Editor)

UNICORN BOOKS

Publisher
UNICORN BOOKS
F-2/16, Ansari Road, Daryaganj, New Delhi-110002
E-mail: info@unicornbooks.in • Website: www.unicornbooks.in
☎ 011-23275434, 23262683

Branch : Mumbai
23-25, Zaoba Wadi Thakurdwar, Mumbai-400002
☎ 022-22010941, 022-22053387
E-mail: rapidex@bom5.vsnl.net.in

Showroom :
★ **PM Publications, New Delhi**
- 10-B, Netaji Subhash Marg, Daryaganj, New Delhi-110002
- 6686, Khari Baoli, Delhi-110006

Distributors :
★ **Pustak Mahal**

Bengaluru: ☎ 080-22234025

Patna: ☎ 0612-3294193

★ **V & S Publishers, Hyderabad**

☎ 040-24737290

ISBN 978-81-7806-296-9

Edition: January, 2012

Printed at : *Param Offsetters, Okhla, New Delhi-110020*

Preface

This TRAILBLAZER Series presents CBSE plus-2 preparatory materials for exam preparation, which includes everything that students need to pass the exams with flying colours. This is a unique solution series which is intended to be the most valuable guide to enable the students brush up the concepts.

The series comprises four subjects — Maths, Physics, Chemistry, and Biology.

UNIQUE FEATURES

- The Series is based on the latest CBSE prescribed Exam Blue Print.
- All the chapters have been designed in Q & A format as per guidelines of CBSE.
- Each chapter contains three sections, such as VSA (Very Short Answer), SA-I & SA-II (Short Answer I & II) and LA (Long Answer).
- At the end of each chapter is a – NUTSHEET (MIND MAP) it includes flow charts.
- HOTS questions at the end of each chapter are given to enhance thought process of the students.
- Previous year's questions papers have been included along with solved Mock Sample Question Papers.

Students are advised to prepare themselves strictly following the CBSE question papers. The answers have been outlined in a very simple language and kept up to the mark as per the requirement of the questions.

This Book is prima facie an essential and useful compendium for all students aspiring to secure high marks in the exams.

Any suggestions, comments and criticisms from the students & teachers towards improving the book will be highly appreciated.

The Publisher

Content

Preface

Blue Print-I,II and III

Design of the Question Paper

1. Solid State 1
2. Solutions 13
3. Electrochemistry 35
4. Chemical Kinetics 58
5. Surface Chemistry 80
6. General Principles and Processes of Isolation of Elements 90
7. The *p*-block Elements 98
8. The *d*- and *f*-block Elements 108
9. Coordination Compounds 118
10. Haloalkanes and Haloarenes 127
11. Alcohols, Phenols and Ethers 142
12. Aldehydes, Ketones and Carboxylic Acids 159
13. Organic Compounds Containing Nitrogen 177
14. Biomolecules 193
15. Polymers 206
16. Chemistry in Everyday Life 217

Mock Test Paper-I 224

Mock Test Paper-II 228

Mock Test Paper-III 231

Solved Sample Paper-I 234

Solved Sample Paper-II 246

Solved Sample Paper-III 259-272

CBSE Papers ..... *(i - xii)*

Sample Question Paper- I

CHEMISTRY

BLUE PRINT

CLASS - XII

Time Allowed : 3 Hrs **Maximum Marks : 70**

S.R.	UNIT	VSA (1)	SAI(2)	SA II(3)	LA (5)	TOTAL
1	Solid State		4(2)			4 (2)
2	Solutions				5 (1)	5 (1)
3	Electrochemistry		2(1)	3(1)		5 (2)
4	Chemical Kinetics	1(1)	4(2)			5 (3)
5	Surface Chemistry	1(1)		3(1)		4 (2)
6	General Principles and processes of isolation of elements			3(1)		3 (1)
7	p-block elements	1(1)	4 (2)	3 (1)		8 (4)
8	d & f- block elements				5 (1)	5 (1)
9	Co-ordination Compounds	1 (1)	2 (1)			3 (2)
10	Haloalkanes and haloarenes	1 (1)		3 (1)		4(2)
11	Alcohols, Phenols & Ethers	1 (1)		3 (1)		4(2)
12	Aldehydes, Ketones & Carboxylic Acids	1 (1)			5 (1)	6 (2)
13	Organic compounds containing Nitrogen		4 (2)			4 (2)
14	Biomolecules	1 (1)		3 (1)		4 (2)
15	Polymers			3 (1)		3 (1)
16	Chemistry in everyday life			3 (1)		3 (1)
	TOTAL:	**8 (8)**	**20(10)**	**27(9)**	**15(3)**	**70(30)**

DESIGN

S No.	Type of Question	Marks for each Question	No. of Questions	Total Marks
1.	Long Answers (LA)	5	3	15
2.	Short Answers-II (SA II)	3	9	27
3.	Short Answers-I (SA-I)	2	10	20
4.	Very Short Answer (VSA)	1	08	08
	Total		**30**	**70**

Sample Question Paper-II

CHEMISTRY

BLUE PRINT

CLASS - XII

Time Allowed : 3 Hrs **Maximum Marks : 70**

S.R.	UNIT	VSA	S.A. I	S.A. II	L.A.	TOTAL
		(1)	(2)	(3)	(5)	
1	Solid State		4(2)		-	4(2)
2	Solutions	-	2(1)	3(1)	-	5(2)
3	Electrochemistry		2(1)	3(1)	-	5(2)
4	Chemical Kinetics	-	-	-	5(1)	5(1)
5	Surface Chemistry	1(1)		3(1)	-	4(2)
6	General Principles and Processes of Extraction of Elements	1(1)	2(1)	-	-	3(2)
7	p- Block Elements	1(1)	2(1)	-	5(1)	8(3)
8	d- and f- Block Elements	-	2(1)	3(1)	-	5(2)
9	Coordination Compounds	-	-	3(1)	-	3(1)
10	Haloalkanes and Haloarenes	2 (2)	2(1)	-	-	4(3)
11	Alcohols ,Phenols & Ethers	1(1)	-	3(1)	-	4(2)
12	Aldehydes,ketones and Carboxylic Acids	1(1)	-	-	5(1)	6(2)
13	Organic Compounds Containing Nitrogen		4 (2)	-	-	4(2)
14	Biomolecules	1(1)	-	3(1)	-	4(2)
15	Polymers			3(1)	-	3(1)
16	Chemistry in everyday Life	-	-	3(1)	-	3(1)
	Total	**8 (8)**	**20(10)**	**27(9)**	**15(3)**	**70(30)**

DESIGN

S No.	Type of Question	Marks for each Question	No. of Questions	Total Marks
1.	Long Answers (LA)	5	3	15
2.	Short Answers-II (SA II)	3	9	27
3.	Short Answers-I (SA-I)	2	10	20
4.	Very Short Answer (VSA)	1	08	08
	Total		**30**	**70**

Sample Question Paper - III

CHEMISTRY

BLUE PRINT

CLASS - XII

Time Allowed : 3 Hrs **Maximum Marks : 70**

S.R.	UNIT	VSA(1)	SA I	SA II	LA	TOTAL
1	Solid State		4(2)			4(2)
2	Solutions	1(1)	4(2)			5(3)
3	Electrochemistry				5(1)	5(1)
4	Chemical Kinetics		2(1)	3(1)		5(2)
5	Surface Chemistry	1(1)		3(1)		4(2)
6	General Principles and Processes of Extraction of Elements	1(1)	2(1)			3(2)
7	p- Block Elements		2(1)	6(2)		8(3)
8	d- and f- Block Elements				5(1)	5(1)
9	Coordination Compounds	1(1)	2(1)			3(2)
10	Haloalkanes and Haloarenes		4(2)			4(2)
11	Alcohols,Phenols & Ethers	1(1)		3(1)		4(2)
12	Aldehydes,ketones and Carboxylic Acids	1(1)			5(1)	6(2)
13	Organic Compounds Containing Nitrogen	1(1)		3(1)		4(2)
14	Biomolecules	1(1)		3(1)		4(2)
15	Polymers			3(1)		3(1)
16	Chemistry in Everyday Life			3(1)		3(1)
	Total	**8(8))**	**20(10)**	**27(9)**	**15(3)**	**70(30)**

DESIGN

S No.	Type of Question	Marks for each Question	No. of Questions	Total Marks
1.	Long Answers (LA)	5	3	15
2.	Short Answers-II (SA II)	3	9	27
3.	Short Answers-I (SA-I)	2	10	20
4.	Very Short Answer (VSA)	1	08	08
	Total		**30**	**70**

CHAPTER

1 SOLID STATE

Syllabus

- *Classification of solids based on different binding forces : molecular, ionic, covalent and metallic solids, amorphous and crystalline solids (elementary idea), crystal lattices and unit cells, calculation of density of unit cell, packing in solids, voids, number of atoms per unit cell in a cubic unit cell, point defects, electrical and magnetic properties.*

TYPES OF CUBIC CRYSTALS AND NUMBER OF ATOMS PER UNIT CELL

The contribution of each atom to the unit cell is :

at corner = $\frac{1}{8}$; at the face = $\frac{1}{2}$; within the body = 1

1. **Simple or Primitive cubic unit cell :** In this unit cell, the points are present at all the corners of a cube. Atom present at each corner contributes 1/8 to each cube because it is shared by 8 cubes.

   The number of atoms present in each unit cell = 8 corner atoms × $\frac{1}{8}$ atom per unit cell

   $$= 1 \text{ atom}$$

2. **Body centred cubic unit cell :** It has points at all the corners as well as at the body centre of the cube.

   The number of atoms present at the corners per unit cell

   $$= 8 \text{ corner atoms} \times \frac{1}{8} \text{ atom per unit cell} = 1$$

   The number of atoms present at the centre of the cube = 1

   ∴ Total number of atoms in bcc arrangement = $1 + 1 = 2$

3. **Face centred cubic unit cell :** It has points at all the corners as well as at the centre of each of the six faces.

   The number of atoms present at corners per unit cell

   $$= 8 \text{ corner atoms} \times \frac{1}{8} \text{ atom per unit cell} = 1$$

   Number of atoms present at faces per unit cell

   $$= 6 \text{ atoms at the faces} \times \frac{1}{2} \text{ atom per unit cell} = 3$$

   ∴ Total number of atoms in ccp or fcc arrangement = $1+3=4$.

Packing Fraction in the Unit Cells

The fraction of the total volume of the unit cell occupied by the atoms present in it is called packing fraction.

(1) Simple cubic unit cell

A simple cubic unit cell contains only one atom and Corner spheres touch each other. Edge length of the cube will be 2 R.

$$\text{Total volume of unit cell} = (2R)^3 = 8R^3$$

$$\text{Volume occupied} = \frac{4}{3}\pi R^3$$

$$\text{\% of occupied space} = \frac{\frac{4}{3}\pi R^3}{8R^3} \times 100 = 52.4\%$$

Hence, the percentage of the occupied space = 52.4%
and, the percentage of unoccupied (empty) space = 100 – 52.4 = 47.6 %.

(2) Body-centred unit cell

A body-centred cubic unit cell contains 2 atoms. If r is the radius of an atom, the volume occupied by two atoms

$$= 2 \times \frac{4}{3} \text{p} r^3 = \frac{8}{3} \text{p} r^3 \qquad ..(i)$$

$$\text{Volume of cubic unit cell} = \frac{64}{3\sqrt{3}} R^3$$

Therefore, $$\text{\% of occupied space} = \frac{\frac{8}{3}\pi R^3}{\frac{64}{3\sqrt{3}} R^3} \times 100 = \frac{8\sqrt{3}}{64} \times 3.14 \times 100 = 68\%$$

Volume of free space = 22%.

Hence, the percentage of the occupied space = 68%
and the percentage of unoccupied (empty) space = 100 – 68 = 32 %

(3) Face-centred unit cell

A face-centred cubic unit cell contains 4 atoms. If r is the radius of an atom, the volume occupied by 4 atoms

$$= 4 \times \frac{4}{3} \pi r^3 = \frac{16}{3} \pi r^3 \qquad ...(i)$$

$$\therefore \qquad a = \frac{4}{\sqrt{2}} r$$

$$\text{The volume of the unit cell} = a^3 = \left(\frac{4}{\sqrt{2}} r\right)^3 = \frac{64 r^3}{2\sqrt{2}}$$

$$\therefore \qquad \text{Packing fraction} = \frac{\text{Volume occupied by atoms}}{\text{Volume of unit cell}} = \frac{\frac{16}{3}\pi r^3}{\frac{64 r^3}{2\sqrt{2}}} = \frac{\sqrt{2}\pi}{6} = 0.74$$

Hence, the percentage of the occupied space = 74%
and the percentage of unoccupied (empty) space = 100 – 74 = 26 %.

Schottky defect

It arises when both the cations and anions are missing from an ideal crystal lattice in equal numbers. The essential conditions for the defect are : (i) sizes of cations and anions should be comparable and (ii) coordination number should be high. Alkali metal halides NaCl and CaCl show this type of defect. This defect results in the increase in electrical conductance of the crystal and decreases density.

Frenkel defect

It arises when a cation is displaced from its normal lattice site to an interstitial site. The essential conditions for this defect are : (i) size of the cation should be smaller than that of the anion and (ii) coordination number should be low. Examples are AgCl, AgBr, ZnS. In this defect, density remains same, lattice energy decreases, conductance increases and dielectric constant also increases.

Piezoelectricity

Certain crystals, e.g. quartz, lead zironate etc. under mechanical strees show alignment of dipoles and produce net dipole moment and this produces electricity.

Pyroelectricity

The property of acquiring electric charges on opposite faces when certain piezoelectric crystal is heated.

Diamagnetism

The property by which a substance is weakly repelled by a magnetic field. For example, benzene, NaCl, TiO_2 etc.

Paramagnetism

The property by which substance is attached by a magnetic field. Examples of compounds showing paramagnetism are O_2, Cu^{2+}, Fe^{3+} etc.

Ferromagnetism

A substance which in solid state only exhibits unusually large paramagnetism and shows permanent magnetism even in the absence of an applied magnetic field is called ferromagnetic substance. Examples are Fe, Ni, CO, CrO, CrO_2, Fe_3O_4, Alnico.

Antiferromagnetism

A substance which exhibits much reduced paramagnetism than expected is called antiferromagnetic substance. Examples are– V_2O_3, Cr_2O_3, O_3, MnO_2, FeO, Fe_2O_3, CoO, CO_3O_4, NiO. In this case, the alignment of magnetic moments are equal and in opposite directions so that the net magnetic moment is zero.

Ferrimagnetism

A substance which exhibits fairly good paramagnetic character is called terrimagnetic substance. In ferrimagnetic substances, the alignment of magnetic moments in opposite directions are not equal. As a result, the substance has a net magnetic moment. Examples are: Fe_2O_3, ferrites.

IMPORTANT FORMULAE AND RELATIONSHIPS

1. Relationship between nearest neighbour distance of an element (d) with edge length (a) of unit cell and radius of atom.

(a) In **simple cubic,** $d = a = 2r, r = \frac{a}{2}$

(b) In **body-centred cubic,** $d = 2r = \frac{\sqrt{3}\,a}{2}, r = \frac{\sqrt{3}\,a}{4}$ for bcc element

(c) In **face-centred cubic,** $d = 2r = \frac{a}{\sqrt{2}}, r = \frac{a}{2\sqrt{2}}$ for fcc element

where, 'd' is distance between nearest neighbours.

2. **For octahedral void :** Radius of octahedral void $(r) = 0.414 \times$ Radius of the atom (R).
3. **For tetrahedral void :** $r = 0.225\,R$
4. **For cubic void :** $r = 0.73\,R$
5. **Density of the unit cell** $= \frac{Z \times m}{a^3 \times N_A}$

where, Z is rank of unit cell (no. of atoms per unit cell), M is molar mass, 'a' is edge length of the cube, a^3 is volume of cube, N_A is Avogadro's number.

Type 1.

Numerical Problems

1. Cr has mono atomic body-centred cubic structure. Its cell edge is 300 pm. What is its density? Atomic mass of Cr = 52, $N_A = 6.023 \times 10^{23}$.

Solution :

For *bcc* element, $Z = 2$, $a = 300 \times 10^{-10}$ cm, $M = 52$ g mol^{-1}, $N_A = 6.023 \times 10^{23}$, $d = ?$

For a cubic crystal, density is given by,

$$d = \frac{Z\,m}{a^3 N_A} = \frac{2 \times 52}{(300 \times 10^{-10})^3 \times 6.023 \times 10^{23}} = 6.39 \text{ g cm}^{-3}.$$

2. An element of atomic mass 98.5 g mol^{-1} occurs in fcc structure. If its unit cell edge length is 500 pm and its density is 5.22 g cm^{-3}, what will be the value of Avogadro's constant ?

Solution :

For fcc structure, $Z = 4$, atomic mass $M = 98.5$ g mol^{-1}, $a = 500 \times 10^{-10}$ cm,
$d = 5.22$ g/ cm^3, $N_A = ?$

Density of a cubic unit cell, $d = \frac{Z\,M}{a^3 N_A}$

$\therefore$ $N_A = \frac{Z\,M}{a^3 d}$

Value of Avogadro's Constant, $N_A = \frac{4 \times 98.5}{(500 \times 10^{-10})^3 \times 5.22} = \frac{394}{125 \times 10^{-24} \times 5.22}$

$= 0.603 \times 10^{24} = 6.03 \times 10^{23}$

3. An element A crystallises in fcc structure. 200 g of this element has 4.12×10^4 atoms. The density of A is 7.2 g cm^{-3}. Calculate the edge length of the unit cell.

Solution :

For fcc structure, $Z = 4, m = 200$ g, $d = 7.2$ g cm^{-3}, $a = ?$

We know that density, $d = \dfrac{ZM}{a^3 \times N_A \times 10^{-30}}$

$$a^3 = \frac{ZM}{d \times N_A \times 10^{-30}} = \frac{4 \times 200}{7.2 \times 4.12 \times 10^{24} \times 10^{-30}} = 27 \times 10^6 \text{ pm}^3$$

Edge length, $a = (27 \times 10^6)^{1/3}$ pm $= 300$ pm

4. Gold (atomic radius = 0.144 nm) crystallises in a face-centred unit cell. What is the length of a side of the cell ?

Solution :

Given : radius, $r = 0.144$ nm; unit cell is fcc,
edge of unit cell, $a = ?$

In face centred unit cell, diagonal of face $= 4r = a\sqrt{2}$ ($\because$ face diagonal $= a\sqrt{2}$)

$$\therefore \qquad a = \frac{4r}{\sqrt{2}} = \sqrt{2}\,r = 2 \times 1.4142 \times 0.144 \text{ nm} = 0.4073 \text{ nm}$$

Length of side of unit cell, $a =$ **0.4073**

Self-Evaluation Numericals

1. An element A crystallises in fcc structure. 200 g of this element has 4.12×10^{24} atoms. The density of A is 7.2 g cm^{-3}. Calculate the edge length of the unit cell. **[Ans. 299.8 pm]**
2. Unit cell of an element (atomic mass 108 u and density 10.5 g cm^{-3}) has an edge length 409 pm. Deduce the type of crystal lattice. [$N_A = 6.02 \times 10^{23}$] **[Ans. $Z = 4$ fcc]**
3. An element A crystallises in fcc structure, 208 g of this element has 4.283×10^{24} atoms. If edge length of the unit cell of this element is 408 pm, calculate its density. **[Ans. 2.86 g cm^{-3}]**
4. A metallic element exists as body-centred cubic lattice. Each edge of the unit cell is 288 pm. The density of metal is 7.2 g cm^{-3}. How many atoms and unit cells are there in 100 g of the metal ? **[Ans. 1.1632×10^{24}, 5.816×10^{23}]**
5. A metal (atomic mass = 50) has a body-centred cubic crystal lattice. The density of the metal is 5.91 g cm^{-3}. Find out the volume of the unit cell. [$N_A = 6.023 \times 10^{23}$] **[Ans. 2.809×10^{-23} cm^3]**

Type 2.

Structure Base Numericals

1. If three elements P, Q and R crystallise in a cubic unit cell with P atoms at the corners, Q atoms at the cubic centre and R atoms at the centre of each face of the cube, then write the formula of the compound.

Solution :

Contribution made by the atoms of P present at all the eight corners of the tube $= 1/8 \times 8 = 1$
Contribution made by the atoms of Q present in the centre of the body $= 1$
Contribution made by the atoms of R present at the centre of all the six faces $= 1/2 \times 6 = 3$
$\therefore$ Formula of the compound $= PQR_3$.

2. In naturally occurring corrundom, the oxide ions form the hexagonal close packing and aluminium ions occupy 2/3rd of the octahedral voids. What is the formula of corrundum?

Solution :

Let the number of oxide ions = 60

Number of Al^{3+} ions = 2/3 × No. of octahedral voids = 2/3 × 60 = 40

The ratio of Al^{3+} ions to O^{2-} ions = 40 : 60 = 2 : 3

∴ Formula of the compound = Al_2O_3

3. In a crystalline solid, the atoms A and B are arranged as follows :

(a) Atoms A are arranged in ccp array.

(b) Atoms B occupy all the octahedral voids and half of the tetrahedral voids. What is the formula of the compound ?

Solution :

We know that in a close packing, the number of octahedral voids is equal to the number of atoms and number of tetrahedral voids is twice the number of atoms. As all the octahedral voids and half the tetrahedral voids are occupied, this means that :

(i) there will be one atom of *B* in the tetrahedral voids

(ii) there will be one atom of *B* in the octahedral void.

Thus, there will be two atoms of *B* corresponding to each atom of A. Hence, the formula of solid = AB_2.

4. Compound is formed by two elements *X* and *Y*. Atoms of the element *Y* (as anions) make ccp and those of the element *X* (as cations) occupy all the octahedral voids. What is the formula of the compound ?

Solution :

Suppose number of atoms *Y* in ccp = *n*

As number of octahedral voids = No. of atoms in ccp

∴ No. of octahedral voids = *n*

As all the octahedral voids are occupied by atoms *X*, therefore, number of atoms *X* = *n*.

∴ Ratio of $X : Y = n : n = 1 : 1$

Hence, the formula of the compound is *XY*.

5. Atoms of element B form hcp lattice and those of the element A occupy 2/3rd of tetrahedral voids. What is the formula of the compound formed by these elements A and B ?

Solution :

Suppose number of atoms *B* in hcp lattice = *n*

As number of tetrahedral voids is double the number of atoms in the close packing, therefore, number of tetrahedral voids = 2*n*

As atoms *A* occupy 2/3rd of the tetrahedral voids, therefore, number of atoms *A* in the lattice

$$= \frac{2}{3} \times 2n = \frac{4n}{3}$$

$$\therefore \quad \text{Ratio of } A : B = \frac{4n}{3} : n = \frac{4}{3} : 1 = 4 : 3$$

Hence, the formula of the compound **A_4B_3**.

Self-Evaluation Numericals

1. A compound is formed by two element X and Y. Atoms of element Y (as anions) make ccp and those of the element X (as cations) occupy all the octahedral viods. What is the formula of the compound. **[Ans.** XY]
2. A compound is formed by two elements M and N. The element N forms ccp and M atom occupy 1/3rd of the tetrahedral voids. What is the formula of the compound ? **[Ans.** M_2N_3]
3. In a solid, oxide ions are arranged in ccp. One-sixth of the tetrahedral voids are occupied by the cations A and one-third of the octahedral voids are occupied by the cations B. What is the formula of the compound ? **[Ans.** ABO_3]

Type 3

1. Analysis shows that nickel oxide has formula $Ni_{0.98}O_{1.00}$. What fractions of the nickel exist as Ni^{2+} and Ni^{3+} ?

Solution :

Let Ni^{2+} be x so that Ni^{3+} will be $0.98-x$. Total charge on the compound must be zero so that,

$$+2x+3(0.98-x)-2=0$$

$$2x+2.94-3x-2=0$$

$$-x=-0.94 \quad \text{or} \quad x=0.94$$

$$\%\text{ of } Ni^{2+} = \frac{0.94}{0.98}\times 100 = 96\%$$

$$\%\text{ of } Ni^{3+} = \mathbf{4\%}$$

2. Analysis shows that a metal oxide has the empirical formula of $M_{0.96}O_{1.00}$. Calculate the percentage of M^{2+} and M^{3+} ions in this crystal.

Solution :

The formula $M_{0.96}O_{1.00}$ shows that M : O = 0.96 : 1.00 = 96 : 100

Thus, if there are 100 O-atoms, then M atoms = 96.

Change on 100 O^{2-} ions = 100 × (–2) = – 200

Suppose M atoms as $M^{2+} = x$.

Then M atoms as $M^{3+} = 96-x$

Total charge on M^{2+} and $M^{3+} = (+2)x + (+3)(96-x) = (288-x)$

As metal oxide is neutral, total charge on cations = total charge on anions.

$$\therefore \quad (288-x)=200 \quad \text{or} \quad x=88$$

$$\therefore \quad \%\text{ of } M \text{ as } M^{2+} = \frac{88}{96}\times 100 = \mathbf{91.7\%}$$

$$\%\text{ of } M \text{ as } M^{3+} = 100-91.7 = \mathbf{8.3\ \%}$$

3. The composition of a sample of Wustite is $Fe_{0.93}\,O_{1.00}$. What percentage of iron is present in the form of Fe(III) ?

Solution :

The ratio of the Fe and O atoms in pure iron oxide (FeO) = 1 : 1

Let x atoms of Fe(II) be replaced by Fe(III) in Wustite.

$\therefore$ No. of Fe(II) atoms present = $(0.93-x)$

Since the oxide is neutral,

Total charge on iron atoms = Charge on oxygen atom

$$2(0.93-x) \div 3x = 2\ ;\ 1.86-2x+3x=2$$

$$x = 2 - 1.86 = 0.14$$

$$\% \text{ of iron(III) in Wustite} = \frac{\text{No. of Fe(III) atoms}}{\text{Total no. of Fe atoms}} \times 100 = \frac{0.14}{0.93} \times 100 = \mathbf{15.05\%}$$

Very Short Answer Type Questions

Q. 1. Give three examples of amorphous solids.

Ans. Glass, rubber and plastics.

Q. 2. How many atoms are present in the unit cell of (*a*) simple cubic lattice (*b*) BCC (*c*) FCC?

Ans. (*a*) 1 (*b*) 2 (*c*) 4

Q. 3. What are interstitials in a crystal?

Ans. Atoms or ions that fill the normal vacant interstitial voids in a crystal are called interstitials.

Q. 4. What is the effect of the presence of schottky. Defects on the density of a crystal?

Ans. The density of the crystal decreases.

Q. 5. What is the coordination number of Na^+ and Cl^- ions in NaCl structure?

Ans. Six.

Q. 6. Name the type of point defect that occurs in a crystal of ZnS.

Ans. Frenkel defect.

Q. 7. How many octahedral voids are there in 1 mole of a compound having cubic close packed structure?

Ans. No. of octahedral voids = No. of atoms in the packing = 1 mole = 6.02×10^{23}.

Q. 8. Find out the number of atoms per unit cell in a face-centred cubic structure having only single atoms at the lattice points.

Ans. For fcc, number of atoms per unit cell =

$$\underset{\text{(corners)}}{8 \times \frac{1}{8}} + \underset{\text{(face-centres)}}{6 \times \frac{1}{2}} = 4$$

Q. 9. Why are solids rigid?

Ans. In a solid, the constituent particles are very closely packed. Hence the forces of attraction among these particles are very strong. So, they are rigid.

Q. 10. A compound is formed by two elements M and N. The element N forms ccp and atoms of M occupy $^1/_3$rd of tetrahedral voids. What is the formula of the compound?

Ans. Suppose the atoms in the ccp = h

$\therefore$ No of tetrahedral voids = $2h$

On-third of the tetrahedral voids are occupied by atoms M, therefore, number of atoms:

$$M = \frac{2n}{3}$$

$\therefore$ Ratio of M : N = $\frac{2n}{3} : n = 2 : 3$

Hence the formula is M_2N_3.

Q. 11. What type of stoichiometric defect is shown by: (*i*) ZnS (*ii*) AgBr?

Ans. (*i*) ZnS shows Frenkel defect because its ions have a large difference in size.

(*ii*) AgBr shown both Frenkel and Schottky defects.

Q. 12. Distinguish between:

(*i*) Hexagonal and monoclinic unit cells.

(*ii*) Face-centred and end-centred unit cells.

Ans. (*i*) For hexagonal unit cell,

$$a = b \neq c,\ \alpha = \beta = 90°,\ \gamma = 120°$$

For monoclinic unit cell,

$$a \neq b \neq c,\ \alpha = \gamma = 90°,\ \beta \neq 90°.$$

(*ii*) A face-centred unit cell has one constituent particle present at the centre of each face in addition of the particles present at the corners.

An end-centred unit cell has one constituent particle each at the centre of any two opposite faces in addition to the particles present at the corners.

Short Answer Type Questions

Q. 1. Describe the term 'amorphous'. Give a few examples of amorphous solids.

Ans. Amorphous solids are those solids in which the constituent particle may have short range order but do not have a long range order. They do not have sharp melting points or definite heats of fusion. *Example : Glass, plastic, rubber, etc.*

Q. 2. Silver crystallises in fcc lattice. If the length of the cell is 4.077×10^{-8} cm and density is 10.5 g cm^{-3}, calculate the atomic mass of silver.

Ans. Given value

$$P = 10.5 \text{ g cm}^{-3}, a = 4.077 \times 10^{-8} \text{ cm}$$

$$No = 6.02 \times 10^{23} \text{ mol}^{-1}, z = 4$$

$$M = \frac{P \times a^3 \times No}{Z}$$

$$= \frac{10.5 \text{ g cm}^{-3} \times (4.077 \times 10^{-8} \text{ cm})^3 \times (6.02 \times 10^{23} \text{ mol}^{-1})}{4}$$

$$= 107.09 \text{ g mol}^{-1}.$$

Q. 3. How many lattice points are there in one unit cell of each of the following lattices?

(*i*) Face-centred cubic (*ii*) Face-centred tetragonal (*iii*) Body-centred cubic

Ans. Lattice points in face-centred cubic or face-centred tetragonal = 8 (at corners) + 6 (at face centres).

However, particles per unit cell $= 8 \times \frac{1}{8} + 6 \times \frac{1}{2} = 4.$

Lattice points in body centred cubic = 8 (at corners) + 1 (at body centre) = 9.

However particles per unit cell $= 8 \times \frac{1}{8} + 1 = 2.$

Q. 4. Explain:—

(*a*) The basis of similarities and differences between metallic and ionic crystals.

(*b*) Ionic crystals are hard and brittle.

Ans. (*a*) *Similarities*:

(*i*) Both ionic and metallic crystals have electrostatic forces of attraction.

(*ii*) Both have high melting point.

(*iii*) In both the cases, the bond is non-directional.

Differences:

(*i*) In ionic crystals, the ions are not free to move. Hence, they cannot conduct electricity in the solid state.

In metals, the valence electrons are free to flow. Hence they can conduct electricity in the solid state.

(*ii*) Ionic bond is strong due to electrostatic forces of attraction.
Metallic bond may be weak or strong depending upon the number of valence electrons and size of the kernels.

(*b*) Ionic crystals are hard because there are strong electrostatic forces of attraction among the oppositely charged ions. They are brittle because ionic bond is non-directional.

Q. 5. Copper crystallizes into a fcc lattice with edge length 3.61×10^{-8} cm. Show that the calculated density is in agreement with its measured value of 8.92 g cm^{-3}.

Ans. Given value—

$$Z = 4$$

Atomic mass of copper, $M = 63.5 \text{ g mol}^{-1}$

$$a = 3.61 \times 10^{-8} \text{ cm}$$

$$No = 6.022 \times 10^{23} \text{ mol}^{-1}$$

$$\therefore \quad P = \frac{Z \times M}{a^3 \times No}$$

$$= \frac{4 \times 63.5 \text{ g mol}^{-1}}{(3.61 \times 10^{-8} \text{ cm})^3 \times (6.022 \times 10^{23} \text{ mol}^{-1})} = 8.97 \text{ g cm}^{-3}.$$

Q. 6. What is 'semiconductor'? Describe the two main types of semiconductors and contrast their conduction mechanisms.

Ans. Substances whose conductance lies in between that of metals and insulators are called semiconductors.
Two main types of semiconductors are *n*-type and *p*-type.

Q. 7. Gold (atomic radius = 0.144 nm) crystallises in face-centred unit cell. What is the length of the side of the cell.

Ans. Given value—

$$r = 0.144 \text{ nm}$$

$$a = ?$$

For fcc, $a = 2\sqrt{2}r$

$$= 2 \times 1.414 \times 0.144$$

$$= 0.407 \text{ nm}$$

Q. 8. Aluminium crystallises in a cubic close packed structure. Its metallic radius is 125 pm.
(*i*) What is the length of the side of the unit cell?
(*ii*) How many unit cells are there in 1.00 cm^3 of aluminium?

Ans. (*i*) ccp = fcc

For fcc, $a = 2\sqrt{2}r$

$$= 2 \times 4.414 \times 125 \text{ pm}$$

$$= 354 \text{ pm}$$

(*ii*) Volume of one unit cell $= (354 \times 10^{-10} \text{ cm})^3$

$$= 4.44 \times 10^{-23} \text{ cm}^3$$

Unit cells in $1 \text{ cm}^3 = \dfrac{1}{4.44 \times 10^{-29}}$

$$= 2.25 \times 10^{22}.$$

Q. 9. Non-stoichiometric cuprous oxide, Cu_2O can be prepared in the laboratory. In this oxide, copper to oxygen ratio is slightly less than 2:1. Can you account for the fact that this substance is a p-type semiconductor.

Ans. The ratio less than 2:1 in Cu_2O shows that some cuprous (Cu^+) ions have been replaced by cupric (Cu^{2+}) ions. To maintain electrical neutrality, every two Cu^+ ions will be replaced by one Cu^{2+} ion thereby creating a hole. As conduction will be due to presence of these positive holes, hence it is a *p*-type semiconductor.

Q. 10. Classify each of the following as being either a p-type or n-type semiconductor:—
(*i*) Ge doped with In (*ii*) *B* doped with Si

Ans. (*i*) Ge is group 14 element and In is group 13 element. Hence an electron deficit hole is created and therefore, it is p-type.

(*ii*) *B* is group 13 element and Si is group 14 elements there will be a free electron. Hence, it is n-type.

Long Answer Type Questions

Q. 1. Explain the following terms with suitable examples :
(*i*) Schottky defect (*ii*) Frenkel defect (*iii*) Interstitials (*iv*) F-centres

Ans. (*i*) *Schottky defect* : If in an ionic crystal of the type $A^+ B^-$, equal number of cations and anions are missing from their lattice sites so that the electrical neutrality is maintained, it is called schottky defect.

Types of compounds exhibiting schottky defects : This type of defect is shown by highly ionic compounds which have—
(*i*) high coordination number.
(*ii*) small difference in the size of cations and anions.
For examples—NaCl, KCl, KBr, CrCl etc.

(*ii*) *Frenkel defect*—If an ion is missing from its lattice site and occupies the interstitial site, electrical neutrality as well as the stoichiometry of the compound are maintained. This type of defect is called *Frenkel defect.*

Types of compounds exhibiting Frenkel defects—This type of defect is present in those compounds which have —
(*i*) low coordination number.
(*ii*) large difference in the size of cations and anions.
For example—AgCl, AgBr, AgI, ZnS due to small size of Ag^+ ion and Zn^{+2} ions.

(*iii*) *Interstitials* : Atoms or ions that fill the normal vacant interstitials voids in a crystal are called interstitials.

(*iv*) *F-centres* : The site where electron is entrapped in the anion vacancy is called F-centre.

Q. 2. Explain the following with suitable examples :
(*i*) Ferromagnetism (*ii*) Paramagnetism
(*iii*) Ferrimagnetism (*iv*) Antiferramagnetism

Ans. (*i*) *Ferromagnetism* : Substances which show permanent magnetism even in the absence of the magnetic field are called ferromagnetic substances. For example : Fe, Ni, Co, Gd and CrO_2 etc.

(*ii*) *Paramagnetism* : Substances which are attracted by the external magnetic field are called paramagnetic substances. For example, O_2, Cu^{2+}, Fe^{3+}, and Cr^{3+}.

(*iii*) *Ferrimagnetism* : Substances which are expected to possess large magnetism on the basis of the magnetic moments of the domains but actually have small net magnetic moment are called ferrimagnetism substances, e.g. Fe_3O_4, Cu, Zn etc.

(*iv*) *Anti-ferramagnetism* : Substances which are expected to possess paramagnetism or ferromagnetism on the basis of magnetic moments of the domains but actually they possess zero net magnetic moment are called anti-ferromagnetic substances. For example, MnO.

Q. 3. In terms of bond theory, what is the difference :

(i) betweeen a conduction and an insulation.

(ii) between a conduction and a semiconductor ?

Ans. (i) The energy gap between the valence bond and conduction bond in an insulator is very large whereas in a conductor, the energy gap is very small or there is overlapping between valence bond and conduction bond.

(ii) In a conductor, there is very small gap or there is overlapping between valence bond and conduction bond but in a semiconductor there is always energy gap between them.

Q. 4. Silver from ccp lattice and x-ray studies of its Gystals show that the edge length of its unit cell is 408.6 pm. Calculate the denity of silver (Atomic mass = 107.94).

Ans. For ccp lattice, $z = 4$ atoms/unit cell, $m = 107.9 \text{ g mol}^{-1}, a = 408.6 \text{ pm} = 408.6 \times 10^{-12}\text{cm}$

$$\therefore \quad P = \frac{4 \times 107.9}{408.6 \times 10^{-12} \times 6.22 \times 10^{23}} = 10.5 \text{ g cm}^{-3}.$$

Higher Order Thinking Skills — Hots Questions

1. Why is melting point of crystalline solid is sharp whereas amorphous solid is not?
2. Why does electrical conductivity in most of the metals decrease with increase in temperature?
3. What is the effect of the presence of Schottky defects on the density of a crystal?
4. (*a*) Calculate the packing efficiency in fcc crystal.
   (*b*) How many octahedral voids are present in fcc crystal?
5. An element crystallines in fcc structure. Its density is 7.2 g cm^{-3}. 208 g of this element has 4.283×10^{24} atoms. Calculate the edge length of unit cell.
6. Example each of the following with a suitable example :
   (i) Paramagnetism
   (ii) Frenkel defect in crystals
7. An element crystallises in fcc structure. Its density is 7.2 g cm^{-3}. 208 g of this element has 4.283×10^{24} atoms. Calculate the edge length of the unit cell. **[Ans. 300 pm]**
8. A metal (atomic mass = 50) has a body-centred cubic crystal lattice. The density of the metal is 5.91 g cm^{-3}. Find out the volume of the unit cell. [$N_A = 6.023 \times 10^{23}$] **[Ans. 2.809×10^{-23} cm³]**
9. Analysis shows that nickel oxide has formula $Ni_{0.98}O_{1.00}$. What fractions of the nickel exist as Ni^{2+} and Ni^{3+} ions ? **[Ans. Ni^{2+} = 96%, Ni^{3+} = 4%]**
10. How many latice points are there in one unit cell of each of the following lattice ?
    (a) face-centred cubic
    (b) face-centred tetragonal
    (c) body-centred cubic.
11. (a) Calculate the packing efficiency in fcc crystal.
    (b) How many octahedral voids are present in fcc crystal ?

❑❑❑

CHAPTER

2 SOLUTIONS

Syllabus

- *Types of solutions, expression of concentration of solutions of solids in liquids, solubility of gases in liquids, solid solutions, colligative properties — relative lowering of vapour pressure, elevation of boiling point, depression of freezing point, osmotic pressure, determination of molecular masses using colligative properties, abnormal molecular mass.*

1. **Henry's Law :** The law states the amount of gas dissolved (a) per unit volume of solvent is directly proportional to its pressure (P) at constant temperature, i.e.,

$$a \propto P$$

or

$$a = KP$$

where P is partial pressure of the gas over the solution and K is proportionality constant.

2. **Applications of Henry's law**
   (i) To minimise the painful effect of deep sea divers due to dissolution of more N_2 in blood when $N_2 + O_2$ mixture was used for breathing. N_2 is replaced by less soluble He.
   (ii) Haemoglobin combines with oxygen in lungs to give oxyhaemoglobin where pressure of O_2 is more and oxyhaemoglobin releases O_2 in tissues where pressure of O_2 is low. This controls cellular activities.

3. **Limitation of Henry's law**
   (i) Pressure is low. At high pressure, the law becomes less accurate and the proportionality constant shows considerable variations.
   (ii) The temperature is not too low.
   (iii) The gas is not highly soluble and
   (iv) The gas neither reacts chemically with the solvent nor dissociate or associates in the solvent.

Type 1. Numerical on the basis of Henry's law

Example 1. If N_2 gas is bubbled through water at 273 K, how many millimoles of N_2 gas would dissolve in 1 litre of water ? Assume that N_2 exerts a partial pressure of 0.987 bar. Given that Henry's law constant for N_2 at 293 K is 76.48 kbar.

Solution : The solubility of gas is related to its mole fraciton in aqueous solution.

The mole fraction of the gas in solution,

$$x_{N_2} = \frac{p_{N_2}}{K_H} = \frac{0.987 \text{ bar}}{76480 \text{ bar}} = 1.29 \times 10^{-5}$$

If n is the number of moles of N_2 in solution and 1 litre of water contains 55.5 mol. then

$$x_{N_2} = \frac{n}{n + 55.5} = \frac{n}{55.5} = 1.29 \times 10^{-5}$$

(n in the denominator is neglected because it is << 55.5)

$\therefore \quad n = 55.5 \times 1.29 \times 10^{-5} = 7.16 \times 10^{-4}$ mol

or $\quad = 7.16 \times 10^{-1}$ m mol $=$ **0.716 m mol.**

Example 2. Henry's law constant for the molarity of methane in benzene at 298 K is 4.27 × 10^5 mm Hg. Calculate the solubility of methane in benzene at 298 K under 760 mm Hg.

Solution : Here, $K_H = 4.27 \times 10^5$ mm, $p = 760$ mm

Applying Henry's law, $p = K_H x$

We have
$$x = \frac{p}{K_H} = \frac{760 \text{ mm}}{4.27 \times 10^5 \text{ mm}} = 1.78 \times 10^{-3}$$

i.e., mole fraction of methane in benzene = **1.78×10^{-3}**.

Example 3. Henry's law constant for CO_2 in water is 1.67×10^8 Pa at 298 K. Calculate the quantity of CO_2 in 500 mL of soda water when packed under 2.5 atm CO_2 pressure at 298 K.

Solution :
$$K_H = 1.67 \times 10^8 \text{ Pa}$$
$$p = 2.5 \text{ atm} = 2.5 \times 101.325 \times 10^3 \text{ Pa} = 2.533 \times 10^5 \text{ Pa}$$

Now,
$$p = K_H x_2$$

or
$$x_2 = \frac{p}{K_H} = \frac{2.533 \times 10^5 \text{ Pa}}{1.67 \times 10^8 \text{ Pa}} = 1.517 \times 10^3$$

$$\text{Moles of water} = \frac{500}{18} = 27.78$$

$$x_2 = \frac{n_2}{n_1 + n_2} = \frac{n_2}{27.78 + n_2} = 1.517 \times 10^{-3}$$

$$n_2 = 0.0419 + 0.0015\, n_2$$

or
$$0.9958\, n_2 = 0.0419$$
$$n_2 = 0.0420$$

Amount of CO_2 dissolved = 0.0420×44 = **1.85 g.**

Type 2. Concentration-based Numerical

(i) $\text{Molarity} = \dfrac{\text{No. of moles of solute}}{\text{Volume of solution in litres or dm}^3}$ $\left\{\begin{matrix} 1 \text{ cm}^3 = 1\text{mL} \\ 1 \text{ dm}^3 = 1 \text{ L} \end{matrix}\right\}$

(ii) $\text{Molality} = \dfrac{\text{No. of moles of solute}}{\text{Mass of solvent in kg}}$

(iii) $\text{Normality} = \dfrac{\text{No. of g eq. of solute}}{\text{Volume of solution in litres or dm}^3}$

(iv) Mole fraction of a component in the solution

$$= \frac{\text{No. of moles of that component}}{\text{Total number of moles of all the components}}$$

(v) Moles = $\dfrac{\text{Mass in g}}{\text{Molar mass}}$

(vi) No. of g eq. = $\dfrac{\text{Mass in g}}{\text{Eq. mass}}$

(vii) The normality equation is $N_1 \times V_1 = N_2 \times V_2$
(For duration from volume V_1 to V_2 or reaction between two reactants)

(viii) The molarity equation is $M_1 \times V_1 = M_2 \times V_2$ (For dilution from volume V_1 to V_2).

(ix) On mixing two non-reacting solutions, final normality or molarity is calculated using
$N_1V_1 + N_2V_2 = N_3V_3 \quad M_1V_1 + M_2V_2 = M_3(V_1 + V_2)$
On mixing acid and base solutions, first calculate gram equivalents neutralised. Final normality = No. of g eq. left/Total volume in L.

Example 4. Calculate the molality and mole fraction of 2.5 g of ethanoic acid (CH_3COOH) in 75 g of benzene.

Solution : Mass of solute (CH_3COOH) = 2.5 g
Mass of solvent (C_6H_6) = 75 g = 0.075 kg
Molar mass of CH_3COOH = 60 g mol^{-1}
Molar mass of C_6H_6 = 78 g mol^{-1}

Calculation of molality :

$$\text{Moles of solute } (CH_3COOH) = \frac{2.5g}{60 \text{ g mol}^{-1}} = 0.0417$$

$$\text{Molality} = \frac{\text{No. of moles of solute}}{\text{Mass of solvent in kg}} = \frac{0.0417 \text{ mol}}{0.075 \text{ kg}}$$

$$= 0.556 \text{ mol kg}^{-1}$$

Calculation of mole fraction :

$$\text{Moles of solute } (n_{CH_3COOH}) = 0.0417 \text{ (calculated above)}$$

$$\text{Moles of solvent } (n_{C_6H_6}) = \frac{75g}{78 \text{ g mol}^{-1}} = 0.961$$

$$\text{Mole fraction of } CH_3COOH \text{ in the solution} = \frac{n_{CH_3COOH}}{n_{CH_3COOH} + n_{C_6H_6}}$$

$$= \frac{0.0417}{0.0417 + 0.961} = \mathbf{0.0416}$$

Example 5. Calculate the molarity and normality of a solution containing 5 g of NaOH in 450 mL solution.

Solution : Mass of NaOH dissolved = 5 g
Volume of the solution = 450 cm^3 = 0.45 L

Calculate of molarity :

$$5 \text{ g of NaOH} = \frac{5}{40} \text{ mole of NaOH} = 0.125 \text{ mole}$$

(∵ Molar mass of NaOH = 40 g mol^{-1})

$$\text{Molarity} = \frac{\text{No. of moles of solute}}{\text{Volume of solution in litres}}$$

$$= \frac{0.125 \text{ mole}}{0.45 \text{ L}} = 0.278 \text{ mol L}^{-1}$$

Hence, molarity of the solution = **0.278 M**

Calculation of normality :

For NaOH, valence factor is 1.

So, N = molarity

⇒ N = **0.278**

Example 6. Calculate the mole fraction of ethylene glycol ($C_2H_6O_2$) and water in a solution containing 20% of $C_2H_6O_2$ by mass.

Solution : 20% of $C_2H_6O_2$ by mass means that 20 g of $C_2H_6O_2$ are present in 100 g of the solution, i.e.

Mass of solute ($C_2H_6O_2$) = 20 g

Mass of solvent (H_2O) = 100 – 20 g = 80 g

Molar mass of $C_2H_6O_2$ = 62 g mol^{-1}

Molar mass of H_2O = 18 g mol^{-1}

$$\therefore \text{No. of moles of } C_2H_6O_2 = \frac{20}{62} = 0.322$$

$$\text{No. of moles of } H_2O = \frac{80}{18} = 4.444$$

∴ Mole fraction of $C_2H_6O_2$ in the solution

$$= \frac{n_{C_2H_6O_2}}{n_{C_2H_6O_2} + n_{H_2O}} = \frac{0.322}{0.322 + 4.444} = \mathbf{0.068}$$

Mole fraction of H_2O in the solution = 1 – 0.068 = **0.932**

4. **Raoult's Law :** Partial vapour pressure of a component (*P'*) is defined as the product of vapour pressure of that component in pure state and its mole fraction in mixture.

$$\therefore \qquad P'_A = P^o_A . X_A \quad \text{and} \quad P'_B = P^o_B . X_B$$

Limitations of Raoult's law

(i) Raoult's law is applicable only to very dilute solutions.

(ii) Raoult's law is applicable to solutions containing non-volatile solute only.

(iii) Raoult's law is not applicable to solutes which dissociate or associate in the particular solution.

5. **Azeotropes :** The solutions which boil at constant temperature and can distil unchanged in composition are called **azeotropes** or **azeotropic mixtures**. The azeotropes distil over as if they were pure liquids. These types of solutions are also called **minimum boiling azeotropes**.
6. **Colligative Properties :** Certain properties of dilute solutions containing non-volatile solute depend only upon the number of particles of the solute present in the solution. Such properties are called colligative properties. Colligative properties are :

(i) Lowering of vapour pressure of the solvent.
(ii) Osmotic pressure of the solution.
(iii) Elevation in boiling point of the solvent.
(iv) Depression in freezing point of the solvent.

7. **Ideal Solutions :** The solutions which obey Raoult's law are called **ideal solutions.**
Examples : n-heptane and *n*-hexane, chlorobenzene and bromobenzene, Ethyl bromide and ethyl iodide.
Such solutions, are not accompanied by any change in enthalpy or volume, i.e.,
$$\Delta H_{mixing} = 0 \quad \text{and} \quad \Delta V_{mixing} = 0$$

8. **Non-ideal Solutions : Non-ideal solutions showing positive deviations from Raoult's law.** If the *A–B* interactions in the solutions are weaker than the *A–A* and *B–B* interactions in the two liquids forming the solution, then the escaping tendency of *A* and *B* types of molecules from the solution becomes more than from pure liquids.
Mathematically, it may be expressed as :
$$p_A > p_A^{\circ} x_A \quad \text{and} \quad p_B > p_B^{\circ} x_B$$
Non-ideal solutions exhibiting negative deviations :
1. $\Delta H_{mixing} = -ve$
2. $\Delta V_{mixing} = -ve$

Non-ideal solutions showing negative deviations from Raoult's law. In such solutions, the A–B interactions are stronger than the A–A and B–B interactions present in the two liquids forming the solution.
For such solution, $\quad p_A < p_A^{\circ} x_A \quad \text{and} \quad p_B < p_B^{\circ} x_B$
Non-ideal solutions exhibiting positive deviations :
1. P_M (observed) > P_M (from Raoult's law)
2. $\Delta H_{mixing} = +ve$
3. $\Delta V_{mixing} = +ve$

Type 3. Relative lowering in vapour pressure :

$$\frac{p^{\circ} - p_s}{p^{\circ}} = \frac{w_A \times 1000}{m_A \times w_B}$$

w_A = weight of solute, $\quad w_B$ = weight of solvent, $\quad m_A$ = mol. mass of solute

$$\text{Molality} = \frac{p^{\circ} - p_s}{p^{\circ}} \times \frac{1000}{m_B}$$

Relative lowering in vapour pressure $\dfrac{p^{\circ} - p_s}{p^{\circ}} = x_A$ (mole fraction of solute)

Example 7. Vapour pressure of water at 293 K is 17.51 mm. Lowering of vapour pressure of a sugar solution is 0.0614 mm. Calculate (i) Relative lowering of vapour pressure (ii) Vapour pressure of the solution and (iii) Mole fraction of water.

Solution : Here, we are given that Vapour pressure of water (p°) = 17.51 mm
Lowering of vapour pressure ($p^{\circ} - p_s$) = 0.0614 mm
(i) Relative lowering of vapour pressure
$$= \frac{p^{\circ} - p_s}{p^{\circ}} = \frac{0.0614 \text{ mm}}{17.51 \text{ mm}} = \mathbf{0.00351}$$
(ii) Vapour pressure of the solution (p_s)

$$p^\circ - p_s = 0.0614\,\text{mm}$$
$$p^\circ = 17.51\,\text{mm}$$
$\therefore$ $$17.51\,\text{mm} - p_s = 0.0614\,\text{mm}$$
or $$p_s = 17.51\,\text{mm} - 0.0614\,\text{mm} = \mathbf{17.4468\,mm}$$

(iii) To calculate mole fraction of water :

$$\text{By Raoult's law } \frac{p^\circ - p_s}{p^\circ} = \frac{n_2}{n_1 + n_2} = x_2$$

$$\text{mole fraction of solute, i.e., } x_2 = \frac{p^\circ - p_s}{p^\circ} = 0.00351$$

$\therefore$ Mole fraction of solvent (water),

$$x_1 = 1 - x_2 = 1 - 0.00351 = \mathbf{0.99649}$$

Example 8. The vapour pressure of pure benzene at a certain temperature is 0.850 bar. A non-volatile, non-electrolyte solid weighing 0.5 g is added to 39.0 g of benzene (molar mass 78 g mol^{-1}). The vapour pressure of the solution then is 0.845 bar. What is the molar mass of the solid substance ?

Solution : Here we are given that $w_2 = 0.5$ g, $w_1 = 39.0$ g, $M_1 = 78$ g mol^{-1}
$p^\circ = 0.850$ bar, $p_s = 0.845$ bar

Substituting these values in the formula

$$\frac{p^\circ - p_s}{p^\circ} = \frac{n_2}{n_1} = \frac{w_2/M_2}{w_1/M_1} = \frac{w_2 M_1}{w_1 M_2} \text{ we get}$$

$$\frac{0.850\text{ bar} - 0.845\text{ bar}}{0.850\text{ bar}} = \frac{0.5\,\text{g} \times 78\,\text{g mol}^{-1}}{39.0\,\text{g} \times M_2}$$

or $$M_2 = \frac{0.5 \times 78}{39.0} \times \frac{0.850}{0.005}\,\text{g mol}^{-1} = \mathbf{170\ g\ mol^{-1}}$$

Example 9. Calculate the mass of a non-volatile solute (molar mass 40 g mol^{-1}) which should be dissolved in 114 g octane to reduce its vapour pressure to 80%.

Solution : $p_s = 80\%$ of $p^\circ = 0.80\,p^\circ$. Solute $= \frac{w}{40}$ mol

$$\text{Solvent (octane)} = \frac{114\,\text{g}}{114\,\text{g mol}^{-1}} = 1\text{ mol (Molar mass of } C_8H_{18} = 114\text{ g mol}^{-1})$$

Now, $$\frac{p^\circ - p_s}{p^\circ} = x_2$$

$\therefore$ $$\frac{p^\circ - 0.80\,p^\circ}{p^\circ} = \frac{w/40}{w/40 + 1}$$

$$0.2\left(\frac{w}{40} + 1\right) = \frac{w}{40} \quad \text{or} \quad \frac{0.8w}{40} = 0.2 \quad \text{or} \quad w = \mathbf{10\ g}$$

Self-Evaluation Numericals

1. Vapour pressure of an aqueous solution of glucose is 750 mm of Hg at 373 K. Calculate the molality and mole fraction of solution. **[Ans. $x_2 = 0.013$, molality = 0.73 m]**
2. How much urea (molar mass = 60 g mol^{-1}) should be dissolved in 50 g of water so that its vapour pressure at room temperature is reduced by 25%. Calculate molality of the solution obtained. **[Ans. 55.556 g, 18.52 m]**
3. Urea forms an ideal solution in water. Determine the vapour pressure of an aqueous solution containing 10% by mass of urea at 40°C (Vapour pressure of water at 40°C = 55.3 mm Hg) **[Ans. 53.52 mm]**
4. A 0.2 percent aqueous solution of a non-volatile solute exerts a vapour pressure of 1.004 bar at 100°C. What is the molar mass of the solute ? (Given : vapour pressure of pure water at 100°C is 1.013 bar and molar mass of water is 18 g mol^{-1}). **[Ans. 4.06 g mol^{-1}]**

Type 4. Elevation in Boiling Point

The difference in the boiling points (D*T*) is called **the elevation of boiling point.**

$$\Delta T = T_1 - T_2.$$

$$\Delta T_b = k_b \times \text{molality} = k_b \times \frac{w_B \times 1000}{m_B \times w_A}$$

Example 10. 0.90 g of a non-electrolyte was dissolved in 87.90 g of benzene. This raised the boiling point of benzene by 0.25°C. If the molecular mass of the non-electrolyte is 103.0 g mol^{-1}, calculate the molal elevation constant for benzene.

Solution : Molal elevation constant, $\Delta T_b = \frac{K_b \times 1000 \times w_B}{w_A \times M_B}$

or $K_b = \frac{\Delta T_b \times w_A \times M_B}{1000 \times w_B}$

$M_B = 103.0$ g mol^{-1}, $w_A = 87.90$ g, $w_B = 0.90$ g, $\Delta T_b = 0.25°$

$\therefore \quad K_b = \frac{0.25 \times 103 \times 87.90}{1000 \times 0.90}$ = **2.515 K m^{-1}**

Example 11. Calculate the boiling point of a solution containing 0.456 g of camphor (mol. mass = 152) dissolved in 31.4 g of acetone (b.p. = 56.30°C) if molal elevation constant per 100 g of acetone is 17.2°C.

Solution : Elevation in boiling point $\Delta T_b = \frac{K_b \times 1000 \times w_B}{w_A \times M_B}$

$M_B = 152$, $w_A = 31.4$ g, $w_B = 0.456$, $K_b = 17.2$ K/mol per 100 g or = 1.72 Km^{-1}

$$\Delta T_b = \frac{1.72 \times 1000 \times 0.456}{31.4 \times 152} = 0.16°$$

Boiling point of solution = 56.30 + 0.16 = **56.46°C**

Example 12. A solution prepared by dissolving 1.25 g of oil of winter green (methyl salicylate) in 99.0 g of benzene has a boiling point of 80.31°C. Determine the molar mass of this compound. (B.P. of pure benzene = 80.10°C and K_b for benzene = 2.53°C kg mol^{-1})

Solution : $$\Delta T_b = \frac{K_b \times 1000 \times w_B}{w_A \times M_B}$$

$$M_B = \frac{K_b \times 1000 \times w_B}{\Delta T_b \times w_A}$$

$K_b = 2.53°C\ kg\ mol^{-1}$, $w_A = 99.0$ g, $w_B = 1.25$ g, $\Delta T_b = 80.31 - 80.10 = 0.21°C$

$$\therefore \quad M_B = \frac{2.53 \times 1000 \times 1.25}{0.21 \times 99.0} = \mathbf{152.1\ g\ mol^{-1}}$$

Example 13. The boiling point of benzene is 353.23 K. When 1.80 g of a non-volatile solute was dissolved in 90 g of benzene, the boiling point raised to 354.11 K. Calculate the molar mass of the solute, K_b for benzene is 2.53 K kg mol^{-1}.

Solution : Here, we are given, $w_2 = 1.80$ g, $w_1 = 90$ g

$$\Delta T_b = 354.11 - 353.23\ K = 0.88\ K$$

$$K_b = 2.53\ K\ kg\ mol^{-1}$$

Substituting these values in the formula,

$$M_2 = \frac{1000\ K_b w_2}{w_1 \Delta T_b}, \text{ we get}$$

$$M_2 = \frac{1000\ g\ kg^{-1} \times 2.53\ K\ kg\ mol^{-1} \times 1.80 g}{90 g \times 0.88\ K} = \mathbf{58\ g\ mol^{-1}}$$

Example 14. 18 g of glucose, $C_6H_{12}O_6$, is dissolved in 1 kg of water in a saucepan. At what temperature will the water boil at 1.013 bar pressure ? K_b for water is 0.52 K kg mol^{-1}.

Solution : Here, we given $w_2 = 18$ g, $w_1 = 1$ kg $= 1000$ g, $K_b = 0.52\ K\ kg\ mol^{-1}$,
M_2 (for glucose, $C_6H_{12}O$) $= 72 + 12 + 96 = 180\ g\ mol^{-1}$

$$\Delta T_b = \frac{100\ K_b w_2}{w_1 M_2}$$

$$= \frac{1000\ g\ kg^{-1} \times 0.52\ K\ kg\ mol^{-1} \times 18 g}{1000\ g \times 180\ g\ mol^{-1}} = 0.052\ K$$

As water boils at 373.15 K at 1.013 bar pressure, therefore, boiling point of solution $= 373.15 + 0.052\ K = \mathbf{373.202\ K}$

Self-Evaluation Numericals

1. Calculate the molar mass of a substance 1.3 g of which whne dissolved in 169 g of water gave a solution boiling at 100.025°C at a pressure of one atmosphere (K_b for water = 0.52 K m^{-1})
[Ans. 160 g mol^{-1}]
2. On dissolving 3.24 g of sulphur in 40 g of benzene, boiling point of solution was higher than that of benzene by 0.81 K. K_b value of benzene is 2.53 K g mol^{-1}. What is the molecular formula of sulphur ? (Atomic mass of sulphur = 32 mol^{-1}) **[Ans. S_8]**
3. A solution of an organic compound is prepared by dissolving 68.4 g in 1000 g of water. Calculate the molecular mass of the compound and osmotic pressure of the solution at 293 K

when elevation in b.pt. is 0.104 and K_b for water is 0.52 K mol^{-1}. **[Ans. 342 g mol^{-1}, 4.5 atm.]**

4. A solution of glycerol ($C_3H_8O_3$), molar mass = 92 g mol^{-1}, in water was prepared by dissolving some glycerol in 500 g of water. This solution has a boiling point of 100.42°C. What mass of glycerol was dissolved to make this solution ? K_b for water = 0.512 K kg mol^{-1}.

[Ans. 37.7 g]

Type 5. Depression in freezing point

When w_B g solute is added in w_A g solute then

$$\Delta T_f = T_2 - T_1 = k_f \times \text{molality}$$

$$\Delta T_f = k_f \times \frac{w_B \times 1000}{m_B \times w_A}$$

If solute is electrolyte then, $$\Delta T_f = i \times \frac{w_B \times 1000}{m_A \times w_B}$$

Example 15. Addition of 0.643 g of a compound to 50 mL of benzene (density 0.879 g/mL) lowers the freezing point from 5.51°C to 5.03°C. If K_f for benzene is 5.12 K kg mol^{-1}, calculate the molar mass of the compound.

Solution : The molar mass, M_B is calculated as : $M_B = \dfrac{K_f \times w_B \times 1000}{w_A \times \Delta T_f}$

$w_B = 0.643$ g, $w_A = (50 \text{ mL}) \times (0.879 \text{ g/mL}) = 43.95$ g

$K_f = 512$ K m^{-1}, $\Delta T_f = 5.51 - 5.03 = 0.48°$

$$M_B = \frac{512 \times 0.643 \times 1000}{43.95 \times 0.48} = \mathbf{156.06}$$

Example 16. Two elements A and B form compounds having molecular formula AB_2 and AB_4. When dissolved in 20 g of benzene, 1 g of AB_2 lowers it by 1.3 K. The molar depression constant for benzene is 5.1 K kg mol^{-1}. Calculate the atomic mass of A and B.

Solution :

Let us first calculate molar masses of AB_2 and AB_4.

For AB_2 compound $$M_B = \frac{K_f \times w_B \times 1000}{w_A \times \Delta T_f}$$

$\Delta T_f = 2.3$ K, $w_B = 1.0$ g, $w_A = 20.0$ g, $K_f = 5.1$ K kg mol^{-1}

$$M_B = \frac{5.1 \times 1.0 \times 1000}{20.0 \times 2.3} = 110.87$$

$$\therefore \quad M_{AB_2} = 110.87$$

For AB_4 compound $\Delta T_f = 1.3$ K, $w_B = 1.0$ g, $w_A = 20.0$ g

$$M_B = \frac{5.1 \times 1.0 \times 1000}{20.0 \times 1.3} = 196.15$$

$$\therefore \quad M_{AB_4} = 196.15$$

Let a is the atomic mass of A and b is the atomic mass of B, then,

$$MAB_2 = a + 2b = 110.87 \quad ...(i)$$

$$MAB_4 = a + 4b = 196.15 \quad ...(ii)$$

Subtracting eqn. (ii) from eqn. (i)

$$-2b = -85.28$$

$$b = 42.64$$

Substituting the value of b in eqn. (i)

$$a + 2 \times 43.64 = 110.87 \quad \text{or} \quad a = 110.87 - 85.28 = 25.59$$

Atomic mass of A = **25.59**

Atomic mass of B = **42.64**

Example 17. 19.5 g of CH_2FCOOH is dissolved in 500 g of water. The depression in the freezing point observed is 1.0°C. Calculate the van't Hoff factor and dissociation constant of fluoroacetic acid. K_f for water is 1.86 K kg mol^{-1}.

Solution : Here, $w_2 = 19.5$ g, $w_1 = 500$ g, $K_f = 1.86$ K kg mol^{-1}, $(\Delta T_f)_{obs} = 1.0°$

$$\therefore \quad M_2\text{ (observed)} = \frac{1000\, K_f w_2}{w_1 \Delta T_f} = \frac{(1000 \text{ g kg}^{-1})(1.86 \text{ K kg mol}^{-1})(19.5 \text{ g})}{(500 \text{ g})\,(1.0 \text{ K})}$$

$$= 72.54 \text{ g mol}^{-1}$$

M_2(Calculated) for CH_2FCOOH = 14+19+45 =78 g mol^{-1}

$$\text{van't Hoff factor (i)} = \frac{(M_2)_{cal}}{(M_2)_{obs}} = \frac{78}{72.54} = 1.0753$$

Calculate of dissociation constant. Suppose degree of dissociation at the given concentration is α. Then

$$CH_2FCOOH \rightleftharpoons CH_2FCOO^- + H^+$$

	CH_2FCOOH	CH_2FCOO^-	H^+	
Intial	C mol L^{-1}	0	0	
At qum.	$C(1-\alpha)$	$C\alpha$	$C\alpha$	Total = $C(1+\alpha)$

$$\therefore \quad i = \frac{C(1+\alpha)}{C} = 1 + \alpha \quad \text{or} \quad \alpha = i - 1 = 1.0753 - 1 = 0.0753$$

$$K_a = \frac{[CH_2FCOO^-][H^+]}{[CH_2FCOOH]} = \frac{C\alpha . C\alpha}{C(1-\alpha)} = \frac{C\alpha^2}{1-\alpha}$$

Taking volume of the solution as 500 mL.

$$C = \frac{19.5}{78} \times \frac{1}{500} \times 1000 = 0.5 \text{ M}$$

$$K_a = \frac{C\alpha^2}{1-\alpha} = \frac{(0.5)(0.0753)^2}{1-0.0753} = \mathbf{3.07 \times 10^{-3}}$$

Example 18. 1.00 g of a non-electrolyte solute dissolved in 50 g of benzene lowered the freezing point of benzene by 0.40 K. The freezing point depression constant of benzene is 5.12 K kg mol^{-1}. Find the molar mass of solute.

Solution : Here, we are given, $w_2 = 1.00$ g, $w_1 = 50$ g, $\Delta T_f = 0.40$ K, $K_f = 5.12$ K kg mol^{-1}

Substituting these value in the formula

$$M_2 = \frac{1000\, K_f w_2}{w_1 \Delta T_f}, \text{ we get}$$

$$M_2 = \frac{1000\text{g Kg}^{-1} \times 5.12 \text{ K kg mol}^{-1} \times 1.0 \text{ g}}{50 \text{ g} \times 0.40 \text{ K}} = \mathbf{256 \text{ g mol}^{-1}}$$

Example 19. 45 g of ethylene glycol ($C_2H_6O_2$) is mixed with 600 g water. Calculate (a) freezing point depression (b) freezing point of the solution.
(K_f for water = 1.86 K kg mol^{-1}; Atomic masses : C = 12, H = 1, O = 16 amu)

Solution : Here, we are given $w_2 = 45$ g, $w_1 = 600$ g, $K_f = 1.86$ K kg mol^{-1}

M_2 (for solute $C_2H_6O_2$) = 24 + 6 + 32 = 62 g mol^{-1}

Substituting these values in the formula,

$$\Delta T_f = \frac{1000\, K_f w_2}{w_1 \times M_2}, \text{ we get}$$

$$\Delta T_f = \frac{1000\text{g Kg}^{-1} \times 1.86 \text{ K kg mol}^{-1} \times 45 \text{ g}}{600 \text{ g} \times 62 \text{ g mol}^{-1}} = 2.25 \text{ K}$$

Freezing point of pure water = 273.15 K

∴ Freezing point of the solution = $T_f^\circ - \Delta T_f = 273.15 - 2.25$ K = **270.9 K**

Example 20. 2.0 g of benzoic acid dissolved in 25.0 g of benzene shows a depression in freezing point equal to 1.62K. Molal depression constant (K_f) of benzene is 4.9K kg mol^{-1}. What is the percentage association of the acid if it forms dimer in the solution?

Solution : Mass of solute (benzoic acid), $w_2 = 2.0$ g

Mass of solvent (benzene), $w_1 = 25.0$ g

Observed $\Delta T_f = 4.62$ K

$K_f = 4.9$ K kg mol^{-1}

∴ Observed molar mass of benzonic acid

$$M_2 = \frac{1000 \times K_f \times w_2}{\Delta T_f \times w_1} = \frac{1000\text{g Kg}^{-1} \times 4.9 \text{ K kg mol}^{-1} \times 2.0 \text{ g}}{1.62 \text{ K} \times 25.0 \text{ g}} = 242 \text{ g mol}^{-1}$$

Calculate molar mass of benzoic acid (C_6H_5COOH)

$= 72 + 5 + 12 + 32 + 1 = 122$ g mol^{-1}

$$\text{van't Hoff factor, } i = \frac{\text{Calculated mol. mass}}{\text{Observed mol. mass}} = \frac{122}{242} = 0.504$$

If a is the degree of association of benzoic acid, then we have

	$2C_6H_5COOH$	$\rightleftharpoons$	$(C_6H_5COOH)_2$
Initial moles	1		0
After association	$1-\alpha$		$\alpha/2$

∴ Total number of moles after association

$$= 1 - \alpha + \frac{\alpha}{2} = 1 - \frac{\alpha}{2}$$

∴ $$i = \frac{1-\alpha/2}{1} = 0.504 \quad \text{or} \quad 1 - \frac{\alpha}{2} = 0.504$$

$$\alpha = (1 - 0.504) \times 2 = 0.496 \times 2 = 0.992$$

or % age association = **99.2%**

Type 6. Osmotic Pressure

1. $\pi = C \cdot RT \quad \Rightarrow \quad C = \dfrac{w \times 1000}{m \times V_{ml}}$

   For electrolyte solution $\quad \pi = i \times c \times RT$

$$\alpha = \frac{i-1}{n-1}$$

2. When solution contains x% solute by mass/volume

$$\pi = \frac{x-10}{m}.RT$$

Example 21. Calculate the osmotic pressure in passcals exerted by a solution prepared by dissolving 1.0 g of polymer of molar mass 185,000 in 450 mL of water at 37°C.

Solution : $\pi = CRT = \dfrac{n}{V} RT$

Here, number of moles of solute dissolved (n)

$$= \frac{1.0\,g}{185{,}000 \text{ g mol}^{-1}} = \frac{1}{185{,}000} \text{mol}$$

$V = 450 \text{ mL} = 0.450 \text{ L}, \quad T = 37°C = 37 + 273 = 310 \text{ K}$
$R = 8.314 \text{ kPa L K}^{-1} \text{ mol}^{-1} = 8.314 \times 10^3 \text{ Pa L K}^{-1} \text{ mol}$
Substituting these values, we get

$$\pi = \frac{1}{185{,}000} \text{mol} \times \frac{1}{0.45 \text{ L}} \times 8.314 \times 10^3 \text{ Pa L K}^{-1} \text{mol}^{-1} \times 310 \text{ K} = \mathbf{30.96 \text{ Pa}}$$

Example 22. Determine the amount of $CaCl_2$ (i = 2.47) dissolved in 2.5 litre of water such that its osmotic pressure is 0.75 atm at 27-C.

Solution : $\pi = i\,CRT = i\dfrac{n}{V} RT$

$$\text{or} \quad n = \frac{\pi \times V}{i \times R \times T} = \frac{0.75 \text{ atm} \times 2.5 \text{ L}}{2.47 \times 0.0821 \text{ L atm K}^{-1}\text{mol}^{-1} \times 300 \text{ K}} = \mathbf{0.0308 \text{ mole}}$$

Molar mass of $CaCl_2 = 40 + 2 \times 35.5 = 111 \text{ g mol}^{-1}$
$\therefore$ Amount dissolved = 0.0308×111 g = **3.42 g**

Example 23. Determine the osmotic pressure of a solution prepared by dissolving 25 mg of K_2SO_4 in 2 litre of water at 25°C, assuming that it is completely dissociated.

Solution : K_2SO_4 dissolved = 25 mg = 0.025 g
Volume of solution = 2 L
$T = 25°C = 298$ K
Molar mass of $K_2SO_4 = 2 \times 39 + 32 + 4 \times 16 = 174 \text{ g mol}^{-1}$

As K_2SO_4 dissociates completely as $K_2SO_4 \longrightarrow 2K^+ + SO_4^{2-}$
i.e., ions produced = 3, $\quad \therefore i = 3$

$$\therefore \quad \pi = i\,CRT = i\frac{n}{V} RT = i \times \frac{w}{M} \times \frac{1}{V} RT$$

$$= 3\times\frac{0.025\,g}{174\text{ g mol}^{-1}}\times\frac{1}{2L}\times 0.0821\text{ L atm K}^{-1}\text{mol}^{-1}\times 298\text{ K} = \mathbf{5.27\times 10^{-3}\ atm.}$$

Numerical Problems

1. Calculate the boiling point of a solution containing 0.45 g of tamphor (mol. wt. 152) dissolved in 35.4 g of acetone (b.p. 56.3°C); K_b per 100 gm of acetone is 17.2°C.

Solution :

Here it is given that

$w = 0.45$ g, $W = 35.4$ g, $m = 152$, $K_b = 17.2$ per 100 gm

Now we know that, $\Delta T_b = \dfrac{100\times K_b\times w}{m\times W}$

(Note that this is an expression when K_b is given per 100 g of the solvent).

Substituting the values in the above expression.

$$\Delta T_b = \frac{100\times 17.2\times 0.45}{152\times 35.4} = 0.146°C$$

Now we know that

B.P. of solution (T) – B.P. of solvent (T_0) = ΔT

$\therefore$ B.P. of solution (T) = B.P. of solvent (T_0) + ΔT

Hence, B.P. of solution = 56.3 + 0.146 = **56.446°C**

2. A solution of 4.5 g of a pure non-electrolyte in 100 g of water was found to freeze at 0.465°C. Determine the molecular weight of the solute.

Solution : $$M_2 = \frac{100\times K_f\times w}{\Delta T_f\times W} = \frac{1000\times 1.86\times 4.5}{100\times 0.465} = \mathbf{180}$$

3. What mass of non-volatile solute (urea) needs to be dissolved in 100 g of water in order to decrease the vapour pressure of water by 5%. What will be the molality of solution ?

Solution :

According to Raoult's law $\dfrac{P° - P}{P°} = \dfrac{wM}{Wm}$

If $P° = 100$ mm, $P = 75$ mm

Then, $$\frac{100-75}{75} = \frac{w\times 18}{100\times 60} \qquad w = 111.1$$

$$\text{Molality} = \frac{w\times 1000}{m\times W} = \frac{111.1\times 1000}{60\times 100} = \mathbf{18.52\ m}$$

Very Short Answer Type Questions

Q. 1. Define the term solution.

Ans. A solution is a homogeneous mixture of two or more chemically non-reacting substances whose composition can be varied within certain limits.

Q. 2. Define molarity.

Ans. Molarity of a solution is the number of moles of the solute dissolved per litre of the solution.

Q. 3. Define molality.

Ans. Molality of a solution is the number of moles of the solute dissolved per kilogram of the solvent.

Q. 4. Which is more concentrated out of 1 molar and 1 molal solution?

Ans. 1 molar solution is more concentrated than 1 molal solution.

Q. 5. What are isotonic solutions?

Ans. Isotonic solutions are the solutions which have same osmotic pressure and also the same molar concentration of the solute.

Q. 6. Name the method for determining the osmotic pressure of a solution.

Ans. Berkley and Hartley's method is used to determine the osmotic pressure of the solution.

Q. 7. What happens to freezing point of water if ethylene glycol is added to it?

Ans. Freezing point of water gets lowered.

Q. 8. Suppose a solid solution is formed between two substances, one whose particles are very large and the other particles are very small. What type of this solid solution is likely to be?

Ans. Interstitial solid solution.

Q. 9. What do you mean by 10% aqueous solution of sodium carbonate?

Ans. It means that 10 g of Na_2CO_3 are present in 100 g of the solution.

Q. 10. Why do gases nearly always tend to be less soluble in liquid as the temperature is raised?

Ans. Dissolution of gas in liquid is an exothermic process [Gas + Solvent $\rightleftharpoons$ Solution + Heat]. As the temperature is increased, equilibrium shifts backward.

Short Answer Type Questions - I

Q. 1. Concentrated nitric acid used in the laboratory is 68% nitric acid by mass in aqueous solution. What should be the molarity of such a sample of the acid if the density of the solution is 1.504 g mL^{-1}?

Ans. 68% nitric acid by mass means that

mass of nitric acid = 68 g

mass of solution = 100 g

molar mass of HNO_3 = 63 g mol^{-1}

$$\therefore \quad 68\text{ g } HNO_3 = \frac{68}{63}\text{ mole} = 1.079\text{ mole}$$

Density of solution = 1.504 g mL^{-1}

$$\therefore \quad \text{Volume of solution} = \frac{100}{1.504}\text{ mL} = 66.5\text{ mL} = 0.0665\text{ L}$$

$$\text{Molarity of the solution} = \frac{\text{moles of the solute}}{\text{volume of solution in L}} = \frac{1.079}{0.0665}\text{ m} = 16.23\text{ M.}$$

Q. 2. The vapour pressure of water is 12.3 K Pa at 300 K. Calculate the vapour pressure of 1 molal solution of a solute in it.

Ans. 1 molal solution means 1 mol of the solute in 1 kg of the solvent (water).

$$\therefore \quad \text{Mol fraction of solute} = \frac{1}{1+55.5} = 0.0177$$

Now,
$$\frac{P^0 - P_S}{12.3} = X_2$$

$$\frac{12.3 - P_S}{12.3} = 0.0177$$

or $$P_S = 12.08 \text{ K Pa.}$$

Q. 3. A 5% solution (by mass) of cane sugar in water has freezing point of 271 K. Calculate the freezing point of a 5% glucose in water if freezing point of pure water is 273.15 K.

Ans. Molality of sugar solution $= \frac{5}{342} \times \frac{1000}{100} = 0.146$

If for sugar solution = 273.15 – 271 = 2.15°

$$\Delta T_F = K_F \times m$$

$$\therefore \quad K_F = \frac{\Delta T_F}{m} = \frac{2.15}{0.146}$$

Molality of glucose solution $= \frac{5}{180} \times \frac{1000}{100} = 0.278$

$$\therefore \quad \Delta T_F \text{ (Glucose)} = \frac{2.15}{0.146} \times 0.278 = 4.09^0$$

$\therefore$ Freezing point of glucose solution = 273.15 – 4.09 = 269.06 K.

Q. 4. Suggest the most important type of intermolecular interaction in the following pairs:

(*i*) *n*-hexane and *n*-octane (*ii*) I_2 and CCl_4

(*iii*) $NaClO_4$ and water (*iv*) Methanol and acetone

(*v*) Acetonitnile (CH_3CH) and acetone (C_3H_6O)

Ans. (*i*) Both are non-polar. Hence, intermolecular interactions in them will be *London dispersion* forces.

(*ii*) Same as (*i*)

(*iii*) $NaClO_4$ gives Na^+ and ClO_4^- ions in the solution while water is polar molecule. Hence, intermolecular interactions in them will be *ion-dipole interaction.*

(*iv*) Both are polar molecules. Hence, intermolecular interactions in them will be *dipole-dipole* interactions.

(*v*) Same as (*iv*)

Q. 5. Calculate the mass percentage of benzene (C_6H_6) and carbon tetrachloride (CCl_4) if 22 g of benzene is dissolved in 122 g of carbon-tetrachloride.

Ans. Mass of solution = mass of benzene + mass of CCl_4 = 22 g + 122 g = 144 g.

Mass of percentage $C_6H_6 = \frac{\text{mass of benzene}}{\text{mass of solution}} \times 100 = \frac{22\,g}{144\,g} \times 100 = 15.28\%.$

Mass percentage of $CCl_4 = \frac{\text{mass of } CCl_4}{\text{mass of solution}} \times 100 = \frac{122}{144} \times 100 = 84.72\%.$

Alternatively, mass percentage of CCl_4 = 100 – mass percentage of C_6H_6 = 100 – 15.28 = 84.72%.

Q. 6. Give three differences between Ideal solution and Non-ideal solution.

Ans.

Ideal Solution	*Non-ideal Solution*
(*i*) $\Delta V \text{ (mixing)} = 0$	(*i*) $\Delta V \text{ (mixing)} \neq 0$
(*ii*) $\Delta H \text{ (mixing)} = 0$	(*ii*) $\Delta H \text{ (mixing)} \neq 0$
(*iii*) They obey Raoult's law at all temperatures and pressures.	(*iii*) They do not obey Raoult's law at all temperatures and pressures.

Q. 7. What role does the molecular interaction play in solution of alcohol and water?

Ans. There is strong hydrogen bonding in alcohol molecules as well in water molecules on mixing, the molecular interactions are weakened. Hence, they show positive deviations from ideal behaviour. As a result, the solution will have higher vapour pressure and lower boiling point than that of water and alcohol.

Q. 8. State Henry's law and mention some of its important applications.

Ans. *Henry's law* : The mass of a gas dissolved in a given volume of the liquid at constant temperature is directly proportional to the pressure of the gas present in equilibrium with the liquid

$$m \propto P$$

$$\boxed{m = KP}$$

where m = mass of the gas dissolved in a unit volume of the solvent

P = Pressure of the gas in equilibrium with the solvent

K = Proportionality constant.

Applications of Henry's law :

1. In the production of carbonated beverages.
2. In the deep sea diving.
3. In the function of lungs.
4. For climbers or people living at high altitudes.

Q. 9. Henry's law constant for the molarity of methane in benzene at 298 K in 4.27×10^5 mm Hg. Calculate the solubility of methane in benzene at 298 K under 760 mm Hg.

Ans.
$$K_H = 4.27 \times 10^5 \text{ mm}$$
$$P = 760 \text{mm}$$

Applying Henry's law

$$P = K_H x$$

$$\therefore \quad x = \frac{P}{K^H} = \frac{760\, mm}{4.27 \times 10^5\, mm} = 1.78 \times 10^{-3}$$

i.e., mole fraction of methane in benzene = 1.78×10^{-3}.

Q. 10. What is the Van't Hoff factor for a compound which undergoes tetramerisation in an organic solvent?

Ans. $4A \longrightarrow A_4$

1 mole of A after association gives $\frac{1}{4}$ mole of A_4.

Hence, $\quad i = \frac{1}{4} = 0.25.$

Short Answer Type Questions [SAQ-II]

Q. 1. Define the term solution. How many types of solutions are formed? Write briefly about each type with an example.

Ans. *Solutions* are homogeneous mixtures of two or more than two components.

Types of Solutions:

Table 2.1

[NCERT Book]

Q. 2. Define the following terms:

(*i*) Mole fraction (*ii*) Molality (*iii*) Molarity (*iv*) Mass percentage

Ans. (*i*) *Mole fraction* : The ratio of the number of moles of one component to the total number of moles of the solution. It is expressed as x. For example—

$$X_A = \frac{n_A}{n_A + n_B} \text{ and } X_B = \frac{n_B}{n_A + n_B}.$$

(*ii*) *Molality* : Same as Q. 3 [VSAQ]

(*iii*) *Molarity* : Some as Q. 3 [VSAQ]

(*iv*) *Mass percentage* : The mass of the component expressed in grams per 100 g of the solution.

$$\text{Mass\% of a component (W/W)} = \frac{\text{Mass of the component in the solution}}{\text{Total mass of the solution}} \times 100.$$

Q. 3. Under what conditions Vant Hoff's factor '*i*' is

(*i*) equal to unity (*ii*) less than 1 and (*iii*) greater than 1?

Ans. Explain the answer.

(*i*) When the solute does not undergo any dissociation or association in the solution i.e., for non-electrolyte solutes.

(*ii*) When the solute undergoes association in the solution.

(*iii*) When the solute undergoes dissociation in the solution.

Q. 4. H_2S a toxic gas with rotten egg like smell is used for qualitative analysis. If the solubility of H_2S in water at STP is 0.195 m, calculate Herry's law constant.

Ans. 0.195 m solution means that 0.195 moles of H_2S is dissolved in 1 kg of water.

Moles of $H_2S = 0.195$

$$\text{Moles of water} = \frac{1000}{18} \; 55.55$$

$$\text{Mole fraction of } H_2S = \frac{0.195}{55.55 + 0.195} = 0.0035$$

Now, $P = K_H X_2$ Pressure = 1.01325 bar

or $$K_H = \frac{P}{X_2} = \frac{1 \text{ bar}}{0.0035} = 289.5 \text{ bar}.$$

Q. 5. Calculate the molarity of each of the following solution:—

(*a*) 30 g of $CO(NO_3)_2 . 6H_2O$ in 4.3 L of solution.

(*b*) 30 mL of 0.5 M H_2SO_4 diluted to 500 mL.

Ans. (*a*) Molar mass of $CO(NO_3)_2 . 6H_2O$

$$= 58.93 + 2 \times 14 + 6 \times 16 + 6 \times 18$$
$$= 290.93.$$

$$\text{Moles of } CO(NO_3)_2 . 6H_2O = \frac{30}{290.93} = 0.103$$

$$\text{Molarity} = \frac{0.103}{4.3} = 0.024 \text{ M}$$

$$M_1V_1 = M_2V_2$$
$$0.5 \times 30 \text{ mL} = M_2 \times 500 \text{ mL}$$
$$\therefore \quad M_2 = \frac{0.5 \times 30}{500} = 0.03 \text{ M}.$$

(*b*)
$$M_1V_1 = M_2V_2$$
$$0.5 \times 30 \text{ mL} = M_2 \times 500 \text{ mL}$$

$$\therefore \quad M_2 = \frac{0.5 \times 30}{500} = 0.03 \text{ M.}$$

Q. 6. If the density of some lake water is 1.25 m mL^{-1} and contains 92 g of Na^+ ions per kg of water. Calculate the molality of Na^+ ions in the lake.

Ans. Mass of Na^+ ions = 92 q

Moles of Na^+ ions $= \frac{92}{23} = 4$

Moles of water = 1 kg

$$\text{Molality} = \frac{\text{Moles of solute}}{\text{Mass of solvent in kg}} = \frac{4}{1} = 4 \text{ m.}$$

Q. 7. If the solubility product of CuS is 6×10^{-16}. Calculate the maximum molarity of CuS in aqueous solution.

Ans. Ksp of CuS = 6×10^{-16}

If S is the solubility, then

$$CuS \rightleftharpoons Cu^{2+} + S^{2-}$$

$$[Cu^{2+}] = S, [S^{2-}] = S$$

$$Ksp = [Cu^{2+}][S^{2-}]$$

$$= S \times S = S^2$$

$$\therefore \text{ Solubility, } \quad S = \sqrt{Ksp} = \sqrt{6 \times 10^{-16}} = 2.45 \times 10^{-8} \text{ M}$$

$\therefore$ Highest molarity = 2.45×10^{-8} M.

Q. 8. Define osmotic pressure. How does it depend upon the temperature and atmospheric pressure?

Ans. Osmotic pressure (π) may be defined as:

The additional pressure which gets exerted on the solution due to the osmosis of pure solvent into it through a semi-permeable membrane.

OR

The extra pressure which has to be applied on the surface of the solution to check the osmosis of pure solvent in toit.

(*i*) Osmotic pressure always increases with the rise in temperature because according to Vant Hoff equation $\pi = CRT$.

(*ii*) The osmatic pressure increases with the increase in atmospheric pressure because as the atmospheric pressure increases, there is a greater tendency of the solvent molecules to pass into the solution through the semi-permeable membrane thereby causing an increase in osmotic pressure.

Q. 9. Calculate the mass of non-volatile solute (molar mass 40 g mol^{-1}) which should be dissolved in 114 g octane to reduce its vapour pressure to 80%.

Ans. $P_S = 80\%$ of $P^0 = 0.80\ P^0$, Solute $= \frac{W}{40}$ mol

$$\text{Solvent (Octane)} = \frac{114\,g}{114\,g\,mol^{-1}} = \text{mol}$$

Molar mass of $C_8H_{18} = 114$ g mol^{-1}.

$$\text{Now,} \quad \frac{P^0 - P_S}{P^0} = X_2$$

$$\therefore \quad \frac{P^0 - 0.80\,P^0}{P^0} = \frac{\frac{W}{40}}{\frac{W}{10}+1}$$

$$0.2\left(\frac{W}{40}+1\right) = \frac{W}{40}$$

$$\frac{0.8\,W}{40} = 0.2$$

$$W = 10\,g.$$

Long Answer Type Questions

Q. 1. State Raoult's law. Why is the vapour pressure of a solvent lowered by the addition of non-volatile solute to it?

(*i*) A solution containing 18 g of non-volatile solute in 200 g of water freezer at 272.07 K.

(*ii*) Calculate the molecular mass of the solute. (Given $K_f = 1.86$ K/m).

Ans. Raoult's law may be stated in two different ways:

(*i*) *Solution containing a non-volatile solute*—According to the law, the vapour pressure of the solution at a given temperature is equal to the product of the vapour pressure of the pure solvent and its mole fraction.

$$P = P^0 \times A$$

Where P = Vapour pressure of solution

P^0 = Vapour pressure of pure solvent.

X_A = Mole fraction of pure solvent

(*ii*) *Solution containing both volatile solute and solvent* : According to Raoult's the vapour pressure of each component in the solution is equal to the product of the vapour pressure of the pure solvent and its mole fraction.

$$PA = P_A{}^0 \times A, \quad P_B = P_B{}^0 \times B$$

When a non-volatile solute is added to a solvent the vapour pressure of the solution gets lowered. Actually, evaporation is a surface phenomenon, i.e. it takes place from the surface of the container. The non-volatile solute particles occupy certain surface area and as a result, the tendency of the solvent molecular to change to vapours decreases.

Numerical :

Mass of the solute $(W_B) = 18\,g$

Mass of water $(W_A) = 200\,g$

$\Delta T_F = 273–272.07 = 0.93\,K$

$K_F = 1.86\,K/m$

$M_B = ?$

$$M_B = \frac{K_F \times W_B \times 1000}{\Delta T_F \times W_A} = \frac{1.86 \times 18 \times 1000}{0.93 \times 200} = 180.$$

Q. 2. Why do we get sometimes abnormal molecular masses of the substances by using colligative properties of the solution? State factors with suitable examples which bring abnormally in results thus obtained.

Ans. *Abnormal molecular masses*—The molecular masses of certain substances as determined experimentally by osmatic pressure, elevation in boiling points, depression in freezing points or relative lowering in vapour pressure are different from those calculated theoretically from their chemical formulae.

In some cases, the determined molecular masses are high while in the other they are less as compared to their normal values. This may be due to the association or the dissociation of the solute molecules in the solution. Therefore, the number of the molecules undergo a change. As the colligative properties depend only upon the number of the particles, they are expected to show certain deviation. These two changes are being discussed below:

1. *Association of solute particles* : When the number of solute particles are less than the expected number then molecules of solute are said to associate, e.g., benzoic acid molecules dimerise in benzene and the molecular weight calculated from depression in freezing point is 244 which is double of 122 (actual molecular weight).

   When $i < 1$, association occurs and theoretical molecular mass is less than calculated from colligative property.

2. *Dissociation of solute particles* : When the number of solute particles are more than the expected number, solute molecules are said to dissociate, e.g., KCl will dissociate into K^+ and Cl^- ions. The molecular mass calculated from depression of freezing point will be less than the true value.

   When $i > 1$, dissociation occurs and theoretical molecular mass is more than calculated from colligative property.

Q. 3. What are ideal and non-ideal solutions? What types of non-idealities are exhibited by cyclohexane- ethanol and acetone-chloroform mixtures? Give reasons for your answer.

Ans. (*i*) *Ideal solutions* : The solutions which obey Raoult's law exactly at all concentrations and at a temperatures are called ideal solutions.

According to Raoult's law, the partial pressure of two components of the solutions are proportional to their mole fractions i.e.

$$P_A = P_A{}^0 \times X_A$$
$$P_B = P_A{}^0 \times X_B$$

Where PA^0 and $P_B{}^0$ are vapour pressure of two liquids, P_A and P_B are the partial vapour pressure of two components and X_A and X_B are their mole fraction in solution. Therefore, for ideal solution, total pressures

$$P = P_A + P_B$$
$$= P_A^0 \times X_A + P_B^0 \times X_B.$$

(*ii*) *Non-ideal solution* : When a solution does not obey Raoult's law over the entire range of concentration, it is called non-ideal solution. For these solutions

$$\Delta H_{mix} \neq 0$$
$$\Delta V_{mix} \neq 0$$

e.g. ethanol and water, chloroform and acetone, ethanol and cyclohexane.

(*a*) *Cyclohexane-ethanol* : Solutions shows positive deviations from Raoult's law. In these solutions the alcohol molecules are held together by hydrogen bonding as shown below:

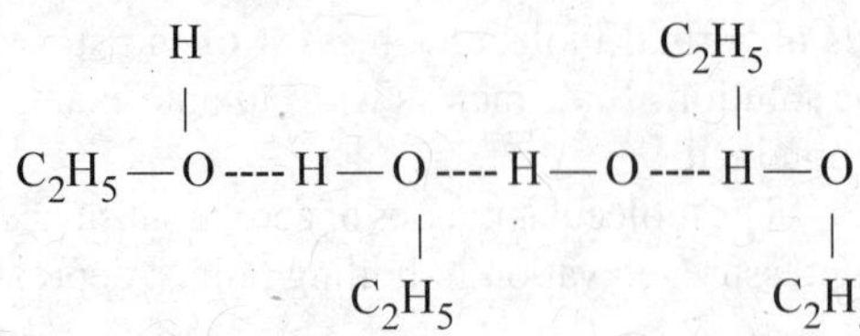

When cyclohexane is added to ethyl alcohol, the molecules of cyclohexane try to occupy the spaces between alcohol molecules. As a result, some hydrogen bonding in alcohol molecules break and the attractive forces become weak. As a result, the vapour pressure of the solution is slightly more on mixing.

The positive deviations have been shown in the Fig. the dotted lines show the ideal behaviour upon mixing while the thick lines show the actual behaviour.

(*b*) *Acetone-Chloroform* : Solutions show negative deviations from Raoult's law as explained below:

When acetone and chloroform are mixed, there are new attractive forces due to intermolecular hydrogen bonding. As a result of new attractive forces, the escaping tendency of each liquid from solution becomes less. Therefore, the vapour pressure of the solution is slightly less than what is expected from an ideal solution.

Thus, $P_A < P_A^0 \times X_A$

$P_B < P_B^0 \times X_B$

The total vapour pressure ($P_A + P_B$) becomes less than the corresponding vapour pressure expected from ideal solution.

Higher Order Thinking Skills Hots Questions

1. Define colligative property.
2. Define azeotropic mixture.
3. Write two differences between osmosis and diffusion.
4. 0.01 m solution of KCl and $BaCl_2$ are prepared in water. The freezing points of KCl is found to be –2°C. What freezing point would you expect for $BaCl_2$ solution assuming both KCl and $BaCl_2$ to be completely ionized. **[Ans. – 3°C]**
5. A 1.2% solution (wt./volume) of NaCl is isotonic with 7.2% solution (Wt./volume) of glucose (molar mass = 180. Calculate the degree of dissociation of NaCl solution. **[Ans. 0.95]**
6. What is meant by positive and negative deviation from Raoult's law and how in the sign of $\Delta_{sol} H$ related to positive and negative deviation from Raoult's law?
7. What is Raoult's law ? By taking suitable examples discuss the factors responsible for the deviation from the law.
8. (a) What is osmotic pressure ? Explain how the molecular mass of a non-volatile solute can be determined from it.

   (b) What is elevation in boiling point ? Explain how the molecular mass of a non-volatile solute can be determined from it.

   (c) What is depression in freezing point ? Explain how the molecular mass of a non-volatile solute is determined from it.
9. (a) Give any two difference between ideal and non-ideal solutions.

   (b) Which of the following solutions will have the highest and which will have the lowest osmotic pressure and why ?

   (i) 0.1 M NaCl (ii) 0.1 M Glucose (iii) 0.1 M $BaCl_2$

10. Calculate the volume of 75% H_2SO_4 by weight (density = 1.80 g/ml) required to prepare 1 L of 0.2 M solution. **[Ans. 14.5 ml]**

11. Two elements A and B form compounds having molecular formulae AB_2 and AB_4. When dissolved in 20 g of benzene, 1.0 g of AB_2 lowers the freezing point by 2.3°C whereas 1.0 g of AB_4, lowers the freezing point by 1.3°C. Calculate the atomic masses of A and B. (K_f for benzene = 5.1 K/m). **[Ans. 25.6, 42.65]**

12. 0.01 m aqueous solution of sodium sulphate depresses the freezing point of water by 0.0284°C. Calculate the degree of dissociation of the salt. (K_f for water = 1.86 K m^{-1})

[Ans. 26.5%]

13. 15 g of an unknown molecular substance was dissolved in 450 g of water. The resulting solution freezing at – 0.34°C. What is the molar mass of the substance ?

[Ans. 182.35 g mol^{-1}]

❑❑❑

CHAPTER

3 ELECTROCHEMISTRY

Syllabus

- *Redox reactions, conductance in electrolytic solutions, specific and molar conductivity, vanations of conductivity with concentration, Kohlrausch's Law, electrolysis and laws of electrolysis (elementary idea), dry cell — electrolytic cells and galvanic cells; lead accumulator, EMF of a cell, standard electrode potential, Nernst equation and its application to chemical cells, fuel cells.*

1. **Role of Salt Bridge :** Salt bridge carries whole of the current across the boundary; moreover the K^+ and NO_3^- ions have the same speed or transport number. Hence, salt bridge with uniform and same mobility of cations and anions minimize the liquid junction potential.
2. **Limitations of salt bridge :** When there is electrolyte solution of silver, mercurous or thallus salt electrolyte solution of silver, mercurous or thallus salt we cannot use KCl in salt bridge because precipitation of corresponding chloride may take place.
3. **Relation between Electrical Energy and Free energy :** Electrical work done by the cell per mole of the reactant consumed is given by nEF^*, where n is the number of electrons liberated at one electrode and n is simply the valency of the metal, E is the e.m.f. of the cell and F^* is Faraday.

   Electrical work done by the cell may be calculated as,

   $$\text{Work done} = \text{Charge} \times \text{Potential} = nFE$$

   Gibbs free energy of a system is a measure of reversible or maximum obtainable work by the system if there is no work due to volume expansion.

   $$-\Delta G = nFE \quad \text{and} \quad -\Delta G^\circ = nFE^\circ$$
4. **Nernst Equation for a Half-Reaction**

   For the half-reaction $aA + ne^- \rightleftharpoons bB$

   the Nernst equation giving the half-cell potential, E is :

   Nernst equation : $$\boxed{E = E^\circ - \frac{RT}{nF}\ln Q}$$

   where, E° = standard reduction potential (when molarity of ions are 1)

   R = gas constant [8.314 472 J/(K-mol) = 8.314 472 (V·C)/(K·mol)]

   T = temperature (K)

   n = number of electrons in the half-reaction

   F = Faraday constant ($9.648\,534\,15 \times 10^4$ C/mol)

   Q = reaction quotient

   Converting the natural logarithm in above Nernst equation to the base 10 logarithm and inserting T = 298.15 K (25.00°C) gives the most useful form of the Nernst equation.

   Nernst equation at 25°C : $$\boxed{E = E^\circ - \frac{0.059\,16\text{ V}}{n}\ln Q}$$

The potential changes by 59.16/n mV for each factor-of-10 change in Q.

5. Standard Electrode Potentials :

In this electrode, H_2 gas at one atmospheric pressure is in contact with H^+ ions having concentration equal to one molar. It is the primary standard electrode.

A plate of Pt metal coated with platinum black is dipped in the acid solution. Now H_2 gas at 25° (298 K) and one atmospheric pressure is passed. Hydrogen gas is adsorbed on the platinum plate. Thus H_2 gas remains in contact with H^+ ions. It is like an electrode in which a metal is in contact with its own metal ions. Standard or normal hydrogen electrode is represented as ;

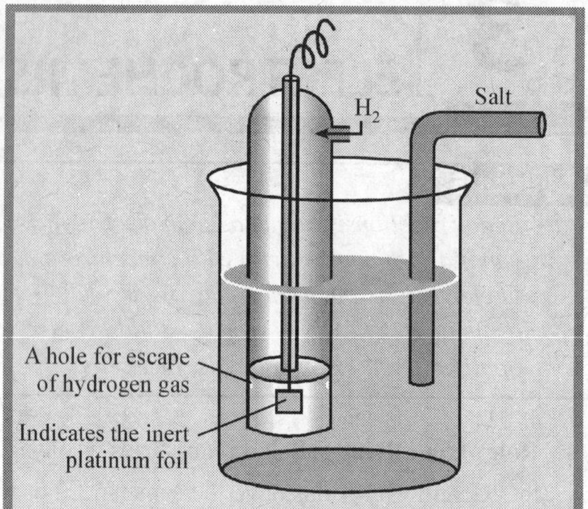

Diagram of a simple standard hydrogen electrode

$\underset{(P=1\,atm)}{Pt, H_2(g)}\,|\,H^+$ (one molar) aqueous

At cathode : $2H^+ + 2e^- \longrightarrow H_2$

At anode : $H_2 \longrightarrow 2H^+ + 2e^-$

Type 1.

$$E_{cell} = E^o_{cell} - \frac{0.059}{n} \log k$$

$$E^o_{cell} = E^o_{cathode} - E^o_{anode}$$

Numerical Problems

1. Write Nernst equation and calculate e.m.f. of the following cells at 298 K :
Fe (s) | Fe^{2+} (0.001 M) || H^+ (1 M) H_2 (1 atm), Pt

Given : $E^o_{Fe^{++}/Fe} = -0.44$, $E^o_{H^+/H_2} = 0$

Solution :

Fe (s) | Fe^{2+} (0.001 M) || H^+ (1 M) H_2 (1 atm), Pt

The electrode reactions and overall cell reactions are :

At anode : $Fe(s) \longrightarrow Fe^{2+}(aq) + 2e^-$

At cathode : $2H^+(aq) + 2e^- \longrightarrow H_2(g)$

$Fe(s) + 2H^+(aq) \longrightarrow Fe^{2+}(aq) + H_2(g)$ (Overall cell reaction)

Since the reaction involves 2 moles of electrons, therefore, $n = 2$ and the Nernst equation at 298 K is :

$$E_{cell} = E^o_{cell} - \frac{0.059}{2} - \log \frac{[Fe^{2+}]}{[H^+]}$$

$$E^o_{cell} = E^o (H^+ | H_2) - E^o (Fe^{2+} | Fe)$$

$$E^\circ(H^+|H_2) = 0.0\,V, \quad E^\circ(Fe^{2+}|Fe) = -0.44\,V$$

$$E^\circ_{cell} = 0.0 - (-0.44) = 0.44\,V$$

$$E_{cell} = 0.44 - \frac{0.059}{2}\log\frac{0.001}{1} = 0.44 + 0.0885 = \mathbf{0.5285\,V}$$

2. Represent the cell in which the following reaction takes place :
$Mg(s) + 2Ag^+(0.0001\,M) \longrightarrow Mg^{2+}(0.130\,M) + 2Ag(s)$
Calculate its E if E° is 3.17 V.

Solution :

The cell may be represented as
$Mg|Mg^{2+}(0.130\,M)||Ag^+(0.0001\,M)|Ag$
The Nernst equation for the cell is

$$E = E^\circ - \frac{0.059}{2}\log\frac{[Mg^{2+}]}{[Ag^+]^2}$$

$$= 3.17 - \frac{0.059}{2}\log\frac{(0.130)}{(0.0001)^2} = 3.17 - 0.21 = \mathbf{2.96\,V}$$

3. Calculate the e.m.f. of cell and unit the cell equation.
$Mg(s)|Mg^{2+}(0.1\,M)||Cu^{2+}(1\times10^{-3}\,M)|Cu(s)$
Given $E^\circ(Cu^{2+}|Cu) = +0.34\,V$
$E^\circ(Mg^{2+}|Mg) = -2.37\,V$

Solution

At anode : $Mg(s) \longrightarrow Mg^{2+}(aq) + 2e^-$
At cathode : $Cu^{2+} + 2e^- \longrightarrow Cu$

$$Mg(s)|Cu^{2+}(aq) \longrightarrow Mg^{2+}(aq) + Cu(s)$$

$$E = E^\circ - \frac{0.059}{2}\log\frac{[Mg^{2+}]}{[Cu^{2+}]}$$

$$E = E^\circ(Cu^{2+}|Cu) - E^\circ(Mg^{2+}|Mg) = 0.34 - (-(2.37) = 2.71\,V$$

$$E = 2.71 - 0.0295\log\frac{0.1}{1\times10^{-3}} = 2.71 - 2\times0.0295 = \mathbf{2.651\,V}$$

Self-Evaluation Numericals

1. Calculate the e.m.f. of the cell at 25°C
$Zn|Zn^{2+}(0.01\,M)||Fe^{2+}(0.005\,M))|Fe$
$E^\circ(Zn^{2+}|Zn) = -0.763\,V)$ and $E^\circ(Fe^{2+}|Fe) = -0.44\,V$ **[Ans. 0.314 V]**
2. Calculate the e.m.f. of the following cell at 298 K,
$Fe|Fe^{2+}(0.1\,M)||Ag^+(0.1\,M)|Ag$
Given : $E^\circ\,Fe^{2+}|Fe = -0.44\,V$ and $E^\circ\,Ag^+|Ag = 0.80\,V$
$(R = 8.31\,J\,K^{-1}\,mol^{-1}, F = 96500\,C\,mol^{-1})$ **[Ans. 1.2105 V]**

Type 2. Determination of Equilibrium Constant

At equilibrium $E_{cell} = 0$

According to, $E_{cell} = E^{o}_{cell} - \frac{0.059}{n} \log k$

$$0 = E^{o}_{cell} - \frac{0.059}{n} \log k_c$$

$$k_c = \text{antilog} \frac{n \times E^{o}_{cell}}{0.059}$$

Numerical Problems

1. Calculate the equilibrium constant for the reaction at 298 K

$Cu(s) + 2Ag^{+}(aq) \longrightarrow Cu^{2+}(aq) + 2Ag(s)$

Given that $E^{o}(Ag^{+}|Ag) = 0.80$ V

and $E^{o}(Cu^{2+}|Cu) = 0.34$ V

Solution :

E^{o}_{cell} is related to equilibrium constant K_c at 298 K as :

$$E^{o}_{cell} = \frac{0.059}{n} \log K_c \quad \text{or} \quad \log K_c = \frac{nE^{o}_{cell}}{0.059}$$

$$E^{o}_{cell} = E^{o}(Ag^{+}|Ag) - E^{o}(Cu^{2+}|Cu) = 0.80 - 0.34 = 0.46$$

or $$\log K_c = \frac{2 \times 0.46}{0.059} = 15.6$$

$$\mathbf{K_c = 3.98 \times 10^{15}}$$

Self-Evaluation Numericals

1. Calculate the equilibrium constant for the reaction,

$$2Fe^{3+} + 2I^{-} \rightleftharpoons 2Fe^{2+} + I_2$$

if $E^{o}_{cell} = 0.235$ V **[Ans. 9.25×10^{7}]**

2. For a cell reaction :

$A(s) + 2B^{+}(aq) \longrightarrow A^{2+}(aq) + 2B(s)$

the equilibrium constant is 1×10^{4}. Calculate E^{o}_{cell}. **[Ans. 0.118V]**

3. Calculate the equilibrium constant for the reaction :

$Cd^{2+}(aq) + Zn(s) \longrightarrow Zn^{2+}(aq) + Cd(s)$

if $E^{o}(Cd^{2+}|Cd) = -0.403$ V and $E^{o}(Zn^{2+}|Zn) = -0.763$ V **[Ans. 1.596×10^{12}]**

Type 3.

For concentration cell

$$E^{o}_{cell} = 0$$

$$E_{cell} = 0 - \frac{0.059}{n} \log k = \frac{0.059}{n} \log \frac{1}{k}$$

Numerical Problems

1. **Calculate the e.m.f. of the following concentration cell at 298 K**
   $Zn \mid ZnSO_4 (0.05\ M) \mid\mid ZnSO_4 (0.5\ M) \mid Zn$

Solution :

$$E_{cell} = \frac{0.0591}{n}\log\frac{C_2}{C_1} = \frac{0.0591}{2}\log\frac{0.5}{0.005} = \mathbf{0.02955\ V}$$

2. **A cell consists of two hydrogen electrodes. The negative electrode is in contact with a solution having 10^{-6} M H^+ ion concentration. Calculate the concentration of H^+ ions at the positive electrode, if the emf of the cell is found to be 0.118 V at 298 K.**

Solution :

Here, $C_1 = 10^{-6}$ M, C_2 = To be calculated

For the given concentration cell, $E_{cell} = \frac{0.0591}{n}\log\frac{C_2}{C_1}$

$$0.118 = \frac{0.0591}{1}\log\frac{C_2}{10^{-6}} \quad \text{or} \quad \log\frac{C_2}{10^{-6}} = 2$$

or $$\frac{C_2}{10^{-6}} = \text{Antilog } 2 = 10^2 \quad \therefore \quad C_2 = 10^2 \times 10^{-6} = \mathbf{10^{-4}\ M}$$

Type 4.

(i) $\Delta G^o = -nF\,E^o_{cell}$

If $A^{6+} \longrightarrow A^{3+} \longrightarrow A^{2+} \longrightarrow A$

$E_{cell} = aV \qquad E^o_{cell} = bV \qquad E^o = cV$

then E^o for $A^{6+} \longrightarrow A$

$$E^o_{cell} = \frac{3a + b + 2c}{8}$$

(ii) $\Delta G^o = -2.303\ RT \log k_c$

Numerical Problems

1. **Calculate the maximum work that can be obtained from the Daniel cell :**
   $Zn \mid Zn^{2+}(aq) \mid\mid Cu^{2+}(aq) \mid Cu$
   Given that $E^o(Zn^{2+} \mid Zn) = -0.76$ V and $E^o(Cu^{2+} \mid Cu) = 0.34$ V

Solution :

The maximum work that can be obtained from a cell is equal to free energy change for the cell reaction.

$$Zn(s) + Cu^{2+}(aq) \longrightarrow Cu(s) + Zn^{2+}(aq)$$

$$E^o_{cell} = E^o\,(\text{cathode}) - E^o\,(\text{anode})$$
$$= E^o\,(Cu^{2+} \mid Cu) - E^o\,(Zn^{2+} \mid Zn) = 0.34 - (-0.76) = 1.10\ V$$

Now, $\Delta G^o = -nFE^o_{cell}$

$E^o_{cell} = 1.10\,V, n = 2, F = 96500\,C$

$\therefore \quad \Delta G^o = -(2\,mol) \times (96500\,C\,mol^{-1}) \times (1.10\,V)$

$= -212{,}300\,CV \qquad (1J = 1C \times V)$

$= -212{,}300\,J$ or **−212.3 kJ**

Thus, 212.3 kJ is the maximum work that can be obtained by the operation of this type cell.

2. The ΔG^o for the Daniel cell has been found to be −212.3 kJ at 25°C. Calculate the equilibrium constant for the cell reaction.

Solution : $\Delta G^o = -RT\ ln\,K_c$

Here, $\Delta G^o = -212.3\,kJ = -212300\,J, T = 298\,K$

$R = 8.314\,J\,K^{-1}\,mol^{-1}) \times 298\,K)\ ln\,K_c$

or $ln\,K_c = \frac{212300}{8.314 \times 298} = 85.69$ or $K_c = \mathbf{1.64 \times 10^{37}}$.

3. Estimate the minimum potential difference needed to reduce Al_2O_3 at 500°C. The free energy change for the decomposition reaction :

$\mathbf{\frac{2}{3}Al_2O_3 \longrightarrow \frac{4}{3}Al + O_2}$ **is $\Delta G = +960$ kJ ($F = 96500\,C\,mol^{-1}$)**

Solution :

$Al_2O_3\,(2Al^{3+} + 3O^{2-}) \longrightarrow 2Al + \frac{3}{2}O_2$

This reaction involves 6 electrons, $n = 6$

$\therefore \quad \frac{2}{3}Al_2O_3 \longrightarrow \frac{4}{3}Al + O_2\,; n = \frac{6 \times 2}{3} = 4e^-$

$\Delta G = -nFE$

$\Delta G = 960 \times 10^3\,J, n = 4, F = 96500\,C\,mol^{-1}$

$\therefore \quad 960 \times 10^3 = -4 \times 96500 \times E$

or $E = -\frac{960 \times 10^3}{4 \times 96500} = -2.487\,V$

$\therefore$ Minimum potential difference needed to reduce

Al_2O_3 = **2.487 V**

Self-Evaluation Numericals

1. Calculate ΔG^o and E_{cell} for the cell
$Al\,|\,Al^{3+}\,(0.01\,M)\,||\,Fe^{2+}\,(0.02\,M)\,|\,Fe$
Given that $E^o\,(Al^{3+}\,|\,Al) = -1.66\,V$ and $E^o\,(Fe^{2+}\,|\,Fe) = -0.44\,V$ **[Ans. 1.209 V, −706.38 kJ]**

2. Write the Nernst equation and calculate the value of ΔG^o for the galvanic cell :
$Cu(s)\,|\,Cu^{2+}\,(0.130\,M)\,||\,Ag^+\,(1.00 \times 10^{-4}\,M)\,Ag(s)$
Given $E^o\,Cu^{2+}\,|\,Cu = 0.34\,V, E^o\,Ag^+\,|\,Ag = 0.80\,V$ **[Ans. − 48.250 kJ]**

Type 5. Electrolysis

1. **Preferential Discharge Theory:** If an electrolytic solution consists of more than one cations or anions and the electrolysis is done, it is observed that all the ions are not discharged at the electrodes simultaneously but certain ions are liberated at the electrodes in preference to others. This is explained by **preferential discharge theory**. According to preferential discharge theory, a cation or anion moves toward cathode or anode which has least discharge potential than other cation or anion present in solution and discharged is corresponding electrode. The decreasing order of discharge potential.

   For cations : $K^+ > Na^+ > Ca^{2+} > Mg^{2+} > Al^{3+} > Zn^{2+} > H^+ > Cu^{2+} > Hg^{2+} > Ag^+$.

   For anions : $SO_4^{2-} > NO_3^- > OH^- > Cl^- > Br^- > I^-$.

2. **Electrolysis of a Solution of Sulphuric Acid:** Electrolysis of 50% H_2SO_4 is done at 0°C using platinum electrodes. Perdisulphuric acid ($H_2S_2O_8$) is formed.

   Cathode (Cu core)   **Anode (Pt)**

$$2H_2SO_4 \longrightarrow 2H^+ + 2HSO_4^-$$

$$2H^+ \xrightarrow{2e} H_2 \qquad 2HSO_4^- \longrightarrow H_2S_2O_8 + 2e$$

$$H_2S_2O_8 + 2H_2O \longrightarrow H_2O_2 + 2H_2SO_4$$

3. **Electrolysis of Aqueous $NaNO_3$:** On electrolysis of aq. solution of $NaNO_3$, O_2 is obtained at anode and H_2 is obtained at cathode.

$$NaNO_3 \longrightarrow Na^+ + NO_3^-$$

$$2H_2O \rightleftharpoons H_3O^+ + OH^-$$

   Discharge potential of OH^- is less than NO_3^-, therefore OH^- is discharged at anode

   Anode : $2OH^- \longrightarrow H_2O + \frac{1}{2}O_2 + 2e$

   Discharge potential of H_3O^+ is less than Na^+; therefore, H_3O^+ is discharge at anode

   Cathode : $2H_3O^+ + 2e \longrightarrow 2H_2O + H_2$

5. **Electrolysis of Na_2SO_4(aq) :**

$$Na_2SO_4 \longrightarrow 2Na^+ + SO_4^{--}$$

$$2H_2O \rightleftharpoons H_3O^+ + OH^-$$

   Discharge potential of OH^- is less than SO_4^{--}, therefore OH^- is discharged at anode

   Anode : $2OH^- \longrightarrow H_2O + \frac{1}{2}O_2 + 2e$

   Discharge potential of H_3O^+ is less than Na^+, therefore H_3O^+ is discharged at anode

   Cathode : $2H_3O^+ + 2e \longrightarrow 2H_2O + H_2$

6. **Faraday's First Law of Electrolysis :** According to this law, amount of substance deposited or dissolved at an electrode will be directly proportional to amount of charge passed through the solution.

$$W \propto Q$$

7. **Faraday's Second Law of Electrolysis :** According to this law, when same amount of charge is passed through different electrolyte solutions, weight of substances deposited at electrodes will be proportional to their chemical equivalent weight.

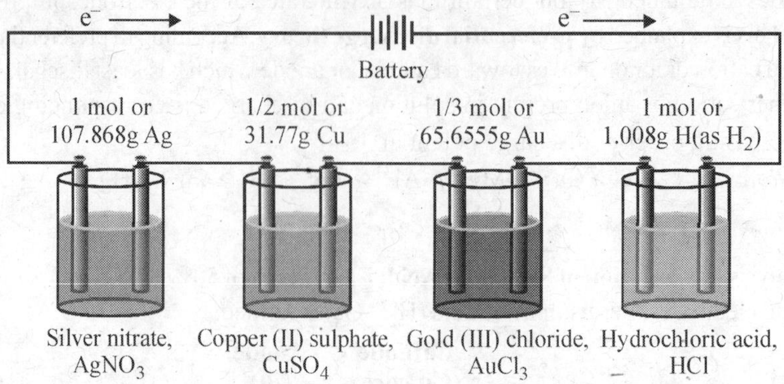

Let same amount of charge is passed through $CuSO_4$ and $AgNO_3$ solutions then

$$\frac{\text{Weight of copper deposited}}{\text{Weight of silver deposited}} = \frac{\text{Equivalent weight of copper (31.8)}}{\text{Equivalent weight of silver (107.88)}}$$

8. **Quantitative Aspects of Electrolysis :**

   (i) Determining the mass of product :

Current and time —($q = i \times t$)→ Charge → Coulombs —(mass of 1 moles / $n \times 96500$)→ $\frac{q \times M}{n \times 96500}$ → Weight

Illustration

If a current of 0.17 A flows for 16 min through the cell $CuSO_4$, how many grams of Cu(s) will be deposited ?

Solution :

$$Cu^{++} + 2e^- \longrightarrow Cu$$

$$q \text{ Charge} = i \times t = 0.17 \times 16 \times 60 = 163.2 \text{ Coulomb}$$

$$2 \times 96500 \text{ Coulombs produce} = 63.5 \text{ g}$$

$$1 \text{ coulomb produce} = \frac{63.5}{2 \times 96500} \text{ gram}$$

$$163.2 \text{ coulomb produce} = \frac{63.5}{2 \times 96500} \times 163.2 = \mathbf{0.0536 \text{ gram}}$$

   (ii) Determine the Length of Electrolysis :

$n \times 96500$ —(devided by mol-mass)→ charge for 1 gram —(× given mass)→ charge for given mass → $t = \frac{q}{i}$

Numerical Problems

1. **How much time is required to produce exactly 1 metric ton (1000 kg) of magnesium by passage of a current of 150,000 amperes through molten $MgCl_2$? Assume a 100% yield of magnesium based on the current.**

Solution :

Step - 1 :

$$24 \text{ grams produced by} = 2 \times 96500\text{ C}$$

$$1 \text{ gram produced by} = 2 \times \frac{2 \times 96500}{24}\text{ C}$$

$$\therefore \ 1000 \text{ kg } (i.e., 10^6 \text{ grams}) \text{ produced by} = \frac{2 \times 96500}{24} \times 10^6 = 8.04 \times 10^9\text{ C}$$

Step - 2 : $q = i \times t \Rightarrow \quad t = \frac{q}{i} = \frac{8.04 \times 10^9}{150{,}000} = 5.36 \times 10^4 \text{ sec} = \mathbf{14.9\ hours}$

2. Calculate the mass of copper deposited by passing a current of 0.3 ampere for 45 minutes in a solution of $CuSO_4$.(Cu = 63.5)

Solution :

At cathode : $\underset{2\,\text{Faraday}}{Cu^{++} + 2e} \longrightarrow \underset{63.5\,\text{gram}}{Cu}$ (reduction)

$$\text{Faraday} = \frac{i \times t}{96500}$$

Given, $i = 0.3$ ampere, $t = 45 \times 60$ seconds

$$F = \frac{0.3 \times 45 \times 60}{96500} = \frac{8.1}{965}$$

Faraday is equal to the moles of electrons taking part in the reaction

$\because$ From 2 faraday copper obtained = 63.5 gram

$\therefore$ From $\frac{8.1}{965}$ copper obtained $= \frac{63.5 \times 8.1}{2 \times 965} = \mathbf{0.266\ gram}$

3. A solution of $CuSO_4$ is electrolysed for 10 minutes with a current of 1.5 amperes. What is the mass of copper deposited at the cathode?

Solution : Current strength (I) = 1.5 A

Time (t) = 10 min = 10 × 60 = 600 s

Quantity of electricity passed = I × t = (1.5 A) × 600 s) = 900 C (A s = C)

Copper is deposited as : $Cu^{2+} + 2e^- \longrightarrow Cu(s)$

2 mol of electrons or 2 × 96500 C of current deposit copper = 63.65 g

$$900 \text{ C of current will deposit copper} = \frac{63.56}{2 \times 96500} \times 900 = \mathbf{0.296\ g.}$$

4. How many coulombs are required to deposit 50 g of aluminium when the electrode reaction is :

$$\mathbf{Al^{3+} + 3e^- \longrightarrow Al}$$

Solution : $Al^{3+} + 3e^- \longrightarrow Al$

1 mol of Al requires 3 mol of electrons or 3 × 96500 C

1 mol of Al = 27 g

27 g of Al required = 3 × 96500 C

$$50 \text{ g of Al required} = \frac{3 \times 96500\text{ C} \times 50}{27} = \mathbf{536111\ C}$$

5. How many coulombs of electricity are required for

(i) oxidation of 1 mol of H_2O to O_2

(ii) oxidation of 1 mol of FeO to Fe_2O_3

(iii) reduction of 1 mol of MnO_4^- to Mn^{2+}

(iv) reduction of 1 mol of Cu^{2+} to Cu^2

(v) reduction of 1 mol of Al^{3+} to Al.

Solution :

(i) Oxidation of H_2O to O_2

$$2H_2O \rightleftharpoons 4H^+ + O_2 + 4e^-$$

Oxidation of 2 mol of H_2O require $= 4 \times 96500$ C

Oxidation of 1 mol of H_2O require $= 2 \times 96500$ C $=$ **1.93×10^5 C**

(ii) Oxidation of 1 mol of FeO to Fe_2O_3

$$Fe^{2+} \longrightarrow Fe^{3+} + e^-$$

Oxidation of 1 mol of Fe^{2+} require $= 1 \times 96500$ C $=$ **96500 C**

(iii) Reduction of 1 mol of MnO_4^- to Mn^{2+}

$$MnO_4^- + 8H^+ + 5e^- \longrightarrow Mn^{2+} + 4H_2O$$

Reduction of 1 mol of MnO_4^- requires $= 5 \times 96500$ C $=$ **4.825×10^5C**

(iv) Reduction of Cu^{2+} to Cu

$$Cu^{2+} + 2e^- \longrightarrow Cu$$

Reduction of 1 mol of Cu^{2+} requires $= 2 \times 96500$ C $=$ **1.93×10^5 C**

(v) Reduction of 1 mol of Al^{3+} to Al

$$Al^{3+} + 3e^- \longrightarrow Al$$

Reduction of 1 mol of Al^{3+} requires $= 3 \times 96500$ C $=$ **2.895×10^5 C**

6. How many hours does it take to reduce 3 mol of Fe^{3+} to Fe^{2+} with 2.0 A current ? (F = 96500 C)

Solution :

Reduction of Fe^{3+} to Fe^{2+}

$$Fe^{3+} + e^- \longrightarrow Fe^{2+}$$

Reduction of 1 mol of Fe^{3+} requires $= 96500$ C

Reduction of 3 mol of Fe^{3+} require $= 3 \times 96500$ C $= 2.895 \times 10^5$ C

Now, Quantity of electricity = Current × Time

$$2.895 \times 10^5 = 2 \times \text{Time}$$

$$\therefore \quad \text{Time} = \frac{2.895 \times 10^5}{2} = 1.4475 \times 10^5 \text{ s}$$

$$= \frac{1.4475 \times 10^5}{60 \times 60} = \textbf{40.21 hours.}$$

7. Two electrolytic cells containing silver nitrate solution and dilute sulphuric acid solution were connected in series. A steady current of 2.5 amp was passed through them till 1.078 g of silver was deposited.

[Ag = 107.8 g mol^{-1}, 1 F = 96500 C]

(i) How much electricity was consumed ?

(ii) What was the weight of oxygen gas liberated ?

Solution :

(i) In first cell, silver is deposited at cathode as

$$Ag^+(aq) + e^- \longrightarrow Ag(s)$$

107.8 g of Ag require electricity = 96500 C

1.078 g of Ag require electricity = **965 C**

(ii) O_2 gas liberated at anode of first cell and second cell according to the equation :

$$2H_2O(l) \longrightarrow 4H^+(aq) + 4e^- + O_2(g)$$

4×96500 C electricity = 1 mol of O_2 at each cell

= 32 g of O_2 at each cell

$$965 \text{ C of electricity} = \frac{32}{4 \times 96500} \times 965$$

= 0.08 g O_2 at each cell

Total amount of O_2 at anode of both cells = 2×0.08 = **0.16 g.**

Type 6.

1. **Conductance (C) :** It is equal to the reciprocal of resistance (R)

$$C = \frac{1}{R}$$

Units of conductance (C) **:** ohm^{-1}, mho or S

2. **Specific Conductivity (κ, Kappa) :**

It is the reciprocal of specific resistance (ρ or resistivity) :

$$\kappa = \frac{1}{\rho} \quad \text{and} \quad R = \frac{\rho \times l}{a} \quad \text{or} \quad \frac{1}{\rho} = \frac{l}{a \times R}$$

or specific conductivity (κ) = conductance (C) $\times \frac{l}{a}$ = conductance × cell constant

3. **Equivalent Conductivity : "*The conductivity of solution containing 1 g equivalent of an electrolyte when placed between two sufficiently large electrodes which are 1 cm apart to each other is known as equivalent conductivity of the solution.*"**

It is denoted by λ_V, where V is the volume of solution in cc containing 1g equivalent of electrolyte.

Thus, $$\lambda_V = K_V \times V = K_V \times \frac{1000}{N}$$

where, N = Normality of solution of electrolyte.

Unit of λ_V is $ohm^{-1} cm^2$ $equivalent^{-1}$ or mho $cm^2 equivalent^{-1}$.

4. **Molecular Conductivity : "*The conductivity of a solution containing 1g mol of the electrolyte when placed between two sufficient large electrodes which are one cm apart to each other is known as molecular conductivity of the solution.*"** It is denoted by μ_V.

$$\mu_V = \kappa_V \times V = \kappa_V \times \frac{1000}{M}$$

where, M= molarity of solution of electolyte

Units of molecular conductivity μ_V : Unit of μ_V is ohm^{-1} cm^2 mol^{-1} or mho $cm^2 mol^{-1}$.

Numerical Problems

1. **0.5 normal solution of a salt placed between two platinum electrodes 2.0 cm. apart and of area of cross section 4.0 sq. cm. has a resistance of 25 ohms. Calculate the equivalent conductivity of solution.**

Solution :

1st Step : Calculation of specific conductivity.

Here, $l = 2.0$ cm, $a = 4.0$ cm^2, R = 25 ohms.

$$\therefore \qquad \text{Conductance G} = \frac{1}{25}\text{ohm}^{-1}$$

$$\text{Call constant} = \frac{l}{a} = \frac{2 \text{ cm}}{4 \text{ cm}^2} = \frac{1}{2}\text{cm}^{-1}$$

∴ Sq. conductivity(κ)

$$= \text{Observed conductance} \times \text{Cell constant}$$

$$= \frac{1}{25}\Omega^{-1} \times \frac{1}{2}\text{cm}^{-1} = 0.02\Omega^{-1}\text{ cm}^{-1}$$

2nd Step : Calculation of equivalent conductivity

$$\Lambda_{eq} = \kappa \times \frac{1000}{c_{eq}}$$

Here, $c = 0.5$ N, $\kappa = 0.02$ ohm^{-1} cm^{-1} (calculated above)

$$\therefore \qquad \Lambda_{eq} = \frac{(0.02\Omega^{-1}\text{cm}^{-1}) \times (1000 \text{ cm}^3\text{L}^{-1})}{(0.5 \text{ g eq L}^{-1})} = \mathbf{40\ \Omega^{-1}\ cm^2\ eq^{-1}\ or\ 40\ S\ cm^2\ eq^{-1}}$$

2. **The electrical resistance of a column of 0.05 M NaOH solution of diameter 1 cm and length 50 cm is 5.55 × 10^3 ohm. Calculate its resistivity, conductivity and molar conductivity.**

Solution :

(i) **Calculation of Resistivity :** Electrical resistance of the solution, R = 5.55 × 10^{3}W

Area of cross-section of the column (a) = $\pi r^2 = 3.14 \times \left(\frac{1}{2}\right)^2$ cm^2

Length of the column (l) = 50 cm

Applying the formula, $R = \rho\frac{l}{a}$

$$\rho = \frac{R \times a}{l} = \frac{(5.55 \times 10^3\ \Omega)(0.785 \text{ cm}^2)}{50 \text{ cm}} = 87.135 \text{ W cm}$$

i.e., Resistivity (ρ) = **87.135 W cm**

(ii) **Calculation of conductivity :**

$$\text{Conductivity } (\kappa) = \frac{1}{\rho} = \frac{1}{87.135\Omega \text{ cm}} = \mathbf{0.01148\ S\ cm^{-1}}$$

(iii) **Calculation of molar conductivity :**

$$\text{Molar conductivity } (\Lambda_m) = \frac{\kappa \times 1000}{\text{Molarity}}$$

$$= \frac{(0.01148 \text{ S cm}^{-1})(1000 \text{ cm}^3\text{L}^{-1})}{(0.05 \text{ mol L}^{-1})} = \mathbf{229.6\ S\ cm^2\ mol^{-1}}$$

3. Resistance of a conductivity cell filled with 0.1 mol L^{-1} KCl solution is 100 W. If the resistance of the same cell when filled with 0.02 mol L^{-1} KCl solution is 520 Ω, calculate the conductivity and molar conductivity of 0.02 M KCl solution. The conductivity of 0.1 M KCl solution is 1.29 S/m.

Solution :

(i) For 0.1 M KCl solution, R = 100 W, k = 1.29 S m^{-1}

Cell constant = Conductivity × Resistance

$$= 1.29\ S\ m^{-1} \times 100\ W = 129\ m^{-1}\ (S = W^{-1}) = \mathbf{1.29\ cm^{-1}}$$

(ii) Conductivity of 0.02 M KCl solution (k)

$$= \frac{\text{Cell constant}}{\text{Resistance}} = \frac{129\ m^{-1}}{520\Omega} = 0.248\ W^{-1}m^{-1} \text{ or } 0.248\ S\ m^{-1}$$

Concentration of the solution = 0.02 M = 0.02 mol L^{-1}

$$= 0.02 \times 10^3\ mol\ m^{-3} = 20\ mol\ m^{-3}$$

$$\text{Molar conductivity} = \frac{\kappa}{c_m} = \frac{0.248\ S\ m^{-1}}{20\ mol\ m^{-3}}$$

$$= 0.0124\ S\ m^2\ mol^{-1} = \mathbf{1.24 \times 10^{-2}\ S\ m^{-2}\ mol^{-1}}$$

$$\text{Alternatively,} \quad \kappa = \frac{\text{Cell const.}}{\text{Resistance}} = \frac{1.29\ cm^{-1}}{520\Omega} = 0.00248\ S\ cm^{-1}$$

$$\Lambda_m = \frac{\kappa}{c_m} = \frac{0.00248\ S\ cm^{-1} \times 1000\ cm^3 L^{-1}}{0.02 mol\ L^{-1}} = \mathbf{124\ S\ cm^2\ mol^{-1}}$$

Type 7.

1. **Kohlrausch's Law :** ***A infinite dilution the ions behave independently of each other and each ion makes a definite contribution towards equivalent conductivity at infinite dilution (λ_∞).***

General expression of Kohlrausch's law

$$A_xB_y \rightleftharpoons xA^+ + yB^-$$

Then,

$$\lambda_\infty = \lambda_{1/x}A^+ + \lambda_{1/y}B^-$$

For Example :

$$NaCl \rightleftharpoons Na^+ + Cl^-$$

$$\lambda_{\infty \text{ for NaCl}} = \lambda_{Na^+} + \lambda_{Cl^-}$$

Numerical Problems

1. **If the molar conductivities at infinite dilution of NaCl, HCl and CH_3COONa (NaAc) are 126.4, 425.9 and 91.0 S cm^2 mol^{-1} respectively, what will be that of acetic acid (HAc) ?**

Solution :

According to Kohlrausch's law, Λ° for $CH_3COOH = \lambda^o_{CH_3COO^-} + \lambda^o_{H^+}$

$$\Lambda° \text{ for NaCl} = \lambda^o_{Na^+} + \lambda^o_{Cl^-} = 126.4\ S\ cm^2\ mol^{-1} \quad ...(i)$$

$$\Lambda° \text{ for HCl} = \lambda^o_{H^+} + \lambda^o_{Cl^-} = 425.9\ S\ cm^2\ mol^{-1} \quad ...(ii)$$

$\Lambda°$ for $CH_3COONa = \lambda^o_{CH_3COO^-} + \lambda^o_{Na^+} = 91.0 \text{ S cm}^2 \text{ mol}^{-1}$ ...(iii)

Adding eqns. (ii) and (iii) and substracting (i), we get

$$\lambda^o_{H^+} + \lambda^o_{Cl^-} + \lambda^o_{CH_3COO^-} + \lambda^o_{Na^+} - \lambda^o_{Na^+} - \lambda^o_{Cl^-} = 425.9 + 91.0 - 126.4 \text{ S cm}^2 \text{ mol}^{-1}$$

or $\quad \lambda^o_{CH_3COO^-} + \lambda^o_{H^+} = 390.5 \text{ S cm}^2 \text{ mol}^{-1}$

i.e. $\quad \Lambda°$ for $CH_3COONa = \mathbf{390.5 \text{ S cm}^2 \text{ mol}^{-1}}$

2. Calculate $\Lambda°$ for $CaCl_2$ and $MgSO_4$ from the following data:

$\lambda°$ ($\text{S cm}^2 \text{ mol}^{-1}$) : $Ca^{2+} = 119.0$, $Mg^{2+} = 106.0$, $Cl^- = 76.3$, $SO_4^{2-} = 160.0$.

Solution : By Kohlrausch law,

$$\Lambda^o_m(CaCl_2) = \lambda^o_{Ca^{2+}} + 2\lambda^o_{Cl^-}$$
$$= 119.0 \text{ S cm}^2\text{mol}^{-1} + 2 \times 76.3 \text{ S cm}^2\text{mol}^{-1}$$
$$= (119.0 + 152.6)\text{S cm}^2 \text{ mol}^{-1} = 271.6 \text{ S cm}^2 \text{ mol}^{-1}$$

$$\lambda^o_m(MgSO_4) = \lambda^o_{Mg^{2+}} + \lambda^o_{SO_4^{2-}}$$
$$= 106.0 \text{ S cm}^2 \text{ mol}^{-1} + 160.0 \text{ S cm}^2 \text{ mol}^{-1} = \mathbf{266 \text{ S cm}^2 \text{ mol}^{-1}}$$

Type 8.

1. **Corrosion :** Corrosion is the oxidative deterioration of a metal, such as the conversion of iron to rust, a hydrated iron (III) oxide of approximate composition $Fe_2O_3 \cdot H_2O$.

   Many metals, particularly iron, undergo corrosion when exposed to air and water. Iron will not rust in dry air or in waιer that is free of dissolved oxygen. Both air and water are involved in the corrosion process. The presence of an electrolyte in the water accelerates corrosion, particularly when the solution is acidic.

   Corrosion is an electrochemical process (See figure). When iron is in contact with water—with even a microscopic drop of water, the iron tends to oxidise and give up electrons.

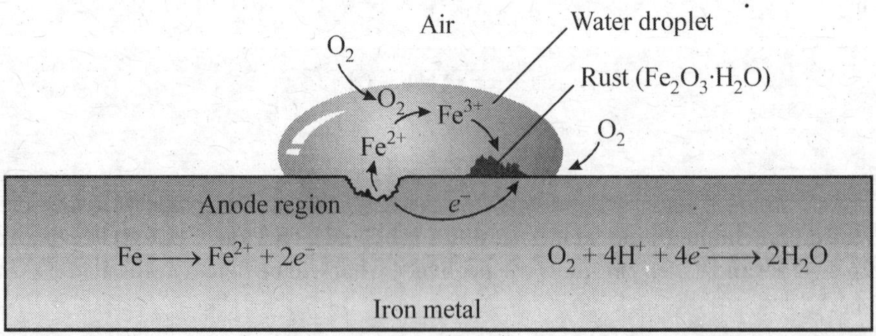

2. **Secondary Cells :** The battery in an automobile is a lead storage battery (also called a lead-acid battery). Its electrodes are lead alloy grids. One set grids is filled with lead (IV) oxide and the other with spongy lead metal. Dilute sulphuric acid serves as the electrolyte. When the battery discharges (delivers a current), the spongy lead is oxidized to lead ions, which

combines with sulphate ions of the electrolyte and coal the lead electrode with insoluble lead sulphate. The anode half-reaction is :

$$Pb(s) + SO_4^{2-}(aq) \longrightarrow PbSO_4(s) + 2e^-$$

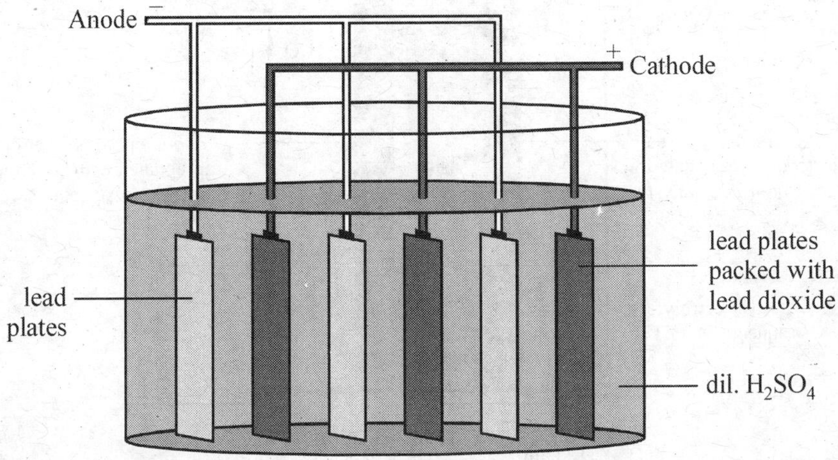

Lead storage battery

Electrons from the lead electrode flow through an external circuit and enter the lead (IV) oxide electrode. The lead (IV) oxide is reduced to lead (III) ions, and water is formed. Again lead ions combine with sulphate ions of the sulphuric acid electrolyte and this plate also becomes coated with lead sulphate. The cathode half-reaction is :

$$PbO_2(s) + 4H_3O^+(aq) + SO_4^{2-}(aq) + 2e^- \longrightarrow PbSO_4(s) + 6H_2O(l)$$

The charge and discharge at the two plates may be summarized as follows. At the lead plate

$$Pb(s) + SO_4^{2-}(aq) \underset{\text{Recharge}}{\overset{\text{Discharge}}{\rightleftharpoons}} PbSO_4(s) + 2e^-$$

At the lead oxide plate :

$$PbO_2(s) + 4H_3O^+ + SO_4^{2-}(aq) + 2e^- \underset{\text{Recharge}}{\overset{\text{Discharge}}{\rightleftharpoons}} PbSO_4(s) + 6H_2O(l)$$

During recharging, hydronium ions and sulphate ions are regenerated.

The net cell reaction of the lead storage battery is obtained by adding the two electrode reactions together.

$$Pb + PbO_2 + 4H_3O^+ + SO_4^{2-} \underset{\text{Recharge}}{\overset{\text{Discharge}}{\rightleftharpoons}} 2PbSO_4 + 6H_2O$$

The potenital of a single standard lead cell is 2.04 volts. The potential falls off slowly as the cell is used. A 12 volt automobile battery contains six lead storage cells.

3. **Fuel Cells :** Fuel cells are galvanic cells in which electrode materials, usually in the form of gases, are supplied continuously and are consumed to produce electricity.

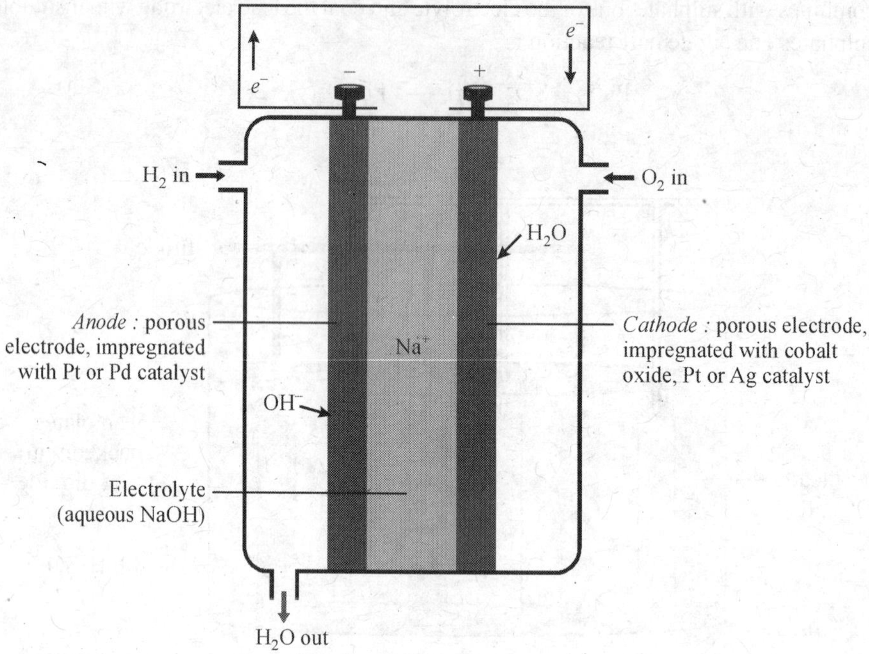

The anode half-reaction is

$$2H_2 + 4OH^- \longrightarrow 4H_2O + 4e^-$$

The cathode half-reaction is :

$$O_2 + 2H_2O + 4e^- \longrightarrow 4OH^-$$

The overall cell reaction is the combination of hydrogen and oxygen to produce water.

Anode : $2H_2 + 4OH^- \longrightarrow 4H_2O + 4e^-$

Cathode : $O_2 + 2H_2O + 4e^- \longrightarrow 4OH^-$

Cell reaction : $2H_2 + O_2 \longrightarrow 2H_2O$

Fuel cells have the potential for providing electricity from methane and other hydrocarbons much more efficienty than steam-driven generators. Thus, a great deal of effort is being spent investigating fuels such as methane and electrode systems for these fuels.c

Very Short Answer Type Questions

Q. 1. What are the units of conductance and specific conductance?

Ans. Conductance has units ohm^{-1} or S and specific conductance has unit ohm^{-1} cm^{-1} or ohm^{-1} m^{-1}.

Q. 2. Define conductivity (K).

Ans. It is the conducting power of all the ions present in one CC solution of the electrolyte.

Q. 3. What will happen to the conductivity of a metal upon heating?

Ans. It will decrease upon heating.

Q. 4. Can an electric current pass through solid sodium chloride?

Ans. No, current cannot pass through solid NaCl because the ions do not move in the solid state.

Q. 5. When the zinc electrode having reduction potential –0.76 V is attached to NHE, will it act as anode or cathode?

Ans. Since reduction potential is negative, oxidation will occur at this electrode. It will act as anode.

Q. 6. What will the effect of dilution on the molar and equivalent conductance of an electrolyte?

Ans. With dilution, more of ions are formed in the solution. Therefore, both molar conductance and equivalent conductance increase upon dilution.

Q. 7. What is the basic difference in a primary and a secondary cell?

Ans. A primary cell cannot be recharged while a secondary cell can be recharged.

Q. 8. Can we determine Λ_m^∞ for weak electrolyte?

Ans. No, it is not possible because the dissociation of weak electrolyte is never complete.

Q. 9. Suggest a list of metals that are extracted electrolytically.

Ans. Sodium, calcium, magnesium, aluminium.

Q. 10. Suggest two materials other than hydrogen that can be used as fuels in fuel cells.

Ans. Methane and methanal.

Short Answer Type Questions – I

Q. 1. How would you determine the standard potential of Mg^{2+} / Mg?

Ans. We will set up a cell consisting of Mg/Mg SO_4(1M) as one electrode (by dipping a magnesium wire in 1M Mg SO_4 solution) and standard hydrogen electrode Pt, H_2 (1 atm) H^+ / (1 M) as the second electrode and measure the EMF of the cell and also note the direction of deflection in the voltmeter. The direction of deflection shows that electrons flow from magnesium electrode to hydrogen electrode, i.e., oxidation takes place on magnesium electrode and reduction on hydrogen electrode. Hence, the cell may be represented as follows —

$$Mg/Mg^{2+}\,(1\text{ m})\,||\,H^+\,(1M)\,/\,H_2\,(1\text{ atm}),\,Pt$$

$$E^o_{cell} = E^o\,H^+,\ \frac{1}{2}\,H_2 - E^o\,Mg^{2+},\,Mg$$

But $\quad E^o\,H^+,\ \frac{1}{2}\,H_2 = 0$

Hence, $\quad E^o\,Mg^{2+},\,Mg = -\,E^o_{cell}$

Q. 2. Can you store copper sulphate solution in a zinc pot?

Ans. Zinc is more reactive than copper. Hence, it displaces copper from copper sulphate solution as follows —

$$Zn(S) + CuSO_4\,(aq) \longrightarrow ZnSO_4\,(sq) + Cu(s)$$

Thus, zinc reacts with $CuSO_4$ solution. Hence, we cannot store copper sulphate solution in a zinc pot.

Q. 3. Consult the table of the standard electrode potentials and suggest three substances that can oxidize ferrous ions under suitable conditions.

Ans. Oxidation of ferrous ions means that the following reaction should occur:—

$$Fe^{2+} \longrightarrow Fe^{3+} + e^-;\ E^0_{ox} = -\,0.77\text{ V}$$

Only those substances can oxidize Fe^{2+} to Fe^{3+} which are stronger oxidizing agents and have positive reduction potentials greater than 0.77 V so that EMF of the cell reaction is positive. This is so for elements lying below Fe^{3+}/Fe^{2+} in the electrochemical series, e.g. Br_2, Cl_2 and F_2.

Q. 4. Calculate the potential of hydrogen electrode in contact with a solution whose pH is 10.

Ans. For hydrogen electrode,

$$H^+ + e^- \longrightarrow \frac{1}{2} H_2$$

Applying Nernst equation,

$$E_{H^+, \frac{1}{2} H_2} = E^0_{H^+, \frac{1}{2} H_2} - \frac{0.0591}{n} \log \frac{1}{[H^+]}$$

$$= 0 - \frac{0.0591}{1} \log \frac{1}{10^{-10}} \quad (\text{pH} = 10 \text{ means } [H^+] = 10^{-10} \text{ M})$$

$$= -0.0591 \times 10 = -0.591 \text{ V}.$$

Q. 5. Calculate the emf of the cell in which the following reaction takes place:—

$$Ni(S) + 2Ag^+ (0.002 \text{ M}) \longrightarrow Ni^{2+} (0.160 \text{ M}) + 2Ag(S)$$

Given that $E^0_{cell} = 1.05 \text{ V}$.

Ans. Applying Nernst equation to the given cell reaction

$$E_{cell} = E^0_{cell} - \frac{0.0591}{n} \log \frac{[Ni^{2+}]}{[Ag^+]^2}$$

$$= 1.05 - \frac{0.0591}{2} \log \frac{0.160}{(0.002)^2}$$

$$= 1.05 - \frac{0.0591}{2} \log (4 \times 10^4)$$

$$= 1.05 - \frac{0.0591}{2} (4.6021) = 1.05 - 0.14 = \mathbf{0.91\ V}$$

Q. 6. Why does the conductivity of a solution decrease with dilution?

Ans. Conductivity of a solution is the conductance of ions present in a unit volume of the solution. On dilution, the number of ions per unit volume decreases. Hence, the conductivity decreases.

Q. 7. Suggest a way to determine the Λ^0_m value of water.

Ans. $\Lambda^0_m (H_2O) = \lambda^0 H^+ + \lambda^0 OH^-$

We determine Λ^0_m (HCl), Λ^0_m (NaOH) and Λ^0_m (NaCl)

Then $\Lambda^0_m (H_2O) = \Lambda^0_m (HCl) + \Lambda^0_m (NaOH) - \Lambda^0_m (NaCl)$

$$= \Lambda^0_m (H^+) + \Lambda^0_m (Cl^-) + \Lambda^0_m (Na^+) + \Lambda^0_m (OH^{-1}) - \Lambda^0_m (Na^+) - \Lambda^0_m (Cl^-)$$

$$\Lambda^0_m (H_2O) = \Lambda^0_m (H^+) + \Lambda^0_m (OH^-).$$

Q. 8. If a current of 0.5 ampere flows through a metallic wire for 2 hours, then how many electrons flow through the wire?

Ans.
$$Q = I \times t$$
$$= (0.5 \text{ ampere}) \times (2 \times 60 \times 60 \text{ S}) = 3600\ l.$$

A flow of 1 F, i.e. 96500 C is equivalent to flow of 1 mole of electrons, i.e. 6.02×10^{23} electrons.

$\therefore$ 3600 C is equivalent to flow of electrons $= \dfrac{6.02 \times 10^{23}}{96500} \times 3600$

$$= 2.246 \times 10^{22} \text{ electrons}.$$

Q. 9. Given the standard electrode potentials $K^+/K = -2.93$ V, $Ag^+/Ag = 0.80$ V, $Hg_2^{2+}/Hg = 0.79$ V, $Mg^2/mg = -2.37$ V, $Cr^{2+}/Cr = -0.74$ V. Arrange these metals in their increasing order of reducing power.

Ans. Higher the oxidation potential, more easily it is oxidised and hence greater is the reducing power. Thus, increasing order of reducing power will be Ag < Hg < Cr < Mg < K.

Q. 10. The conductivity of 0.20 M solution of KCl at 298 K is 0.0248 S cm^{-1}. Calculate its molar conductivity.

Ans. Given value $K = 0.0248 \text{ S cm}^{-1}$

Molarity = 0.20 M

$$\Lambda_m = \frac{K \times 1000}{\text{Molarity}} = \frac{0.0248 \text{ S cm}^{-1} \times 1000 \text{ cm}^3 \text{ L}^{-1}}{0.20 \text{ mol L}^{-1}} = \mathbf{124 \text{ S cm}^2 \text{ mol}^{-1}}.$$

Short Answer Type Questions – II

Q. 1. What is the difference between e.m.f. and potential difference?

Ans. Differences between e.m.f. and potential difference :

E.M.F.	Potential difference
1. It is the potential difference between the true electrodes of an electrochemical cell when no current is flowing in the circuit, i.e., in an open circuit.	1. It is difference of the electrode potentials of the two electrodes of an electrochemical cell when the cell is sending current through the circuit.
2. It is maximum voltage obtainable from the cell.	2. It is less than the maximum voltage obtainable from the cell (i.e., E.M.F. of the cell).
3. It is responsible for the flow of steady current in the cell.	3. It is not responsible for the flow of steady current in the cell.

Q. 2. The cell in which the following reaction occurs:

$$2Fe^{3+} + 2e^- \longrightarrow 2\,Fe^{2+}$$

or

$$2I^- \longrightarrow I_2\, 2e^-.$$

Ans. For the given cell reaction, $n = 2$

$$\Delta rG^0 = -nFE^0_{cell}$$
$$= -2 \times 96500 \times 0.236 \text{ J}$$
$$= -45.55 \text{ KJ mol}^{-1}.$$
$$\Delta rG^0 = -2.303 \text{ RT} \log Kc$$

$$\therefore \quad \log Kc = -\frac{\Delta rG^0}{2.303 \text{RT}}$$

$$= \frac{-45.55 \text{ KJ mol}^{-1}}{2.303 \times 8.314 \times 10^{-3} \text{ KJK}^{-1} \text{ mol}^{-1} \times 298 \text{ K}} = 7.832$$

$$\therefore \quad Kc = \text{Antilog}(7.983) = 9.616 \times 10^7.$$

Q. 3. The resistance of a conductivity cell containing 0.001m KCl solution at 298 K is 1500 Ω what is the cell constant if conductivity of 0.001m KCl solution at 298 K is 0.146×10^{-3} S cm^{-1}?

Ans. Cell constant $= \dfrac{\text{Conductivity}}{\text{Conductance}} = \text{Conductivity} \times \text{Resistance}$

$$= 0.146 \times 10^{-3} \text{ S cm}^{-1} \times 1500\, \Omega = 0.219 \text{ cm}^{-1}.$$

Q. 4. Depict the galvanic cell in which the reaction

$$Zn(S) + 2Ag^+(aq) \longrightarrow Zn^{2+}(aq) + 2Ag(S)$$

takes place, further shows:—

(*i*) Which of the electrode is negatively charged?

(*ii*) The carriers of the current in the cell.

(*iii*) Individual reaction at each electrode.

Ans. The cell may be represented as:

$$Zn(s) \mid Zn^{2+}(aq) \parallel Ag^+(aq) \mid Ag(S)$$

(*i*) Zinc electrode (anode)

(*ii*) Current will flow from silver to zinc in the external circuit.

(*iii*) At anode: $Zn(S) \longrightarrow Zn^{2+} + 2e^-$

At cathode: $Ag^+(aq) + e^- \longrightarrow Ag(S)$.

Q. 5. Define conductivity and molar conductivity for the solution of an electrolyte. Discuss their variation with concentration.

Ans. 1. *Conductivity*—The conductivity of solutions of different electrolytes in the same solvent and at a given temperature differ due to difference in charge and size of the ions in which they dissociate, the concentration of ions or ease with which the ions more under potential gradient.

2. *Molar Conductivity*—It is defined as the conducting power of all the ions produced by one gram mole of an electrolyte in a solution. It is denoted by Λ_m

$$\Lambda_m = \frac{K}{C} \times 1000 \text{ S cm}^2 \text{ mol}^{-1}$$

Where 'K' is electrolytic conductivity of solution

'C' is concentration of solution.

The unit of Λ_m is Ω^{-1} cm^2 mol^{-1} or S cm^2 mol^{-1}.

Variation of conductivity and molar conductivity with concentration—Both conductivity and molar conductivity change with change in concentration of electrolyte.

1. *Conductivity*—always decreases with decrease in concentration both for weak as well as strong electrolytes.
2. *Molar conductivity*—increases with decrease in concentration.

Long Answer Type Questions

Q. 1. (*i*) Give three differences, between electrochemical and electrolytical cells.

(*ii*) Calculate the electrode potential of a zinc electrode dipped in 0.1 m $ZnSO_4$ solution at 25°C.

Given that: $E^o_{Zn/Zn^{2+}} = 0.76$ V.

Ans. (*i*)

Electrochemical cell	Electolytic cell
1. Chemical energy is converted into electrical energy.	1. Electrical energy is converted into chemical energy.
2. The cell reaction is spontaneous.	2. The cell reaction is non-spontaneous.
3. Two electrolytes are used.	3. Only, one electrolyte is used.

(*ii*) $Zn^{2+}(aq) + 2e^- \rightleftharpoons Zn(s)$

$$E_{zn} = E^0_{zn} + \frac{0.0591}{2} \log [Zn^{2+}]$$

$$= -0.76 + \frac{0.0591}{2} \log (10^{-1}) = -0.76 - \frac{0.0591}{2} \log 10$$

$$E_{zn} = -0.76 - \frac{0.0591}{2} \times 1 = -0.76 - 0.0295 = -0.7895 \text{ V.}$$

∴ Oxidation potential of Zn electrode = +0.7895 V.

Q. 2. (*i*) Explain Faraday's First and Second law of electrolysis.

(*ii*) Calculate the molar conductance of NH_4OH at infinite dilution (Λ^0m). If (Λ^0m) for NH_4Cl, NaOH and NaCl are 129.80, 217.40 and 108.45 Ω^{-1} cm^2 mol^{-1} respectively.

Ans. (*i*) *Faraday's First Law of Electrolysis*—The amount of substance deposited during electrolysis is directly proportional to quantity of electricity paned.

$$W \propto Q$$
$$W = ZQ$$

Where Z in electrochemical equivalent of the substance.

Faraday's Second Law of Electrolysis—It states that when the same quantity of electricity is passed through different electrolytes connected in series, the masses of the substances produced at the respective electrodes will be in the ratio of their equivalent masses.

Suppose there are two voltameters containing $CuSO_4$ and $AgNO_3$ solutions connected in series. Let a certain current is passed through them for sometime. According to Faraday's second law of electrolysis :

$$\frac{\text{Mass of Cu deposited}}{\text{Mass of ag deposited}} = \frac{\text{Eq.mass of Cu}}{\text{Eq.mass of Ag}}.$$

(*ii*) $\Lambda^{\infty}_m (NH_4OH) = \Lambda^0_m (NH_4Cl) + \Lambda^0_m (NaOH) - \Lambda^0_m (NaCl)$

$= 129.80 + 217.40 - 108.45$

$= 238.75 \; \Omega^{-1} \; cm^2 \; mol^{-1}$.

Q. 3. State and explain Kohlrausch's law. How would you calculate the molar conductance of acetic acid at infinite dilution with the help of this law?

Ans. This law states that :

At infinite dilution when dissociation is complete, each ion makes a definite contribution towards molar conductivity of the electrolyte irrespective of the nature of the other ion with which it is associated. This means that the molar conductivity at infinite dilution for a given salt can be expressed as the sum of the individual contribution from the ions of the electrolyte i.e.

$$\Lambda^{\infty}_m (AB) = \Lambda^{\infty}_m (A^+) + \Lambda^{\infty}_m (B^-)$$

Where $\Lambda^{\infty}_m (A^+)$ and $\Lambda^{\infty}_m (B^-)$ are called limiting ionic molar conductances. For examples,

$$\Lambda^{\infty}_m (NaCl) = \Lambda^{\infty}_m (Na^+) + \Lambda^{\infty}_m (Cl^-)$$

Application of Kohlrausch's law for the determination of limiting molar conductance of acetic acid—

We know that it is not possible to determine accurately Λ^{∞}_m value for a weak electrolyte by extrapolation of Λ^{∞}_m versur $\sqrt{C}$ graph. However, it can be calculated easily by using

Kohlrausch's law. For example, the molar conductance at infinite dilution of CH_3COOH can be calculated from the values of molar conductances at infinite dilution of CH_3COONa, HCl and NaCl (Strong electrolytes) as follows:—

$$\Lambda_m^{\infty}(CH_3COOH) = \Lambda_m^{\infty}(CH_3COO^-) + \Lambda_m^{\infty}(H^+)$$

$$\Lambda_m^{\infty}(CH_3COOH) = \Lambda_m^{\infty}(CH_3COO^-) + \Lambda_m^{\infty}(Na^+) + \Lambda_m^{\infty}(H^+) + \Lambda_m^{\infty}(Cl^-) - \Lambda_m^{\infty}(Na^+) - \Lambda_m^{\infty}(Cl^-)$$

$$\Lambda^{\infty}(CH_3COOH) = \Lambda_m^{\infty}(CH_3COONa) + \Lambda_m^{\infty}(HCl) - \Lambda_m^{\infty}(NaCl)$$

Q. 4. Discuss the electrochemical theory of rusting.

Ans. The rusting of iron can be explained on the basis of electrochemical theory which involves oxidation and reduction reaction.

According to this theory, it is believed that non-uniform surface of metal or impurities present in iron behaves like small electric cells (called corrosion couples) in the presence of water containing dissolved oxygen or CO_2. A film of moisture with dissolved CO_2 acts as electrolytic solution covering the metal surface at various places.

In these small electrolytic cells, pure ion acts as anode while cathodes are impure portions. The overall rusting involves the following steps:—

Oxidation occurs at the anodes of each electrochemical cell, therefore, at each anode iron is oxidised to Fe^{2+} ions.

At anode—

$$Fe(S) \longrightarrow Fe^{2+}(aq) + 2e^- \qquad (i)$$

At the cathode of each cell, the electrons are taken up by hydrogen ions (reduction takes places) the H^+ ions are obtained either from water or from acidic substances in water:—

$$H_2O \rightleftharpoons H^+ + OH^- \qquad (ii)$$

or

$$CO_2 + H_2O \longrightarrow H^+ + HCO_3^- \qquad (iii)$$

At Cathode:

$$H^+ + e^- \longrightarrow H \qquad (iv)$$

The hydrogen atoms on the iron surface reduce dissolved oxygen:

$$4H + O_2 \longrightarrow 2H_2O \qquad (v)$$

Therefore, the overall reaction at cathode of different electrochemical cells may be written as—

$$4H^+(aq) + O_2(g) + 4e^- \longrightarrow 2H_2O(l) \qquad (vi)$$

The overall redox reaction may be written by multiplying reaction at anode, Eq. (*i*) by Z and adding reaction at cathode Eq. (iv) to equalize number of electrons lost and gained, i.e.,

Oxidation half reaction

$$Fe(S) \longrightarrow Fe^{2+}(aq) + 2e^-] XZ$$

Reduction half reaction

$$4H^+(aq) + O_2(g) + 4e^- \longrightarrow 2H_2O(l)$$

Overall cell reaction

$$2Fe(S) + 4H^+(aq) + O_2(g) \longrightarrow 2Fe^{2+}(aq) + 2H_2O(l)$$

The ferrous ions are oxidized further by atmospheric oxygen to Fe^{3+} (as Fe_2O_3) and form rust.

$$4Fe^{2+} + O_2(g) + 4H_2O \longrightarrow 2Fe_2O_3 + 8H^+$$

and

$$Fe_2O_3 + xH_2O \longrightarrow \underset{\text{(Rust)}}{2Fe_2O_3 . xH_2O}$$

The H^+ ions produced above are also used for reaction (*iv*)

$$4Fe^2 + O_2 + 4H_2O \longrightarrow 2Fe_2O_3 + 8H^+(aq)$$

$$Fe_2O_3 + xH_2O \longrightarrow Fe_2O_3 . xH_2O$$

Drop of moisture

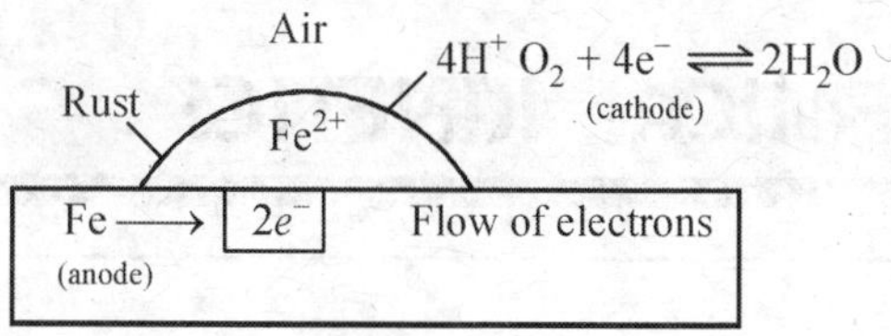

Higher Order Thinking Skills Hots Questions

1. What are the signs of ΔG, K and E^0_{cell} for a spontaneous cell reaction?

2. Write Nernst equation for the electrode reaction

$$M^{n+}(aq) + ne^- \longrightarrow M(s)$$

3. Why does electrolysis of aqueous solution of NaBr and NaI give Br_2 and I_2 respectively whereas that of NaF gives O_2 instead of F_2?

4. Calculate equilibrium constant for the reaction

$$Fe(s) + Cd^{2+}(aq) \longrightarrow Fe^{2+}(aq) + Cd(s)$$

Given: $E^0(Cd^{2+}/Cd) = -0.40\ V, E^0(Fe^{2+}/Fe) = -0.44\ V.$ **Ans. 22.7**

5. (*a*) Describe standard hydrogen electrode and give one of its applications.

(*b*) A Voltaic cell is set up at 25°C with the following half cells:

Al/Al^{3+} (0.001 M) and Ni/Ni^{2+} (0.50 M)

Calculate the cell voltage

$$\left[E^o_{Ni^{2+}/Ni} = -0.25\ V, E^o_{Al^{3+}/Al} = +1.66\ V\right]$$ **Ans. 1.463 V**

6. What are fuel cells ? Give one example.

7. What are the units of conductivity ?

8. Why does blue colour of copper sulphate solutions get discharged when iron rod is dipped into it, given : $E°(Cu^{2+} | Cu) = +0.34\ V; E°(Fe^{2+} | Fe) = -0.44\ V.$

9. Can we store

(i) $CuSO_4$ solution in zinc vessel ?

(ii) $FeSO_4$ solution in silver vessel ?

Give suitable explanation in support of your answer.

10. (a) Define molar conductivity and specific conductivity and give the relationship between them.

(b) Calculate the e.m.f. of the following cell at 298 K :

Given $E°(Cu^{2+} | Cu) = +0.34\ V, E°(Mg^{2+} | Mg) = -2.37\ V.$

11. Explain why the electrolysis of aqueous solution of NaCl gives H_2 at cathode and Cl_2 at anode ? Write overall reaction.

$E°Na^+ | Na = -2.71\ V; E°\ H_2O | H_2 = -0.83\ V, E°\ Cl | 2Cl^- = 1.36\ V, E°\ H^+ + O_2 | H_2O = 1.23\ V)$

12. Write cell reactions which occur in lead stronger battery :

(i) when battery is in use

(ii) when the battery is on charging.

13. What are primary cells ? How do they differ from stornger batteries ?

❑❑❑

CHAPTER

4 CHEMICAL KINETICS

Syllabus

- *Rate of a reaction (average and instantaneous), factors affecting rates of reaction; concentration, temperature, catalyst; order and molecularity of a reaction; rate law and specific rate constant, integrated rate equations and half life (only for zero and first order reactions); collision theory (elementary idea, no mathematical treatment).*

1. **Rate of Reaction :** The change in any one of the reactants or products per unit time.
Consider a hypothetical reaction :

$$R \longrightarrow P$$

(i) The rate of disappearance or decrease in concentration of R (reactants) :

$$\text{Rate of reaction} = \frac{\text{Decrease in concentration of R}}{\text{Time taken}}$$

(ii) The rate of increase in concentration of P (products) :

$$\text{Rate of reaction} = \frac{\text{Increase in concentration of P}}{\text{Time taken}}$$

2. **Unit of rate of reaction :** The concentrations of reactants and products are often exprressed in mol litre^{-1} and the time in second or minute.

$$\text{Rate} = \frac{d[\text{Product}]}{dt} = -\frac{d[\text{Reactant}]}{dt}$$

This unit of rate will be mol litre^{-1} time^{-1} or mol litre^{-1} sec^{-1} or mol litre^{-1} min^{-1}.

3. **The instantaneous rate of a reaction is its rate at a particular moment in its course. It is the average rate over an arbitrarily short period of time.**
Thus, to obtain instantaneous rate, one has to consider the average rate when time interval is smallest (say) dt.

$$A \longrightarrow B$$

or $\quad r_{\text{instantaneous}}$ for disappearance of A $= \frac{-d[A]}{dt}$

$r_{\text{instantaneous}}$ for formation of B $= \frac{-d[B]}{dt}$

$$\text{Instantaneous rate} = -\frac{d[A]}{dt} = -\frac{d[B]}{dt}$$

Type 1. Order of Reaction-based Numerical

Example 1. A chemical reaction 2A $\longrightarrow$ 4B + C in gaseous phase shows an increase in

concentration of B by 5×10^{-3} M in 10 second. Calculate.

(a) rate of appearance of B

(b) rate of the reaction

(c) rate of disappearance of A

Solution : Rate of appearance of B $= \frac{\text{Increase in [B]}}{\text{time}} = \frac{5\times10^{-3}}{10} = \mathbf{5 \times 10^{-4}\ M\ s^{-1}}$

Also rate of reaction $= -\frac{1}{2}\frac{d[A]}{dt} = \frac{1}{4}\frac{d[B]}{dt} = \frac{1}{4}\times5\times10^{-4} = \mathbf{1.25 \times 10^{-4}\ M\ s^{-1}}$

and rate of disappearance of A $= -\frac{d[A]}{dt} = \frac{1}{2}\frac{d[B]}{dt} = \frac{1}{2}\times5\times10^{-4}$

$= \mathbf{2.5 \times 10^{-4}\ M\ s^{-1}}$

Example 2. The reaction $2N_2O_5 \longrightarrow 4NO_2 + O_2$ shows an increase in concentration of NO_2 by 20×10^{-3} mol litre^{-1} in 5 second. Calculate (i) rate of appearance of NO_2, (ii) rate of reaction, and (iii) rate of disappearance of N_2O_5.

Solution : Increase in concentration of $NO_2 = 0 \times 10^{-1}$ mol litre^{-1}, time taken = 5 sec.

(i) Rate of appearance of $NO_2 = \frac{\Delta[NO_2]}{\Delta t} = \frac{20\times10^{-3}}{5}$

$= \mathbf{4 \times 10^{-3}\ mol\ litre^{-1} sec^{-1}}$

(ii) Rate of reaction $= -\frac{1}{2}\frac{\Delta[N_2O_2]}{\Delta t} = \frac{1}{4}\frac{\Delta[NO_2]}{\Delta t} = \frac{\Delta[O_2]}{\Delta t}$

$= \frac{1}{4} \times 4 \times 10^{-3} = \mathbf{1 \times 10^{-3}\ mol\ litre^{-1}\ sec^{-1}}$

(iii) Rate of disappearance of $N_2O_5 = -\frac{\Delta[N_2O_5]}{\Delta t} = \frac{1}{2}\frac{\Delta[NO_2]}{\Delta t} = \frac{1}{2}\times4\times10^{-3}$

$= \mathbf{2 \times 10^{-3}\ mol\ litre^{-1}\ sec^{-1}}$.

4. **Order of reaction :** The sum of the power to which the concentration terms are raised in the rate law equation to express the observed rate of the reaction.
   If the rate of a reaction,

$$aA + bB + cC \longrightarrow \text{Products}$$

is given by the rate law as : Rate $= -\frac{dx}{dt} = k\,[A]^x\,[B]^y\,[C]^z$

then, the order of the reaction, n is :

$$n = x + y + z$$

Example 3. The reaction $A + 2B \longrightarrow C$ obeys the rate equation

$$\mathbf{Rate = k\,[A]^{1/2}\,[B]^{3/2}}$$

What is the order of the reaction?

Solution : The rate law of the given reaction is

$$\text{Rate} = k[A]^{1/2}\,[B]^{3/2}$$

$\therefore$ The order of reaction with respect to A $= \frac{1}{2}$

The order of reaction with respect to B $= \frac{3}{2}$

Overall order of reaction $= \frac{1}{2} + \frac{3}{2} = 2$.

Example 4. **For the reaction A + B $\longrightarrow$ D, it has been found experimentally that the rate of reaction gets doubled on doubling the concentration of A and the rate increases 4 times on doubling the concentration of B. Write the rate law and find the order of the reaction.**

Solution Since the rate of reaction gets doubled on doubling the concentration of A, the rate is directly proportional to the concentration of A. Moreover, as the concentration of B is doubled, the rate increases 4 times. This implies that the rate is proportional to the square of concentration of B. Therefore, the rate law should be

$$\text{Rate} = k\,[A]\,[B]^2$$

The given reaction is of order 1 with respect to A and of order 2 with rspcet to B. Hence, overall order of reaction = 1 + 2 = 3.

Example 5. **The following data were obtained for the reaction :**

$$2NO_2(g) + F_2(g) \longrightarrow 2NO_2F$$

Experiment	Initial conc.		Initial rate
	$[NO_2]_0$	$[F_2]_0$	Mol L^{-1} min^{-1}
1	0.20	0.05	6.0×10^{-3}
2	0.40	0.05	1.2×10^{-2}
3	0.80	0.10	4.8×10^{-2}

Determine (i) order of reaction, (ii) rate law
(iii) rate of reaction when $[NO_2] = 0.50$ mol L^{-1} and $[F_2] = 0.60$ mol L^{-1}.

Solution The initial rate expression may be written as :

$$(\text{Rate})_0 = k[NO_2]^p\,[F_2]^q$$

Comparing experiments 1 and 2, we get

$$(\text{Rate})_1 = k(0.2)^p\,(0.05)^q = 6.0 \times 10^{-3} \quad \text{...(i)}$$

$$(\text{Rate})_2 = k(0.4)^p\,(0.05)^q = 1.2 \times 10^{-2} \quad \text{...(ii)}$$

Dividing Eq. (ii) by Eq. (i)

$$\frac{(\text{Rate})_2}{(\text{Rate})_1} = \frac{k(0.4)^p(0.05)^q}{k(0.2)^p(0.05)^q} = \frac{1.2\times10^{-2}}{6.0\times10^{-3}}$$

or $\quad (2)^p = 2$

$\therefore \quad p = 1$

Thus, order with respect to NO_2 is 1.

Comparing experiments 2 and 3,

$$(\text{Rate})_2 = k(0.4)^p\,(0.05)^q = 1.2 \times 10^{-2} \quad \text{...(iii)}$$

$$(\text{Rate})_3 = k(0.8)^p\,(0.10)^q = 4.8 \times 10^{-2} \quad \text{...(iv)}$$

Dividing Eq. (iv) by Eq. (iii), we get :

$$\frac{k(0.8)^p(0.10)^q}{k(0.4)^p(0.05)^q} = \frac{4.8\times10^{-2}}{1.2\times10^{-2}}$$

$$(2)^p(2)^q = 4$$

Now, we have obtained $p = 1$ for the reaction, so that

$$(2)^1(2)^q = 4 \quad \text{or} \quad (2)^n = 2 \text{ or } q = 1$$

Thus, order w.r.t. F_2 is 1

(i) Order of reaction = 1 + 1 = 2

(ii) Rate law for the reaction is

$$\text{Rate} = k[NO_2][F_2]$$

(iii) Rate of reaction, when $[NO_2] = 0.50 \text{ mol L}^{-1}$ and $[F_2] = 0.60 \text{ mol L}^{-1}$.

Let us first calculate, k from first run.

$$\text{Rate} = k[NO_2][F_2]$$

$$6.0\times10^{-3} \text{ mol L}^{-1}\text{ min}^{-1} = k(0.20 \text{ mol L}^{-1})\times(0.05 \text{ mol L}^{-1})$$

or $$k = \frac{60\times10^{-3}}{0.20\times0.05} = \text{mol L}^{-1}\text{ min}^{-1} = 60 \text{ mol}^{-1}\text{ L min}^{-1}$$

Substituting the values of k, $[NO_2]$ and $[F_2]$

$$\text{Rate} = 6.0\times(0.5)\times(0.60) = \mathbf{0.18 \text{ mol L}^{-1}\text{ min}^{-1}}$$

Problem 1. The following results have been obtained during the kinetic studies of the reaction:

$$2A + B \longrightarrow C + D$$

Experiment	[A]/mol L^{-1}	[B]/mol L^{-1}	Initial rate of formation of D/mol L^{-1} min^{-1}
I	0.1	0.1	6.0×10^{-3}
II	0.3	0.2	7.2×10^{-2}
III	0.3	0.4	2.88×10^{-1}
IV	0.4	0.1	2.40×10^{-2}

Determine the rate law and the rate constant for the reaction.

[**Ans.** Rate = $k[A][B]^2$, Rate constant $k = 56.0 \text{ mol}^{-2}\text{ L}^2\text{ min}^{-1}$]

Problem 2. The reaction between A and B is first order with respect to A and zero order with respect to B. Fill in the blanks in the following table :

Experiment	[A]/mol L^{-1}	[B]/mol L^{-1}	Initial/mol L^{-1} min^{-1}
I	0.1	0.1	2.0×10^{-2}
II	–	0.2	4.0×10^{-2}
III	0.4	0.4	–
IV	–	0.2	2.0×10^{-2}

Ans. The rate expression will be : Rate = $k[A]^1[B]^0 = k[A]$

For expt. I, $2.0 \times 10^{-2} = \text{mol L}^{-1} \text{min}^{-1} = k(0.1 \text{ M})$ or $k = \mathbf{0.2 \ min^{-1}}$

For expt. II, $4.0 \times 10^{-2} \text{ mol L}^{-1} \text{min}^{-1} = 0.2 \text{ min}^{-1} [A]$ or $[A] = \mathbf{0.2 \ mol \ L^{-1}}$

For expt. III, Rate $= (0.2 \text{ min}^{-1}) (0.4 \text{ mol L}^{-1}) = \mathbf{0.05 \ mol \ L^{-1} \ min^{-1}}$

For expt. IV. $2.0 \times 10^{-2} \text{ mol L}^{-1} \text{min}^{-1} = 0.2 \text{ min}^{-1} [A]$ or $[A] = \mathbf{0.1 \ mol \ L^{-1}}$.

Type 2. First Order-based Numerical

For first order reaction : $$k = \frac{2.303}{t} \log \frac{a}{a-x}$$

and $$t_{50\%} = \frac{0.693}{k} \quad \text{or} \quad k = \frac{0.693}{t_{50\%}}$$

Example 6. A first order reaction is found to have a rate constant, $k = 5.5 \times 10^{-14} \text{ s}^{-1}$. Find the half-life of the reaction.

Solution : For a first order reaction,

$$t_{1/2} = \frac{0.693}{k} = \frac{0.693}{5.5 \times 10^{-14} \text{ s}^{-1}} = \mathbf{1.26 \times 10^{13} \ s}$$

Example 7. The initial concentration of N_2O_5 in the first order reaction, $N_2O_5(g) \longrightarrow 2NO_2(g) + 1/2 \ O_2(g)$, was 1.24×10^{-2} mol L^{-1} at 318 K. The concentration of N_2O_5 after 60 minutes was 0.20×10^{-2} mol L^{-1}. Calculate the rate constant of the reaction at 318 K.

Solution : $$k = \frac{2.303}{t} \log \frac{[A]_0}{[A]} = \frac{2.303}{t} \log \frac{[N_2O_5]_0}{[N_2O_5]_t}$$

$$= \frac{2.303}{60 \text{ min}} \log \frac{1.24 \times 10^{-2} \text{ mol L}^{-1}}{0.2 \times 10^{-2} \text{ mol L}^{-1}} = \frac{2.303}{60} \log 6.2 \text{ min}^{-1}$$

$$= \frac{2.303}{60} \times 0.7924 \text{ min}^{-1} = \mathbf{0.0304 \ min^{-1}}$$

Example 8. The decomposition of $N_2O_5(g)$, i.e., $N_2O_5(g) \longrightarrow 4NO_2(g)$ is a first order reaction with a rate constant of 5×10^{-4} sec^{-1} at 45°C. If initial concentration of N_2O_5 is 0.25 M, calculate its concentration after 2 min. Also calculate half life for the decomposition of $N_2O_5(g)$.

Solution : $k = 5 \times 10^{-4} \text{sec}^{-1}, a = 0.25 \text{ M}, (a-x) = ?, t = 2 \text{ min} = 120 \text{ sec}$

According to a first order kinetic equation, $k = \frac{2.303}{t} \log \frac{a}{a-x}$

$$\therefore \quad 5 \times 10^{-4} = \frac{2.303}{120} \log \frac{0.25}{(a-x)} \quad \text{or} \quad \log \frac{0.25}{(a-x)} = 0.026$$

$$\therefore \quad \frac{0.25}{a-x} = \text{Antilog } 0.026 = 1.062 \quad \text{or} \quad (a-x) = \frac{0.25}{1.062} M = \mathbf{0.235 \ M}$$

$$t_{1/2} = \frac{0.693}{k} = \frac{0.693}{5 \times 10^{-4} \text{ sec}^{-1}} = 1386 \text{ sec} = \mathbf{23 \ min \ 6 \ sec.}$$

Type 3.

For first order reaction 90% part of reaction take place in x min and 50% part take place in y min. Relation between $t_{90\%}$ and $t_{50\%}$:

For 50% $$k = \frac{0.693}{t_{1/2}} \quad \text{...(i)}$$

For 90% part of reaction $a = 100$, $x = 90$, $a - x = 10$

$$k = \frac{2.303}{t_{90\%}} \log \frac{100}{10} = \frac{2.303}{t_{90\%}} \log 10 = \frac{2.303}{t_{90\%}} \quad \text{...(ii)}$$

From eq. (i) and (ii) $$\frac{0.693}{t_{1/2}} = \frac{2.303}{t_{90\%}}$$

$$t_{90\%} = \frac{2.303}{0.693} \times t_{1/2} = 3.32 \times t_{1/2}$$

Example 9. A first order reaction is 20% complete in 10 minutes. Calculate the time for 75% completion of the reaction.

Solution : For first order reaction, $k = \frac{2.303}{t} \log \frac{a}{a-x}$

For 20% part of reaction, $a = 100$, $x = 20$, $a - x = 80$

$$k = \frac{2.303}{t_{20\%}} \log \frac{100}{80} = \frac{2.303}{t_{20\%}} \log \frac{10}{8} = \frac{2.303}{t_{20\%}} \times 0.096 \quad \text{...(i)}$$

For 75% part of reaction,

$$k = \frac{2.303}{t_{75\%}} \log \frac{100}{4} = \frac{2.303 \times 2 \times 0.3010}{t_{75\%}} \quad \text{...(ii)}$$

From Eq. (i) and Eq. (ii)

$$\frac{2.303 \times 2 \times 0.3010}{t_{75\%}} = \frac{2.303 \times 0.096}{t_{20\%}}$$

$$t_{75\%} = \frac{2 \times 3010}{0.096} \times t_{20\%} = 6.27 \times t_{20\%}$$

$$= 6.27 \times 10 = \mathbf{62.7\ \%}$$

Example 10. A first order reaction is 15% complete in 20 minutes. How long will it take to complete 60% ?

Solution : According to first order reaction

$$k = \frac{2.303}{t} \log \frac{a}{a-x}$$

For 15% part of reaciton, $a = 100$, $a - x = 85$

$$k = \frac{2.303}{t_{15\%}} \log \frac{100}{85} = \frac{2.303}{t_{15\%}} \times 0.07 \quad \text{...(i)}$$

For 60% part of reaction, $a = 100, \quad a - x = 85$

$$k = \frac{2.303}{t_{60\%}} \log \frac{100}{60} = \frac{2.303}{t_{60\%}} \times 0.40 \qquad \text{...(ii)}$$

From Eq. (i) and Eq. (ii)

$$\frac{2.303}{t_{15\%}} \times 0.07 = \frac{2.303}{t_{60\%}} \times 0.40$$

$$\Rightarrow \qquad t_{60\%} = \frac{0.40}{0.07} \times t_{15\%}$$

$$t_{60\%} = 5.71 \times t_{15\%} = 5.71 \times 10 = 114.7 \text{ min}$$

Example 11. For a first order reaction, show that the time required for 99% completion of a first order reaction is twice the time required for the completion of 90%.

Solution : For first order reaction, $t = \frac{2.303}{k} \log \frac{a}{a - x}$

99% completion means that x = 99% of a = 0.99 a

$$t_{99\%} = \frac{2.303}{k} \log \frac{a}{a - 0.99a} = \frac{2.303}{k} \log 10^2 = 2 \times \frac{2.303}{k}$$

90% completion means that $x = 90\%$ of $a = 0.90\ a$

$$\therefore \qquad t_{90\%} = \frac{2.303}{k} \log \frac{a}{a - 0.99a} = \frac{2.303}{k} \log 10 = \frac{2.303}{k}$$

$$\therefore \qquad \frac{t_{99\%}}{t_{90\%}} = \left(\frac{2 \times 2.303}{k}\right) \bigg/ \left(\frac{2.303}{k}\right) = 2$$

or $\qquad t_{99\%} = 2 \times t_{90\%}$

Example 12. A first order reaction takes 40 min for 30% decomposition. Calculate $t_{1/2}$.

Solution : 30% decomposition means that $x = 30\%$ of $a = 0.30\ a$

A reaction is of 1st order,

$$k = \frac{2.303}{t} \log \frac{a}{a - x} = \frac{2.303}{40 \text{ min}} \log \frac{a}{a - 0.30a} = \frac{2.303}{40} \times \log \frac{10}{7} \text{ min}^{-1}$$

$$= \frac{2.303}{40} \times 0.1549 \text{ min}^{-1} = 8.918 \times 10^{-3} \text{ min}^{-1}$$

For a 1st order reaction, $t_{1/2} = \frac{0.693}{k} = \frac{0.693}{8.918 \times 10^{-3} \text{ min}^{-1}} = \mathbf{77.7\ min.}$

Example 13. Show that in case of a first order reaction, the time required for 99.9% for the reaction to take place is about ten times than that required for half the reaction.

Solution : For reaction of first order,

$$t_{1/2} = \frac{2.303}{k} \log \frac{a}{a - \frac{a}{2}} = \frac{2.303}{k} \log 2 = \frac{2.303}{k} (0.3010)$$

$$t_{99.9\%} = \frac{2.303}{k}\log = \frac{a}{a-0.999a} = \frac{2.303}{k}\log 10^{-3} = \frac{2.303}{k}\times 3$$

$$\therefore \quad \frac{t_{99.9\%}}{t_{1/2}} = \frac{3}{0.3010} = \mathbf{10}$$

Problem 1. The thermal decomposition of a compound is of first order. If 50% of the compound is decomposed in 120 minutes, how long will it take for 90% of the compound to decompose ? **[Ans. 399 min.]**

Problem 2. A first order reaction takes 69.3 minutes for 50% completion. Calculate the time required for 80% completion of the reaction. **[Ans. 161 min.]**

Problem 3. The three-fourth of a first order reaction is completed in 32 minutes. What is the half-life period of the reaction? **[Ans. 16 min.]**

Problem 4. 60% of a first order reaction was completed in 60 min. When was it half completed? **[Ans. 45.3 min.]**

Type 4.

Radioactive decay is first order reaction which follow first order kinetic equation.

$$k = \frac{0.693}{k}\log\frac{[N]_0}{[N]} = \frac{0.693}{t_{1/2}}$$

Relation between t_{age} and $t_{1/2}$

$$\frac{0.693}{t_{1/2}} = \frac{2.303}{t_{age}}\log\frac{[N]_0}{[N]}$$

$$t_{age} = \frac{2.303}{0.693}\times t_{1/2}\log\frac{[N]_0}{[N]}$$

$$= 3.32\times t_{1/2}\log\frac{[N]_0}{[N]}$$

Example 14. The half-life period for radioactive decay of ^{14}C is 5730 year. An archaeological artefact contained wood had only 80% of ^{14}C found in a living tree. Estimate the age of the sample.

Solution : Decay constant, $k = \dfrac{0.693}{t_{1/2}}$

$t_{1/2} = 5730$ years

$$\therefore \quad k = \frac{0.693}{5730y} = 1.209\times 10^{-4}\ \text{year}^{-1}$$

Since the rate of counts is proportional to the number of ^{14}C atoms in the sample,

$N_0 = 100, \quad N = 80$

Now, $$t = \frac{2.303}{k}\log\frac{N_0}{N} = \frac{2.303}{1.209\times 10^{-4}}\log\frac{100}{80}$$

$$= \frac{2.303}{1.209 \times 10^{-4}} \times 0.0969 = \mathbf{1846\ years.}$$

Example 15. During nuclear explosion, one of the products is ^{90}Sr with half life of 28.1 % y. If 1 μg of ^{90}Sr was absorbed in bone of a newly born baby instead of calcium, how much of it will remain after 10 years and 60 years if it is not lost metabolically ?

Solution : As radioactive disintegrations follow first order kinetics,

$$\text{Decay constant of } ^{90}\text{Sr } (k) = \frac{0.693}{t_{1/2}} = \frac{0.693}{281\,y} = 2.466 \times 10^{-2}\ y^{-1}$$

To calculate the amount left after 10 years.

$a = 1$ μg, $t = 10$ years, $k = 2.466 \times 10^{-2}\ y^{-1}$, $(a-x) = ?$

$$k = \frac{2.303}{t} \log \frac{a}{a-x}$$

$$2.466 \times 10^{-2} = \frac{2.303}{10} \log \frac{1}{(a-x)} \quad \text{or } \log(a-x) = -0.1071$$

or $\quad (a-x) = \text{Antilog} = \bar{1}.8929 = \mathbf{0.7814\ \mu g}$

To calculate the amount left after 60 years.

$$2.466 \times 10^{-2} = \frac{2.303}{60} \log \frac{1}{a-x}$$

or $\quad \log(a-x) = -0.6425$

to $\quad (a-x) = \text{Antilog } \bar{1}.3575 = \mathbf{0.2278\ \mu g.}$

Type 5. First order pressure kinetic equation

Suppose a first order decomposition reaction

	A(g) ⟶	B (g) +	C(g)
$t = 0$	p^0		
At time t	$p^0 - x$	x	x

At time t total pressure is p_t

$$p_t = p^0 + x \Rightarrow x = p_t - p^0$$

Kinetic equation $\quad k = \frac{2.303}{t} \log \frac{p^0}{p^0 - x}$

Now, $\quad p^0 - x = p^0 - (p_t - p^0) = p^0 - p_t + p^0 = 2p^0 - p_t$

So, $\quad k = \frac{2.303}{t} \log \frac{p^0}{2p^0 - p_t}$

Example 16. The following data were obtained during the first order thermal decomposition of N_2O_5 (*g*) at constant volume.

$$\mathbf{2\,N_2O_5(g) \longrightarrow 2\,N_2O_4(g) + O_2(g)}$$

S.No.	Time/s	Total pressure (atm)
1	0	0.5
2	100	0.512

Calculate the rate constant.

Solution :

$$2\,N_2O_5(g) \longrightarrow 2\,N_2O_4(g) + O_2(g)$$

Initial: N_2O_5 = 0.5 atm

After 100 s : N_2O_5 = $0.5 - 2p$, N_2O_4 = $2p$, O_2 = p

$$P_{Total} = (0.5-2p)+2p+p = 0.5+p = 0.512 \text{ atm} \quad (Given)$$

$\therefore \quad p = 0.012$ atm

Thus, initial pressure of N_2O_5 $(P_0) = 03.5$ atm

Pressure of N_2O_5 after 100 s $(P_{N_2O_5}) = 0.5 - 2 \times 0.012 = 0.476$ atm

$$k = \frac{2.303}{t}\log\frac{(P_{N_2O_5})_0}{P_{N_2O_5}} = \frac{2.303}{100\,s}\log\frac{0.5 \text{ atm}}{0.476 \text{ atm}}$$

$$= \mathbf{4.98 \times 10^{-4} s^{-1}}$$

Example 17. For the decomposition of azoisopropane to hexane and nitrogen at 543 K, the following data is obtained.

t (sec)	P (mm of Hg)
0	35.0
360	54.0
720	63.0

Calculate the rate constant.

Solution : Let initial pressure of azoisopropane $= p_1$

Let x atm of azoisopropane decreases at time t so that

$$(CH_3)_2CHNH = NHCH(CH_3)_2 \longrightarrow N_2 + C_6H_{14}$$

At $t = 0$: p_i, 0, 0

At time $= t$: $(p_i - x)$ atm, x atm, x atm

$$p_t = p_i - x + x + x = p_i + x$$

or $\quad x = p_t - p_i$

$$p\text{ (azoisopropane)} = p_i - x = p_i - (p_t - p_i) = 2p_i - p_t$$

$$k = \frac{2.303}{t}\log\frac{[A]_0}{[A]} = \frac{2.303}{t}\log\frac{p_i}{2p_i - p_t}$$

At time 360 s $\quad k = \dfrac{2.303}{360}\log\dfrac{35.0}{(2\times 35.0 - 54)}$

$$= \frac{2.303}{360}\log\frac{35.0}{16} = \frac{2.606}{360}\times 0.3399 = \mathbf{2.17 \times 10^{-3}\ s^{-1}}$$

Example 18. The following data were obtained during the first order thermal decomposition of SO_2Cl_2 at a constant volume.

$$\mathbf{SO_2Cl_2\ (g) \longrightarrow SO_2\ (g) + Cl_2(g)}$$

Experiment	Time/s^{-1}	Total pressure/atm
1	0	0.5
2	100	0.6

Calculate the rate of the reaction when total pressure is 0.65 atm.

Solution :
$$k = \frac{2.303}{t}\log\frac{p_i}{(2p_i - p_i)} = \frac{2.303}{100}\log\frac{0.5}{(2\times 0.5 - 0.6)}$$

$$= \frac{2.303}{100}\log\frac{0.5}{0.4} = \frac{2.303}{100}\times 0.0969 = 2.23\times 10^{-23}\text{s}^{-1}$$

Now, Rate $= p\,SO_2Cl_2$

Pressure of SO_2Cl_2 when total pressure = 0.65 atm.

$$p\,SO_2\,Cl_2 = 2p_i - p_t$$
$$= 2\times 0.5 - 0.65 = 0.35 \text{ atm}$$

$\therefore$ Rate $= 2.23\times 10^{-3}\times 0.35 = \mathbf{7.805\times 10^{-4}\ atm\ s^{-1}}$

Type 6.

1. **Arrhenius Equation :** Arrhenius proposed a quantitative relationship between rate constant and temperature as:

$$k = Ae^{-E_a/RT}$$

This equation is called, Arrhenius equation in which constant A is known as **Arrhenius factor or frequency factor**.

$$\log k = \log A - \frac{E_a}{2.303RT}$$

2. Alternatively, E_a and A can be determined by measuring the values of rate constant at two different temperatures. Let k_1 and k_2 are the rate constants for the reaction at two different temperature T_1 and T_2 respectively. Then,

$$\log k_1 = \log A - \frac{E_a}{2.303RT_1} \quad ...(i)$$

and
$$\log k_2 = \log A - \frac{E_a}{2.303RT_2} \quad ...(ii)$$

Subtracting Eq. (i) from eqn. (ii), we get

$$\log k_2 - \log k_1 = \frac{E_a}{2.303R}\left[\frac{1}{T_1} - \frac{1}{T_2}\right]$$

or
$$\log\frac{k_2}{k_1} = \frac{E_a}{2.303R}\left[\frac{1}{T_1} - \frac{1}{T_2}\right]$$

or
$$\log\frac{k_2}{k_1} = \frac{E_a}{2.303R}\left[\frac{T_2 - T_1}{T_1\times T_2}\right].$$

Example 19. The first order rate constant for the decomposition of ethyl iodide by the reaction:

$$C_2H_5I\,(g) \longrightarrow C_2H_4\,(g) + HI\,(g)$$

at 600 K is 1.60×10^{-5} s^{-1}. Its energy of activation is 209 kJ/mol. Calculate the rate constant of the reaction at 700 K.

Solution : Here, $T_1 = 600$ K, $k_1 = 1.60 \times 10^{-5}$ s^{-1}, $T_2 = 700$ K, $k_2 = ?$, $E_a = 209$ kJ mol^{-1}

Applying Arrhenius equation,

$$\log \frac{k_2}{k_1} = \frac{E_a}{2.303\,R}\left(\frac{1}{T_1} - \frac{1}{T_2}\right)$$

or

$$\log k_2 = \log k_1 + \frac{E_a}{2.303\,R}\left(\frac{T_2 - T_1}{T_1 T_2}\right)$$

$$= \log(1.60 \times 10^{-5}) + \frac{209000 \text{ J mol}^{-1}}{2.303 \times 8.314 \text{ J K}^{-1}\text{mol}^{-1}}\left(\frac{700 - 600}{600 \times 700}\right)$$

$$= (-5 + 0.2041) + 2.5989 = -2.197 = \bar{3}.8030$$

$$k_2 = \text{Antilog } \bar{3}.8030 = \mathbf{6.353 \times 10^{-3}\ s^{-1}}$$

Example 20. Rate constant *k* of a reaction values with temprerature according to the equation

$$\log k = \text{constant} - \frac{E_a}{2.303\,R}\frac{1}{T}$$

where, E_a is the energy of activation for the reaction. When a graph is plotted for log *k* versus 1/*T*, a straight line with a slop – 6670 K is obtained. Calculate the energy of activation for this reaction. State the units ($R = 8.314$ J K^{-1} mol^{-1})

Solution :

$$\text{Slope of the line} = \frac{E_a}{2.303\,R} = -6670 \text{ K}$$

or

$$E_a = 2.303 \times 8.314\ (\text{J K}^{-1}\text{mol}^{-1}) \times 6670 \text{ K}$$

$$= \mathbf{127711.4\ J\ mol^{-1}}.$$

Example 21. The rate constants of a reaction at 500 K and 700 K are 0.02 s^{-1} and 0.07 s^{-1} respectively. Calculate the values of E_a and A.

Solution :

$$\log \frac{k_2}{k_1} = \frac{E_a}{2.303\,R}\left(\frac{T_2 - T_1}{T_1 T_2}\right)$$

$$\log \frac{0.07}{0.02} = \frac{E_a}{2.303 \times 8.314 \text{ JK}^{-1}\text{mol}^{-1}} \times \frac{700\text{K} - 500\text{K}}{700\text{K} \times 500\text{K}}$$

$$\log 3.5 = \frac{E_a}{2.303 \times 8.314 \text{J K}^{-1}\text{mol}^{-1}} \times \frac{200\text{K}}{700\text{K} \times 500\text{K}}$$

or

$$E_a = \frac{0.5441 \times 2.303 \times 8.314 \times 700 \times 500}{200} \text{ J mol}^{-1} = \mathbf{18.23\ kJ\ mol^{-1}}$$

Further,

$$\log k = \frac{E_a}{2.303\,R} + \log A$$

or

$$\log A = \log k + \frac{E_a}{2.303\,RT}$$

Substituting $T = 500$ K, $k = 0.02$ s^{-1}, we get

$$\log A = \log 0.02 + \frac{18231.4 \text{ J mol}^{-1}}{2.303 \times 8.314 \text{ J K}^{-1}\text{mol}^{-1} \times 500\text{K}}$$

$$= -\log 50 + 12.4095 = -1.699 + 1.904 = 0.205$$

$$A = \text{Antilog}\,(0.205) = \mathbf{1.603}$$

Example 22. The rate constant of a reaction is 1.2×10^{-3} sec^{-1} at 30°C and 2.1×10^{-3} sec^{-1} at 40°C. Calculate the energy of activation of the reaction.

Solution : Here we are given that :

$$k_1 = 1.2 \times 10^{-3} \text{ sec}^{-1}, \quad T_1 = 30 + 273 = 303 \text{ K},$$

$$k_2 = 2.1 \times 10^{-3} \text{ sec}^{-1}, \quad T_2 = 40 + 273 = 313 \text{ K}$$

Substituting these values in the equation :

$$\log \frac{k_2}{k_1} = \frac{E_a}{2.303\,R}\left(\frac{T_2 - T_1}{T_1 T_2}\right), \text{ we get}$$

$$\log \frac{2.1 \times 10^{-3}\, s^{-1}}{1.2 \times 10^{-3}\, s^{-1}} = \frac{E_a}{2.303 \times 8.314 \text{ J K}^{-1}\text{mol}^{-1}} \times \left(\frac{313\text{K} - 303\text{K}}{303\text{K} \times 313\text{K}}\right)$$

$$\log \frac{2.1}{1.2} = \frac{E_a}{2.303 \times 8.314} \times \frac{10}{303 \times 313 \text{ (J mol}^{-1})}$$

This on solving gives

$$E_a = 44126.3 \text{ J mol}^{-1} = \mathbf{44.13 \text{ kJ mol}^{-1}}$$

Example 23. The slope of the line in the graph of log k (k = rate constant) versus $\frac{1}{T}$ for a reaction is – 5841 K. Calculate the energy of activation for this reaction. (R = 8.314 J K^{-1} mol^{-1})

Solution : The slope of the line in the plot of log k vs $\frac{1}{T}$ is given by

$$\text{slope} = \frac{E_a}{2.303\,R}$$

$$\therefore \quad E_a = -2.303 \times \text{R} \times \text{Slope of the line}$$

$$= -2.303 \times 8.314 \times (-5841) = 111838.4 \text{ J mol}^{-1} = \mathbf{111.8 \text{ k J mol}^{-1}}$$

Example 24. The rate constant of a first order reaction becomes 5 times when the temperature is raised from 350 K to 400 K. Calculate the activation energy for the reaction. (Gas constant R = 8.314 J K^{-1} mol^{-1}).

Solution : In the present case,

$$T_1 = 350 \text{ K}, \ T_2 = 400 \text{ K}, \ k_2 = 5 \times k_1 \text{ and } R = 8.314 \text{ J K}^{-1} \text{ mol}^{-1}$$

According to Arrhenius equation,

$$\log_{10} \frac{k_2}{k_1} = \frac{E_a}{2.303\,R}\left[\frac{1}{T_1} - \frac{1}{T_2}\right]$$

Substituting the values, we get

$$\log_{10} \frac{5 \times k_1}{k_1} = \frac{E_a}{2.303 \times 8.314}\left[\frac{1}{350} - \frac{1}{400}\right]$$

or

$$0.6990 = \frac{E_a}{19.147} \times \frac{50}{350 \times 400}$$

or $\quad E_a = \dfrac{0.6990 \times 19.147 \times 350 \times 400}{50} = 37474.5 \text{ J mol}^{-1}$

or $\quad E_a = \mathbf{37.47\ kJ\ mol^{-1}}$

Example 25. The rate constant for the first order decomposition of H_2O_2 is given by the following equation :

$$\log k = 14.34 - 1.25 \times 10^4 \text{ K/T}$$

Calculate E_a for this reaction and at what temperature will its half-period be 256 minutes?

Solution : According to Arrhenius equation, $k = Ae^{-E_a/RT}$

or $\quad \ln k = \ln A - \dfrac{E_a}{RT}$

or $\quad \log k = \log A - \dfrac{E_a}{2.303\,RT}$

Comparing with the given equation,

$$\frac{E_a}{2.303\,RT} = \frac{1.25 \times 10^4\ K}{T}$$

or $\quad E_a = 2.303\ \text{R} \times 1.25 \times 10^4\ \text{K}$

$$= 2.303 \times (8.314\ \text{J K}^{-1}\ \text{mol}^{-1}) \times 1.25 \times 10^4\ \text{K} = \mathbf{239.34\ kJ\ mol^{-1}}$$

When $t_{1/2} = 256$ min, $k = \dfrac{0.693}{256 \times 60\,s} = 4.51 \times 10^{-5}\ \text{s}^{-1}$

Substituting this value in the given equation,

$$\log(4.51 \times 10^{-5}) = 14.34 - \frac{1.25 \times 10^4\ \text{K}}{\text{T}}$$

i.e., $\quad (-5 + 0.6542) = 14.34 - \dfrac{1.25 \times 10^4\ \text{K}}{\text{T}}$

or $\quad \dfrac{1.25 \times 10^4\ \text{K}}{\text{T}} = 18.6858$ or $\text{T} = \mathbf{669\ K}$

Example 26. The time required for 10% completion of a first order reaction at 298 K is equal to that required for its 25% completion at 308 K. If the value of A is $4 \times 10^{10}\ s^{-1}$, calculate k at 318 K and E_a.

Solution : $\quad k_{298\text{K}} = \dfrac{2.303}{t_1} \log \dfrac{a}{a - 0.10a}$

$$= \frac{2.303}{t_1} \log \frac{10}{9} = \frac{2.303}{t_1}(0.0458) = \frac{0.1055}{t_1} \text{ or } \frac{0.1055}{k_{298\text{K}}}$$

$$k_{308\text{K}} = \frac{2.303}{t_2} \log \frac{a}{a - 0.25a}$$

$$= \frac{2.303}{t_2} \log \frac{4}{3} = \frac{2.303}{t_2}(0.125) = \frac{0.2879}{t_2} \text{ or } t_2 = \frac{0.2879}{k_{308\text{K}}}$$

But $t_1 = t_2$. Hence, $\frac{0.1055}{k_{298K}} = \frac{0.2879}{k_{308K}}$ or $\frac{k_{308K}}{k_{298K}} = 2.7289$

Now, applying Arrhenius equation,

$$\log \frac{k_{308K}}{k_{298K}} = \frac{E_a}{2.303R}\left(\frac{T_2 - T_1}{T_1 T_2}\right)$$

$$\therefore \quad \log(2.7289) = \frac{E_a}{2.303 \times 8.314 \text{ J K}^{-1}\text{mol}^{-1}} \times \frac{(308-298)\text{K}}{298\text{K} \times 308\text{K}}$$

$$0.4360 = \frac{E_a}{2.303 \times 8.314} \times \frac{10}{298 \times 308} \quad \text{or} \quad E_a = 76.623 \text{ kJ mol}^{-1}$$

Calculate of k at 318 K

$$\log k = \log A - \frac{E_a}{2.303RT}$$

$$= \log(4 \times 10^{10}) - \frac{7623 \text{ JK}^{-1} \text{ mol}^{-1}}{2.303 \times 8.314 \text{ JK}^{-1}\text{mol}^{-1} \times 318\text{K}}$$

or $\quad k = \text{Antilog}(-1.9822)$

$= \text{Antilog}(\bar{2}.0178) = \mathbf{1.042 \times 10^{-2} s^{-1}}$

Very Short Answer Type Questions

Q. 1. Explain the rate law.

Ans. It is a mathematical expression which gives us the experimentally determined rate of a reaction in terms of molar concentrations of reactants which actually influence their rate of a reaction.

Q. 2. Define activation energy.

Ans. It is the excess energy in addition to the energy already possessed by the reactants so that their energy becomes equal to the threshold energy.

Q. 3. Does the value of rate constant depend upon initial molar concentration of reacting species?

Ans. No, it does not depend upon the initial molar concentration of reacting species.

Q. 4. What is the rate determining step in a multistep reaction?

Ans. The slowest step in the reaction is the rate determining step.

Q. 5. Calculate half-life period for first order reaction when specific rate constant is 2 min^{-1}.

Ans. $t_{1/2} = \frac{0.693}{K} = \frac{0.693}{2} = 0.3456$ minutes.

Q. 6. Give one example of a zero order reaction.

Ans. $H_2 + Cl_2 \xrightarrow{hv} 2HCl$.

Q. 7. Why reaction rate does not remain constant throughout the reaction?

Ans. Reaction rate depends upon the molar concentration of the reacting species. As the molar concentration changes, the reaction rate also changes.

Q. 8. For a reaction, $A + B \longrightarrow$ Product, the rate law is given by: $r = K[A]^{1/2}[B]^2$. What is the order of the reaction?

Ans. Order of reaction $= \frac{1}{2} + 2 = 2\frac{1}{2}$ or 2.5.

Q. 9. Mention the factors that affect rate of a chemical reaction.

Ans. 1. Nature of the reactants

2. Concentration of the reactants
3. Temperature
4. Presence of catalyst
5. Surface area of the reactants
6. Presence of light.

Q. 10. Can order of a reaction be fractional? Give example.

Ans. Yes, order of a reaction can be fractional.

For example,

$$CH_3CHO(g) \longrightarrow CH_4(g) + CO(g)$$

Reaction Rate $= K[CH_3CHO]^{3/2}$ and order of reaction $= \frac{3}{2}$.

Short Answer Type Questions – I

Q. 1. For the reaction $R \longrightarrow P$, the concentration of a reactant changes from 0.03 M to 0.02 M in 25 minutes. Calculate the average rate of reaction using units of time both in minutes and seconds.

Ans. $$\text{Average Rate} = -\frac{\Delta[R]}{\Delta t}$$

$$= -\frac{[R_2]-[R_1]}{t_2 - t_1} = -\frac{0.002\,M - 0.030\,M}{25\,min} = -\frac{0.01M}{25\,min} = 4 \times 10^{-4}\,M\,min^{-1}$$

or $$= -\frac{0.01M}{25 \times 605} = 6.66 \times 10^{-6}\,MS^{-1}.$$

Q. 2. The conversion of the molecules X to Y follows second order kinetics. If the concentration X is increased to three times, how will it affect the rate of formation of Y?

Ans. For the reaction,

$X \longrightarrow Y$, as it follows second order

$$\text{Rate} = K[X]^2 = Ka^2.$$

If concentration of X is increased three times, now

$$[X] = 3a\,mol\,L^{-1}$$

$$\therefore \quad \text{Rate} = K(3a)^2 = 9\,Ka^2$$

Thus, the rate of reaction will becomes 9 times. Hence, the rate of formation of y will increase 9 times.

Q. 3. Find the three-fourth life $t_{3/4}$ of a first order reaction when for it $K = 74.\times 10^{-5}\,sec^{-1}$.

Ans. For a first order reaction

$$t = \frac{2.303}{K}\log\frac{a}{(a-x)}$$

$$t_{3/4} = \frac{2.303}{7.4\times10^{-5}} \log\frac{a}{\left(a-\frac{3}{4}a\right)} = \frac{2.303}{7.4\times10^{-5}} \log 4$$

$$= \frac{2.303\times0.6020}{7.4\times10^{-5}} = 1.87\times10^{4}\text{ sec.}$$

Q. 4. How will you distinguish between reaction rate and rate constant of a reaction?

Ans. *Differences between Reaction rate and Reaction rate constant—*

Rate of reaction	Reaction rate constant
1. It is the speed with which reactants are converted into products. It is measured as the rate of decrease of concentration of reactants or rate of increase of concentration of products with time.	1. It is the proportionality constant in the rate law and is defined as the rate of reaction when the concentration of the reactants is unity.
2. It depends upon the initial concentration of the reactants.	2. It is independent of the initial concentration of the reactants.

Q. 5. The rate expression for the chemical

$$\text{reaction} - 2NO_2Cl \longrightarrow 2NO_2 + Cl_2$$

is given as : Rate = K $[Na_2Cl]$

Propose a possible mechanism for the above reaction and give the order of the reaction.

Ans. Since the rate of the reaction depends upon the conc. of NO_2Cl, the mechanism of the reaction may be proposed as

(*i*) $NO_2Cl \longrightarrow NO_2 + Cl$ (slow)

(*ii*) $NO_2Cl + Cl \longrightarrow NO_2 + Cl_2$ (fast)

The first step is slow and therefore is rate controlling step. The rate law for the reaction in

$$\text{Rate} = K[NO_2Cl]$$

So that the order of reaction in one.

Q. 6. A first order reaction is 75% complete in 60 minutes. Calculate the half-life of the reaction.

Ans. For the first order reaction

$$K = \frac{2.303}{t}\log\frac{a}{a-x}.$$

Let the initial concentration = a.

$$x = \frac{75}{1000}a = 0.75\,a, t = 60\text{ min}$$

$$\therefore \quad K = \frac{2.303}{60}\log\frac{a}{a-0.75a} = \frac{2.303}{60}\log\frac{1}{0.25}$$

$$= \frac{2.303}{60}\log 4 = 0.0231\text{ min}^{-1}.$$

Now, half-life period, $t_{1/2} = \frac{0.693}{K} = \frac{0.693}{0.0231} = 30$ min.

Q. 7. What is energy of activation? How is the rate of constant of a reaction related to its activation energy?

Ans. *Activation energy*— It is the minimum energy that the reacting molecules must possess before undergoing a reaction.

The rate constant of a reaction is related to its activation energy by Arrhenius equation as

$$K = Ae^{-Ea/RT}$$

where A is a constant of proportionality, E_a is activation energy and T is absolute temperature.

Q. 8. A reaction is second order with respect to a reactant. How is the rate of reaction affected if the concentration of the reactant is

(*i*) doubled (*ii*) reduced to half.

Ans. (*i*) When concentration of reactant is doubled the rate becomes 4 times.

(*ii*) When concentration is reduced to ½, the rate becomes ¼ times.

Q. 9. A first order reaction has a rate constant $1.15 \times 10^{-3}\ S^{-1}$. How long will 5 g of this reactant take to reduce to 3g?

Ans. Here, $[A_0] = 5g$, $[A] = 3g$, $K = 1.15 \times 10^{-3}\ S^{-1}$

$$t = \frac{2.303}{t} \log \frac{[A_0]}{[A]} = \frac{2.303}{1.15 \times 10^{-3}\ S^{-1}} \log \frac{5g}{3g}$$

$$= 2.00 \times 10^3 (\log 1.667)\ S = 2.0 \times 10^3 \times 0.2219\ S = 443.8\ S = 444\ S$$

Q. 10. The decomposition of dimethyl ether leads to the formation of CH_4, H_2 and CO and the reaction rate is given by Rate = $K\ [P_{CH_3}\ OCH_3]^{3/2}$.

If the pressure is measured in bar and time in minutes, then what are the units of the rate and rate constants?

Ans. In terms of pressures,

$$\text{Units of rate} = \text{bar min}^{-1}$$

$$\text{unit of K} = \frac{\text{Rate}}{[P_{CH_3}COCH_3]^{3/2}} = \frac{\text{bar min}^{-1}}{\text{bar}^{3/2}} = \text{bar}^{-1/2}\ \text{min}^{-1}.$$

Short Answer Type Questions - II

Q. 1. (*i*) Find the order of reaction if rate = $K[A]^{3/2}\ [B]^{-1}$.

(*ii*) Identify the reaction order if $K = 9.3 \times 10^{-4}$ mol litre^{-1} sec^{-1}.

Ans. (*i*) Order = $\frac{3}{2} - 1 = \frac{1}{2}$. (*ii*) Zero order.

Q. 2. The rate constant for the decomposition of hydrocarbons is $2.148 \times 10^{-5}\ S^{-1}$ at 546 K. If the energy of activation is 179.9 KJ/mol. What will be the value of pre-exponential factor?

Ans.

$$\log K = \log A - \frac{Ea}{2.303\,RT}$$

$$\log A = \log K + \frac{Ea}{2.303\,RT} = \log 2.418 \times 10^{-5} + \frac{179.9 \times 10^3}{2.303 \times 8.314 \times 546}$$

$$= -4.616 + 17.208 = 12.592$$

$$A = 3.90 \times 10^{12}\ S^{-1}.$$

Q. 3. What will be the effect of temperature on rate constant?

Ans. Rate constant of a reaction is nearly doubled with rise in temperature by 10°C. The exact dependence of the rate constant of temperature is given by Arrhenius equation. $K = Ae^{-Ea/RT}$ where A is called frequency factor and Ea is the activation energy of the reaction.

Q. 4. The decomposition of NH_3 on platinum surface

$$2NH_3(g) \xrightarrow{Pt} N_2(g) + 3H_2(g)$$

is zero order with $K = 2.5 \times 10^{-4}$ mol L^{-1} S^{-1}. What are the rates of production of N_2 and H_2?

Ans. $2NH_3 \longrightarrow N_2 + 3H_2$

$$\text{Rate} = -\frac{1}{2}\frac{d[NH_3]}{dt} = +\frac{d[N_2]}{dt} = +\frac{1}{3}\frac{d[H_2]}{dt}$$

For zero order reaction rate K

$$-\frac{1}{2}\frac{d[NH_3]}{dt} = +\frac{d[N_2]}{dt} = \frac{1}{3}\frac{d[H_2]}{dt} = 2.5 \times 10^{-4}\ \text{mol L}^{-1}\ S^{-1}$$

$\therefore$ $$\text{Rate of Production of } N_2 = \frac{d[H_2]}{dt} = 2.5 \times 10^{-4}\ \text{mol L}^{-1}\ S^{-1}.$$

$$\text{Rate of Production of } H_2 = \frac{d[H_2]}{dt}$$

$$= 3 \times (2.5 \times 10^{-4}\ \text{mol L}^{-1}\ S^{-1}) = 7.5 \times 10^{-4}\ \text{mol L}^{-1}\ S^{-1}.$$

Q. 5. A decomposition of A into product has value of K as $4.5 \times 10^3\ S^{-1}$ at 10°C and energy of activation 60 KJ mol^{-1}. At what temperature would K be $1.5 \times 10^4\ S^{-1}$?

Ans. $K_1 = 4.5 \times 10^3\ S^{-1}$, $T_1 = 10 + 273\ K = 283\ K$

$K_2 = 1.5 \times 10^4\ S^{-1}$, $T_2 = ?$

$Ea = 60$ KJ mol^{-1}

Applying Arrhenius equation

$$\log\frac{K_2}{K_1} = \frac{Ea}{2.303R}\left(\frac{T_2 - T_1}{T_1 T_2}\right)$$

$$\log\frac{1.5\times10^4}{4.5\times10^3} = \frac{60000\ \text{J mol}^{-1}}{2.303\times8.314\ \text{JK}^{-1}\ \text{mol}^{-1}}\left(\frac{T_2 - 283}{283\ T_2}\right)$$

or $$\log 3.333 = 3133.63\left(\frac{T_2 - 283}{283\ T_2}\right)$$

or $$\frac{0.5228}{3133.63} = \frac{T_2 - 283}{283\ T_2}$$

or $$0.0473\ T_2 = T_2 - 283$$

or $$0.9528\ T_2 = 283$$

or $$T_2 = \frac{283}{0.9528} = 297\text{K} = 297 - 273°\text{C} = 24°\text{C}$$

Long Answer Type Questions

Q. 1. What is first order reaction? Derive the equation for the rate constant of a first order reaction and show that $t_{1/2}$ in independent of initial concentration.

Ans. Reaction which follow rate $= k\,.\,(A)$ is known as first order of reaction

$$A \longrightarrow B$$

$t=0$ $\quad a$

At $\quad a-x \quad x$

Now, $$\frac{dx}{dt} \propto a-x = k\,(a-x)$$

where, k = rate constant.

$$\frac{dx}{a-x} = k \times dt$$

$$\int \frac{dx}{a-x} = \int k.dt$$

$$-\log_e a-x = kt+c \quad \text{....(i)}$$

when, $t=0$ $\quad a-x=a$

$$-\log_e a = k \times 0 + c$$

$\Rightarrow$ $$c = -\log_e a$$

Value of c on puting eqn. (i)

$$-\log_e a-x = k\,t - \log_e a$$

$$kt = \log_e \frac{a}{a-x}$$

$\Rightarrow$ $$k = \frac{1}{t}\log_e \frac{a}{a-x} = \frac{2.203}{t}\log_{10} \frac{a}{a-x}$$

According to kinetic equation,

$$k = \frac{2.303}{t}\log\frac{a}{a-x}$$

when, $\quad t = t_{50\%},\ a-x = a/2$

$$k = \frac{2.303}{t_{50\%}}\log\frac{a}{a/2} = \frac{2.303}{t_{50\%}}\log 2 = \frac{0.693}{t_{50\%}}$$

This reaction shows that half-life period of first order reaction is independent of initial concentration.

Q. 2. What is a zero order reaction? Give an example. Derive expression for K and $t_{1/2}$ for a zero order reaction. What type of plot will you get for this order?

Ans. *Zero order reaction*—It is a reaction whose rate is independent of concentration of all the reactants.

Example— $H_2 + Cl_2 \xrightarrow{h\nu} 2HCl$

Let us consider a general first order reaction—

$$A \longrightarrow \text{Products}$$

If it is a reaction of zero order,

$$\text{Rate} = -\frac{d[A]}{dt} = K\,[A]^0 = K$$

or $$d[A] = -Kdt$$

Integrating both sides, we get

$$[A] = -Kt + I \qquad ...(i)$$

Where I is a constant of integration

At $t = 0,\ [A] = [A]_0$

$\therefore$ $[A]_0 = I$

Substituting this value of I in eqn. (*i*), we get

$$[A] = -Kt + [A]_0 \qquad ...(ii)$$

or $$Kt = [A]_0 - [A]$$

or $$\boxed{K = \frac{1}{t}\{[A]_0 - [A]\}} \qquad ...(iii)$$

When $[A] = [A_0]/2$, $t = t_{1/2}$ substituting these values in equ. (*iii*) we get

$$t_{1/2} = \frac{1}{K}\{[A]_0 - [A_0]/2\} = \frac{[A_0]}{2K}$$

i.e., $$\boxed{t_{1/2} = \frac{[A_0]}{2K}}$$

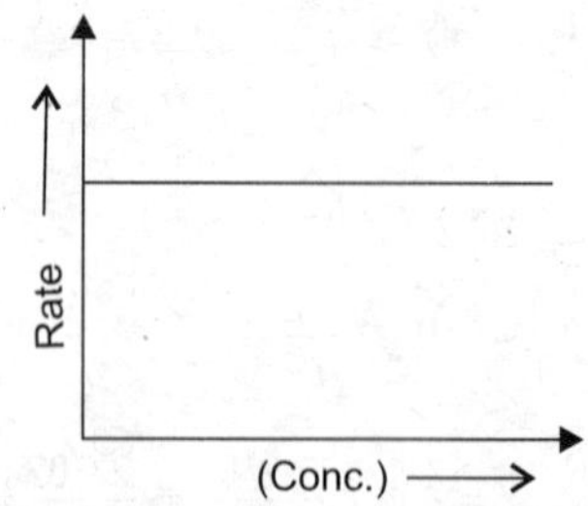

The plot of rate against conc. will be a straight line parallel to concentration axis.

Q. 3. Calculate the half-life of a first order reaction from their rate constants given below:—

(*a*) 200 S^{-1} (*b*) 2 min^{-1} (*c*) 4 $year^{-1}$

Ans. Half-life period of a first orde1 reaction is given by $t_{1/2} = \frac{0.693}{K}$.

(*a*) $t_{1/2} = \frac{0.693}{200\,S^{-1}} = 0.346 \times 10^{-2}$ S.

(*b*) $t_{1/2} = \frac{0.693}{2\,min^{-1}} = 0.346$ min.

(*c*) $t_{1/2} = \frac{0.693}{4\,year^{-1}} = 0.173$ years.

Q. 5. (*i*) Give the important differences between order and molecularity of reaction:

Ans. (*i*)

Order	Molecularity
1. Order is the sum of the powers of the concentration terms in the rate law expression.	1. Molecularity is the number of reacting species undergoing simultaneous collisions in the elementary or simple reaction.

2. Order of a reaction is determined experimentally.	2. Molecularity is a theoretical a theoretical concept.
3. Order of a reaction need not be a values whole number i.e. it can have fractional values also.	3. Molecularity has whole number only, i.e., 1, 3 etc.
4. Order of a reaction can be zero.	4. Molecularity of a reaction cannot be zero.

(*ii*) The decomposition of a hydrocarbon follows the equation

$$K = (4.5 \times 10^{11}\ S^{-1})\ e^{-28000\ K/T}.$$

Calculate Ea.

Ans. According to Arrhenim equation,

$$K = Ae^{-Ea/RT}$$

$$\therefore \quad -\frac{Ea}{RT} = -\frac{28000\,K}{T}$$

or $$Ea = 28000\,K \times R = 28000\,K \times 8.314\,J\,K^{-1}\,mol^{-1}$$

$$= 232.79\,KJ\,mol^{-1}.$$

Higher Order Thinking Skills Hots Questions

1. State any one condition under which a biomolecular reaction may be kinetically of first order.
2. The specific rate of reaction is 4.2×10^{-3} mol L^{-1} S^{-1}. What is the order of reaction?
3. Discuss the effect of (*i*) Catalyst and (*ii*) Concentration on the rate of reaction.
4. The time required for 10% completion of a first order reaction at 298 K is equal to that requested for its 25% completion at 308 K. If the value of A is $4 \times 10^{10}\ S^{-1}$, calculate K at 318 K and Ea.

   [**Ans.:** Ea = 76.623 KJ mol^{-1}, K = – 1.9822].
5. The following data were obtained during the first order thermal decomposition of SO_2Cl_2 at a constant volume:—

   $$SO_2Cl_2\,(g) \longrightarrow SO_2\,(g) + Cl_2\,(g).$$

Experiment	Time/S	Total pressure/atom.
1	0	0.5
2	100	0.6

Calculate the rate of reaction when total pressure is 0.65 atm.

[Am – K = $2.2316 \times 10^{-3}\ S^{-1}$]

❑❑❑

CHAPTER

5

SURFACE CHEMISTRY

Syllabus

- *Adsorption—physisorption and chemisorption; factors affecting adsorption of gases on solids; colloids distinction between true solutions, colloids and suspensions; lyophilic, lyophobic, multimolecular and marcromolecular colloids; properties of colloids; Tyndall effect, Brownian movement, electrophoresis, coagulation; emulsion—types of emulsions.*

1. **Adsorption :** *The change of concentration at a surface brought about by the action of residual surface forces is known as* ***adsorption****.*

   Adsorption is a surface phenomenon and is due to the presence of unbalanced forces on the surfaces of solids and liquids. In the interior of solids and liquids, the molecular forces are balanced but these forces are not completely balanced on their surfaces.

2. **Absorption :** *The phenomenon in which adsorbate penetrates into the bulk (interior) of adsorbent and gets distributed throughout the lattice of the adsorbent is called* ***absorption****.*

3. **Difference between adsorption and absorption :** The main points of difference between adsorption and absorption are summarised in Table.

	Adsorption	Absorption
1.	It is a surface phenomenon. The adsorbate gets deposited only at the surface of adsorbent.	It is a bulk phenomenon. The absorbate penetrates into the interior of absorbent and gets uniformly distributed.
2.	The concentration of adsorbate on the surface of adsorbent is different from that in the bulk of adsorbent.	The concentration of absorbate is the same throughout the bulk of the absorbent.
3.	The rate of adsorption is high in the beginning and then decreases gradually as the equilibrium is reached.	Absorption proceeds with a uniform rate.

4. **Type of Adsorption :**

   (*i*) **Physical adsorption :** If the force operative in the adsorption process are weak van der Waals' forces, the phenomenon is called **physical adsorption** or **physisorption** or **van der Waals' adsorption**.

   (*ii*) **Chemical adsorption :** When the gas molecules get attached to the surface of adsorbent through strong valence bond forces, the adsorption is called **chemical adsorption** or **chemisorption.**

5. Distinction between Physical and Chemical Adsorption :

	Characteristics	Physical Adsorption	Chemical Adsorption
1.	Nature of operative forces	Weak vander Waals' forces	Strong valence bond forces
2.	Specificity	Non-speciofic	Highly specific
3.	Occurrence	At ordinary temperatures	At relatively higher temperature
4.	Reversibility	Reversible	Irreversible
5.	Heat of adsorption	Low (about 40 kJ mol^{-1})	High (400 kJ mol^{-1})
6.	Nature of adsorbed layer	Multilayer	Mono layer
7.	Effect of temperature	Decreases with increases in temperature	First increases and then decreases with increase in temperature
8.	Activation energy	Almost equal to zero	High
9.	Process of adsorption	Rapid	May be rapid or slow

6. **Tyndall Effect :** When an intense converging beam of light is passed through a colloidal solution kept in dark, the path of the beam gets illuminated with a bluish light. This phenomenon is called **Tyndall effect** and the illuminated path is known as **Tyndall cone**. The phenomenon was first observed by **Tyndall** in 1869.

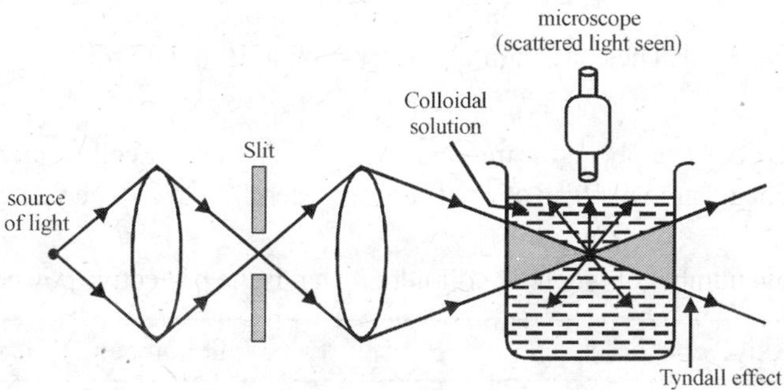

Tyndall effect

7. **Brownian Movement :**
   (i) The continuous zig-zag movement of the colloidal particles in a colloidal solution is known as Brownian movement. This movement arises due to bombardment of the dispersed particles by molecules of the medium.
   (ii) Brownian motion is observed up to a particle size of 0.5 micron. The Brownian movement depends upon the size of sol particles.

$$\text{Brownian moment} \propto \frac{1}{\text{size of particle}}$$

8. **Electrophoresis**
   (i) The migration of colloidal particles under the influence of electrical field and the phenomenon was named as cataphoresis or electrophoresis.

(ii) The phenomenon of electrophoresis clearly indicates that the colloidal particles carry a particular type of charge.

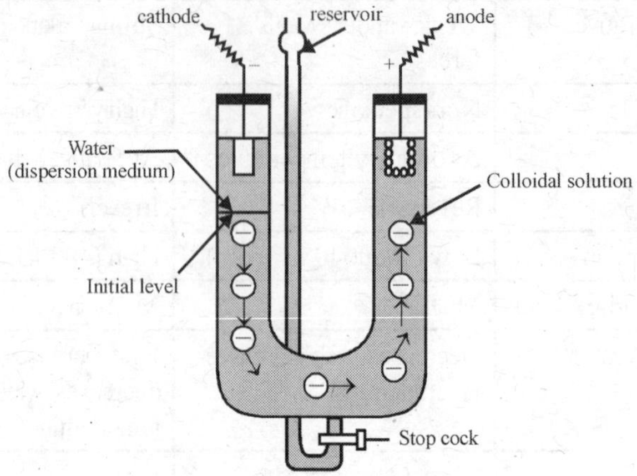

Electrophoresis

9. **Hardy-Schulze Rule :** According to this rule—
   (i) Greater is the valence of effective ion, more is its coagulating power.
   (ii) More is the coagulating power, lesser is coagulation value.
   (iii) Thus coagulating power of cations is in the order :

$$Al^{3+} > Ba^{2+} \text{ or } Mg^{2+} > Na^{+} \text{ or } K^{+}$$

   (iv) For negative sol, The coagulating power of anion is in the order :

$$[Fe(CN)_6]^{4-} > PO_4^{3-} > SO_4^{2-} > Cl^{-}$$

10. **Gold Number:** Gold number is the minimum weight of protective colloid in milligrams which prevents the coagulation of 10 ml of a red gold sol when 1 ml of a 10 percent solution of NaCl is added to it.

Maller the gold number of lyophilic colloid, greater is the protective power.

Protective colloid	Gold number
Gelatin	0.005 – 0.01
Casein	0.01 – 0.02
Haemoglobin	0.03 – 0.07
Albumen	0.1 – 0.2
Gum Arabic	0.15 – 0.25
Potato starch	20 – 25

Example 1.

Coagulation of 200 ml gold sol is prevented by the addition of 0.50 g of starch to it before adding 1 ml of 10% NaCl solution. What is the gold number of starch?

Solution :

$\because$ For 200 ml gold sol starch required = 0.50 g.

$\therefore$ For 10 ml gold sol starch required $= \frac{0.5 \times 10}{200} = 0.025\text{ g} = 25\text{ mg}$

Gold number = **25**

11. **Micelles :** The particles of colloidal size formed due to aggregation of several units of stearate ions of soap molecules (surfactants) in a dispersion medium are called '**micells**'. A concentrated solution of soap in water is a miceller system. Such substances are also called associated colloids.

12. **Emulsions :** Emulsions are the colloidal solutions in which both the dispersed phase and the dispersion medium are liquids. In other words, emulsions are liquid-liquid colloidal systems. Any two immiscible liquids form an emulsion. *Example :* Milk is a naturally occurring emulsion in which the particles (or globules) of liquid fats are dispersed in water.

    *The substances which are added to stabilize the emulsions are called **emulsifier** or **emulsifying agent**.* The substances that are commonly used as emulsifying agents are gum, soap of different forms, gelatin, albumin.

Very Short Answer Type Questions

Q. 1. What is adsorption?

Ans. The phenomenon of attracting and retaining the molecules of a substance on the surface of a liquid or a solid resulting into a higher concentration of the molecules on the surface is called adsorption.

Q. 2. Is adsorption exothermic or endothermic?

Ans. Exothermic.

Q. 3. Is chemisorption reversible or irreversible?

Ans. Irreversible.

Q. 4. What is physical adsorption?

Ans. If the adsorbate is held on a surface by weak Vanderwaals forces, the adsorption is called physical adsorption.

Q. 5. Why are powdered substances more effective adsorbent than their crystalline forms?

Ans. Powdered substances have greater surface area as compared to their crystalline forms, so greater the surface area, greater is the adsorption.

Q. 6. Why is it necessary to remove CO when ammonia is obtained by Haber's process?

Ans. CO acts as a poison for the catalyst used in the manufacture of ammonia by Haber's process, hence it is necessary to remove it.

Q. 7. Is a colloidal system homogeneous or heterogeneous?

Ans. It is heterogeneous.

Q. 8. Are the sols of metals hydrophobic or hydrophilic?

Ans. They are hydrophobic.

Q. 9. Define Brownian movement.

Ans. Brownian movement involves zig-zag motion of colloidal particles.

Q. 10. What are emulsions?

Ans. Emulsions are colloidal dispersion of liquids in liquids.

Q. 11. Give the expression of Freundich isotherms.

Ans. $\frac{x}{m} = KP^{1/n}$ or $\log \frac{x}{m} = \log K + \frac{1}{n} \log P$.

Q. 12. What do x and m represent in the following expression?

$$\frac{x}{m} = KP^{1/n}$$

Ans. x = mass of adsorbate
m = mass of adsorbent

Q. 13. To which colloidal system does milk belong?

Ans. Liquid in liquid or oil in water (Emulsion).

Q. 14. How will you obtain a colloidal sol of arsenious oxide solution?

Ans. Arsenious sulphide is obtained by passing H_2S through arsenious sulphide.

Q. 15. Give an example of an associated colloid.

Ans. Soap and detergents.

Q. 16. What is the range of particle size in colloidal solution in nm?

Ans. 1–1000 nm.

Q. 17. What is ZSM–5? What is its formula?

Ans. ZSM–5 is a zeolite sieve of molecular poroity 5. Its formula is

$$Hx\,[(AlO_2)x\,(SiO_2)96\text{–}x]\,.\,16H_2O$$

Q. 18. What are the physical states of dispersed phase and dispersion medium of froth?

Ans. Dispersed phase = Gas
Dispersion medium = Liquid

Q. 19. How does an increase in temperature affect both physical as well as chemical adsorption?

Ans. With increase of temperature, physical adsorption decreases while chemisorption first increases and then decreases.

Q. 20. Write down the heterogeneous catalyst involved in the polymerisation of ethylene.

Ans. $TiCl_4$ + trialkyl aluminum (zeigler – Natta catalyst).

Q. 21. Give one example of each of positive and negative sol.

Ans. Positive Sol : $Fe(OH)_3$
Negative Sol : As_2S_3

Q. 22. Arrange the solutions : true solution, colloidal solution and suspension in the decreasing order of their particle size.

Ans. Suspension > Colloidal solution > True solution.

Short Answer Type Questions – I

Q. 1. Why are substances like platinum and palladium often used for carrying out electrolysis of aqueous solutions?

Ans. Platinum and palladium are often used for carrying out electrolysis because these are inert in nature and the products of electrolysis easily get absorbed and deposited over these metals. Therefore, products can be easily collected.

Q. 2. Why is the role of desorption in the process of catalysis?

Ans. In the process of catalysis, when desorption occurs from the surface of the catalyst, the surface becomes ready to adsorb fresh reactants and act as a catalyst.

Q. 3. Why is adsorption always exothermic?

Ans. Adsorption occurs because of attraction between adsorbate and adsorbent molecules and therefore, energy is always released during adsorption. Hence, adsorption is an exothermic process.

Q. 4. Distinguish between the meaning of the terms adsorption and absorption. Give one example of each.

Ans. 1. *Adsorption*—It is a phenomenon in which there is higher concentration of another substance on the surface than in the bulk. For example, Silica gel adsorbs water vapour.

2. *Absorption*—It is a phenomenon in which the molecules of a substance are uniformly distributed throughout the body of the other substance. For example, Anhydrous calcium chloride adsorbs water.

Q. 5. What are lyophilic and lyophobic sols? Give one example of each type. What is hydrophobic sol easily coagulated?

Ans. 1. *Lyophilic sols*— Lyophilic sols are easily prepared by directly mixing with the liquid dispersion medium e.g. starch solution.

2. *Lyophobic sols*—Lyophobic sols cannot be prepared directly. They can be prepared only by special methods, e.g. metals, sulphides etc.

The stability of hydrophobic sol is only due to the presence of charge on the colloidal particles. If charge is removed, e.g., by addition of suitable electrolytes, the particles will come nearer to each other to form aggregate, i.e., they will coagulate and settle down. On the other hand, the stability of hypophilic sol is due to charge as well as solution of the colloidal particles. Both the factors have to be removed to bring about their coagulation.

Q. 6. Explain what is observed :

(*i*) when a beam of light is passed through a colloidal solution.

(*ii*) an electrolyte, NaCl is added to ferric hydroxide sol.

(*iii*) electric current is passed through a colloidal sol.

Ans. (*i*) Scattering of light by the colloidal particles takes place and the path of light becomes visible (Tyndall effect).

(*ii*) The positively charged colloidal particles of $Fe(OH)_3$ get coagulated by the oppositely charged Cl^- ions provided by NaCl.

(*iii*) On passing an electric current, colloidal particles move towards the oppositely charged electrode where they lose their charge and get coagulated.

Q. 7. Explain the following terms with suitable examples

(*i*) Alcosol (*ii*) Aerosol (*iii*) Hydrosol

Ans. (*i*) *Alcosol*—It is a colloidal dispersion having alcohol as the dispersion medium, e.g., collodion (a colloidal sol of cellulose nitrate in ethyl alcohol).

(*ii*) *Aerosol*—It is a colloidal dispersion of a liquid in a gas, e.g. fog.

(*iii*) *Hydrosol*—It is a colloidal sol of a solid in water as the dispersion medium, e.g. starch sol or gold sol.

Q. 8. What are emulsions? What are their different types? Give one example of each type.

Ans. An emulsion is a colloidal dispersion in which both the dispersed phase and the dispersion medium are liquids.

Types of emulsions—Emulsions may be classified into two types :

(*i*) *Emulsion of oil in water* (o/w) in which oil is the dispersed phase and water is the dispersion medium, e.g., milk, vanishing cream.

(*ii*) *Emulsion of water in oil* (w/o) in which water is the dispersed phase and oil is the dispersion medium, e.g., CoCl liver oil, butter.

Q. 9. Explain the following terms:

(*i*) Electrophoresis (*ii*) Coagulation (*iii*) Dialysis (*iv*) Tyndall effect

Ans. (*i*) *Electrophoresis*—The movement of colloidal particles under the influence of an electric field is called electrophoresis or cataphoresis.

Electrophorsis can be used to find out the nature of the charge that the colloidal particles carry.

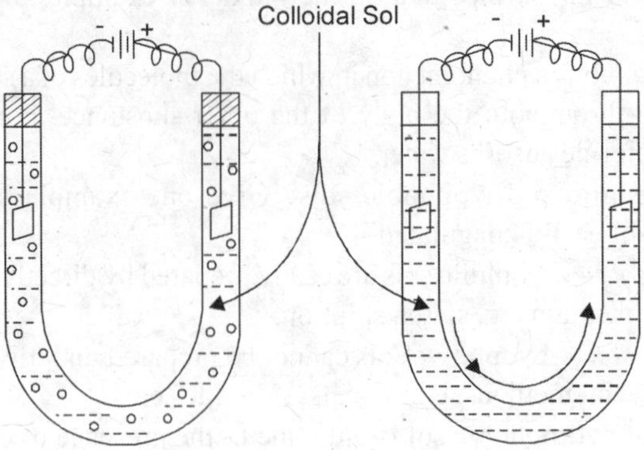

(*a*) Before electrophoresis (*b*) After Electrophoresis (For negatively charged colloidal particles)

Fig. 5.1

(*ii*) *Coagulation*—Coagulation or precipitation is a process of aggregating together the colloidal particles so as to change them into large-sized particles which ultimately settle as a precipitate.

Coagulation is generally brought about by the addition of electrolytes when an electrolyte is added to a colloidal sol, the particles of the solution take up the ions which are oppositely charged and thus get neutralised. The neutral particles then start accumulating to form particles of larger size which settle down.

(*iii*) *Dialysis*—The method used to separate the impurities from the colloidal solution is called dialysis.

Its principle is based upon the fact that colloidal particles cannot pass through a parchment of cellophane membrane while the ions of the electrolyte can pass through it. The colloidal solution is taken in a bag made of cellophane or parchment. The impurities slowly diffuse out of the bag leaving behind pure colloidal solution.

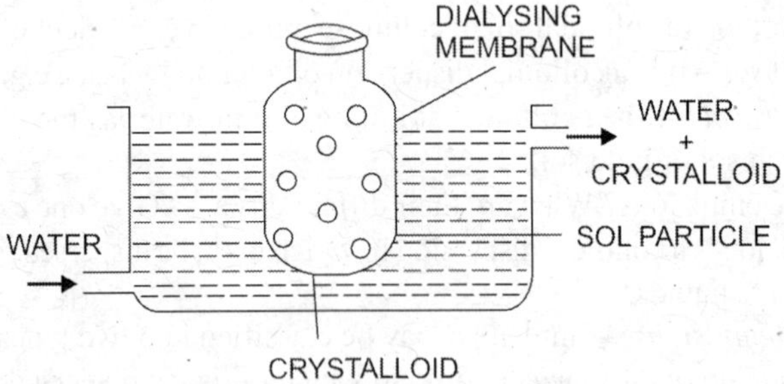

Fig. 5.2

(*iv*) *Tyndall effect* : When a strong beam of light is passed through a true solution placed in a beaker, in a dark room, the path of the light does not become visible. However, if the light is passed through a sol, placed in the same room, the path of the light becomes visible when viewed from a direction at right angle to that of the incident beam. This phenomenon was studied for the first time by Tyndall and therefore, it is called *Tyndall* effect. The *Tyndall* effect is due to the scattering of light by colloidal particles, i.e., these particles first absorb the incident and then a part of it gets scattered of them.

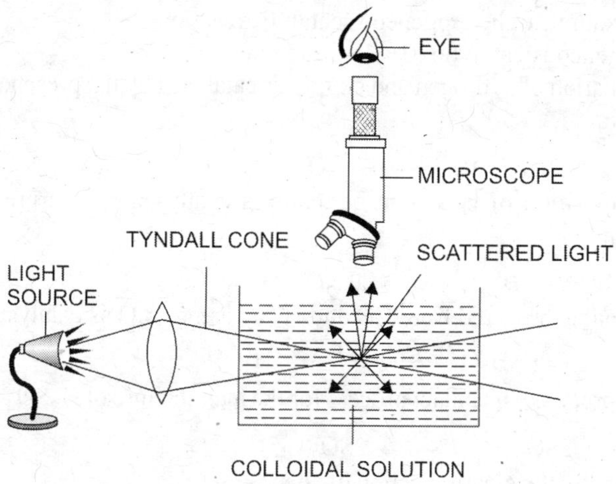

Fig. 5.3

Q. 10. What is heat of adsorption? Give the effect of temperature on physical adsorption and chemical adsorption.

Ans. *Heat of adsorption*: It is the heat change that takes place when 1 mole of a substance gets adsorbed on the surface of the another substance.

Effect of temperature :

(*a*) Physical adsorption—
[Same as Q. No. 19 [VSAQ]]

(*b*) Chemical adsorption—
[Same as Q. No. 19 [VSAQ]]

Short Answer Type Questions - II

Q. 1. Differentiate between homogeneous and heterogeneous catalysis with one example of each.

Ans. In the homogeneous catalysis, the reactants and the catalyst are all present in the same phase. But in heterogeneous catalysis these constitute different phases.

For example :

(*i*) Oxide of nitrogen (NO) acts as homogeneous catalyst in the oxidation of SO_2 to SO_3 in the contact process.

$$2SO_2 + O_2 \xrightarrow{NO_2} 2SO_3$$

(*ii*) Nickel (Ni) acts as the heterogeneous catalyst in the reaction of steam on methane to form carbon monoxide and hydrogen.

$$CH_4 + \underset{\text{(steam)}}{H_2O} \xrightarrow[1273\,K]{Ni} CO + 3H_2$$

Q. 2. Define zeolites with an example. Define peptization.

Ans. *Zeolite* is the nature given to some alumina silicates of metals with formula, $M_{x/n}[(AlO_2)x(SiO_2)y] . ZH_2O$ where n is the charge on the metal cation M^{n+}, which is usually Na^+, K^+ or Ca^{2+} and Z is the number of water molecules of hydration which is highly variable.

Peptization is the process of converting a precipitate into a colloidal sol by the addition of a suitable electrolyte to it. For example, a colloisal solution of ferric hydroxide is formed by adding a small amount of $FeCl_3$ to the precipitate. The precipitate adsorbs

Fe^{3+} ions form the electrolyte on its surface to form colloidal sol.

$$Fe(OH)_3 + Fe^{3+} \rightarrow [Fe(OH)_3]Fe^{3+}$$

Q. 3. Give four example of heterogeneous catalytic reactions.

Ans. The heterogeneous catalytic reactions are:

(*i*) Combination of hydrogen and oxygen is catalysed by the presence of finely divided platinum.

$$2H_2 + O_2 \xrightarrow{Pt} 2H_2O$$

(*ii*) Decomposition of hydrogen peroxide is catalysed by the presence of colloidal platinum.

$$2H_2O_2 \xrightarrow{Pt} 2H_2O + O_2$$

(*iii*) Methonal is prepared from CO and H_2 by using ZnO as catalyst.

$$CO + H_2O \xrightarrow{ZnO/Cr_2O_3} CH_3OH$$

(*iv*) SO_3 is prepared in contact process for the manufacture of H_2SO_4 by using platinum.

$$2SO_2 + O_2 \xrightarrow{Pt} 2SO_3$$

Q. 4. Describe briefly the clearing action of soap.

Ans. *Clearing action of soap*— Soap or detergents have been used as cleaning agents. The soaps are sodium salts of long chain fatty acids..They have a polar end $COO^- Na^+$ and non-polar end made of long chain hydrocarbons which may be —$C_{15}H_{31}$, —$C_{17}H_{33}$, —$C_{17}H_{35}$ etc.

This may be represented as the polar end which is water soluble and non-polar end which is soluble in organic solvents and acids. When the cloth is dipped in aqueous soap solution, the soap and dirt come in contact with each other. The non-polar end (tail) is directed towards the oil or grease present on the cloth and polar end (head) is directed towards water. In the manner, each oil droplet is surrounded by a number of negatively charged carboxylations. Since simple charges repel each other, the oil droplet are prevented from coming in contact with each other. As a result, oil droplets break up and more small droplets are formed. The hand rubbing or the agitation due to the washing machine causes dispersion of the oil or grease throughout the soapy water. In thisway, grease or dirt are removed from the surface of the cloth.

Q. 5. What is Freundlich adsorption isotherm? Explain it.

Ans. *Freundlich adsorption isotherm*— A graph between the amount of the gas adsorbed per gram of he adsorbent (x/m) and the equilibrium pressure of the adsorbate at constant temperature is called the **adsorption isotherm**. The behaviour of adsorption with pressure can be expressed by adsorption isotherm as shown in Fig. 5.4. The inspection of the graph reveals the following facts—

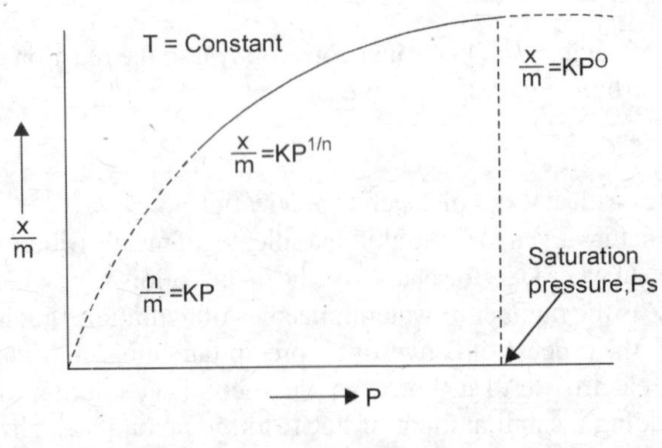

variation of $\frac{x}{m}$ with increase in pressure at constant temperature (Freundlich adsorption isotherm)

(*i*) *At low pressure*— The graph is almost straight line which indicates that $\frac{x}{m}$ is directly proportional to the pressure. This may be expressed as:—

$$\frac{x}{m} \propto P \quad \text{or} \quad \frac{x}{m} = KP \qquad ...(i)$$

where K is a constant.

(*ii*) *At high pressure*— The graph becomes almost constant which means that $\frac{x}{m}$ becomes independent of pressure. This may be expressed as:

$$\frac{x}{m} = \text{constant}$$

$$\text{or} \quad \frac{x}{m} \propto P^0 \qquad [\because P^0 = 1]$$

$$\frac{x}{m} = KP^0 \qquad ...(ii)$$

(*iii*) Thus, in the intermediate range of pressure, $\frac{x}{m}$ will depend upon the power of pressure which lies between 0 to 1 *i.e.* fractional power of pressure. This may be expressed as:

$$\text{or} \quad \frac{x}{m} \propto P^{1/n}$$

$$\text{or} \quad \frac{x}{m} = KP^{1/n} \qquad ...(iii)$$

where n can take any value between 1 and a larger integer depending upon the pressure. The above relationship is also called *Freundlich's adsorption isotherm.*

Higher Order Thinking Skills — Hots Questions

1. Give an example of an associated colloid.
2. Why is sky blue in colour?
3. Name the method by which gold sol can be prepared.
4. What is meant by a 'shape-selective catalyst'? Give an example in which shape selectivity of a catalyst is exhibited.
5. What happens when an electric field is applied to colloidal dispersion? Give reasons.
6. Explain the following terms with an example of each:
   (*i*) Emulsification (*ii*) Chemisorption
7. (a) What are micelles ? How do they differ from ordinary colloidal particles ? Give two examples of micelles forming substances.
   (b) State Hardy-Schulze rule.
   (c) State the principle of electrodialysis.
8. What is the adsorption isotherm? Distinguish between Freundlich adsorption isotherm and Langmuir adsorption isotherm with the help of appropriate graphs.
9. What is demulsificaiton ? Name two demulsifiers.
10. What are lyophilic and lyophobic sols ? Give one example of each type. Why is hydrophobic sols easily coagulated ?

❑❑❑

CHAPTER

6 GENERAL PRINCIPLES AND PROCESSES OF ISOLATION OF ELEMENTS

Syllabus

- *Principles and methods of extraction—concentration, oxidation, reduction, electrolytic method and refining; occurrence and principles of extraction of aluminium, copper, zinc and iron.*

Very Short Answer Type Questions

Q. 1. Name the most abundant element in the earth's crust.

Ans. Aluminium (Al).

Q. 2. Why do some metals occur in the native state?

Ans. Metals like Au and Pt, which are not reactive, i.e. not attacked by O_2, moisture and CO_2 of the air, occur in the native state.

Q. 3. Give one important ore of aluminium.

Ans. Bauxite ($Al_2O_3 . 2H_2O$).

Q. 4. What is the role of a stabilizer in froth floation process?

Ans. Chemical compounds like cresols and aniline which tend to stabilize the froth are called froth stabilizers.

Q. 5. What is the role of graphite rod in the electrometallurgy of aluminium?

Ans. The graphite rod is useful in the electrometallurgy of aluminium for reduction of alumina to aluminum

$$2Al_2O_3 + 3C \longrightarrow 4Al + 3CO_2.$$

Q. 6. Out of carbon and CO_2, which is a better reducing agent for ZnO?

Ans. Carbon.

Q. 7. Given two examples of ores which can be concentrated by magnetic separation method.

Ans. 1. Haematite – Fe_2O_3 2. Magnetite – $Fe_3\,O_4$

Q. 8. Out of C and CO which is better reducing agent for ZnO?

Ans. C is better reducing agent for ZnO

$$ZnO + C \xrightarrow{1673\,K} Zn + CO.$$

Q. 9. Name the method used for refining of (*i*) nickel (*ii*) zirconium.

Ans. (*i*) Nickel — Mond's process, (*ii*) Zirconium — Van-Ankel method

Q. 10. At a site, low grade copper ores are available and zinc and iron scraps are also available. Which of the two scraps will be more suitable for reducing the leached copper ore and why?

Ans. The E^0 value for the redox couple Zn^{2+}/Zn (–0.76V) is more negative than that of Fe^{2+}/Fe (–0.441) redox couple. Therefore, zinc is more reactive than iron and hence reduction will be faster in case if zinc scraps are used. But zinc is a costlier metal than iron so using iron scarps would be more economical.

Short Answer Type Questions - I

Q. 1. Differentiate between "minerals" and "ores".

Ans. 1. *Minerals*—The naturally occurring chemical substances in form of which the metals occur in the earth along with impurities are called minerals.

2. *Ore*— The mineral from which the metal can be extracted conveniently and economically is called an ore. All ores are minerals but all minerals are not ores.

Q. 2. Why is the reduction of a metal oxide easier if the metal formed is in the liquid state at the temperature of reduction?

Ans. Entropy is higher when a metal is in the liquid state than when it is in the solid state. Therefore, the value of entropy change (ΔS) of the reduction process is more on the +ve side when metal formed is in the liquid state and metal oxide being reduced is in the solid state. Since the value of $T\Delta S$ increases and that of ΔH remains constant, the value of ΔrG^0 ($\Delta G = \Delta H - T\Delta S$) becomes more on the –ve side and hence the reduction becomes easier.

Q. 3. What is the role of depressant in froth floatation process?

Ans. The depressants are used to prevent certain types of particles from forming the froth with bubbles in froth floation process. This helps to separate two sulphide ores.

For example, in case of an ore containing zinc sulphide (ZnS) and lead sulphide (PbS), sodium cyanide (NaCN) is used as a depressant. It forms a layer of zinc complex $Na_2[Zn(CN)_4]$ with ZnS on the surface of ZnS and therefore, prevents it from forming the froth. Therefore, it acts as a depressant.

$$4NaCN + ZnS \longrightarrow \underset{\text{Sod. tetraxanozincate (II)}}{Na_2[Zn(CN)_4]} + Na_2S$$

Q. 4. Copper can be extracted by hydrometallurgy but not zinc. Explain.

Ans. Zinc is more electropositive ($E^0 = -0.76V$) and therefore, is highly reactive metal. Hence, it cannot be easily displaced from its solution of $ZnSO_4$.

On the other hand, copper is less electropositive ($E^0 = +0.34V$) and can be readily displaced from its solution by some more active metal such as zinc.

Q. 5. Why is copper matte put in silica lined converter?

Ans. The copper matte containing Cu_2S and FeS is put in silica lined convertor. Some silica is also added and hot our blast is blown to convert remaining FeS to FeO, which is removed as slag with silica,

$$2FeS + 3O_2 \longrightarrow 2FeO + 2SO_2\uparrow$$

$$FeO + \underset{\text{Silica}}{SiO_2} \longrightarrow \underset{\text{Slag}}{FeSiO_3}$$

When the whole of iron has been removed as slag, some of the Cu_2S undergoes oxidation to form Cu_2O which then reacts with more Cu_2S to form copper metal

$$2Cu_2S + 3O_2 \longrightarrow 2Cu_2O + 2SO_2\uparrow$$

$$2Cu_2O + Cu_2S \longrightarrow 6Cu + SO_2\uparrow$$

Thus, copper matte is heated in silica lined converter to remove FeS present in matte as $FeSiO_3$ slag.

Q. 6. (*a*) What is the role of cryolite in the metallurgy of aluminium?

(*b*) How is leaching carried out in case of low grade copper ores?

(*c*) Why is zinc not extracted from zinc oxide through reduction using CO?

Ans. (*a*) Cryolite is added to bauxite ore before electrolysis because of the following reasons:—

(*i*) It acts as a solvent.

(*ii*) It lowers the melting point of alumina to about 1173K.

(*iii*) Addition of cryolite to alumina increases the electrical conductivity.

(*b*) Copper is leached out from low grade copper by using acid in the presence of air when copper goes into the solution as Cu^{2+} ions

$$2Cu + 2H_2SO_4 + O_2 \longrightarrow 2CuSO_4 + 2H_2O$$

or $$Cu + 2H^+ + \frac{1}{2}O_2 \longrightarrow Cu^{2+} + H_2O$$

(*c*) In Ellingham diagram, the $\Delta G^0 r$ Vs T plot representing CO, CO_2 lies above ΔG^0 Va T plot of Zn, ZnO. Therefore, CO cannot act as reducing agent for the reduction of ZnO.

Q. 7. What is the role of graphite in the electrometallurgy of aluminium?

Ans. In the electrometallurgy of aluminium a fused mixture of alumina, cryolite and fluorspar (CaF_2) is electrolysed using graphite as anode and graphite lined iron as cathode. During electrolysis, Al is liberated at the cathode while CO and CO_2 are liberated at the anode.

At Cathode: $$Al^{3+} \text{ (melt)} \longrightarrow Al$$

At anode: $$C + O^{2-} \longrightarrow CO + 2e^-$$
$$C + 2O^{2-} \longrightarrow CO_2 + 4e^-$$

Since graphite is much cheaper than any metal; therefore, graphite is used as the anode.

Q. 8. How is cast iron different from pig iron?

Ans. The iron obtained from blast furnace is called *pig iron*. It contains about 4% carbon and many other impurities (e.g., S, P, Si, Mn) in small amounts.

Cast iron is made by melting pig iron with scrap iron and cake using hot air blast. It has slightly lower carbon content (about 3%) and is extremely hard and brittle.

Q. 9. Giving examples, differentiate between 'roasting' and 'calcination'.

Ans.

Calcination	*Roasting*
1. In calcination, the concentrated ore is heated in the absence of air e.g., $Fe_2O_3 . 3H_2O \xrightarrow{\Delta} Fe_2O_3 + 3H_2O\uparrow$ (Limonite → Ferric oxide)	1. In roasting, the concentrated ore is heated in regular supply of air below the melting point of metal $2ZnS + 3O_2 \longrightarrow 2ZnO + 2SO_2\uparrow$ (Zinc blende → Zinc oxide)
2. It is used for carbonate and oxide ores.	2. It is used for sulphide ores.
3. Moisture and organic impurities are removed.	3. Volatile impurities are removed as oxide SO_2, P_2O_5, Ar_2O_5 etc.

Q. 10. Name the common elements present in the anode mud in electrolytic refining of copper. Why are they so present ?

Ans. The anode mud in the electrolytic refining of copper contains antimony, selenium, tellurium, silver, gold and platinum. These are present as impurities in blinter copper. These are less reactive and not affected by $CuSO_4 - H_2SO_4$ solution and hence settle down under anode as anode mud.

Short Answer Type Questions – II

Q. 1. Outline the principles of refining of metals by the following methods:

(*i*) Zone refining (*ii*) Electrolytic refining (*iii*) Vapour phase refining

Ans. (*i*) *Zone refining* : This method is based upon the principle that the impurities are more soluble in the molten state (melt) than in the solid state of the metal. This method is extremely useful for producing semiconductor and other metals of very high purity, e.g., germanium, silicon, boron, gallium and indium.

(*ii*) *Electrolytic refining* : A large number of metals such as copper, silver, gold, lead, nickel, chromium, zinc, aluminium, etc, are refined by this method.

In this method, transfer of pure metal from the anode to the cathode takes place. The voltage applied for electrolysis is such that the impurities of more basic metals (more electropositive metals) remain in the solution as ions whereas impurities of less basic metals (less electropositive metals) settle down under the anode as anode mud or anode sludge.

(*iii*) *Vapour-phase refining* : In this method, the crude metal is freed from impurities by first converting it into a suitable volatile compound by heating it with a specific regent at a lower temperature and then decomposing the volatile compound at some higher temperature to give the pure metal. This method is illustrated by the following two processes: (*i*) Mond process, (*ii*) Van-Arkel method. These methods are used for refining of nickel, zirconium etc.

Q. 2. Write down the reactions taking place in different zones in the blast furnace during the extraction of iron.

Ans. *Reactions taking place in the furnace*: The following reactions occur in the blast furnace.

(*i*) *Zone of combustion* : Near the tuyeres, coke burns to form CO_2

$$C + O_2 \longrightarrow CO_2; \ \Delta H = -393.3 \text{ KJ}$$

Here the temperature is around 2170 K.

(*ii*) *Zone of heat absorption* : This is lower part of the furnace and the temperature here is between 1423–1673K. As CO_2 formed near tuyeres moves up, it meets the descending charge. The coke present in the charge reduces CO_2 to CO.

$$CO_2 + C \longrightarrow 2CO\ ; \ \Delta H = +163.2 \text{ KJ.}$$

(*iii*) *Zone of slag formation* : It is the middle part of the furnace. The temperature here is around 1123 K. In this region, limestone decomposes to form CaO and CO_2

$$CaCO_3 \xrightarrow{1123\text{ K}} CaO + CO_2$$

$$CaO + SiO_2 \xrightarrow{1123\text{ K}} \underset{\text{Calcium silicate (slag)}}{CaSiO_3}$$

(*iv*) *Zone of reduction* : This is the upper part of the furnace. The temperature here is between 500–900 K. Here the ores are reduced to FeO by CO.

$$Fe_2O_3 + CO \xrightarrow{500\text{-}900\text{ K}} 2FeO + CO_2$$

$$Fe_3O_4 + CO \xrightarrow{500\text{-}900\,K} 3FeO + CO_2$$

But the further reduction of FeO to Fe by CO occurs around 1123K.

$$FeO + CO \xrightarrow{1123\,K} Fe + CO_2$$

(v) *Zone of fusion*—This is the lower part of the furnace. Temperature here is in between 1423–1673 K. In this region, spongy iron melts and dissolves some C, S, P, Si, Mn etc.

Q. 3. Explain:

(1) Zone refining (2) Column chromatography

Ans. (1) *Zone refining*—This method is used for metal which are required to very high purity. For example, extremely pure silicon, germanium, baron, gallium and indium are refined by this method.

This method is based on the principle that the impurities are more soluble in the metal than in the solid state of the metal. Therefore, an impure metal on solidification will deposit crystals of pure metals and the impurities will remain behind in the molten part of the metal. In this method, the impure metal is cast into a thin bar. A circular mobile heater is fixed at one end of the rod of impure metal. One zone of the bar is melted by a circular mobile heater in the atmosphere of a noble gas like argon. At the heated zone, the metal is shown in the figure. As the heater moves slowly, the impurities also move into the adjacent molten part. In this way, the impurities are made to move into one end which is finally cut off and discarded. The molten metal present at the colder region solidifies in the mean time since it is away from a heater. Thus, we get completely pure metal by this method.

This method is specially useful for producing semiconductors at very higher purity.

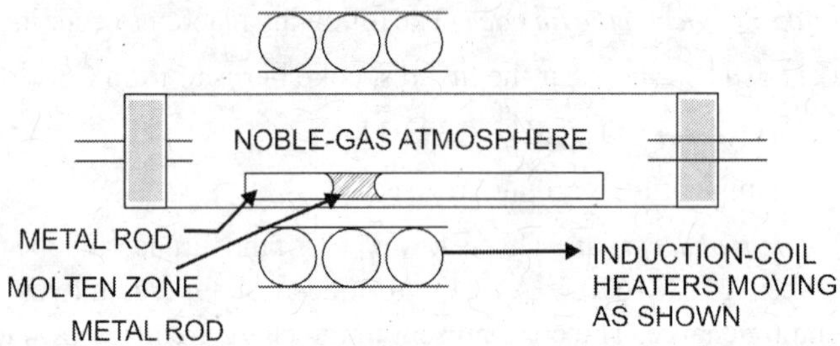

Fig. 6.1

(2) *Column chromatography* : Column chromatography is one of the simplest chromatographic techniques and is widely used.

In column chromatography, an adsorbent such as alumina (Al_2O_3), silica gel or some iron exchange resin is packed in a column. (same as in Fig. 6.2).

This forms the stationary phase. The mixture to be separated is dissolved in a suitable solvent (mobile phase) and applied to the top of the column.

"Different components of the mixture are adsorbed to different extents depending upon their polarity." Later the adsorbed components are extracted (eluted) from the column with a suitable solvent. The component which is more strongly adsorbed on the column than a component which is weakly adsorbed. In this way, the various components of the mixture separated as they travel through the absorbent.

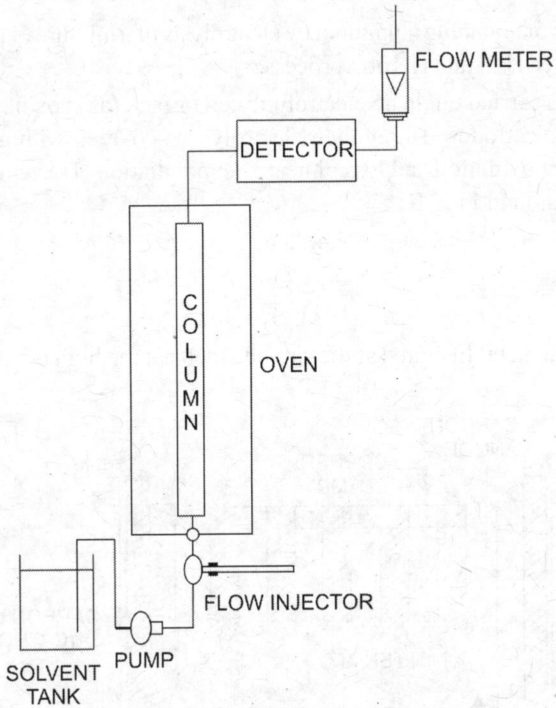

Fig. 6.2

Q. 4. What is the significance of leaching in the extraction of aluminium?

Ans. Aluminium usually contains silica (SiO_2), iron oxide (Fe_2O_3) and titanium oxide (TiO_2) as impurities.

These impurities can be removed by the process of leaching. During leaching the powdered bauxite ore is heated with concentrated (45%) solution of NaOH at 473–52316, when alumina dissolves a sodium meta-aluminate and silica (SiO_2) as sodium silicate leaving $Fe_2O_3.TiO_2$ and other impurities behind.

$$\underset{\text{Alumina}}{Al_2O_3} + 2NaOH + 3H_2O \xrightarrow{473-523\,K} \underset{\text{Sodium meta-aluminate}}{2Na[Al(OH)_4]}$$

$$\underset{\text{Silica}}{SiO_2} + 2NaOH \xrightarrow{473-523\,K} \underset{\text{Sodium silicate}}{Na_2SiO_3 + H_2O}$$

The impurities are filtered off and the solution of sodium meta-aluminate is neutralized by passing CO_2.

$$2Na[Al(OH)_4] + CO_2 \longrightarrow Al_2O_3\,xH_2O\uparrow + 2NaHCO_3$$

Hydrated alumina, detained is filtered, washed and finally heated to about 1473K to get pure alumina (Al_2O_3)

$$Al_2O_3\,.\,xH_2O \xrightarrow{1473\,K} Al_2O_3 + xH_2O.$$

Q. 5. Describe extraction of aluminium from alumina.

Ans. *Extraction of aluminium from alumina* : Fused alumina (Al_2O_3) is a bad conductor of electricity. So, cryolite and fluorspar (CaF_2) are added to purified alumina.

—The process of obtaining aluminum by electrolysis of a mixture of purified alumina and cryolite is called Hall and Heroult process.

This process is carried out in an electrolytic cell or tank (as shown in Fig.) made of iron using carbon electrodes. The molten electrolyte is covered with a layer of powdered coke to prevent oxidation and loss of heat due to radiation. The temperature of the bath is maintained around 1173 K.

At cathode– $Al^{3+} + 3e^- \longrightarrow Al$

At anode– $C + O^{2-} \longrightarrow CO + 2e^-$

$C + 2O^{2-} \longrightarrow CO_2 + 4e^-$

The aluminium metal liberated at the cathode melts at the high temperature (1173 K) of the tank.

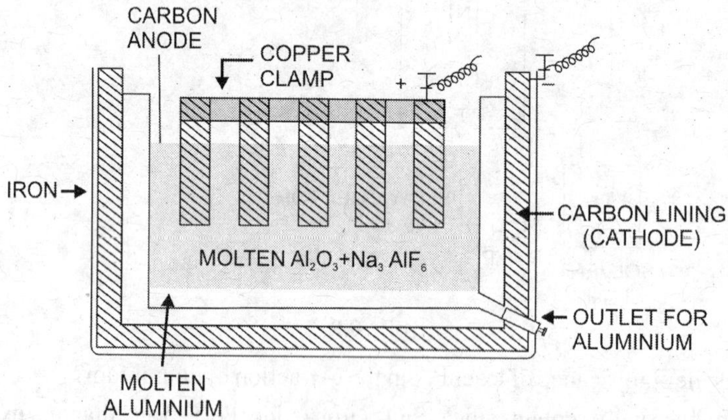

Fig. 6.3

Q. 6. Describe the principle of each of the following process in detail?

(*a*) Mond's process (*b*) Van-Ankel method

Ans. (*a*) *Mond's process* : It is used for refining of nickel when impure nickel is heated in a current of CO at 330–350K, it forms volatile nickel tetracarbonyl complex leaving behind the impurities

$$\underset{\text{Impure nickel}}{Ni + 4CO} \xrightarrow{330-350\,K} \underset{\text{Nickel tetracarbonyl}}{Ni\,(CO_4}$$

$$Ni(CO)_4 \xrightarrow{450-470\,K} \underset{\text{pure nickel}}{Ni + 4CO}$$

(*b*) *Van-Ankel method*–This method is very useful for preparing ultra-pure metals by removing all the oxygen and nitrogen present in the form of impurity in certain metals such a zirconium and titanium.

In this method, crude zirconium is heated in an evacuated vessel with iodine at 870 K.

$$\underset{\text{Impure zirconium}}{Zr + 2I_2} \xrightarrow{870\,K} ZrI_4 \xrightarrow[\text{Tungsten filament}]{2075\,K} \underset{\text{Pure zirconium}}{Zr + 2I_2}$$

Higher Order Thinking Skills Hots Questions

1. Name sulphide ore of copper and silver.
2. Which metals are generally extracted by electrolytic processes? Which positions these metals generally occupy in the periodic table?
3. Metals like Cu, Ag, Zn, Hg and Pb occur in nature as sulphides rather than oxides? Why?
4. Give the uses of aluminium, copper, zinc and iron.
5. Explain the following :
   (*i*) Zinc but not copper is used for the recovery of Ag from $[Ag(CW)_2]^-$.
   (*ii*) Partial roasting of sulphide ore is done in metallurgy of copper.
6. Write short notes on the following giving example :
   (*i*) Magnetic separation
   (*ii*) Aluminathermic process
   (*iii*) Liquation
7. Name the reducing agent used in aluminothermic (thermite) process.
8. What is the role of depressant in froth floatation process ?
9. What is the role of cryolite in the metallurgy of aluminium ?
10. Name the metals which are associated with the following terms in their extraction from ores :
    (*i*) Bessemer's converter
    (ii) Blast furnace
    (iii) Aluminothermic process
    (iv) Magnetic separation
11. Give one example of the following for extraction of metal
    (*i*) Auto-reduction
    (ii) H_2 is used as reducing agent.
12. Write short notes on the following giving one example :
    (*i*) Roasting (ii) Calcination (ii) Smelting.

❑❑❑

CHAPTER

7 THE *p*-BLOCK ELEMENTS

Syllabus

- ***Group 15 elements :*** *General introduction, electronic configuration, occurrence, oxidation states, trends in physical and chemical properties; nitrogen—preparation, properties and uses; compounds of nitrogen: preparation and properties of ammonia and nitric acid. Phosphorus—allotropic forms; compounds of phosphorus: preparation and properties of phosphine, halides (PCl_3, PCl_5) and oxoacids (elementary idea only).*
- ***Group 16 elements :*** *General introduction, electronic configuration, oxidation staes, occurrence, trends in physical and chemical properties; simple oxides; Ozone. Sulphur—allotropic forms; compounds of sulphur: sulphuric acid: industrial process of manufacture, properties and uses, oxoacids of sulphur (structures only).*
- ***Group 17 elements :*** *General introduction, electronic configuration, oxidation states, occurrence, trends in physical and chemical properties; compounds of halogens, hydrochloric acid, interhalogen compounds, oxoacids of halogens (structures only).*
- ***Group 18 elements :*** *General introduction, electronic configuration. Occurrence, trends in physical and chemical properties, uses.*

Very Short Answer Type Questions

Q. 1. Which of the two has higher boiling point, NH_3 or PH_3?

Ans. NH_3 forms H-bonds but PH_3 does not and hence boiling point of NH_3 is higher than that of PH_3.

Q. 2. Name three allotropes of phosphorus? Which of the three is most reactive?

Ans. White or yellow, red and black. White phosphorus is most reactive.

Q. 3. Which of the following is more covalent: $SbCl_5$ or $SbCl_3$?

Ans. $SbCl_5$ due to higher oxidation state.

Q. 4. What is oleum? What is the oxidation state of sulphur in it?

Ans. $H_2S_2O_7$, the oxidation state of sulphur is +6.

Q. 5. What is laughing gas? How is it prepared?

Ans. N_2O. It is prepared by heating ammonium nitrate, i.e.,

$$NH_4NO_3 \xrightarrow{\Delta} N_2O + 2H_2O$$

Q. 6. Nitric oxide becomes brown when released in air.

Ans. When nitric oxide, NO is released in air. It becomes brown due to the formation of NO_2, which is a brown gas.

$$O + O_2 \longrightarrow \underset{\text{(brown)}}{2NO_2}$$

Q. 7. Name the promoter used in Haber's process.

Ans. Molybdenum.

Q. 8. Write the order of thermal stability of the hydrides of group 16 elements?

Ans. $H_2O > H_2S > H_2Se$.

Q. 9. Complete the following reactions:

(*i*) $C_2H_4 + O_2 \longrightarrow$ (*ii*) $4Al + 3O_2 \longrightarrow$

Ans. (*i*) $C_2H_4 + 3O_2 \longrightarrow 2CO_2 + 2H_2O$ (*ii*) $4Al + 3O_2 \longrightarrow 2Al_2O_3$

Q. 10. Write the reactions of F_2 and Cl_2 with water.

Ans. Fluorine reacts vigorously with water giving oxygen and ozone.

$$2F_2 + 2H_2O \longrightarrow 4HF + O_2$$
$$3F_2 + 3H_2O \longrightarrow 6HF + O_3$$

Chlorine reacts slowly with water giving oxygen.

$$2Cl_2 + 2H_2O \longrightarrow 4HCl + O_2$$

Q. 11. Which neutral molecule would be isoelectronic with ClO^-? Is that molecule a Lewis base?

Ans. ClO^- is isoelectronic with ClF. Yes, it is a Lewis base.

Q. 12. Arrange the following in the decreasing order of electron affinity.

F, Cl, I, Br

Ans. Cl > F > Br > I.

Q. 13. Why is helium used in diving apparatus?

Ans. Helium is used as a diluent for oxygen in diving apparatus because of its low solubility in blood.

Q. 14. Which one of the following does not exist?

(*a*) $XeOF_4$ (*b*) NeF_2 (*c*) XeF_2 (*d*) XeF_6

Ans. NeF_2.

Q. 15. Why has it been difficult to study the chemistry of radon?

Ans. Radon is radioactive and has very short half-life period. Therefore, it is difficult to study the chemistry of radon.

Short Answer Type Questions - I

Q. 1. Why are pentahalides more covalent than trihalides?

Ans. In pentahalides, the oxidation state is more (+5) than in trihalides (+3). As a result of higher positive oxidation state of central atom, they have larger polarizing power and can polarise the halide ion (X^-) to a greater extent than in corresponding trihalide.

Since larger the polarisation, larger is the covalent character; therefore, pentahalides are more covalent than trihalides.

Q. 2. Why is N_2 less reactive at room temperature?

Ans. In molecular nitrogen (N_2), there is a triple bond between two nitrogen atoms and it is non-polar in character, due to the presence of a triple bond, it has very high bind dissociation energy (941.4 KJ mol^{-1}) and therefore, it does not react with other elements under normal conditions and is unreactive. However, it may react at higher temperatures.

Q. 3. Phosphine has lower boiling point than ammonia. Give reason.

Ans. Ammonia exists as associated molecule due to its tendency to form hydrogen bonding. Therefore, it has high boiling point unlike NH_3, PH_3 molecules are not associated through hydrogen bonding in liquid state. This is because of low electronegativity of P than N. As a result, the boiling point of PH_3 is lower than that of NH_3.

Q. 4. Though nitrogen exhibits +5 oxidation state, it does not form pentahalides. Give reasons.

Ans. Nitrogen belongs to second period and has only s- and p-orbitals. It does not have d-orbitals in its valence shell and therefore, it cannot extend its octet that is why nitrogen does not form pentahalides.

Q. 5. Why does NO_2 dimerise? Explain.

Ans. NO_2 contains odd number of valence electrons it behaves as a typical molecule. In the liquid and solid state, it dimerises to form stable N_2O_4 molecule, with even number of electrons. Therefore, NO_2 is paramagnetic, while N_2O_4 is diamagnetic in which two unpaired electrons get paired.

Q. 6. Why does ammonia act as a Lewis base?

Ans. Nitrogen atom in NH_3 has one lone pair of electrons which is available for donation. Therefore, it acts as a Lewis base.

Q. 7. What happens when—

(*a*) Concentrated H_2SO_4 is added to calcium fluoride?

(*b*) SO_3 is passed through water?

Ans. (*a*) It forms hydrogen fluoride

$$CaF_2 + H_2SO_4 \longrightarrow CaSO_4 + 2HF$$

(*b*) Sulphuric acid is formed.

$$SO_3 + H_2O \longrightarrow H_2SO_4$$

Q. 8. Mention the conditions required to maximise the yield of ammonia.

Ans. Ammonia is formed according to the reaction:-

$$N_2 + 3H_2 \rightleftharpoons 2NH_3, \quad \Delta H^0 = -46.1 \text{ KJ mol}^{-1}$$

The condition for maximum yield of ammonia are:-

(*i*) Low temperature of the order of about 700K.

(*ii*) High pressure of 200×10^5Pa (about 200 atm.)

(*iii*) Presence of catalyst such as iron oxide with small amount of K_2O and Al_2O_3.

Q. 9. Why does O_3 act as a powerful oxidising agent?

Ans. Ozone acts as a powerful oxidising agent because it has higher energy content and decomposes readily to give atomic oxygen as:—

$$O_3 \longrightarrow O_2 + O$$

Therefore, ozone can oxidise a number of non-metals and other compounds. For example:-

$$PbS + 4O_3 \longrightarrow PbSO_4 + 4O_2$$

Q. 10. Noble gases have low boiling points. Explain.

Ans. Noble gases are monoatomic gases and are held together by weak vander waal's forces (dispersion forces). Therefore, they are liquefied at very low temperatures. Hence they have low boiling points.

Short Answer Type Questions – II

Q. 1. H_3PO_3 is diprotic (or dibasic). Why?

Ans. Its structure is

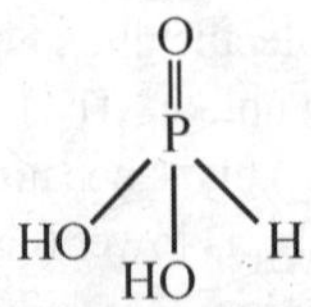

Since it contains only two ionizable H atoms which are present as OH groups, it behaves as a dibasic acid.

Q. 2. What is the covalence of nitrogen in N_2O_5?

Ans. Covalency depends upon the number of shared pairs of electrons. Now in N_2O_5, each nitrogen atom has four shared pairs of electrons as shown below :

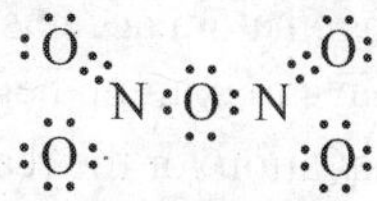

Q. 3. Deduce the molecular shape of BrF_3 on the basis of VSEPR theory.

Ans. No. of electrons in the valence shell of the central Br atom = 7.

No. of electrons provided by three F atoms = 3 × 1 = 3.

Total no. of electrons around the central atom = 7 + 3 = 10.

In BrF_3 structure, there are three Br—F bonds.

∴ No. of lone pairs = 5 – 3 = 2

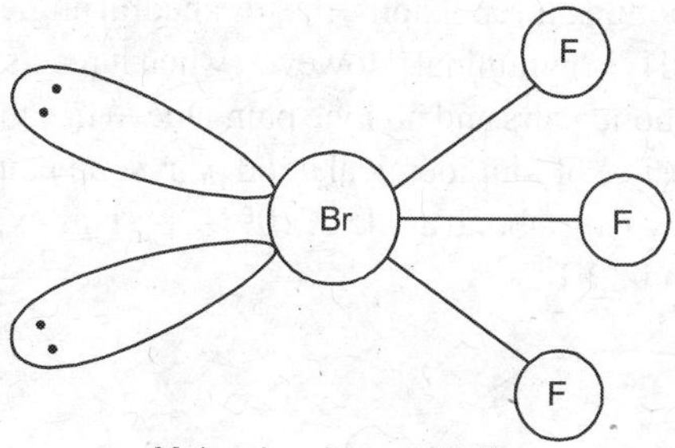

Molecular shape of BrF_3

On the basis of VSEPR theory, a molecule with three bond pairs and two lone pairs must be T-shaped. (*i.e.*, distorted triangle bipyramidal)

The two lone pairs will occupy equatorial positions to minimize lone pair-lone pair repulsions which are much stronger than lone pair-bond pair and bond pair-bond pair repulsion. Further, the axial F atoms will be slightly bent towards the equatorial F atom to minimize the lone pair-bond pair repulsions. Therefore, the shape of BrF_3 would be slightly bent T.

Q. 4. Elements of group 16 generally show lower value of first ionization enthalpy compared to the corresponding elements of group 15. Why?

Ans. This is because of the following two reasons :

(*i*) Due to extra stability of the exactly half filled P-orbitals electronic configuration of group 15 elements, they require larger amount of energy to remove an electron as compared to those of group 16 elements.

(*ii*) After removal of an electron, the group 16 elements yield species which have more stable exactly half-filled p-orbitals electronic configuration while this is not so in case of group 15 elements.

Q. 5. H_2S is less acidic than H_2Te. Why?

Ans. As the size of the element increases down the group, E–H bond-length increases and hence E–H bond dissociation energy decreases. In other words, H–S bond dissociation energy is higher than that of H–Te bond dissociation energy and hence H–S bond breaks less easily than H–Te bond. Therefore, H_2S is a weaker acid than H_2Te.

Q. 6. Halogens have maximum negative electron gain enthalpy. Explain why?

Ans. Halogens have the smallest size in their respective periods and, therefore, have high effective nuclear charge. As a result, they readily accept one electron to acquire the stable electronic configuration of the nearest noble gas. In other words, large amount of energy is released when a halogen atom accepts an electron to form the corresponding halide ion and thus halogens have maximum negative electron gain enthalpies.

Q. 7. Write the balanced chemical equation for the reaction of Cl_2 with hot and concentrated NaOH? Is this reaction a disproportionation reaction? Justify.

Ans.

$$\overset{0}{3Cl_2} + 6NaOH\,(conc.) \xrightarrow{Hot} 5Na\overset{-1}{Cl} + Na\overset{+5}{Cl}O_3 + 3H_2O$$

This is an example of a disproportionation reaction because the oxidation state of chlorine decreases from zero in Cl_2 to -1 in NaCl and increases from zero in Cl_2 to $+5$ in $NaClO_3$.

Q. 8. Bond angle in PH_4^+ is higher than that in PH_3. Why?

Ans. P in PH_3 in Sp. hybridized. It has three bond pairs and one lone pair around *p* due to stronger lone pair bond pair repulsions, the tetrahedral angle decreases from 109°–28′ to 93.6°. As a result, PH_3 is pyramidal. However, when it reacts with a proton, it forms PH_4^+ ion which has four bond pairs and no lone pair. Due to the absence of lone pair-bond pair repulsions and presence of four identical bond pair-bond pair interactions, PH_4^+ assumes tetrahedral geometry with a bond angle of 109°–28′. This explains why the bond angle in PH_4^+ is higher than in PH_3.

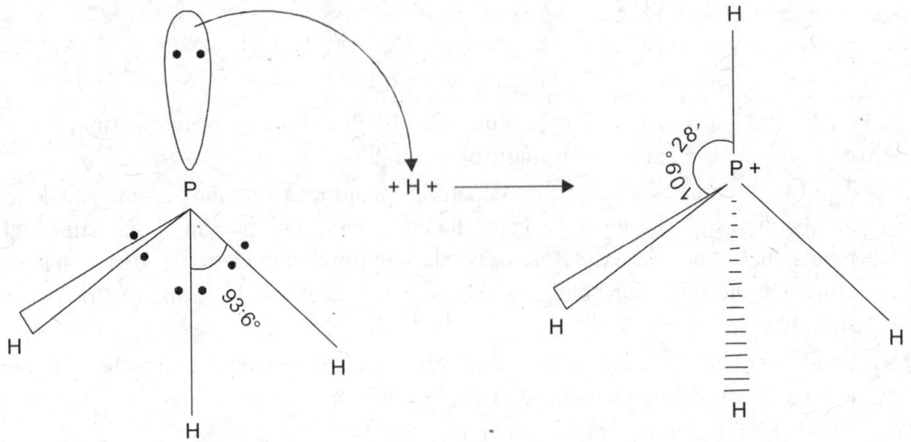

PH_3 molecule (Pyramidal) | PH_4^+ ion Tetrahedral)

Q. 9. Complete the following reaction :

(*i*) $C_2H_4 + O_2 \longrightarrow$ (*ii*) $4Al + 3O_2 \longrightarrow$

Ans. (*i*) C_2H_4 undergoes combustion to form CO_2 and H_2O

$$C_2H_4 + 3O_2 \xrightarrow{heat} 2CO_2 + 2H_2O$$

(*ii*) Al combines with O_2 to form alumina

$$4Al + 3O_2 \xrightarrow{heat} 2Al_2O_3.$$

Q. 10. How are XeF_2, XeF_4 and XeF_6 obtained ?

Ans. All these xenon fluorides are prepared by direct reaction between Xe and F_2 under different conditions as shown below :

$$Xe + F_2 \xrightarrow{673K,\ 1\,bar} XeF_2$$
(Excess)

$$Xe + 2F_2 \xrightarrow{873K,\ 7\,bar} XeF_4$$
(1 : 5 ratio)

$$Xe + 3F_2 \xrightarrow{573K,\ 60-70\,bar} XeF_6$$
(1 : 20 ratio)

Long Answer Type Questions

Q. 1. Describe Ostwald process for the manufacture of nitric acid. Give uses.

Ans. *Theory* :

(*i*) NH_3 is oxidised to NO by air or O_2 at 2070 K in the presence of Rt or Rh – Pd alloy.

$$4NH_3 + SO_2 \longrightarrow 6H_2O + 4NO.$$

(*ii*) Nitric oxide formed is cooled and allowed to come in contact with oxygen or air when it is oxidised to NO_2

$$2NO + O_2 \longrightarrow 2NO_2.$$

(*iii*) The nitrogen dioxide formed is dissolved in water in the presence of air or oxygen when nitric acid is obtained

$$4NO_2 + 2H_2O + O_2 \longrightarrow 4HNO_3.$$

Working of the plant— The outlines of the plant and its working are shown in the Fig.

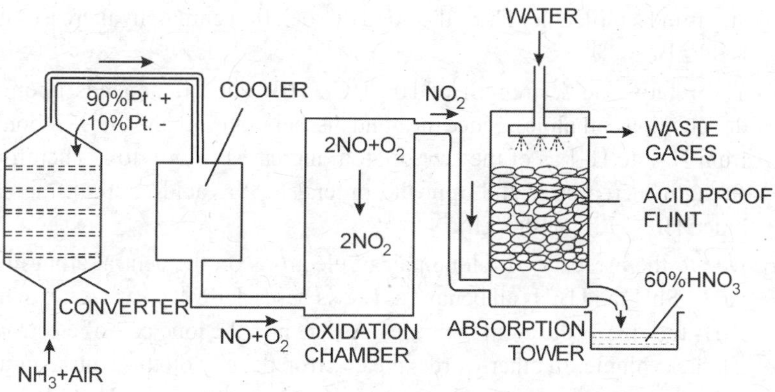

Fig. Ostwald process for the manufacture of nitric acid.

(*i*) *Oxidation of ammonia*—Ammonia prepared by Haber's process is mixed with 10 times its volume of pure, dust, free, dry air. The mixture is passed through a converter made of either steel or aluminium with platinum gauge placed in it. The temperature of the converter is kept at about 1070°C.

$$4NH_3 + 5O_2 \longrightarrow 6H_2O + 4NO + \text{heat}$$

(*ii*) *Oxidation of nitric oxide*—The nitric oxide coming out of the converter is cooled and passed through a chamber where it mixes with oxygen and oxidised to nitrogen dioxide. It is called oxidising chamber.

$$2NO + O_2 \longrightarrow 2NO_2$$

(*iii*) *Absorption of nitrogen peroxide*—The nitrogen dioxide from oxidation chamber is absorbed in water in the presence of oxygen.

$$2H_2O + 4NO_2 + O_2 \longrightarrow 2HNO_3$$

This solution of NHO_3 is concentrated further.

Uses of nitric acid :

(*i*) Nitric acid is needed in the manufacture of ammonium nitrate and basic calcium nitrate which are needed as fertilizers.

(*ii*) In the manufacture of explosives and pyrotechnics such as gun cotton, nitroglycerine, T.N.T., picric acid etc.

(*iii*) In the manufacture of artificial silk.

(*iv*) As an oxidiser in rocket fuels.

(*v*) As a reagent in the laboratory.

Q. 2. Arrange the following in order of property indicated for each set:

(*i*) F_2, Cl_2, Br_2, I_2 – increasing bond dissociation enthalphy.

(*ii*) HF, HCl, HBr, HI – increasing acid strength.

(*iii*) NH_3, PH_3, AsH_3, SbH_3, BiH_3 – increasing base strength.

Ans. (*i*) Bond dissociation enthalphy should decrease as the bond distance increases from F_2 to I_2 due to the increase in the size of the atom as we move from F to I. However, the F–F bond dissociation enthalphy is smaller than that of Cl–Cl and even smaller than that of Br-Br. This is due to the reason that the F atom is very small and hence the three lone pairs of electrons on each F atom repel the bond pair holding the F-atoms in F_2 molecule. Thus, the bond dissociation enthalphy increases in the order: $I_2 < F_2\ Br_2 < Cl_2$.

(*ii*) The relative acid strength of HF, HCl, HBr and HI depends upon their bond dissociation enthalpies. Since the bond dissociation enthalpy of H–X bond decreases from H–F to H–I as of the size of atom increases from F to I. Therefore, the acid strength increases in the opposite order, i.e., the acid strength increases in the order: HF < HCl < HBr < HI.

(*iii*) Due to the presence of a lone pair of electrons on the central atom in NH_3, PH_3, ArH_3, SbH_3 and BiH_3 all behave as Lewis bases. However, as we move from NH_3 to BiH_3 the size of the atom increases. As a result, the lone pair of electrons occupies a larger volume. In other words, the electron density on the central atom decreases and hence the basic strength decreases as we move from NH_3 to BiH_3. Thus, the basic strength increases in the order:

$$BiH_3 < SbH_3 < ArH_3 < PH_3 < NH_3.$$

Q. 3. (*a*) Explain giving reasons for each of the following:—

(*i*) Nitrogen exists as diatomic molecule N_2 whereas phosphorus exists as tetratomic molecule P_4.

(*ii*) SF_6 is known but SH_6 is not known.

(*b*) Write the balanced equation for the following reaction:—

(*i*) $BrO_3 + F_2 + OH^- \longrightarrow$ (*ii*) $XeF_6 + KF \longrightarrow$

Ans. (*a*) (*i*) The size of nitrogen atom is quite small. As a result, two nitrogen atoms can be linked to each other by three covalent bonds in order to complete the octets of both the nitrogen atoms as $N \equiv N$. However, phosphorus being large in size has less tendency to form three bonds. Therefore, P atom completes its octet by sharing its valence electrons with three other P atoms. As a result, it exists as P_4 molecule.

(*ii*) Both SF_6 and SH_6 are expected to be hexavalent and this is possible by promoting the filled electrons of 3s and 3p orbitals to vacant 3d orbitals.

	3s	3p			3d				
S	↑↓	↑↓	↑	↑					
S	↑↓	↑	↑	↑	↑	↑			

(Hexavalent)

Fluorine is highly electronegative and can easily cause the promotion of electrons from the filled to the vacant orbitals. However, hydrogen is less electronegative than that of sulphur and therefore, it cannot cause promotion of electrons. Thus, SH_6 is not possible.

(*b*) (*i*) $BrO_3^- + F_2 + 2OH^- \longrightarrow BrO_4^- + F^- + H_2O$

(*ii*) $XeF_6 + 2KF \longrightarrow K_2[XeF_8]$

Q. 4. (*a*) Assign a reason for each of the following statements:—

(*i*) SCl_6 is not known but SF_6 is known.

(*ii*) Not all bonds in a molecule of PCl_5 are equivalent.

(*iii*) Perchloric acid is a stronger acid than sulphuric acid.

(*iv*) Of all the noble gases only xenon is known to form established chemical compounds.

(*b*) Write the structural formula for the following:

(*i*) SF_4 (*ii*) XeO_3

(*c*) Complete the following reaction equation:—

(*i*) $XeF_6 + H_2O \longrightarrow$ (*ii*) $Ca(OCl)_2 + 4HCl \longrightarrow$

Ans. (*a*) (*i*) Due to small size of S, Cl atoms cannot be accommodated around 4*x* S atom. But small 4*x* F atoms can be easily accommodated around S atom to form SF_6. Moreover, because of low electronegativity of Cl, it cannot easily cause promotion of electrons in S to form S(VI).

(*ii*) In PCl_5 all bonds are not equal. Three equatorial P–Cl bonds are smaller than two axial P–Cl bonds. This is because of greater repulsions on axial position than on equatorial positions.

(*iii*) Perchloric acid is stronger acid than sulphuric acid because of greater stability of its conjugate base (ClO_4^-).

(*iv*) Only xenon involves in chemical compounds because–

(*a*) The first ionisation enthalphy of xenon is low in comparison to other noble gases.

(*b*) The atomic radius of xenon is large. As a result, among noble gases, only xenon can lose electron and form compounds.

(*b*) (*i*) SF_4 has trigonal bipyramidal geometry with one position occupied by a lone pair.

(*ii*) XeO_3 has pyramidal geometry.

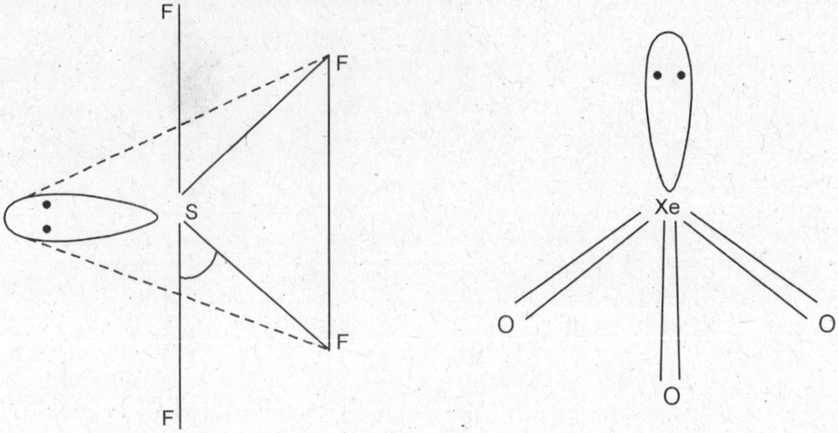

Fig.

(*c*) (*i*) $XeF_6 + 3H_2O \longrightarrow XeO_3 + 6HF$

(*ii*) $Ca(OCl)_2 + 4HCl \longrightarrow CaCl_2 + 2H_2O + 2Cl_2$

Q. 5. Describe the manufacture of H_2SO_4 by contact process?

Ans. *Theory*—The manufacture of H_2SO_4 by the contact process involves the following steps:—

1. Production of SO_2 by burning sulphur or roasting iron pyrites:

$$S_8 + 8O_2 \longrightarrow 8SO_2$$

$$\underset{\text{Iron pyrites}}{4FeS_2} + 11O_2 \longrightarrow 2Fe_2O_3 + 8SO_2$$

2. Catalytic oxidation of sulphur dioxide by air to give sulphur trioxide.

$$2SO_2(g) + O_2(g) \rightleftharpoons 2SO_3(g); \ \Delta 8H^0 = -196.6 \text{ KJ mol}^{-1}$$

This step is the key step in the manufacture of H_2SO_4. The favourable conditions for the maximum yield of SO_3 are:—

(*i*) *High pressure :* Since the forward reaction proceeds with decrease in number of moles; therefore, high pressure will favour the reaction. (Pressure about 2 bars)

(*ii*) *Low temperature*— Since the forward reaction is exothermic; therefore, low temperature will favour the reaction. The reaction is carried out at an optimum temperature of 720K.

(*iii*) *Use of catalyst* : To increase the rate of reaction at low temperature, a catalyst is to be used. The commonly used catalysts are platinum or V_2O_5.

(*iv*) *Purity of gases* : To prevent poisoning of catalyst, the gases must be free from the impurities of As_2O_3, dust particles and moisture.

(*v*) *Excess of oxygen*—To have maximum yield of SO_3, O_2 is used in excess.

3. Absorption of sulphur trioxide in 98% sulphuric acid to form oleum

$$SO_3 + H_2SO_4 \longrightarrow H_2S_2O_7 \text{ (Oleum)}$$

4. Dilution of oleum to get sulphuric acid of desired concentration:

$$H_2S_2O_7 + H_2O \longrightarrow 2H_2SO_4$$

The sulphuric acid obtained by the contact process is generally of 96–98% purity.

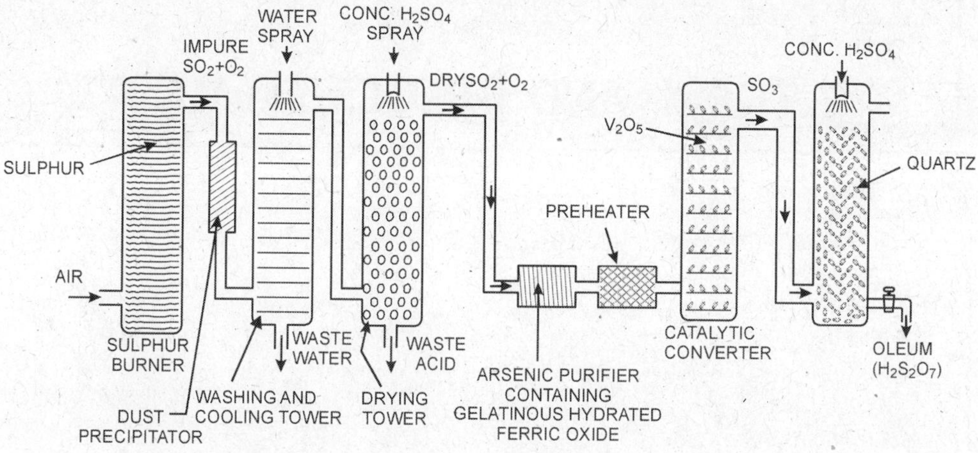

Higher Order Thinking Skills Hots Questions

1. Why is NH_3 liquid where as PH_3 gas?
2. Compare giving reasons, the oxidising powers of F_2 and Cl_2.
3. Give reasons for the differences in the following :
   (*i*) Acidic character of hydrides of group 16 increases down the group.
   (*ii*) Stabilities of +2 oxidation state of tin and lead.
4. (*a*) Arrange the hydrides of group 15 in increasing order of basic strength.
   (*b*) Why does Xe form compounds whereas Ne does not?
   (*c*) Arrange hydrogen halides in increasing order of their boiling points.
5. (*i*) Xe has the highest polarising power. Why?
   (*ii*) Halogens are coloured. Why?
   (*iii*) Noble gases are mostly chemically inert. Why?
   (*iv*) Nitrogen does not form pentahalide. Why?
   (*v*) Bismuth is a strong oxidising agent in pentavalent state. Why?
6. Complete and balance the following chemical equations :
   (*i*) $Fe + H_2O\,(cold) \longrightarrow$ (*ii*) $BrO_3^- + F_2 + OH^- \longrightarrow$
   (*iii*) $Li + N_2\,(cold) \longrightarrow$ (*iv*) $Ca_3P_2 + H_2O \longrightarrow$
   (*v*) $CuO + NH_3 \xrightarrow{\Delta}$

❑❑❑

CHAPTER

8 THE *d*- AND *f*-BLOCK ELEMENTS

Syllabus

- *General introduction, electronic configuration, occurrence and characteristics of transition metals, general trends in properties of the first row transition metals—metallic character, ionization enthalpy, oxidation states, ionic radii, colour, catalytic property, magnetic properties, interstitial compounds, alloy formation. Preparation and properties of $K_2Cr_2O_7$ and $KMnO_4$.*
- ***Lanthanoids** — Electronic configuration, oxidation states, chemical reactivity and lanthanoid contraction.*
- ***Actionids** — Electronic configuration, oxidation state.*

Very Short Answer Type Questions

Q. 1. Write the electronic configuration of last but one element of 3d series.

Ans. Cu (29) – $1S^2\ 2S^2\ 2p^6\ 3S^2\ 3p^6\ 3d^{10}\ 4S^1$.

Q. 2. Write the formula of a compound where the transition metal is in +7 oxidation state.

Ans. $KMnO_4$.

Q. 3. Why are Cd^{2+} salts white?

Ans. The electronic configuration of

Cd^{2+} salts is $4d^{10}$

Since there are no unpaired electrons in 4d sub-shell.

∴ These salts are white.

Q. 4. Write the electronic configuration of Cr^{2+} and find the number of unpaired electrons in it. (For Cr, Z = 24)

Ans. Cr (24) = $1S^2\ 2S^2\ 2p^6\ 3S^2\ 3p^6\ 3d^5\ 4S^1$

$Cr^{2+} = 1S^2\ 2S^2\ 2p^6\ 3S^2\ 3p^6\ 3d^4$

∴ Number of unpaired electrons = 4.

Q. 5. Write the oxidation states of samarium.

Ans. +2 and +3.

Q. 6. Name three precious metals belonging to transition metals.

Ans. Gold (Au), Silver (Ag), Platinum (Pt).

Q. 7. What are the main oxidation states exhibited by lanthanides?

Ans. The main oxidation state of lanthanides is +3 which is exhibited by all lanthanides. In addition, some elements also exhibit +2 and +4 oxidation states. However, +3 oxidation state is more stable than +2 and +4 in aqueous solution and in its compounds.

Q. 8. Write electronic configurations of Fe^{2+} and Fe^{3+} (z = 26). Which of the two has larger paramagnetic character?

Ans. *Electronic configuration of Fe^{2+} and Fe^{3+}*

Fe^{2+} : [Ar] $3d^6$

Fe^{3+} : [Ar] $3d^5$

Fe^{3+} has 5 unpaired electrons while Fe^{2+} has four unpaired electrons. Therefore, Fe^{3+} has larger paramagnetic character.

Q. 9. The size of the trivalent cations in the lanthanide series decreases steadily as the atomic number increases. What is this known as?

Ans. Lanthanide contraction.

Q. 10. Why does a transition series contain 10 elements?

Ans. Transition elements involve the filling of 3d-subshell. Since the 3d-subshell can have maximum of 10 electrons. Therefore, the transition series contains 10 elements.

Short Answer Type Questions - I

Q. 1. On what ground can you say that scandium (z = 21) is a transition element but zinc (z = 30) is not?

Ans. Sc ($z = 21$) contains incompletely filled 3d orbital ($3d^1$) whereas zinc contains completely filled d-orbitals ($3d^{10}$). Hence, by definition scandium is a transition element but zinc is not.

Q. 2. Name a transition element which does not exhibit variable oxidation states.

Ans. Scandium (z = 21) has the electronic configuration $3d^1\ 4S^2$ and shows an oxidation state of +3 only; it does not show variable oxidation states.

Q. 3. Write down the electronic configuration of

(*i*) Cr^{3+} (*ii*) Cu^+ (*iii*) Co^{2+} (*iv*) Mn^{2+}

(*v*) Pm^{3+} (*vi*) Ce^{4+} (*vii*) Lu^{2+} (*viii*) Th^{4+}

Ans. (*i*) $Cr^{3+} = [Ar]^{18}3d^3$ (*ii*) $Cu^+ = [Ar]^{18}3d^{10}$

(*iii*) $Co^{2+} = [Ar]^{18}3d^7$ (*iv*) $Mn^{2+} = [Ar]^{18}3d^5$

(*v*) $Pm^{3+} = [Xe]^{54}4f^4$ (*vi*) $Ce^{4+} = [Xe]^{54}$

(*vii*) $Lu^{2+} = [Xe]4f^{14}5d^1$ (*viii*) $Th^{4+} = [Rn]^{86}$

Q. 4. Why are Mn^{2+} compounds more stable than Fe^{2+} compounds towards oxidation to their +3 state?

Ans. Electronic configuration of Mn^{2+} is $3d^5$ which is half-filled and hence stable. Therefore, 3rd ionization enthalpy is very high, i.e., 3rd electron cannot be lost easily. In case of Fe^{2+}, electronic configuration is $3d^6$. Hence, it can lose one electron easily to give the stable configuration $3d^5$.

Q. 5. Which is a stronger reducing agent Cu^{2+} or Fe^{2+} and why?

Ans. Cr^{2+} is a stronger reducing agent than Fe^{2+} because E° Cr^3/Cr^2 is –ve (–0.41V) whereas E°Fe^{3+}/Fe^{2+} is +ve (+ 0.77V). Thus, Cr^{2+} is easily oxidized to Fe^{3+} but Fe^{2+} cannot be easily oxidised to Fe^{2+}. Hence, Cr^{2+} is stronger reducing agent than Fe^{2+}.

Q. 6. Calculate the 'spin only' magnetic moment of M^{2+}(aq) ion (z = 27).

Ans. Electronic configuration of M atom with z = 27 is [Ar] $3d^7\ 4S^2$.

∴ Electronic configuration of M^{2+} atom will be z = 27 is [Ar] $3d^7 4S^2$.

[Ar] $3d^7$, *i.e.*, ↑↓ ↑↓ ↑ ↑ ↑

Thus, it has three unpaired electrons.

∴ Spin only magnetic moment (μ) = $\sqrt{n(n+2)}$

$$\text{B.M.} = \sqrt{3(3+2)}$$

$$= \sqrt{15}\ \text{B.M.} = 3.87\text{B.M.}$$

Q. 7. What is meant by disproportionation of an oxidation state? Give an example.

Ans. When in a reaction, the oxidation state of an element in a compound increases in one of the products and decreases in the other product, it is said to undergo disproportionation of oxidation state. For example,

$$\overset{\text{VI}}{3MnO_4^{2-}} + 4H^+ \longrightarrow \overset{\text{VII}}{2MnO_4^-} + \overset{\text{IV}}{MnO_2} + 2H_2O$$

In this example, Mn(VI) in $MnO_4{}^{2-}$ changes to Mn(VII) in the product $MnO_4{}^-$ and to Mn(IV) in the product MnO_2.

Q. 8. What is lanthanoid contraction? What are the consequences of lanthanoid contraction?

Ans. There is steady decrease in the atomic and ionic radii as the atomic number increases. It is because, for every additional proton in the nucleus, the corresponding electron goes into the 4f shell which is too diffused to screen the nucleus as effectively as more localised inner shell. Hence, the attraction of the nucleus for the outermost electrons increases steadily with the atomic number of the lanthanoids. This contraction in size is quite regular. This is called *lanthanoid contraction.*

Consequences of lanthanoid contraction—

(*i*) Difficulty in separation of lanthanoids.

(*ii*) Similarity, in size of elements belonging to same group of second and third transition series.

(*iii*) Effect on the basic strength of hydroxides.

Q. 9. What are interstitial compounds?

Ans. The interstitial compounds are formed by occupying vacant spaces (interstitials) in a lattice by smaller size atoms like carbon, hydrogen and nitrogen etc. For example, steel and cast iron become hard by forming interstitial compounds with carbon.

Q. 10. How is the variability in oxidation states of transition metals different from that of the non-transition metals? Illustrate with examples.

Ans. The variability in oxidation states of transition metals is due to the incomplete filling of d-orbitals in such a way that their oxidation states differ from each other by unity, e.g., Fe^{2+} and Fe^{3+}, Cu^+ and Cu^{2+} etc. In case of non-transition elements, the oxidation states differ by units of two, e.g., Pb^{+2} and Pb^{+4}, Sn^{2+} and Sn^{4+} etc.

In transition elements, the higher oxidation states are more stable for heavier elements in a group.

For example, in group 6, Mo (VI) and W (VI) are more stable than Cr (VI). In P-block elements, the lower oxidation states are more stable for heavier members due to inert pair effect. For example, in group 16, Pb (II) is more stable than Pb (IV).

Short Answer Type Questions - II

Q. 1. Compare the stability of +2 oxidation state for the elements of the first transition series.

Ans. The decreasing negative electrode potentials of M^{2+}/M in the first transition series shows that in general, the stability of +2 oxidation state decreases from left to right. The decrease in the negative electrode potentials is due to increase in the sum $IE_1 + IE_2$. The greater stability of +2 state for Mn is due to half-filled d-subshell (d^5) in Mn^{2+} and that of Zn is due to completely filled of subshell (d^{16}) in Zn^{2+}.

Q. 2. Explain—

(*i*) Transition metals form alloys with other transition metals.

(*ii*) Transition metals have high melting and boiling points.

Ans. (*i*) Transition metals form a large variety of alloys. This is due to the fact that transition metals have almost similar sizes and therefore, the atoms of a metal can easily substitute the atoms of other metals in their lattices. For example, manganese dissolves in molten iron to form manganese steel. The alloys formed are hard, having high melting points. These are also resistant to corrosion in comparison to the parent metals.

(*ii*) The melting and boiling points of transition metals are high because that the atoms of these elements are held together by strong forces. This is due to the strong interaction of electrons in the partially filled d-subshells.

In general, larger the number of unpaired d-electrons, stronger is the bonding between the atoms.

Q. 3. Give three important differences between lanthanides and actinides.

Ans.

Lanthanides	Actinides
1. Lanthanides show mainly +3 oxidation state except in a few cases where it is +2 and +4.	1. In addition to +3 oxidation state actinides also show higher oxidation states such as +4, +5, +6 and +7.
2. The tendency to form complexes is less.	2. They have a greater tendency to form complex.
3. Except promethium, these are non-radio active.	3. All the actinides are radioactive.

Q. 4. What are transition elements? Which of the d-block elements are not regarded as transition elements?

Ans. *Transition elements-* According to the definition, the atoms of transition elements or one of its ions have incomplete d-subshells. These constitute three complete series and one incomplete series.

The end member of each series, zinc, calcium and mercury are not regarded as transition elements. The reason is that these atoms have completely filled d-orbitals and do not have partly filled d-subshells as given below:

Zn (z = 30) [Ar] $3d^{10}\,4s^2$

Cd (z = 48) [Kr] $4d^{10}\,5s^2$

Hg (z = 80) [Xe] $4f^{14}\,5d^{10}\,6s^2$

Q. 5. Write chemical equations for the conversion of

(*i*) Chromite ore to sodium chromate.

(*ii*) Pyrolusite to potassium manganate.

(*iii*) Potassium permanganate to manganese dioxide.

Ans. (*i*) $4FeCr_2O_7 + 16NaOH + 7O_2 \longrightarrow 8Na_2CrO_4 + 2Fe_2O_3 + 8H_2O$

Chromite ore — Sodium chromate

(*ii*) $MnO_2 + 4KOH + O_2 \xrightarrow{\text{Fuse}} 2K_2MnO_4 + 2H_2O$

Pyrolusite — Potassium manganate

(A) Blackish brown — (B) –Green coloured

(*iii*) $4KMnO_4 + 2H_2O \longrightarrow 4MnO_2 + 4KOH + O_2$

Pot. permanganate — Manganese dioxide

Q. 6. Account for the following:

(*i*) Of the lanthanides, cerium (Atomic No.58) forms tripositive ion Ce^{4+} in aqueous solutions.

(*ii*) Transition metals have high enthalpy of atomization.

(*iii*) Scandium forms no coloured ions yet it is regarded as a transition element.

Ans. (*i*) Cerium [z = 58] has the electronic configuration:-

$Ce: [Xe]\,4f^1 5d^1 6s^2$

By losing four electrons, it forms stable configuration of noble gas Xe [f^0 configuration]. Therefore, it forms +4 oxidation state:-

$Ce^{4+}: [Xe]\,4f^0$

(*ii*) The transition metals have high melting and boiling points. These suggest that the atoms of these elements are held together by strong forces and have high enthalpy of atomization.

(*iii*) Scandium, Sc (z = 21) has the electronic configuration of [Ar] $3d^1\,4S^2$. It has partially filled d-configuration and, therefore, is regarded as a transition metal. However, Sc^{3+} ion has the electronic configuration of Ar (3d°). Since it does not have partially filled d-electron, it is not coloured.

Q. 7. (*i*) Copper (I) compounds are white and diamagnetic while copper (II) compounds are coloured and paramagnetic and form coloured compounds. Explain.

(*ii*) Why is copper (At. No. 29) considered a transition metal?

Ans. (*i*) In copper (I) ion, all orbitals are completely filled ($1s^2\,2s^2\,2p^6\,3s^2\,3p^6\,3d^{10}$) and therefore, it is diamagnetic and forms white compounds, copper (II) ion has electronic configuration $1s^2\,2s^2\,2p^6\,3s^2\,3p^6\,3d^9$ (has one unpaired electron) and therefore, it is paramagnetic and forms coloured compounds.

(*ii*) This is because copper in oxidation state +2, i.e. Cu^{2+} has incompletely filled *d*-subshell ($3d^9$).

Q. 8. Compare the chemistry of actinoids with that of lanthanoids with special reference to—

(*i*) Electronic configuration (*ii*) Oxidation state

(*iii*) Atomic and ionic sizes (*iv*) Chemical reactivity

Ans. (*i*) *Electronic configuration*—The general electronic configuration of lanthanoids is $[Xe]^{54}\,4f^{1-14}\,5d^{0-1}\,6s^2$ whereas that of actinoids is $[Rn]^{86}\,5f^{1-14}\,6d^{0-1}\,7s^2$. Thus, lanthanoids belong to 4f-series whereas actinoids belong to 5f-series.

(*ii*) *Oxidation state*—Lanthanoids show limited oxidation states (+2, +3, +4) out of which +3 is most common. This is because of large energy gap between 4f, 5d and 6s subshells. On the other hand, actinoids show a large number of oxidation states because of small energy gap between 5f, 6d and 7s subshells.

(*iii*) *Atomic and ionic sizes*—Both show decrease in size of their atoms or ions in +3 oxidation state. In lanthanoids, the decrease is called lanthanoid contraction whereas in actinoids it is called actinoid contraction.

(*iv*) *Chemical reactivity*—

1. *Lanthanoids*–The first few members of the series are quite reactive, almost like calcium. However, with increasing atomic number, their behaviour becomes similar to that of aluminium.
2. *Actinoids*–They are highly reactive metals especially in the finely divided state. Few properties of actinoids are—
   (*a*) They react with boiling water to give a mixture of oxide and hydroxide.
   (*b*) They combine with most of the non-metals at moderate temperature.
   (*c*) All these metals are attacked by HCl but the effect of HNO_3 is very small due to the formation of protective oxide layer on their surface.

Long Answer Type Questions

Q. 1. Discuss the variation of the following properties in the first transition series—

(*i*) Atomic radii (*ii*) Ionisation energies

Ans. *Variation of properties in first transition series*—

(*i*) *Atomic radii*—The atomic radii of the transition elements are in between those of s- and p-block elements. As we move in a particular series, the atomic radius decreases with increase in atomic number. However, this decrease in atomic radius becomes small after midway. The variation of ionic radii of the first transition series with atomic number is shown below:

Element	Sc	Ti	V	Cr	Mn	Fe	CO	Ni	Cu	Zn
Atomic radius (PM)	164	147	135	130	135	126	125	125	128	133

This is due to the reason that in the beginning, the atomic radius decreases because with increase in atomic number, there is increase in the nuclear charge. However, the added d-electrons enter the penultimate shell and screen and outermost s-electrons. As the number of d-electrons increases the screening effect increases. This neutralizer effect of increased nuclear charge and consequently atomic radii remain almost same after chromium.

(*ii*) *Ionisation energies*—The first ionisation energies of the transition elements are higher than those of s-block elements but are lesser than those of p-block elements. The ionisation energies increase as we move across each series, though not very regularly.

The increase in ionisation energy along a given transition series is due to the effect of increasing nuclear charge. As a result, the outer electrons are attracted with greater force. Consequently, ionisation energy is expected to increase. However, in case of transition elements, the addition of electron takes place to the penultimate i.e. (n–1)d subshell and this also increases the screening effect. With the increase in electrons in (n–1)d subshell. The outer electrons in *ns* subshell are shielded more and more. Thus, the effect of increasing nuclear charge is opposed by the screening effect of the nucleus and therefore, ionistion energy increases. The variation of ionisation energy is plotted in Fig.

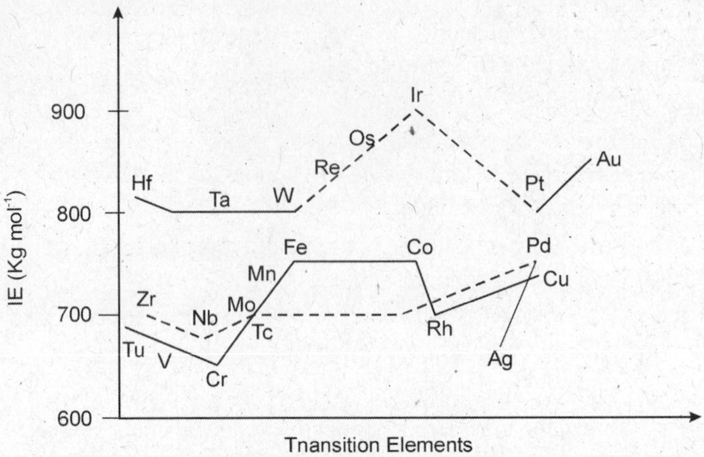

Fig. 8.1 Transition Elements

Q. 2. Describe the preparation of $KMnO_4$ from pyrolusite ore by electrochemical method. Discuss its important properties and uses.

Ans. *Preparation of $KMnO_4$*— $KMnO_4$ is prepared on a large scale from pyrolusite. It is fused with KOH in the presence of air forming a green mass of $KMnO_4$.

$$2MnO_2 + 4KOH + O_2 \longrightarrow \underset{\text{Pot. manganate}}{2K_2MnO_4} + 2H_2O$$

Potassium manganate is oxidised electrochemically to permanganate ion in the cathode compartment.

$$K_2MnO_4 \rightleftharpoons 2K^+ + MnO_4^{2-}$$
$$H_2O \rightleftharpoons H^+ + OH^-$$

Anode:

$$MnO_4^{-2} \longrightarrow MnO_4^- + e^-$$

At cathode:

$$H^+ + e^- \longrightarrow H$$
$$H + H \longrightarrow H_2$$

Properties— The important properties of $KMnO_4$ are discussed below:—

1. It is dark violet crystalline solid having a metallic lustre.
2. It is slightly soluble in water.
3. When heated strongly, it decomposes to give oxygen.

$$2KMnO_4 \longrightarrow K_2MnO_4 + MnO_2 + O_2$$

4. *Oxidising character*— $KMnO_4$ acts as a powerful oxidising agent in neutral alkaline or acidic solution because it liberates nascent oxygen as—

Neutral solution—

$$2KMnO_4 + H_2O \longrightarrow 2KOH + 2MnO_2 + 3O$$

or $$MnO_4^- + 2H_2O + 3e^- \longrightarrow MnO_2 + 4OH^-$$

Alkaline solution—

$$2KMnO_4 + 2KOH \longrightarrow 2K_2MnO_4 + H_2O + O$$

or $$MnO_4^- + e^- \longrightarrow MnO_4^{2-}$$

Acidic solution—

$$2KMnO_3 + 3H_2SO_4 \longrightarrow K_2SO_4 + 2MnSO_4 + 3H_2O + 5O$$

or $$MnO_4^- + 8H^+ + 5e^- \longrightarrow Mn^{2+} + 4H_2O$$

It is frequently used in acidic medium in the laboratory.

For example—

1. It oxidises H_2S to S.

$$2KMnO_4 + 3H_2SO_4 \longrightarrow K_2SO_4 + 2MnSO_4 + 2H_2O + 5O$$
$$H_2S + O \longrightarrow H_2O + S] \times 5$$
$$2KMnO_4 + 3H_2SO_4 + 5H_2S \longrightarrow K_2SO_4 + 2MnSO_4 + 3H_2O + 5S$$

2. Its oxidises sulphur dioxide to sulphuric acid.

$$2KMnO_4 + 3H_2SO_4 \longrightarrow K_2SO_4 + MnSO_4 + 3H_2O + 5O$$
$$SO_2 + H_2O \longrightarrow H_2SO_4] \times 5$$
$$2KMnO_4 + 5SO_2 + 2H_2O \longrightarrow K_2SO_4 + 2MnSO_4 + 2H_2SO_4$$

Uses of $KMnO_4$— It is used:

1. As an oxidising agent in the laboratory and in industry.
2. As an disinfectant germicide and deodorant.
3. In qualitative and quantitative analysis.
4. For purification of water.
5. It is used for testing 4 maturation in organic chemistry and is known as Baeyer's reagent.

Q. 3. Complete the following reactions:—

(*i*) $MnO_4^- + SO_2 + H_2O \longrightarrow$ (*ii*) $Na_2Cr_2O_7 + KCl \longrightarrow$

(*iii*) $FeCr_2O_4 + Na_2CO_3 + O_2 \longrightarrow$ (*iv*) $MnO_2 + KOH + O_2 \longrightarrow$

(*v*) $K_2Cr_2O_7 \xrightarrow{\text{heat}}$

Ans. (*i*) $2MnO_4^- + 5SO_2 + 2H_2O \longrightarrow 2Mn^{2+} + 5SO_4^{2-} + 4H^+$

(*ii*) $Na_2Cr_2O_3 + 2KCl \longrightarrow K_2Cr_2O_7 + 2NaCl$

(*iii*) $4FeCr_2O_4 + 8Na_2CO_3 + O_2 \longrightarrow 8Na_2CrO_4 + 2Fe_2O_3 + 8CO_2$

(*iv*) $2MnO_2 + 4KOH + O_2 \longrightarrow 2K_2MnO_4 + 2H_2O$

(*v*) $4K_2Cr_2O_7 \xrightarrow{\text{heat}} 4K_2CrO_4 + 2Cr_2O_3 + 3O_2$

Q. 4. (*a*) Give the chemical reactions when any chloride is heated with solid $K_2Cr_2O_7$ and Conc. H_2SO_4.

Or

Give the chemistry of chromyl chloride test.

(*b*) Give the following reaction:—

(*i*) In alkaline medium $KMnO_4$ oxidizes I^- to iodates.

(*ii*) In acidic medium $KMnO_4$ oxidizes I^- to I_2.

(*iii*) Effect of heat on $KMnO_4$.

Ans. (*a*) When any chloride is heated with solid $K_2Cr_2O_3$ and H_2SO_4 then orange red vapours of chromyl chloride are formed

$$K_2Cr_2O_3 + 2H_2SO_4 \longrightarrow 2KHSO_4 + 2CrO_3 + H_2O$$
$$KCl + H_2SO_4 \longrightarrow KHSO_4 + HCl] \times 4$$
$$CrO_3 + 2HCl \longrightarrow CrO_2Cl_2 + H_2O] \times 2$$

$$K_2Cr_2O_3 + 4KCl + 6H_2SO_4 \longrightarrow 2CrO_2Cl_2\uparrow + 6KHSO_4 + 3H_2O$$

(*b*) (*i*) $I^- + 2MnO_4^- + H_2O \longrightarrow IO_3^- + 2MnO_2 + 2OH^-$

(*ii*) $10I^- + 2MnO_4^- + 16H^+ \longrightarrow 2Mn^{2+} + 5I_2 + 8H_2O$

(*iii*) $2KMnO_4 \xrightarrow{\Delta} K_2MnO_4 + MnO_2 + O_2$

Q. 5. Complete the following reactions:—

(*i*) $MnO_2 + K_2CO_3 + O_2 \longrightarrow$

(*ii*) $K_2Cr_2O_7 \xrightarrow{heat}$

(*iii*) $KMnO_4 \xrightarrow{heat}$

(*iv*) $K_2MnO_4 + Cl_2 \longrightarrow$

(*v*) $SO_2 + MnO_4^- + H_2O \longrightarrow$

Ans. (*i*) $2MnO_2 + 2K_2CO_3 + O_2 \longrightarrow \underset{\text{Pot. manganate}}{2K_2MnO_4} + 2CO_2$

(*ii*) $4K_2Cr_2O_7 \xrightarrow{heat} 4K_2CrO_4 + 2Cr_2O_3 + 2O_2$

(*iii*) $2KMnO_4 \xrightarrow{heat} K_2MnO_4 + MnO_2 + O_2$

(*iv*) $2K_2MnO_4 + Cl_2 \longrightarrow 2KCl + 2KMnO_4$

(*v*) $5SO_2 + 2MnO_4^- + 2H_2O \longrightarrow 2Mn^{2+} + 5O_4^{-2} + 4H^+$

Q. 6. (a) How is potassium dichromate prepared from chromite? How does it react with

(*i*) acidified ferrous sulphate solution

(*ii*) Potassium iodide solution

(*iii*) hydrochloric acid

(*iv*) Conc. H_2SO_4 and soluble metal chloride ?

(*b*) The orange colour of potassium dichromate changes to yellow on the addition of alkali. On acidifying the yellow solution, the colour again changes to orange red. Explain.

Ans. (*a*) Potassium dichromate is prepared from chromite ($FeCr_2O_4$) by fusing with molten alkali in the presence of air—

$$4FeCr_2O_4 + 16NaOH + 7O_2 \longrightarrow 8Na_2CrO_4 + 2Fe_2O_3 + 8H_2O$$

The solution of sodium chromate is filtered and acidified with dil. H_2SO_4 giving sodium dichromate.

$$2Na_2CrO_4 + 2H^+ \longrightarrow Na_2Cr_2O_7 + 2Na^+ + H_2O$$

Sodium dichromate is more soluble and less stable than potassium dichromate. Potassium dichromate is prepared by mixing a hot conc. solution of $Na_2Cr_2O_7$ and KCl in equimolar quantities.

$$Na_2Cr_2O_7 + 2KCl \longrightarrow K_2Cr_2O_7 + 2NaCl.$$

Reactions:—

(*i*) $K_2Cr_2O_7$ oxidises ferrous sulphate to ferric sulphate.

$$6FeSO_4 + K_2Cr_2O_3 + 7H_2SO_4 \longrightarrow 3Fe_2SO_4 + Cr_2(SO_4)_3 + K_2SO_4 + 7H_2O$$

(*ii*) $F_2Cr_2O_7 + 6KI + 7H_2SO_4 \longrightarrow 3K_2SO_4 + Cr_2(SO_4)_3 + 7H_2O + 3I_2$

(*iii*) $K_2Cr_2O_7 + 14HCl \longrightarrow 2KCl + 2CrCl_3 + 7H_2O + 3Cl_2$

(*iv*) $K_2Cr_2O_7 + 4NaCl + 6H_2SO_4 \longrightarrow 2KHSO_4 + 4NaHSO_4 + 2CrO_2Cl_2 + 3H_2O$

(*b*) $K_2Cr_2O_7$ on heating with alkalies (KOH) changes to potassium chromate

$$K_2Cr_2O_7 + 2KOH \longrightarrow \underset{\substack{\text{Pot. chromate} \\ \text{(yellow)}}}{2K_2CrO_4} + H_2O$$

On acidifying, the yellow colour change back to orange red due to reversible reaction

$$2K_2CrO_4 + H_2SO_4 \longrightarrow \underset{\text{(Orange)}}{K_2Cr_2O_7} + K_2SO_4 + H_2O$$

Higher Order Thinking Skills Hots Questions

1. Name a transition metal which does not exhibit variation in oxidation state in its compounds.

2. What is general electronic configuration of lanthanoids?

3. Explain why

(*i*) E^0 for Mn^{3+}/Mn^{2+} couple is more positive than that of Fe^{3+}/Fe^{2+}. (At. No. of Mn = 25, Fe = 26)

(*ii*) Ce^{3+} can be easily oxidised to Ce^{4+} (At. No. of Ce = 58).

4. With the help of ionic equation describe what happens when

(*i*) pH of a solution of dichromate ion is raised.

(*ii*) Potassium manganate is electrochemically oxidised.

5. Account for the following :

(*a*) Transition elements have higher boiling points.

(*b*) Zn, Cd and Hg are normally not regarded as transition elements.

(*c*) Sc forms no coloured ions yet it is regarded as transition element.

(*d*) Transition elements show variable oxidation states.

(*e*) Zn resembles with Hf.

❑❑❑

CHAPTER

9

COORDINATION COMPOUNDS

Syllabus

- *Coordination compounds—Introduction, ligands, coordination number, colour, magnetic properties and shapes, IUPAC nomenclature of mononuclear coordination compounds. Bonding; isomerism, important of coordination compounds (in qualitative analysis, extraction of metals and biological systems).*

Very Short Answer Type Questions

Q. 1. Write IUPAC name of [CO$(NH_3)_5(CO_3)$]Cl.

Ans. Pentaamminecarbonatocobalt (III) chloride.

Q. 2. Name the ligands in $[Co(NH_3)_5Br]^{2+}$ ion.

Ans. Ammonia, NH_3 and Bromide ion, Br^-.

Q. 3. Write IUPAC name of $[Pt(NH_3)_2Cl_2]Cl_2$.

Ans. Diamminedichloroplatinum (II) chloride.

Q. 4. Draw the structures and write hybridisation in $[Ni(CO)_4]$.

Ans.

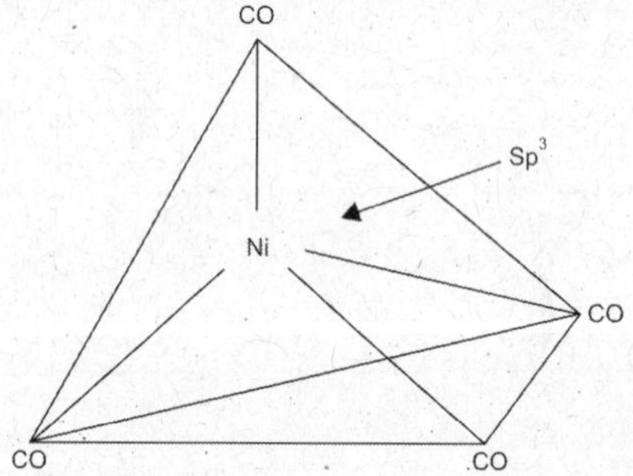

Q. 5. What are organometallic compounds? Give one example.

Ans. The compounds which contain at least one direct metal carbon bond are called organometallic compounds. For example.

CH_3-Mg-Br (Methyl magnesium bromide)

Q. 6. What is the difference between inner and outer complexes?

Ans. In the inner complex, (n–i)d orbitals take part in d^2sp^3 hybridisation.

In outer complex, nd orbitals take part in sp^3d^2 hybridisation

Q. 7. Draw the structure and write the hybridisation in cis-$[Co(NH_3)_4Cl_2]^+$.

Ans.

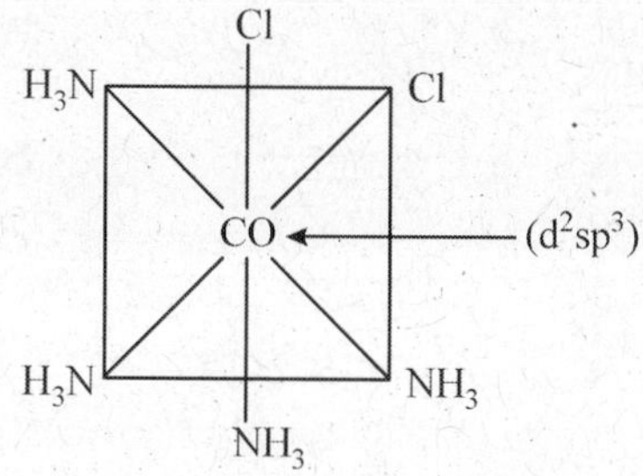

Q. 8. What are chelates?

Ans. When a bidentate or polydentate ligands attached to central metal atom/ion results in the formation of a ring, the complex is called chelate or chelate complex.

Q. 9. Write the structure of potassium hexafluoroplatinate (IV).

Ans. $K_2[Pt F_6]$.

Q. 10. Give central metal ion, ligands, oxidation state and coordination number in the complex:—

$[Cr(NH_3)_4(ONO)Cl]NO_3$.

Ans. Central metal ion — Cr^{3+}

Ligands — NH_3, ONO^-, Cl^-

Oxidation state — +3

Coordination number — 6

Q. 11. Which of the following is square planar?

(*i*) $[Ni(CN)_4]^{2-}$ (*ii*) $Ni(CO)_4$ (*iii*) $Pt(NH_3)_2Cl_2$

Ans. $Pt(NH_3)_2Cl_2$.

Q. 12. Give one example of a linkage isomer.

Ans. $[Co(NH_3)_5ONO]Cl_2$, $[Co(NH_3)_5NO_2]Cl_2$.

Q. 13. What is coordination number of iron in the complexes:— $[Fe(CN)_6]^{3-}$ and $[Fe(CO)_5]$?

Ans. $[Fe(CN)_6]^{3-}$, C.N. = 6, $[Fe(CO)_5]$, C.N. = 5

Q. 14. Draw structures of geometrical isomers of $[Fe(NH_3)_2(CN)_4]^-$.

Ans.

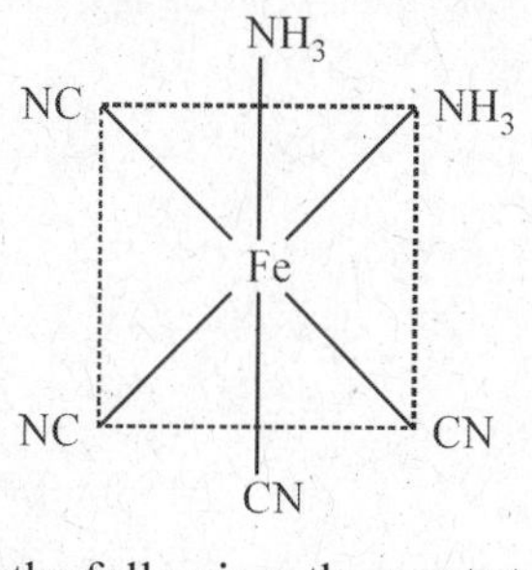

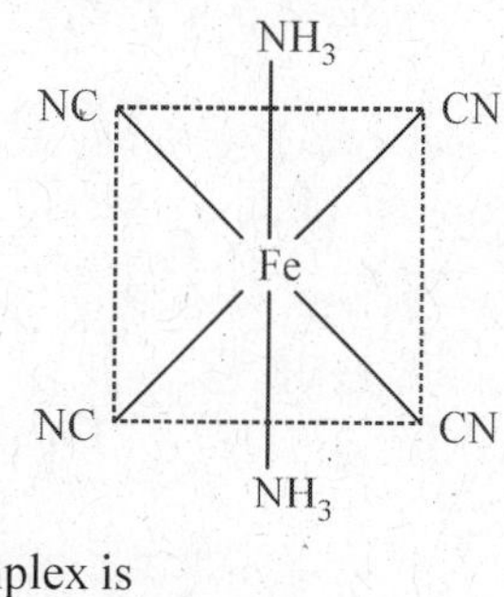

Q. 15. Amongst the following, the most stable complex is

(*i*) $[Fe(H_2O)_6]^{3+}$ (*ii*) $[Fe(NH_3)_6]^{3+}$

(*iii*) $[Fe(C_2O_4)_3]^{3-}$ (*iv*) $[FeCl_6]^{3-}$

Ans. $[Fe(C_2O_4)_3]^{3-}$

(Fe in is +3 state. As $C_2O_4^{2-}$ is didentate chelating ligand, it forms chelate rings and hence is the most stable.)

Q. 16. The oxidation number of cobalt in $K[CO(CO)_4]$ is

(*i*) +1 (*ii*) +3 (*iii*) –1 (*iv*) –3

Ans. $K^+[CO(CO)_4]^{-1}$

$$\therefore \quad n + 0 = -1$$
$$n = -1$$

Hence (*iii*) is the correct answer.

Short Answer Type Questions – I

Q. 1. $[NiCl_4]^{2-}$ is paramagnetic while $[Ni(CO)_4]$ is diamagnetic though both are tetrahedral. Why?

Ans. In $[NiCl_4]^{2-}$, Cl^- is weak ligand and oxidation of Ni is +2, its configuration is $3d^8\ 45°$.Cl^- cannot pair up the electrons in 3d orbitals. Hence, it is paramagnetic.

In $[Ni(CO)_4$, Ni is in zero oxidation state with the configuration $3d^8\ 4s°$. In the presence of CO ligand, the 4s electrons shift to 3d to pair up 3d electrons. Thus, there is no unpaired electron present. Hence, it is diamagnetic.

Q. 2. Out of the following two coordination entities which is chiral (optically active)?

(*a*) cis. – $[CrCl_2(OX)_2]^{3-}$, (*b*) trans–$[CrCl_2(OX)_2]^{3-}$.

Ans.

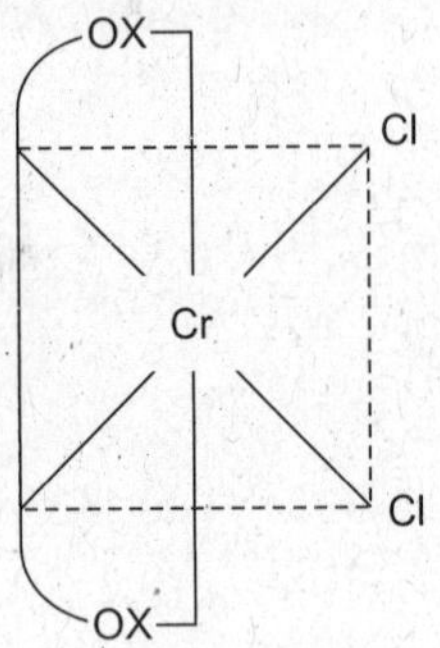

cis-optically active

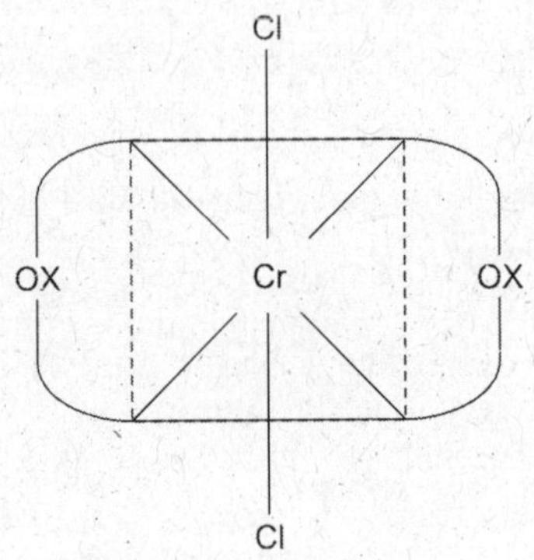

trans-optically inactive (Because its mirror image is superimposable).

Q. 3. Predict the number of unpaired electrons in square planar $[Pt(CN)_4]^{2-}$ ion.

Ans. Pt (Z = 78) lies in group 10 with the configuration $5d^9 6s^1$.

	5d					6s	6p		
Pt atom (z = 78) In ground state	↑↓	↑↓	↑↓	↑↓	↑↓	↑			
Pt^{2+}	↑↓	↑↓	↑↓	↑	↑				

For square planar shape, the hybridsation is dsp^2. Hence, the unpaired electrons in 5*d* pair up to make one *d*-orbital empty for dsp^2 hybridisation. Thus, there is no unpaired electron.

Q. 4. Specify the oxidation numbers of the metals in the following coordination entities:

(*i*) $[Co(H_2O)(CN)(CN)_2]^{2+}$ (*ii*) $[PtCl_4]^{2-}$

(*iii*) $[Cr(NH_3)_3Cl_3$ (*iv*) $[CoBr_2(CN)_2]^+$

Ans. (*i*) $x+(0)+(-1)+(0)=+2$
$x-1=+2$
$x=+2+1$
$x=+3.$

(*ii*) $x-4=-2$
$x=-2+4$
$x=+2.$

(*iii*) $x+0+3(-1)=0$
$x-3=0$
$x=+3.$

(*iv*) $x+2(-1)+0=+1$
$x-2=+1$
$x=+1+2$
$x=+3.$

Q. 5. Explain with two examples each of the following coordination entity, ligand, coordination number, coordination polyhedron, homoleptic and heterolephtic.

Ans. (*i*) *Coordination entity*—The central atom and the ligands which are directly attached to it are enclosed in square brackets and are collectively termed as the coordination sphere or coordination entity.

For example— $\underbrace{[CU(NH_3)_4]}_{\text{Co-ordination entity}}SO_4$

(*ii*) *Ligand*—The molecules or ions attached to the central metal atom or ion are called ligands, e.g. in complex $[Ni(NH_3)_6]^{2+}$, NH_3 molecules are ligands.

(*iii*) *Coordination number*—The total number of ligands attached to the central ion is called coordination number e.g. $[Ag(CN)_2]^2$, The co-ordination numbers of Ag is 2.

(*iv*) *Coordination polyhedron*—The spatial arrangement of the ligand atoms which are directly attached to the central atom/ion in called coordination polyhedron around the central atom/ion. e.g., $[PtCl_4]^{2-}$ is square planar.

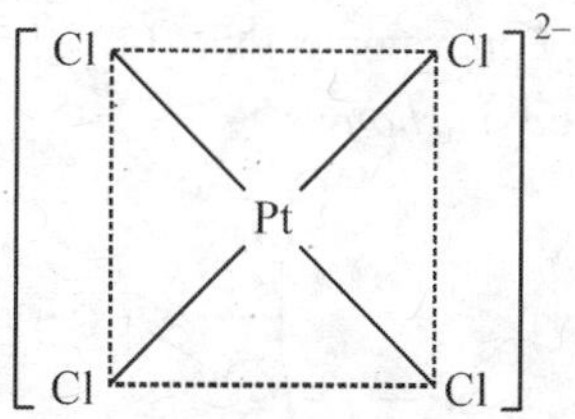

(*v*) *Homoleptic and Heteroleptic complexes* : Complexes in which the metal atom or ion is linked to only one type of ligands are called homoleptic complexes, e.g., $[Co(NH_3)_6]^{3+}$.

The complexes in which the metal atom or ion is linked to more than one kind of ligands are called heteroleptic complexes, e.g., $[Co(NH_3)_4Cl_2]^+$.

Q. 6. Write all the geometrical isomers of [Pt (NH_3) (Br) (Cl) (Py)] and how many of these will exhibit optical isomerism?

Ans. Three isomers are possible as follows:

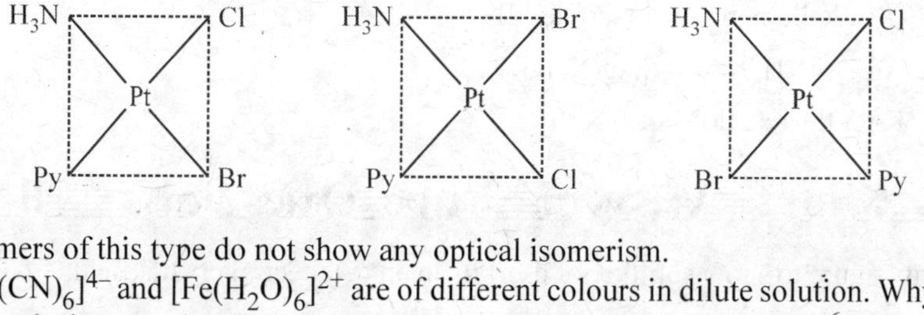

Isomers of this type do not show any optical isomerism.

Q. 7. $[Fe(CN)_6]^{4-}$ and $[Fe(H_2O)_6]^{2+}$ are of different colours in dilute solution. Why?

Ans. In both the complexes, Fe is in +2 state with the configuration $3d^6$, i.e., it has four unpaired electrons. As the ligands H_2O and CN^- possess different crystal field splitting energy (Δ_0), they absorb different components of the visible light (VIBGYOR) for d–d transition. Hence, the transmitted colours are different.

Q. 8. Discuss the salient features of valence bond theory.

Ans. *Valence bond theory*—This theory was proposed by Pouling. The salient features of the valence bond theory are:—

1. The central metal atom or ion maker available a number of vacant orbitals for the formation of coordination bonds with appropriate ligands.
2. The number of vacant orbitals made available for forming coordinate bonds is equal to the coordination number of the metal.
3. The appropriate orbitals (s, p or d) of the metal hybridise to form hybrid orbitals. There hybrid orbitals adopt definite geometries. For example—

   sp^3 Tetrahedral
   dsp^2 Square planar
   sp^3d^2 or d^2sp^3 Octahedral
4. Each ligand has at least one orbital containing a lone pair of electrons.
5. A covalent bond is formed by the overlap of vacant hybrid orbital of metal and filled orbital of ligand ($M \leftarrow L$). The bond is coordinate bond.

Q. 9. (*a*) What are metal carbonyls?

(*b*) Draw structures of three important metal carbonyls.

Ans. (*a*) *Metal carbonyls*—Metal carbonyls are organometallic compounds in which carbonyls (CO) act as ligands. In these compounds, the metalcarbon bond possesses both σ and π-character. For example, $[Ni(CO)_4]$, $[Fe(CO)_5]$, $(Cr(CO)_6]$.

(*b*) *Structures of some metal carbonyls*—

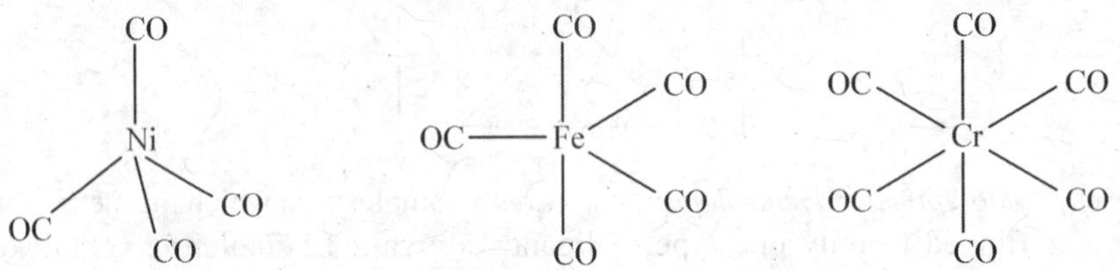

Q. 10. (*a*) Write IUPAC name of the following:

(*i*) $[Cr(NH_3)_6]Cl_3$

(*ii*) $Na_3[Fe(C_2O_4)_3]$

(*b*) Give the value of K for $Ag^+ + 4NH_3 \rightleftharpoons [Ag(NH_3)_4]^+$.

Ans. (*a*) (*i*) Hexaammine chromium (III) chloride

(*ii*) Sodium trioxalato ferrate (III)

(*b*) $Ag^+ + 4NH_3 \rightleftharpoons [Ag(NH_3)_4]^+$

K for the reaction is 1.6×10^7.

Short Answer Type Questions - II

Q. 1. Draw figure to show splitting of d-orbits in an octahectral crystal field.

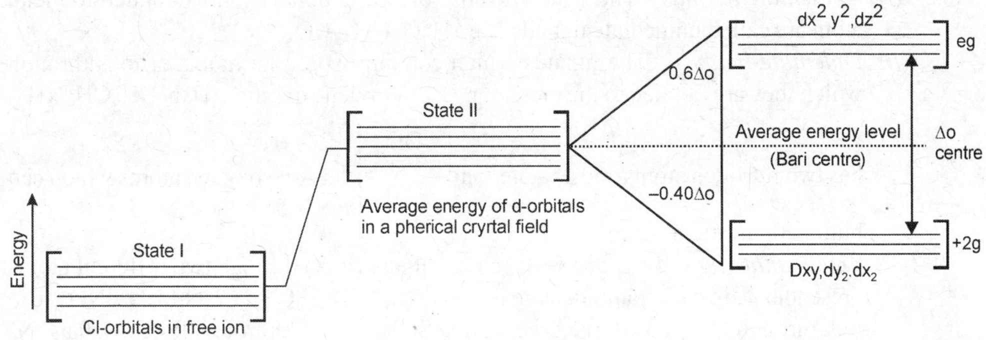

Splitting of d-orbitals in an octahedral crystal field

Splitting of d-orbitals in an octahedral crystal field.

Q. 2. Explain the bonding in co-ordination compounds in terms of Werner's postulates.

Ans. *Werner's coordination theory*—The important postulates of Werner's theory of co-ordination compounds are:—

(1) Metals possess two different types of valencies called (*a*) primary or principal or ionizable valency (*b*) secondary or non-ionizable valency.

(*a*) Primary valencies are those which a metal exhibits in the formation of its simple salts. It is also called oxidation state for example: $PtCl_4$, the primary valency of Pt is 4.

(*b*) Secondary valencies are those which a metal atom or cation exercises towards neutral molecules or negative groups in the formation of its complex ions. The secondary valency is also termed as the coordination number of the metal cation. e.g., In $[Pt(NH_3)_6]Cl_4$, the secondary valency of Pt is 6.

(2) Every metal atom has a tendency to satisfy both its primary and secondary valencies.

(3) The ligands satisfying secondary valencies are always directed towards fixed positions in space thereby giving a definite geometry to the complex but the primary valencies are non-directional. Secondary valencies determine the stereochemistry of the complex.

Q. 3. Using IUPAC norms, write the formulae of the following:

(*i*) Tetrahydroxozincate (II) (*ii*) Potassium tetrachloridopalladate (II)
(*iii*) Diamminedichloridoplatinum (II) (*iv*) Potassium tetracyanonickelate (II)
(*v*) Pentaammine nitrito–O–cobalt (II)

Ans. (*i*) $[Zn(OH)_4]^{2-}$ (*ii*) $K_2[PdCl_4]$ (*iii*) $[Pt(NH_3)_2Cl_2]$
(*iv*) $K_2[Ni(CN)_4]$ (*v*) $[Co(NH_3)_5(ONO)]^{2+}$

Q. 4. Using IUPAC norms, write the systematic names of the following:—

(*i*) $[Co(NH_3)_6]Cl_3$ (*ii*) $[PtCl(NH_3)_2(NH_2CH_3)]Cl$
(*iii*) $[Ti(H_2O)_6]^{3+}$ (*iv*) $[Co(NH_3)_4Cl(NO_2)]Cl$
(*v*) $[Mn(H_2O)_6]^{2+}$

Ans. (*i*) Hexamminocobalt (III) chloride
(*ii*) Diamminechlorido (methyl amine) platinum (II) chloride
(*iii*) Hexaaquatitanium (III) ion
(*iv*) Tetraamminechloridonitrio-N-Cobalt (III) chloride.
(*v*) Hexaaquamanganere (II) ion.

Q. 5. What is meant by unidentate, didentate and ambidentate ligands? Give two examples for each.

Ans. (*i*) *Unidentate ligands*—The ligands whose only one donor atom is bonded to metal atom are called unidentate ligands, e.g., H_2O, NH_3, CO, CN^-.

(*ii*) *Didentate ligands*—The ligands which contain two donor atoms or ions through which they are bonded to the metal ion, e.g.–ethylene diamine ($H_2N\,CH_2CH_2NH_2$) has two nitrogen atoms and oxalate ion $\left[\begin{array}{l} COO^- \\ | \\ COO^- \end{array}\right]$ has two oxygen atoms which can bind with the metal atom.

(*iii*) *Ambidentate ligand*—Ligands which can ligate (link) through two different atoms present in it are called ambidentate ligands e.g., NO_2^-, SCN^-, CNO^-, CN^-, NO_2^- can link through 'N' as well as oxygen while SCN^- can link through 'S' as well as 'N' atom.

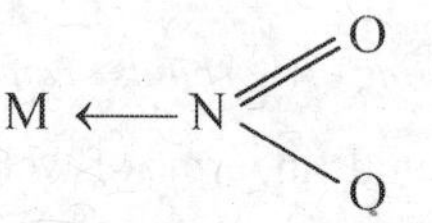

Nitrite-N

Nitrito-O

Q. 6. How many ions are produced from the complex, $CO(NH_3)_6Cl_2$ in solution?

(*i*) 6 (*ii*) 4 (*iii*) 3 (*iv*) 2

Ans. Coordination number of cobalt = 6. Ilence, the complex is $[Co(NH_3)_6]Cl_2$. It ionizes in the solution as—

$$[Co(NO_3)_6]Cl_2 \xrightarrow{+aq} [CO(NH_3)_6]^{2+} + 2Cl^-$$

Hence, three ions are produced. So the correct answer is (iii).

Q. 7. What is meant by chelate effect? Give an example.

Ans. When a didentate or a polydentate ligand contains donor atoms positioned in such a way that when they coordinate with the central metal ion, a five or a NH membered ring is formed, the effect is called chelate effect. As a result, the stability of the complex increases. For example,

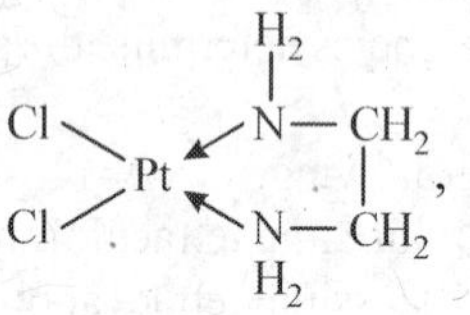

, i.e., $[Pt\,Cl_2(en)]$

Q. 8. What is meant by stability of a coordination compound in solution? State the factors which govern stability of complexes.

Ans. *Stability of co-ordination compound*: The formation of coordiantion compound involves Lewis acid-base reaction between the metal ion and the ligands. If the interaction is strong, the complex formed would be thermodynamically more stable.

For example—

$$M^{a+} + nL^{n-} \longrightarrow [MLn]^{b+}$$

where a^+, x^- and b^+ are the charges on the metal, ligand and complex respectively.

The stability constant for the above reaction is—

$$K = \frac{[MLn]^{b+}}{[M^{a+}][L^{x-}]^n}$$

The magnitude of the stability constant gives an indication of the stability of the complex in solution.

For example, $Cu^{+} + 4NH_3 \rightleftharpoons [Cu(NH_3)_4]^{2+}$
(Stability constant $\beta = 4.5 \times 10^{11}$)

Factors affecting the stability of a complex ion—

(*i*) Charge on the central metal ion.
(*ii*) Nature of the metal ion.
(*iii*) Basic nature of the ligand.
(*iv*) Presence of chelate rings.
(*v*) Effect of multidentate cyclic ligands.

Q. 9. (*a*) Illustrate the following with an example each:
(*i*) Linkage isomerism (*ii*) Co-ordination isomerism
(*b*) Why is $[NiCl_4]^{2-}$ Paramagnetic? [Ni = 28]

Ans. (*a*) (*i*) *Linkage isomerism*—The isomerism in which a ligand can form linkage with metal through different atoms, e.g., nitro group ($-NO_2$) can link to metal either through nitrogen atom or through oxygen atom. For example,

$[Co(NH_3)_5 ONO]Cl_2$

and pentaamminenitrito-O-cobalt (III) chloride

$[Co(NH_3)_5 NO_2]Cl_2$

pentaamminenitrito-N-cobalt (III) chloride are linkage isomers.

(*ii*) *Coordination isomerism*—This type of isomerism occurs when both the cations and anions are complexes and these differ in the co-ordination of ligands. For example, $[Co(NH_3)_6][Cr(C_2O_4)_3]$ and $[Cr(NH_3)_6][Co(C_2O_4)_3]$ are coordiantion isomers.

(*b*) *Bonding* $[NiCl_4]^{2-}$—In this case, Nickel is in +2 oxidation state and the configuration is $3d^8$. Since the molecule is tetrahedral, it involves sp^3 hybridisation as shown below:

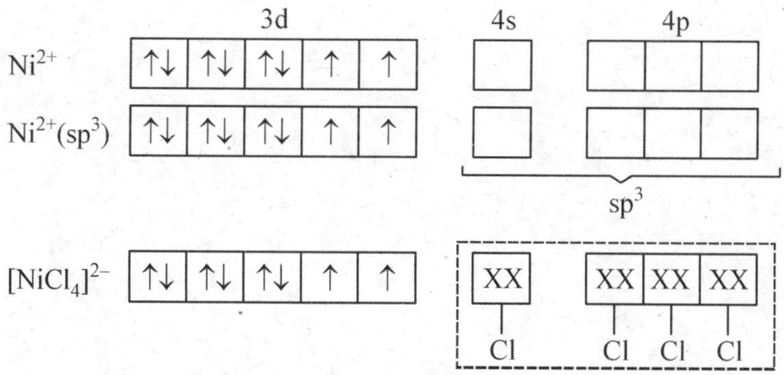

Each of the hybridised orbitals receives a pair of electrons from a Cl^- ion. The compound is paramagnetic because it contains unpaired electrons.

Q. 10. (*a*) What is spectrochemical series? Explain the difference between a weak field ligand and a strong field ligand.
(*b*) What is crystal field splitting energy?

Ans. (*a*) *Spectrochemical series*—The arrangement of ligands in order of their increasing field strengths, i.e., increasing crystal field splitting energy values is called spectrochemical series.

Difference between a weak ligand and a strong field ligand—The ligand with small value of CFSE (Δ_0) are called weak field ligands whereas those with large value of

CFSE are called strong field ligands.

(*b*) When ligands approach a transition metal ion, the d-orbitals split into two sets, one with lower energy and the other with higher energy. The difference of energy between the two sets of orbitals is called crystal field splitting energy.

Higher Order Thinking Skills Hots Questions

1. Name the ionisation isomer of $[Cr(H_2O)_5Br]SO_4$.
2. What is the coordination number of Fe in [Fe(EDTA)]?
3. Write all the isomers of $[Co(NH_3)_5SCN]Cl_2$.
4. Explain the structure and magnetic behaviour of the species $[Ni(CO)_4]$ molecule.
5. Account of the following:
   $[Cr(NH_3)_6]^{3+}$ is paramagnetic and octahedral whereas $[Ni(CN)_4]^{2-}$ is diamagnetic and square planar.
6. Explain each of the following observations:
   (*i*) Tetrahedral Ni(II) complexes are paramagnetic but square planar Ni(II) complexes are diamagnetic.
   (*ii*) Only transition metals are known to form π-complexes.

❑❑❑

CHAPTER

10 HALOALKANES AND HALOARENES

Syllabus

- ***Haloalkanes :*** *Nomenclature, nature of C—X bond, physical and chemical properties, mechanism of substitution reactions.*
- ***Haloarenes :*** *Nature of C—X bond, substitution reactions (directive influence of halogen for monosubstituted compounds only)*
Uses and environmental effects of dichloromethane, trichloromethane, tetrachloromethane, iodoform.

Type 1. Name Reactions

1. **Carbylamine reaction:** This reaction is given by primary amines. Secondary and tertiary amines do not give this reaction.
Therefore, this reaction is used as a test to distinguish a primary amine from other amines. A primary amine is heated with chloroform and alcoholic solution of KOH. An offensive smelling corresponding isocyanide (carbylamine) is formed.

$$RNH_2 + CHCl_3 + 3KOH \longrightarrow RNC + 3KCl + 3H_2O$$

$$\underset{\text{ethylamine}}{C_2H_5NH_2} + CHCl_3 + 3KOH \longrightarrow \underset{\text{ethylisocyanide}}{C_2H_5NC} + 3KCl + 3H_2O$$

$$\underset{\text{aniline}}{C_6H_5NH_2} + CHCl_3 + 3KOH \longrightarrow \underset{\text{phenylisocyanide}}{C_6H_5NC} + 3KCl + 3H_2O$$

2. **Diazotisation :** This reaction is given mainly by aromatic primary amino compounds. The aromatic primary amino compound is treated with cold solution of nitrous acid. Nitrous acid is prepared by the action of dil. HCl or dil. H_2SO_4 on $NaNO_2$ and used as such. A diazonium salt is formed. This reaction is called diazotisation.

$$C_6H_5NH_2 + HNO_2 + HCl \xrightarrow{273-278K} \underset{\text{benzene diazonium chloride}}{C_6H_5N_2^+Cl^-} + 2H_2O$$

$$C_6H_5NH_2 + HNO_2 + H_2SO_4 \xrightarrow{273-278K} \underset{\text{benzene diazonium hydrogen sulphate}}{C_6H_5N_2^+HSO_4^-} + 2H_2O$$

3. **Sandmeyer reaction :** Benzenediazonium chloride is treated with CuCl/HCl, CuBr/HBr or CuCN/KCN. Chlorobenzene, bromobenzene or benzonitrile (phenyl cyanide) is formed respectively. The halogen atom attached to copper enters the benzene ring.

$$C_6H_5N_2^+Cl^- \xrightarrow{CuCl/HCl} C_6H_5Cl + N_2$$

$$C_6H_5N_2^+Cl^- \xrightarrow{CuBr/HBr} C_6H_5Br + N_2$$

$$C_6H_5N_2^+Cl^- \xrightarrow{CuCN/KCN} C_6H_5CN + N_2$$

4. **Wurtz reaction :** Alkyl halides react with sodium in the presence of ether to form alkanes.

$$CH_3\boxed{I + 2Na + I}CH_3 \xrightarrow{\text{ether}} CH_3CH_3 + 2NaI$$

$$C_2H_5\boxed{Br + 2Na + Br}C_2H_5 \xrightarrow{\text{ether}} \underset{n\text{-butane}}{C_2H_5C_2H_5} + 2NaI$$

5. **Swarts reaction :** Fluoro alkanes are prepared by treating alkyl chlorides or bromides with salts such as mercurous fluoride (Hg_2F_2), silver fluoride (AgF), Cobalt fluoride (CoF_3) or antimony trifluoride (SbF_3). This reaction is known as Swarts reaction.

$$2CH_3CH_2Cl + \underset{\text{Mercurous fluoride}}{Hg_2F_2} \longrightarrow \underset{\text{Fluoroethane}}{2CH_3CH_2F} + Hg_2Cl_2$$

$$CH_3Br + AgF \longrightarrow CH_3F$$

6. **Substitution nucleophilic unimolecular (S_N1) :** S_N1 reaction in presence of in polar protic (hydroxylic) solvents such as water, alcohol, acetic acid, etc.

Reaction :

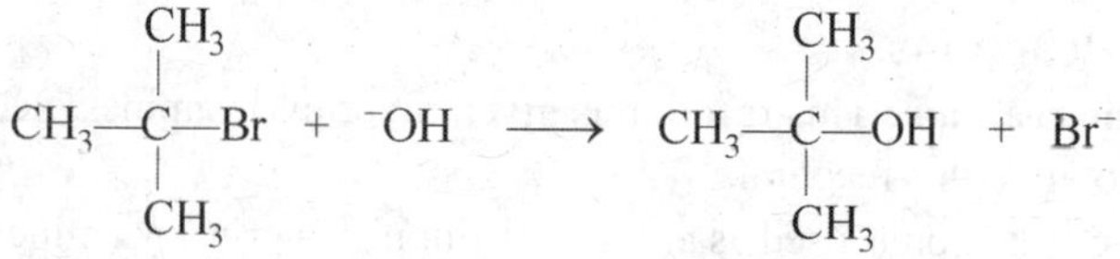

tert-Butyl bromide or 2-Bromo-2-methylpropane → *tert*-Butyl alcohol or 2-Methylpropan-2-ol

Mechanism :

Step I. This step is slow and reversible and hence is the rate-determining step of the reaction.

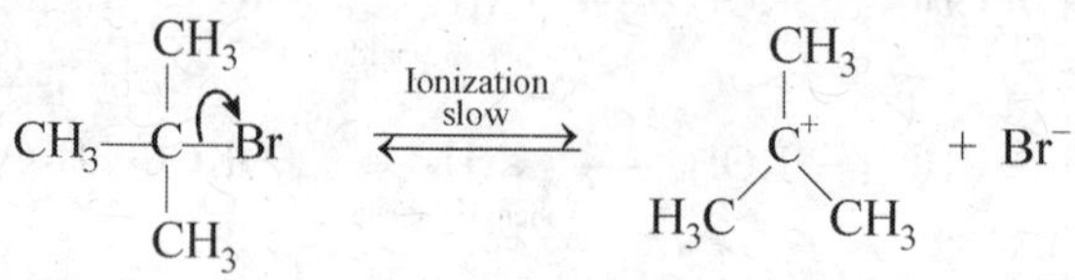

$$\text{Rate} = k[(CH_3)_3CBr].$$

Step II. In the second step, the carbocation being a reactive chemical species, is immediately attacked by the nucleophile OH^- ion to give the substitution product.

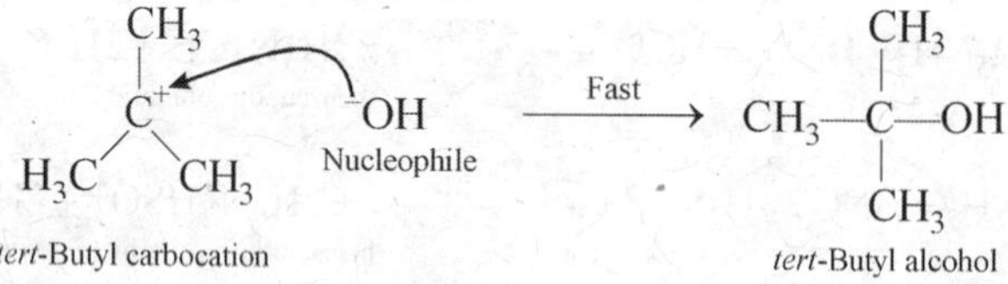

tert-Butyl carbocation → *tert*-Butyl alcohol (Substitution product)

6. **Substitution nucleophilic bimolecular (S_N2) :**
Mechanism :

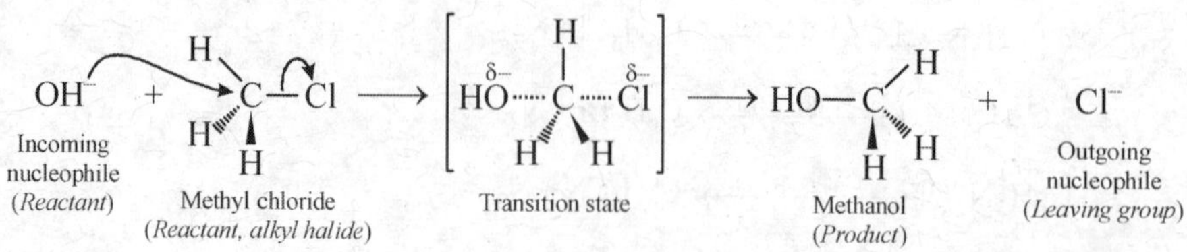

Type 2. Reasoning Type Questions

1. Out of $C_6H_5CH_2Cl$ and $C_6H_5CHClC_6H_5$ which is more easily hydrolysed by aqueous KOH ?

Ans. $C_6H_5CH_2Cl$ is a 1° aralkyl halide while $C_6H_5CH(Cl)C_6H_5$ is a 2° aralkyl halide.

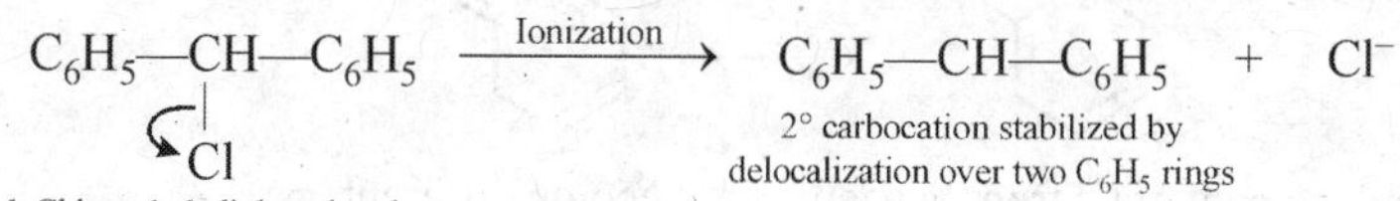

1-Chloro-1, 1-diphenylmethane

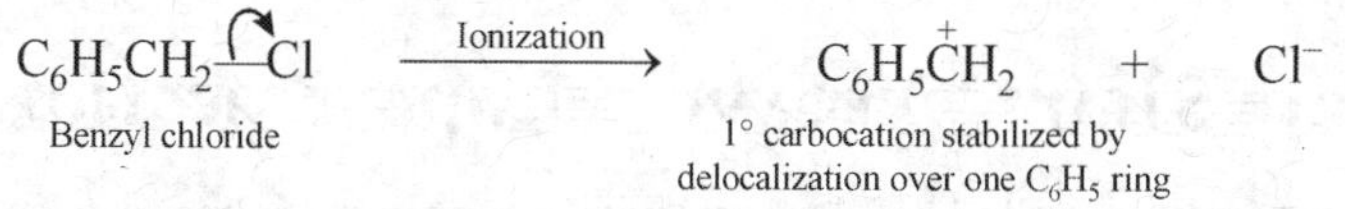

Benzyl chloride

In S_N1 reaction, the reactivity depends upon the stability of carbocations since the carbocation $C_6H_5\overset{+}{C}HC_6H_5$ is more stable due to more resonating structure (7) than the carbocation, $C_6H_5\overset{+}{C}H_2$ (resonating structure 4). Therefore $C_6H_5CHClC_6H_5$ is more easily hydrolysed by aqueous KOH than $C_6H_5CH_2Cl$.

2. p-Dichlorobenzene has higher m.p. and solubility than those of o- and m-isomers. Discuss.

Ans. The melting point of *p*-isomer of dichloro benzene is higher than that of *o*- and *m*-isomers. This is because, *p*-isomer has symmetrical structure and therefore, its molecules can easily pack closely in crystal lattice. Hence, it has stronger intermolecular forces of attraction than o- and m-isomer.

3. Explain why the dipole moment of chlorobenzene is lower than that of cyclohexyl chloride ?

Ans. Due to greater *s*-character, a sp^2-hybrid carbon is more electronegative than a sp^3-hybrid carbon. Therefore, the sp^2-hybrid carbon of C—Cl bond in chlorobenzene has less tendency to release electrons to Cl than a sp^3-hybrid carbon of cyclohexyl chloride.

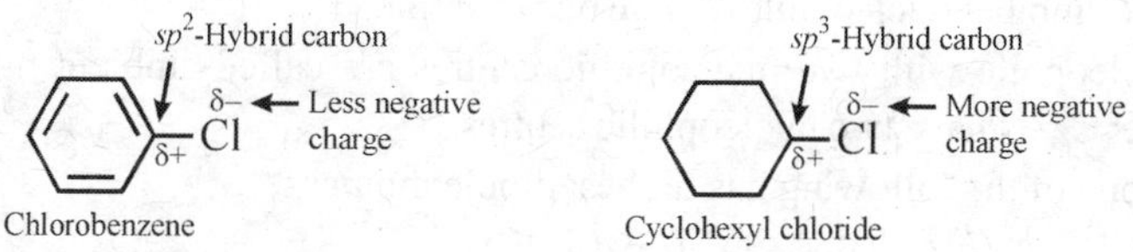

Chlorobenzene   Cyclohexyl chloride

Greater is electronegativity difference, greater is dipole moment.

4. Alkyl halides, though polar, are immiscible with water ?

Ans. Alkyl halides are polar molecules, therefore, their molecules are held together by dipole-dipole attraction. The molecules of H_2O are held together by H-bonds. Since the new forces of attraction between water and alkyl halide molecules are weaker than the forces of attraction already existing between alkyl halide-alkyl halide molecules and water-water molecules, therefore, alkyl halides are immiscible (not soluble) with water.

5. Grignard reagents should be prepared under anhydrous conditions ?

Ans. Grignard reagents are very reactive. They react with moisture present in the apparatus or the starting materials, i.e., R—X, Mg and the solvent (ether or THF).

$$\underset{\text{Grignard reagent}}{\overset{\delta-}{R}—\overset{\delta+}{Mg}\overset{\delta-}{X}} + H—OH \longrightarrow R—H + Mg(OH)X$$

Therefore, Grignard reagents must be prepared under anhydrous conditions.

6. Haloarenes are less reactive than alkyl halides toward nucleophilic addition reaction.

Ans. Due to resonance C—X bond become stronger and shorter.

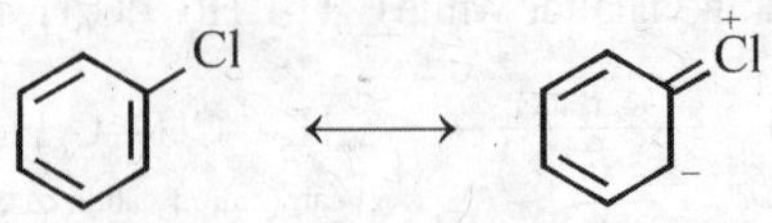

Therefore, replacement of Cl from benzene ring become different.

Very Short Answer Type Questions

Q. 1. What happens when an alkyl halide reacts with magnesium in the presence of dry other?

Ans. Grignard reagent is detained.

$$\underset{\text{Alkyl halide}}{R-X+Mg} \xrightarrow{\text{dry ether}} \underset{\substack{\text{Alkyl magnesium halide} \\ \text{(Grignard reagent)}}}{R-Mg-X}$$

Q. 2. How does iodobenzene react with copper powder? What is the name of the reaction?

Ans. 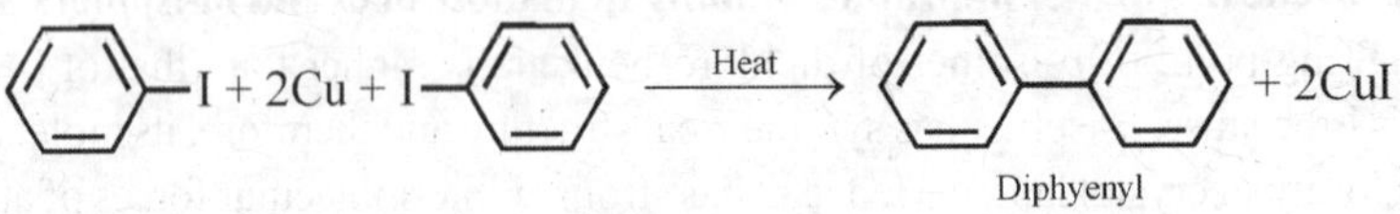

Diphyenyl

Q. 3. Chloroform contains chlorine but gives no reaction with $AgNO_3$ solution. Why?

Ans. $CHCl_3$ contains Cl but it is bonded to carbon by covalent bond and therefore, it is not in ionic form. Hence it does not combine with $AgNO_3$ solution.

Q. 4. How can you test the purity of chloroform?

Ans. Pure chloroform does not give white precipitate with $AgNO_3$ solution.

Q. 5. What are ambient nucleophiles? Give one example.

Ans. The nucleophile with two nucleophilic centres are called ambient nucleophiles. For example: $C \equiv N$ have two nucleophilic centres.

Q. 6. Which one of the following has highest dipole moment?

(*a*) CH_2Cl_2 (*b*) $CHCl_3$ (*c*) CCl_4.

Ans. (*b*)

Q. 7. Which compound in each of the following pains will react faster in Sw^2 reaction with OH^-? (*i*) CH_3Br or CH_3I (*ii*) $(CH_3)_3CCl$ or CH_3Cl.

Ans. (*i*) CH_3I reacts faster than CH_3Br in Sw^2 reaction with OH^- ion, because I^- ion is a better learning group than Br^- ion.

(*ii*) CH_3Cl will react at a faster rate than $(CH_3)_3CCl$ in a Sw^2 reaction with OH^- ion because 1° alkyl halides are more reactive than test-alkyl halides in Sw^2 reaction.

Q. 8. Give the IUPAC and the trivial name of $C_6H_6Cl_6$.

Ans. Trivial name: benzene hexachloride; IUPAC: 1, 2, 3, 4, 5, 6-hexachlorocyclohexane.

Q. 9. What is an asymmetric carbon?

Ans. A carbon which is attached to four different atoms/groups is called asymmetric carbon.

Q. 10. What is the condition to be satisfied for a compound to be chiral?

Ans. Its mirror image should be non-superimposable.

Q. 11. What do prefixes (+), (–) and (±) before an organic compound mean?

Ans. Prefixes (+), (–) and (±) imply dextrorotatory, laevorotatory and racemic modification.

Q. 12. An acid of molecular formula, $C_5H_{10}O_2$ is optically active. What is its structure?

Ans.

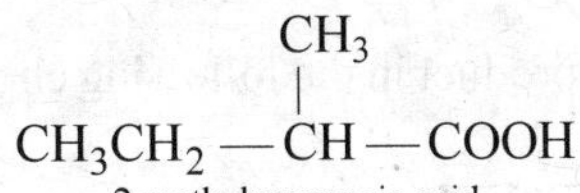

2-methylpropanoic acid

Q. 13. Give IUPAC name of the following organic compound:

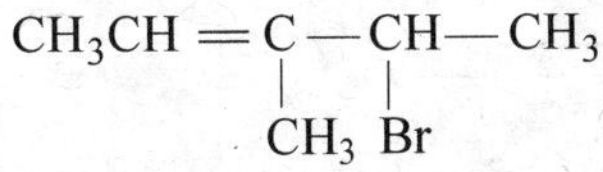

Ans. 4-bromo-3-methylpent-2-ene.

Q. 14. Write a chemical reaction in which the iodide ion replaces the diazonium group in a diazonium salt.

Ans. 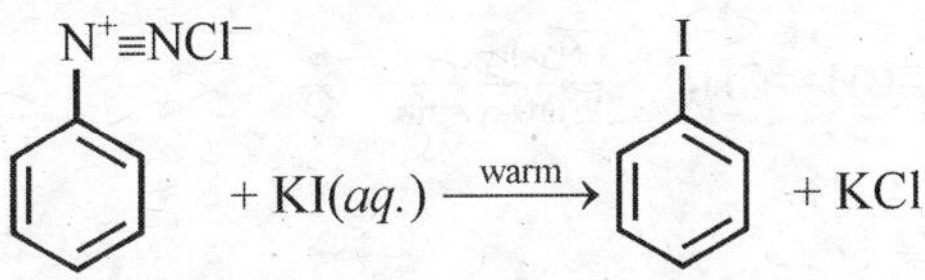

Q. 15. Arrange the following in order of their increasing reactivity in nucleophilic substitution reaction:

$$CH_3F, CH_3I, CH_3Br, CH_3Cl$$

Ans. Reactivity increases as the carbon halogen bond dissociation energy decreases, i.e.,

$$CH_3F < \text{and} < CH_3Br < CH_3I$$

Short Answer Type Questions – I

Q. 1. What are enantiomers?

Ans. Molecules which are non-superimposable mirror images of each other are called enantiomers. For example, I and II are enantiomers of butan-2-ol because (II) is not superimposable on (I) and (I) is not superimposable.

Mirror

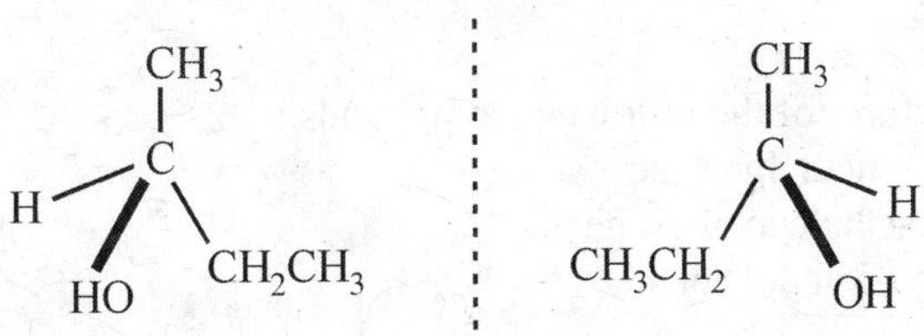

(I) (II)

Q. 2. Write the structural formulae and IUPAC names of all the possible optically active halides having the molecular formula $C_5H_{11}Br$.

Ans. $C_5H_{11}Br$ has three optically active isomers. These are:

$CH_3CH_2CH_2-\overset{\overset{Br}{|}}{CH}-CH_3$ 2-bromapentane

$CH_3CH_2-\overset{\overset{CH_3}{|}}{CH}-CH_3Br$ 1-bromo-2-methylpentane

$CH_3-\overset{\overset{CH_3}{|}}{CH}-\overset{\overset{Br}{|}}{CH}-CH_3$ 2-bromo-3-methylbutane

Q. 3. Write the formula of main product in the following chemical reactions:—

(*i*) $(CH_3)_2CH-Cl \xrightarrow[\text{dry ether}]{Na}$

(*ii*) $CH_3Br + AgF \xrightarrow{\Delta}$

(*iii*) $CH_3CH_2Br + NaI \xrightarrow{\text{dry acetone}}$

(*iv*) 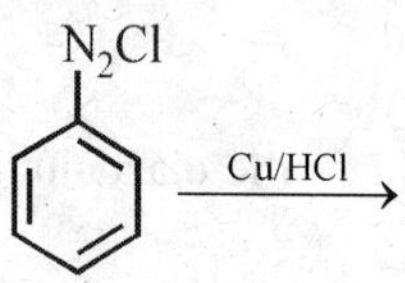

Ans. (*i*) $\underset{\underset{CH_3}{|}}{CH_3-CH}-\vdots\, Cl-2Na+Cl\,\vdots-\underset{\underset{CH_3}{|}}{CH}-CH_3 \xrightarrow[\text{(Wurtz reaction)}]{\text{Na/dry ether}}$

$CH_3-\underset{\underset{CH_3}{|}}{CH}-\underset{\underset{CH_3}{|}}{CH}-CH_3 + 2NaCl$

2,3-dimethylbutune

(*ii*) $CH_3-Br + AgF \xrightarrow[\text{(Swarts reaction)}]{\Delta} CH_3F + AgBr$

Bromomethane Fluoromethane

(*iii*) $CH_3CH_2-Br + NaI \xrightarrow[\text{(Finkelitein reaction)}]{\text{Dryacetonc, }\Delta} CH_3-CH_2-I + NaBr$

Bromomethane Iodoethane

(*iv*) 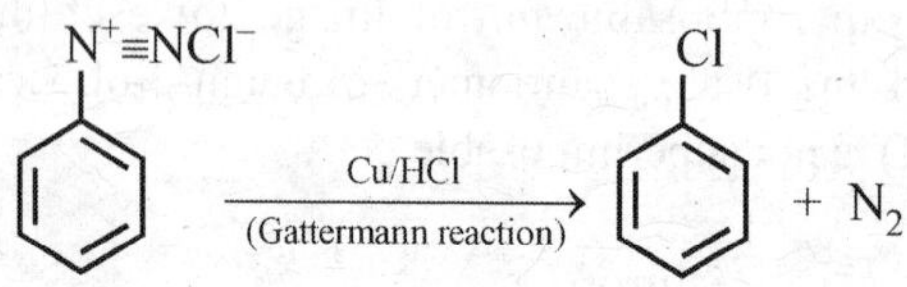

Bengenediazonium chloride

Q. 4. Write the structures of the following compounds :

(*i*) 2-Chloro-3-methylpentane

(*ii*) 1-chloro-4-ethylcyclohexane

(*iii*) 4-*tert*-Butyl-3-iodoheptane

Ans. (*i*) $\overset{1}{CH_3}-\underset{\underset{Cl}{|}}{\overset{2}{CH}}-\underset{\underset{CH_3}{|}}{\overset{3}{CH}}-\overset{4}{CH_2}\,\overset{5}{CH_3}$

2-chloro-3-methylpentane

(*ii*) 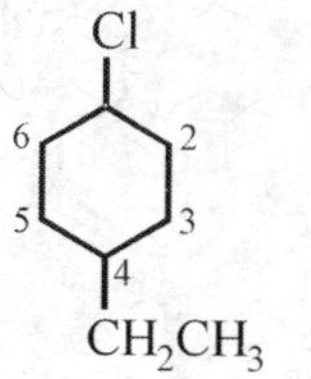

1-chloro-4-ethylcyclohexane

(*iii*) $\overset{1}{C}H_3-\overset{2}{C}H_2-\underset{I}{\overset{3}{C}H}-\underset{H_3C-\underset{CH_3}{C}-CH_3}{\overset{4}{C}H}-\overset{5}{C}H_2-\overset{6}{C}H_2-\overset{7}{C}H_3$

4-tert-butyl-3-iodoheptane

Q. 5. Why is H_2SO_4 not used during the reaction of alcohols with KI?

Ans. H_2SO_4 is an oxidising agent. It oxidises HI produced during the reaction to I_2 and thus prevents the reaction I_2 and then prevents the reaction between an alcohol and HI to form an alkyl iodide.

So H_3PO_4 is used instead of H_2SO_4.

$$2KI + H_2SO_4 \longrightarrow 2KHSO_4 + 2HI$$

$$2HI + H_2SO_4 \longrightarrow H_2O + I_2 + SO_2$$

$$\underset{\text{Ethanol}}{CH_3CH_2OH} + KI + H_3PO_4 \xrightarrow{\Delta} \underset{\text{Iodoethane}}{CH_3CH_2-I} + KH_2PO_4 + H_2O$$

Q. 6. How will you bring about the following conversions?

(*i*) Ethanol to but-1-yne

(*ii*) Ethane to bromoethene

(*iii*) Propene to 1-nitropropane

(*iv*) Toluene to benzyl alcohol

Ans. (*i*) $\underset{\text{Ethanol}}{CH_3CH_2OH} \xrightarrow[-SO_2,-HCl]{SOCl_2,\ Pyridine} \underset{\text{Chloroethane (A)}}{CH_3-CH_2-Cl}$

$$\underset{\text{Acetylene}}{HC\equiv CH} + NaNH_2 \xrightarrow[-NH_3]{Liq.\ NH_3, 196\,K} \underset{\text{Sod. acetylide (B)}}{HC\equiv C^-Na^+}$$

$$CH_3-CH_2-Cl + HC\equiv \bar{C}Na^+ \longrightarrow \underset{\text{But-1-yne}}{CH_3CH_2-C\equiv CH} + NaCl$$

(*ii*) $\underset{\text{Ethane}}{CH_3-CH_3} + Br_2 \xrightarrow[-HBr]{hv, 520-670\,K} \underset{\text{Bromoethane}}{CH_3CH_2-Br} \xrightarrow[-HBr]{KOH(alc), \Delta} \underset{\text{Ethene}}{CH_2=CHBr}$

$$\xrightarrow{Br_2/CCl_4} \underset{\text{1, 2-Dibromoethane}}{BrCH_2-CH_2Br} \xrightarrow[-HBr]{KOH(alc), \Delta} \underset{\text{Bromoethene}}{CH_2=CHBr}$$

(*iii*) $\underset{\text{Propene}}{CH_3-CH-CH_2} \xrightarrow[\text{Peroxide effect}]{HBr, ROOR} \underset{\text{1-bromopropane}}{CH_3-CH_2-CH_2Br} \xrightarrow[-AgBr]{AgNO_2, C_2H_5OH/H_2O}$

$$\underset{\text{1-Nitropropane}}{CH_3CH_2CH_2NO_2}$$

(iv)

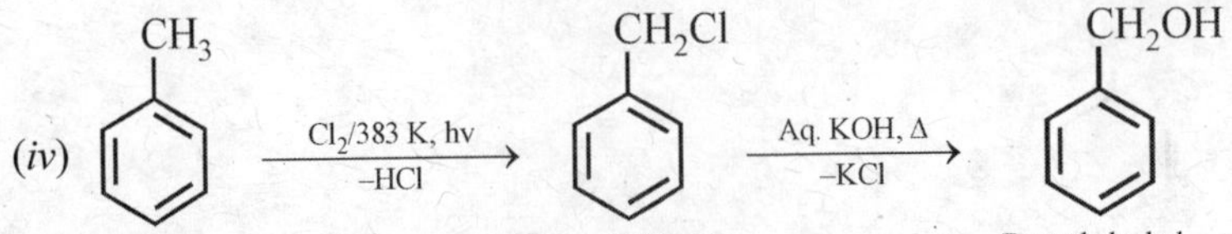

Totluene — Benzyl Chloride — Benzyl alcohol

Q. 7. How is DDT prepared?

Ans. DDT is prepared by heating chloral with chlorobenzene in the presence of conc. H_2SO_4.

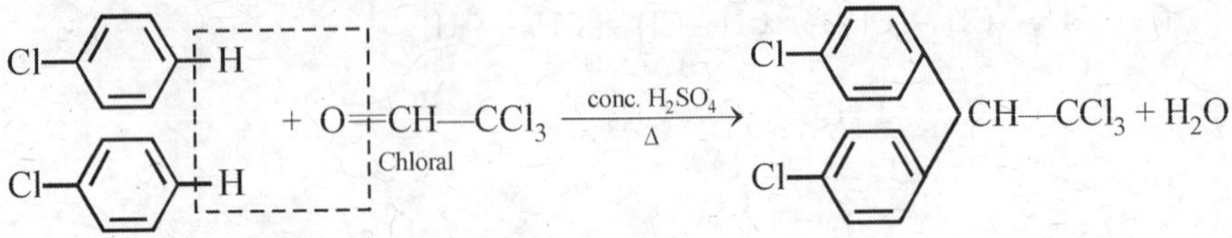

DDT

It is a cheap but powerful insecticide.

Q. 8. Write the mechanism of the reaction :

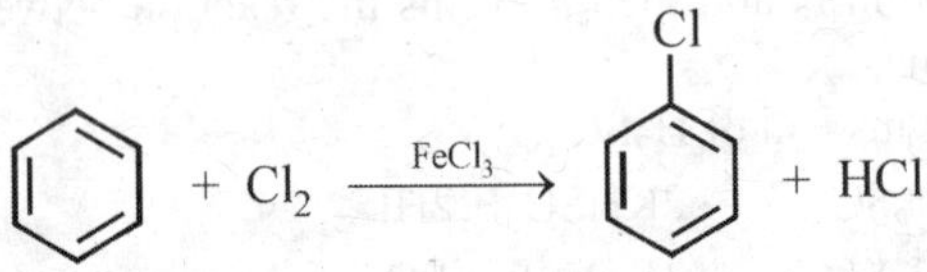

Ans. It is an electrophilic substitution reaction and involves three steps:—

Step I—*Generation of electrophile:*

$$Cl{-}Cl + FeCl_3 \longrightarrow \overset{\delta^+}{Cl}{------}\overset{\delta^-}{FeCl_4}$$

Electrophile

Step II—*Formation of σ-complex or carbocation intermediate.*

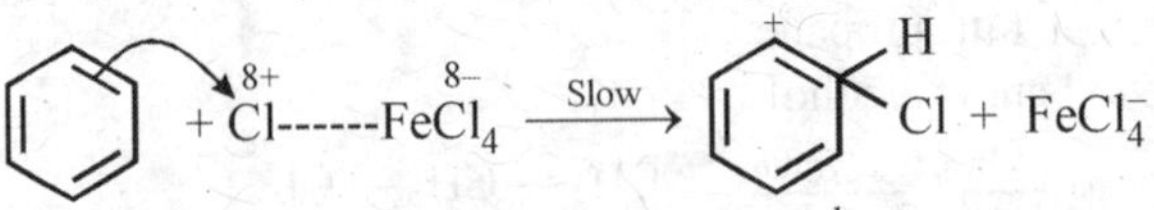

σ-complex

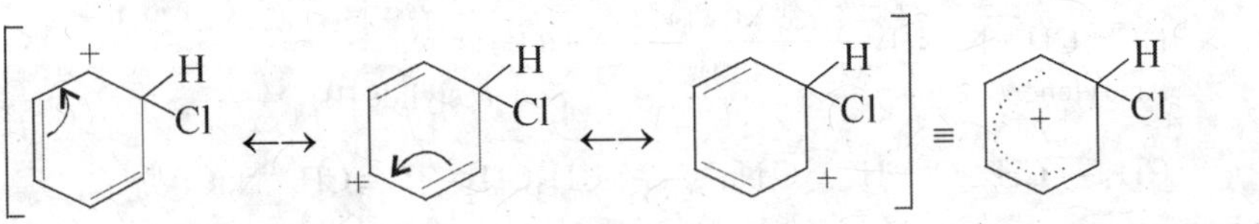

Resonance hybrid

Step III—Loss of a *proton from the carbocation intermediate* :

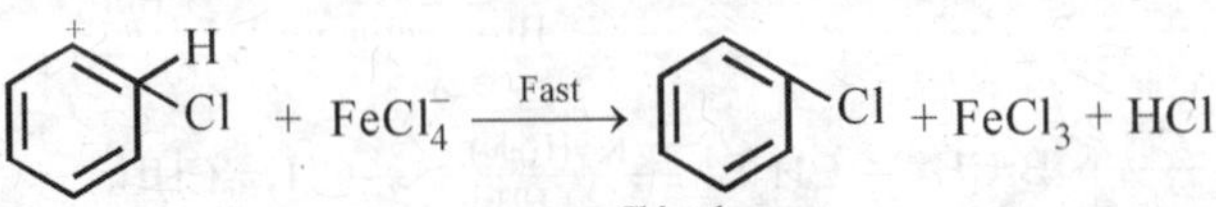

Chlorobenzene

Q. 9. Benzyl chloride is more reactive than chlorobenzene towards nucleophilic substitution. Explain.

Ans. In the molecule of benzyl chloride, the electron pairs on the chlonine atom are not in a position to conjugate with the π-electrons of the ring.

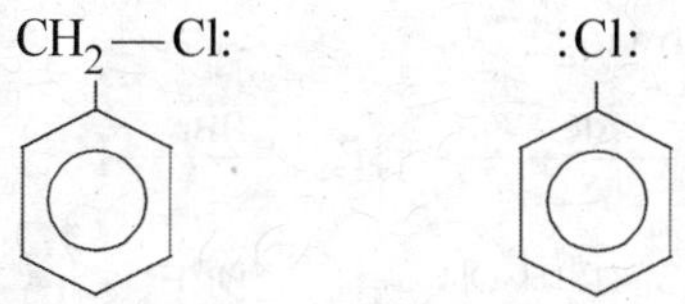

Whereas electron pairs on the chlorine atom are in conjugation with the π-electrons of the ring in the molecules of chlorobenzene. Consequently, the C–Cl bond in chlorobenzene acquires some double bond character, which is not present in benzyle chloride. As a result, the reactivity of benzyl chloride is more than the chlorobenzene.

Q. 10. How will you distinguish between:

(*a*) Methanol and ethanol
(*b*) Propane 1–ol and propan–2–ol
(*c*) Benzyl chloride and chlorobenzene
(*d*) *n*-butyl amine and di-ethyl amine.

Ans. (*a*) Ethanol will give iodoform test while methanal does not.
(*b*) Propan-2-ol will give iodoform test while propane 1-ol does not.
(*c*) Benzyl chloride gives white precipitate with $AgNO_3$ while chlorobenzene does not.
(*d*) *n*-Butylamine will give carbylamine test while diethyl amine will give liberamannitroso test.

Q. 11. Write the IUPAC names of the following compounds :

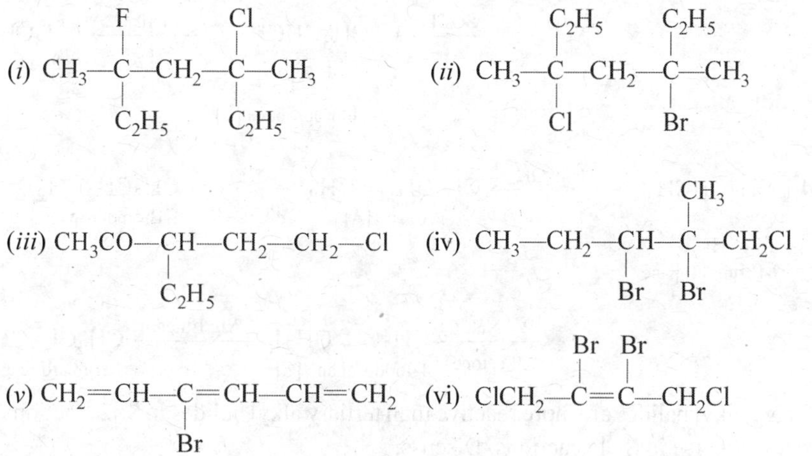

Ans. (*i*) 3-chloro-5-fluoro-3, 5-dimethylheptane
(ii) 3-bromo-5-chloro-3-, 5-dimethylheptane
(iii) 5-chloro-3-ethylpentan-2-one
(iv) 2,3-dibromo-1-chloro-2-methylpentane
(v) 3-bromohexa-1, 3, 5-triene
(vi) 2,3-dibromo-1, 4-dichlorobut-2-ene

Q. 12. Haloalkanes are insoluble in water but are soluble in benzene. Explain.

Ans. Haloalkanes are insoluble in water due to the lack of hydrogen bonding with H_2O moelcules. As a result, the magnitude of attractive forces remain less than the attractive force in the H_2O molecules which are hydrogen bonded. However, haloalkanes dissolve in organic solvents like benzene since the solubility is based on the same principle.

Q. 13. Complete the missing links in the following :

(*i*) $CH_3CH_2CH_2OH \xrightarrow{PBr_3} [A] \xrightarrow{\text{Alc. KOH}} [B] \xrightarrow{HBr} [C] \xrightarrow{NH_3} [D]$

(ii) $CH_3CH_2CH_2I \xrightarrow{\text{Alc. KOH}} [A] \xrightarrow{H^+/H_2O} [B] \xrightarrow{SOCl_2} [C] \xrightarrow{LiAlH_4} [D]$

(iii) $CH_3CHBrCH_3 \xrightarrow{\text{Alc. KOH}} [A] \xrightarrow[\text{Peroxide}]{HBr} [B] \xrightarrow[\text{Acetone}]{NaI} [C] \xrightarrow[\text{Ether}]{Mg} [D]$

Ans. (i) $\underset{\text{Propan-1-ol}}{CH_3CH_2CH_2OH} \xrightarrow{PBr_3} \underset{\text{1-Bromopropane [A]}}{CH_3CH_2CH_2Br} \xrightarrow{\text{Alc. KOH}} \underset{\text{Propene [B]}}{CH_3CH=CH_2}$

$\xrightarrow{HBr} \underset{\text{2–Bromopropane [C]}}{CH_3\underset{\underset{Br}{|}}{C}HCH_3} \xrightarrow{NH_3} \underset{\text{Propan-2-amine [D]}}{CH_3\underset{\underset{NH_2}{|}}{C}HCH_3}$

(ii) $\underset{\text{1-Iodopropane}}{CH_3CH_2CH_2I} \xrightarrow{\text{Alc. KOH}} \underset{\text{Propene [A]}}{CH_3CH=CH_2} \xrightarrow{H^+/H_2O} \underset{\text{Propan-2-ol [B]}}{CH_3\underset{\underset{OH}{|}}{C}HCH_3}$

$\xrightarrow{SOCl_2} \underset{\text{2-Chloropropane [C]}}{CH_3\underset{\underset{Cl}{|}}{C}HCH_3} \xrightarrow[(H)]{LiAlH_4} \underset{\text{Pr opane [D]}}{CH_3CH_2CH_3}$

(iii) $\underset{\text{2-Bromopropane}}{CH_3\underset{\underset{Br}{|}}{C}HCH_3} \xrightarrow{\text{Alc. KOH}} \underset{\text{Propene [A]}}{CH_3CH=CH_2} \xrightarrow[\text{Peroxide}]{HBr} \underset{\text{1-Bromopropane [B]}}{CH_3CH_2CH_2Br}$

$\xrightarrow[\text{(Acetone)}]{NaI} \underset{\text{1-Iodopropane [C]}}{CH_3CH_2CH_2I} \xrightarrow{\text{Mg/Ether}} \underset{\text{Grignard reagent [D]}}{CH_3CH_2CH_2MgI}$

Q. 14. Primary alkyl halides are more reactive than tertiary alkyl halides in S_N2 reactions but the order is reverse in S_N1 reactions. Discuss.

Ans. In S_N2 reactions, the substitution is completed in a single step involving a transition state and the size of the alkyl group handers the attack of the attacking nucleophile. Since the steric hindrance is maximum in tertiary alkyl halides and least in primary alkyl halides, therefore the tertiary alkyl halides are the least reactive while primary are the maximum reactive.

In S_N1 reactions, the substitution is completed in two steps in which the slow step involves the cleavage of alkyl halide to form a carbocation. Since the tertiary carbocation is the maximum stable while primary is the least stable, therefore the former is the maximum reactive while the latter has the least tendency to take part in S_N1 reactions.

Q. 15. Which of the following will respond more to S_N2 reaction in the following pairs ?

(a) 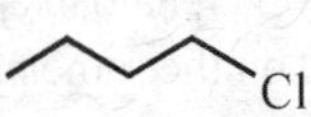 and 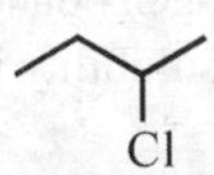

(b) 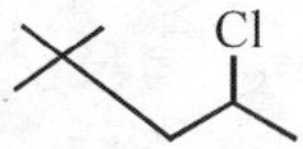 and 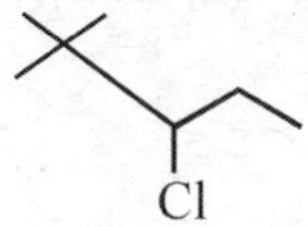

(c) 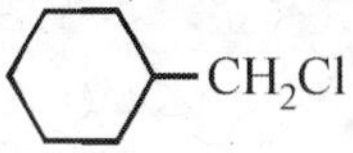 and 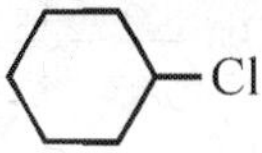

Ans. (a)  : Back side attack of the nucleophile in this molecule is easter as compared to the second due to least steric hindrance.

(b) 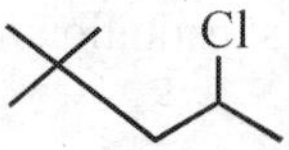 : Reason same as given above.

(c) 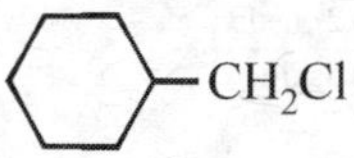 : Reason same as given above.

Short Answer Type Questions - II

Q. 1. What is saytzeff rule? Illustrate with an example.

Ans. If a haloalkane is such that it can undergo elimination in two different ways due to the availability of different types of β-hydrogens, then the more highly substituted alkene (i.e., alkene having lesser number of hydrogen atoms on the doubly bonded carbon atoms) is the major product. This is called saytzeff rule.

$$\underset{\text{2-bromobutane}}{CH_3-\overset{\beta}{C}H_2-\underset{Br}{\underset{|}{\overset{\alpha}{C}H}}-\overset{\beta}{C}H_3} \xrightarrow[-KCl]{KOH(alc.),\ \Delta} \begin{cases} \underset{\substack{\text{But-2-ene (81\%)}\\ \text{(more stable)}}}{CH_3-CH=CH-CH_3} \\ \underset{\substack{\text{But-1-ene (19\%)}\\ \text{(less stable)}}}{CH_3-CH_2-CH=CH_2} \end{cases}$$

Q. 2. State whether the following is optically active or inactive. Give reasons: (*i*) 2, 3-dimethyl-2, 3-dibromobutane (*ii*) 3, 4-dibromo-3, 4-dimethylpentene, (*iii*) 2-bromopentan-2-ol.

Ans. (*i*) $CH_3-\underset{CH_3}{\overset{Br}{\overset{|}{\underset{|}{C}}}}-\underset{CH_3}{\overset{Br}{\overset{|}{\underset{|}{C}}}}-CH_3$ does not contain chiral carbon, hence is optically inactive.

(*ii*) $CH_3-\underset{Br}{\overset{CH_3}{\overset{|}{\underset{|}{C}}}}-\underset{Br}{\overset{CH_3}{\overset{|}{\underset{|}{{}^{*}C}}}}-CH=CH_2$ contains one chiral carbon, hence is optically active.

(*iii*) $HOCH_2-\underset{Br}{\underset{|}{{}^{*}CH}}-CH_2\,CH_2\,CH_3$ contains one chiral carbon, hence is optically active.

Q. 3. Write the major product of the following reaction :

(*a*) $CH_2{=}CHBr \xrightarrow[\text{alcohol}]{AgCN}$

(*b*) 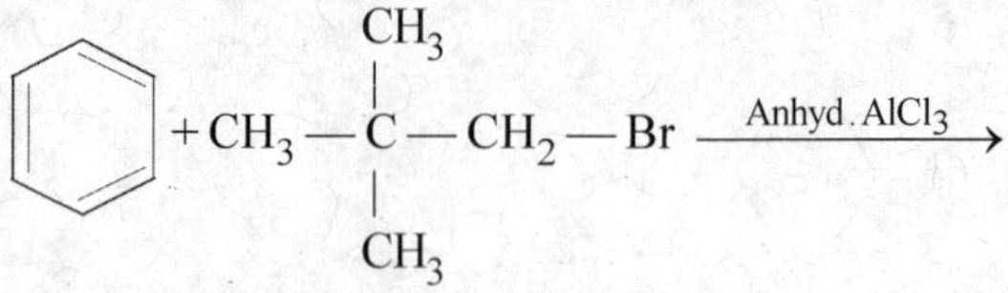

Ans. (*a*) $CH_2{=}CHBr \xrightarrow[\text{alcohol}]{AgCN}$ No reaction
(Vinyl halides)

Since vinyl halides are unreactive towards nucleophilic substitution reaction.

(b) 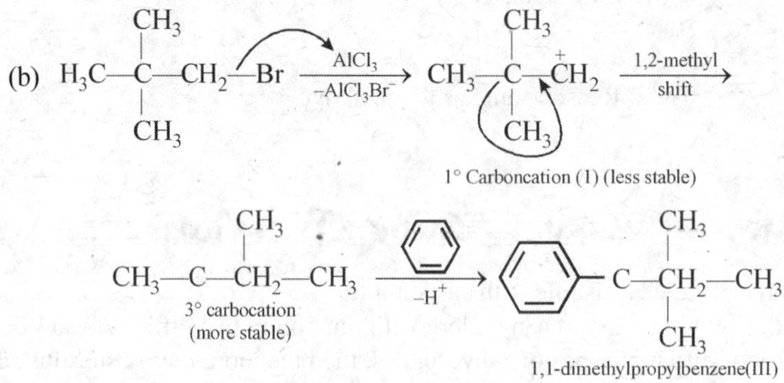

Q. 4. (*i*) 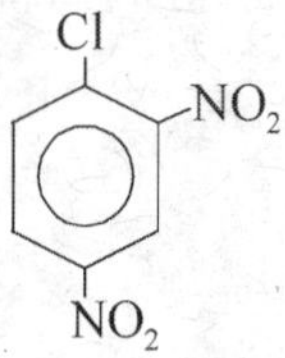 $+Na_2CO_3 + H_2O \longrightarrow C$. Identify C.

(*ii*) Predict the product of the reaction

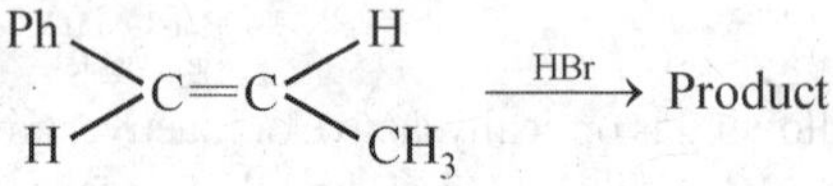

Ans. (*i*)

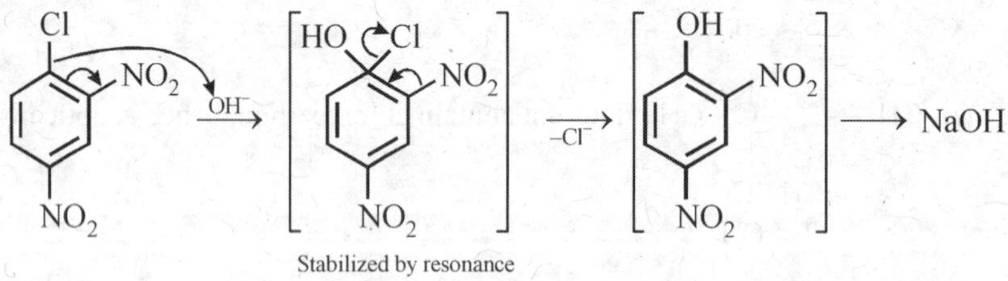

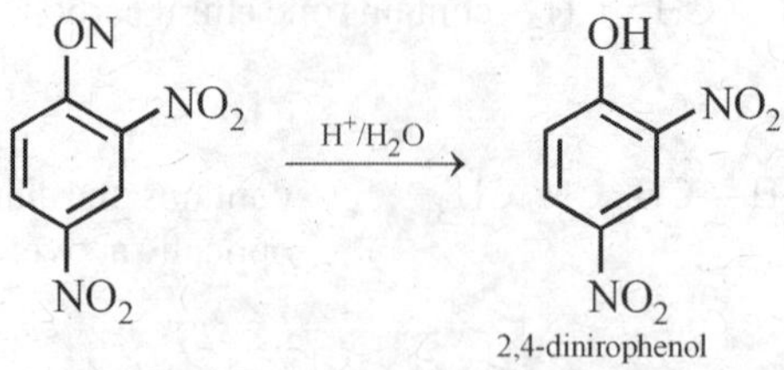

(*ii*)

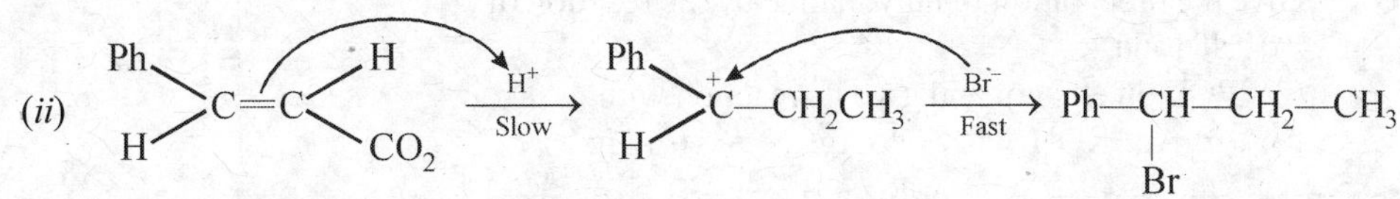

1-bromo-1-phenylpropane(II)

Q. 5. Write IUPAC names of the following :

(*a*)

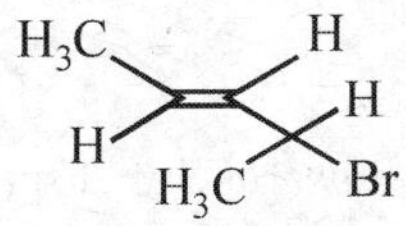

(*b*) $CH_3—C(CH_3)_2—CH_2Br$

(*c*)

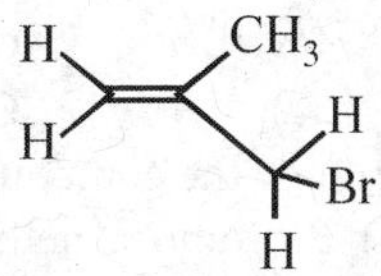

Ans. (*a*)

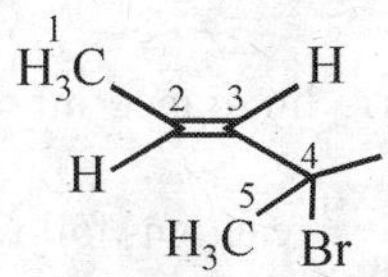

4-bromopent-2-ene

(*b*) $H_3C—C(CH_3)_2—CH_2—Br$

1-bromo-2, 2-dimethylpnpane (i)

(c)

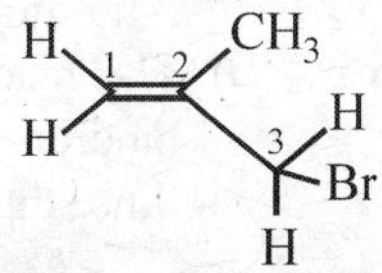

3-bromo-2-methylpropene

Q. 6. (*i*) A hydrocarbon C_5H_{10} does not react with chlorine but gives a single monochloro compound, C_5H_9Cl in bright sunlight. Identify the hydrocarbon.

(*ii*) Write the isomers of the compound having formula C_4H_9Br.

Ans. (*i*)

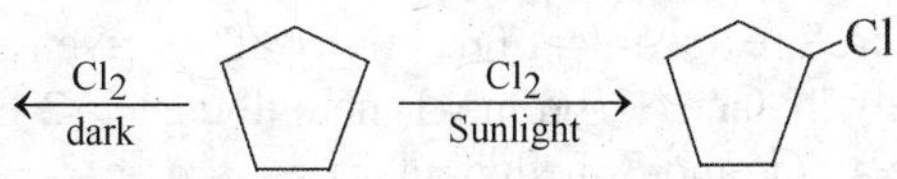

Cyclopentane (C_5H_{10}) Monochloro-cyclopentane (C_5H_9Cl)

(*ii*) This compound is saturated. It has the following four isomers:

(*a*) $CH_3—CH_2—CH_2—CH_2—Br$

1-bromobutane

(*b*) $\overset{4}{C}H_3—\overset{3}{C}H_2—\overset{2}{C}H(Br)—\overset{1}{C}H_3$

2-bromobutane

(*c*) $\overset{3}{C}H_3—\overset{2}{C}H(CH_3)—CH_2Br$

1-Bromo-2-methylpropane

(*d*) $CH_3—{}_2C(Br)(^1CH_3)(^3CH_3)$

2-bromo-2-methylpropane

Q. 7. Give the preparation of alkyl halide by the reaction of :

(*i*) HCl and

(*ii*) PCl_5 on ethanol and give its reaction with

(*a*) Aq. KOH (*b*) AgCN (*c*) Mg

Ans. (*i*) $C_2H_5OH + HCl \xrightarrow[\Delta]{\text{Anhy.}\, ZnCl_2} C_2H_5Cl + H_2O$

(*ii*) $C_2H_5OH + PCl_5 \xrightarrow{\Delta} C_2H_5Cl + HCl + POCl_3$

(*a*) $C_2H_5Cl + KOH\,(aq.) \longrightarrow C_2H_5OH + KCl$

(*b*) $C_2H_5Cl + AgCN \longrightarrow C_2H_5CN + AgCl$

(*c*) $C_2H_5Cl + Mg \longrightarrow C_2H_5—Mg—Cl$

Q. 8. Arrange the compounds of each set in order of reactivity towards Sw^2 displacement:—

(*i*) 2-bromo-2 methylbutane, 1-bromopentane, 2-bromopentane

(*ii*) 1-bromo-3 methylbutane, 2-bromo-2 methylbutane, 2 bromo-3-methylbutane

(*iii*) 1-bromobutane, 2-bromo-2, 2, dimethylpropane, 1-bromo-2-methlbutane, 2-bromo-3-methylbutane.

Ans. (*i*) The reactivity in Sw^2 reactions depends upon steric hindrance more the steric hindrance slower the reaction.

Since due to steric reasons, the order of reactivity in Sw^2 reactions follows the order : $1° > 2° > 3°$.

Therefore, the order of reactivity of the given alkyl bromides is:

1-bromopentane > 2-bromopentane > 2-bromo-2-methylbutane.

(*ii*) Due to steric reasons, the order of reactivity of alkyl halides in Sw^2 reactions follows the order :

$1° > 2° > 3°$, therefore the order of reactivity of the given alkyl bromides is:—

2-bromo-3-methylbutane > 2-bromo-3-methylbutane > 2-bromo-2-methylbutane.

(*iii*) 1-bromobutane > 1-bromo-3-methylbutane > 1-bromo-2-methylbutane > 1-bromo-2, 2-dimethylpropane.

Since in case of 1° alkyl halides, steric hindrance increases in the order: n-alkyl halide alkyl halide with a substituent at any position other than the β-position, two substituents at the β-position, therefore, the reactivity decreases in the same order. Thus, the reactivity of the given alkyl bromides decreases.

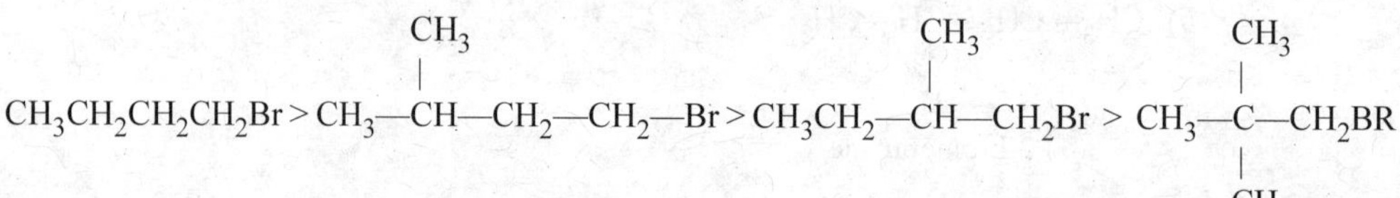

1-bromobutane 1-bromo-3-methylbutane 1-bromo-2-methylbutane 1-bromo-2, 2, dimethylpropane

Q. 9. Give the uses of Freon 12, DDT, carbon tetrachloride and iodoform.

Ans. *Uses of Freon 12*:

(*i*) As a refrigerant.

(*ii*) As a propellant in aerosols and foams.

Uses of DDT—

(*i*) As a insecticide.

(*ii*) It is widely used for sugarcane and fodder crops and to kill mosquitoes and other insects.

Uses of carbon tetrachloride—

(*i*) It is used in the manufacture of refrigerants and propellants for aerosol cans.

(*ii*) It is used as a solvent in the manufacture of pharmaceuticals.

Uses of iodoform—

(*i*) Iodoform was earlier used as an antiseptic for dressing wounds.

(*ii*) It is used in the preparation of certain pharmaceuticals.

Q. 10. What happens when:—

(*i*) n-butyl chloride in treated with alcoholic KOH.

(*ii*) bromobenzene is treated with Mg in the presence of dry ether.

(*iii*) chlorobenzene is subjected to hydrolysis.

(*iv*) ethyl chloride is treated with aqueous KOH.

(*v*) methyl bromide is treated with sodium in presence of dry ether.

Ans. (*i*) $\underset{\text{n-butylchlohide}}{CH_3CH_2—CH_2—CH_2Cl} + KOH\,(alc.) \xrightarrow[\text{(Dehydrohalogenation)}]{\Delta}$

$$\underset{\text{But-1-ene.}}{CH_3—CH_2—CH=CH_2} + KCl + H_2O$$

(*ii*) $\underset{\text{Bromobenzene}}{C_6H_5—Br} + Mg \xrightarrow[\text{(Grignard reaction)}]{\text{Dry ether}} \underset{\text{Phenylmagnesium bromide}}{C_6H_5—Mg—Br}$

(*iii*) $\underset{\text{Chlorobenzene}}{C_6H_5—Cl} + NaOH\,(aN) \xrightarrow{\Delta}$ No reaction

(*iv*) $\underset{\text{Ethyl Chloride}}{CH_3—CH_2—Cl} + KOH\,(aq.) \xrightarrow[\Delta]{\text{Hydrolysis}} \underset{\text{Ethyl alcohol}}{CH_3\,CH_2—OH} + KCl$

(*v*) $\underset{\text{Methyl bromide}}{CH_3—\boxed{Br + 2Na + Br}—CH_3} \xrightarrow[\text{(wirty reaction)}]{\text{dry ether}} \underset{\text{Ethane}}{CH_3—CH_3} + 2\,NaBr$

Higher Order Thinking Skills Hots Questions

1. Arrange the following in increasing order of boiling point:

(*i*) Bromomethane, bromoform, chloromethane, dibromomethane.

(*ii*) Propane, 1-chloropropane, isoprophyl chloride, 1-chlorobutane.

2. How will you obtain 1-bormopropane from propene?

3. Suggest one convenient method for the synthesis of the following:

(*i*) 1-Iodobutane from 1-butene.

(*ii*) Sec-propyl bromide from isobutyric acid.

4. Write short notes on :

(*a*) Wurtz reaction

(*b*) Carbylamine reaction

(*c*) Wurty-Fitting reaction

5. What is meant by SN^1 and SN^2 mechanism? Illustrate with the help of example and discuss the stereochemistry involved. (3)

6. How will you distinguish between: (3)

(*i*) Chlorobenzene and benzyl chloride?

(*ii*) Methanol and ethanol.

(*iii*) Ethylamine and diethylamine.

❑❑❑

CHAPTER

11 ALCOHOLS, PHENOLS AND ETHERS

Syllabus

- ***Alcohols :*** *Nomenclature, methods of preparation, physical and chemical properties (of primary alcohols only); identification of primary, secondary and tertiary alcohols; mechanism of dehydration, uses of methanol and ethanol.*
- ***Phenols :*** *Nomenclature, methods of preparation, physical and chemical properties, acidic nature of phenol, electrophylic substitution reactions, uses of phenols.*
- ***Ethers :*** *Nomenclature, methods of preparation, physical and chemical chemical properties, uses.*

Type 1. Name Reactions

1. **Coupling reaction :** Diazonium salts react with phenols or aromatic amines. A new compound of the general formula Ar—N=N—Ar is formed. These compounds are coloured crystalline solids. Phenols give coupling reactions in alkaline medium while amines react in weakly acidic medium.

   (a) Coupling with phenol : It is done in alkaline medium. (pH = *p* – 10).

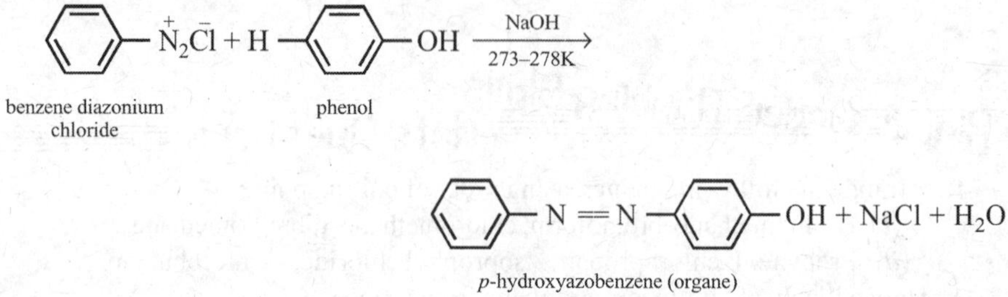

2. **Reimer-Timann reaction :** Phenol is treated with chloroform in the presence of aqueous KOH at 340 K. Main product is *o*-hydroxy benzaldehyde (salicyl aldehyde). Some p-derivative is also formed.

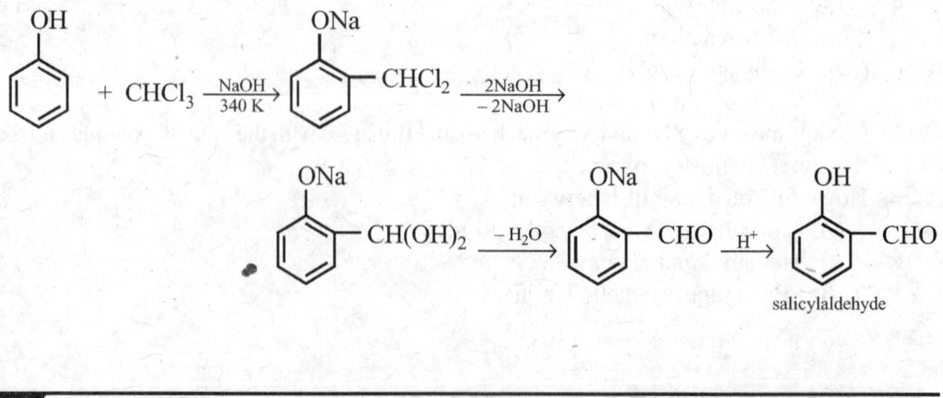

3. **Williamson Synthesis :** . A primary alkyl halide is treated with sodium alkoxide (RO^-Na^+) or sodium phenoxide (C_6H_5ONa) to give sym. or unsym. ether.

$$R'—X + Na^+O^-R \longrightarrow R'—O—R + NaX$$

$$\underset{\text{sod.ethoxide}}{C_2H_5Br + Na^+O^-C_2H_5} \longrightarrow \underset{\text{diethyl ether}}{C_2H_5OC_2H_5} + NaBr$$

4. **Schotten-Baumann reaction :** The process of benzoylation of compounds containing active hydrogen such as phenol, aniline, etc. with benzoyl chloride in the presence of aqueous NaOH is called Schotten—Basumann reaction. For example,

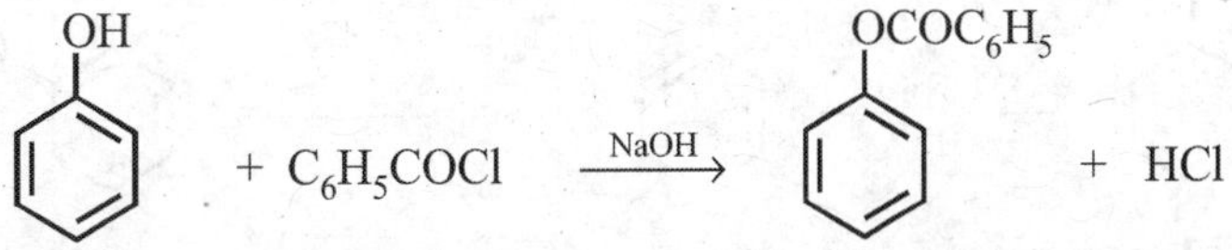

Phenol   Benzoyl chloride   Phenyl benzoate

5. **Transesterification :** When an ester is treated with excess of another alcohol (other than the one from which the ester has been derived) in presence of a base such as the corresponding sodium or potassium alkoxide or an acid (H_2SO_4 or HCl) as catalyst, a new ester and a new alcohol are formed.

$$\underset{\text{Ester}}{R—\overset{\overset{\displaystyle O}{\|}}{C}—OR'} + \underset{\text{Alcohol}}{R''—OH} \xrightleftharpoons[\text{Reflux}]{H^+ \text{ or } R''—ONa,} \underset{\text{New ester}}{R—\overset{\overset{\displaystyle O}{\|}}{C}—OR''} + \underset{\text{New alcohol}}{R'—OH}$$

Example :

$$\underset{n\text{-Butyl acetate}}{CH_3COOC_4H_9} + \underset{\substack{\text{Ethyl alcohol}\\(\textit{Lower alcohol})}}{C_2H_5OH} \xrightleftharpoons{C_2H_5ONa} \underset{\text{Ethyl acetate}}{CH_3COOC_2H_5} + \underset{\substack{n\text{-Butyl alcohol}\\(\textit{Higher alcohol})}}{C_4H_9OH}$$

6. **Cumene Process :** Cumene reacts with air at high temperature by a radical mechanism to form cumene hydroperoxide, which is converted into phenol and acetone by treatment with acid.

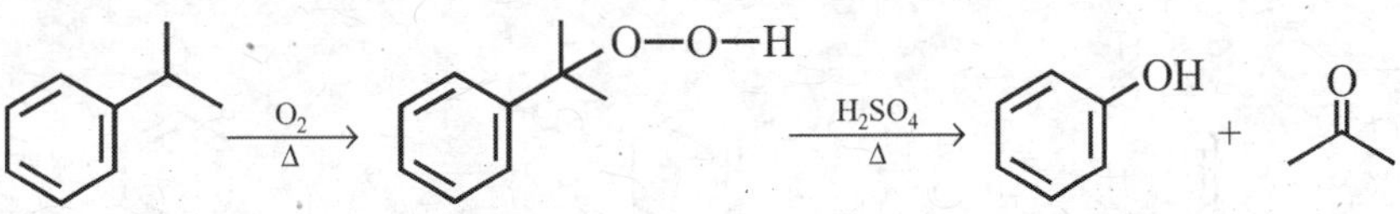

Cumene   Cumene hydroperoxide   Phenol   Acetone

7. **Oxymercuration reduction :** Alkenes react with mercuric acetate in a mixture of tetrahydrofuran (THF) and water to give (hydroxyalkyl) mercury compound, involving addition of—OH and —HgOAc to the double bond. This is called **oxymercuration**. In the second step, sodium borohydride reduces —HgOAc and replaces it with hydrogen. This called **demercuration**.

$$>C=C< + H_2O + \underset{\text{Mercuric acetate}}{Hg(OAc)_2} \xrightarrow{\text{Oxymercuration}} —\underset{OH}{\overset{|}{\underset{|}{C}}}—\underset{HgOAc}{\overset{|}{\underset{|}{C}}}— \xrightarrow[\text{Demercuration}]{NaBH_4} \underset{\text{Alcohol}}{—\underset{OH}{\overset{|}{\underset{|}{C}}}—\underset{H}{\overset{|}{\underset{|}{C}}}—}$$

8. **Kolbe's Reaction :** Sodium salt of phenol reacts with CO_2 under high pressure of 4-7 atm. at about 400 K to form salicylic acid.

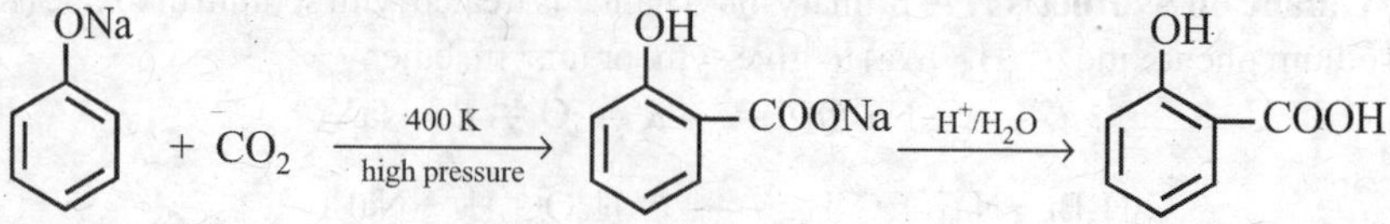

salicylic acid

Type 2. Conversion

1. Phenol to Asprin

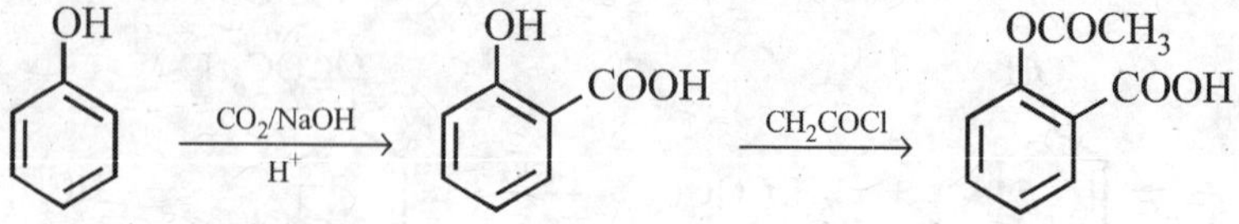

2. Propanol-1 to propanol-2

$$CH_3—CH_2—CH_2—OH \xrightarrow{H_2SO_4} CH_3—CH=CH_2 \xrightarrow[H_2SO_4]{H_2O} CH_3—\underset{\displaystyle OH}{\underset{|}{CH}}—CH_3$$

3. Propanol-2 to propanol-1

$$CH_3—\underset{\displaystyle OH}{\underset{|}{CH}}—CH_3 \xrightarrow{H_2SO_4} CH_3—CH=CH_2 \xrightarrow[H_2O_2/OH^-]{BH_3/THF} CH_3—CH_2—CH_2—OH$$

4. Benzoic acid to phenol

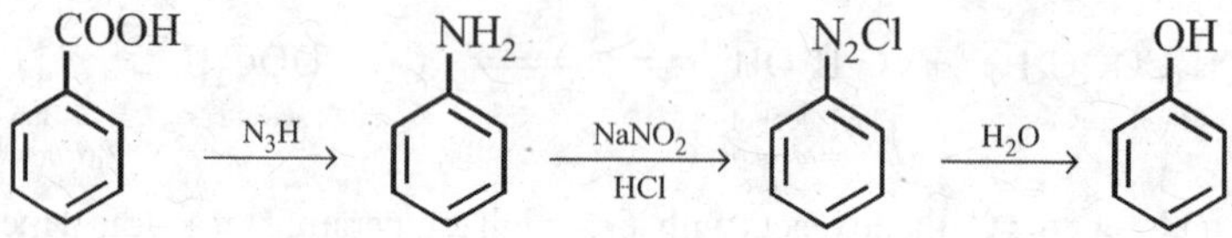

5. Phenol to 1,3,5-tri-nitrophenol

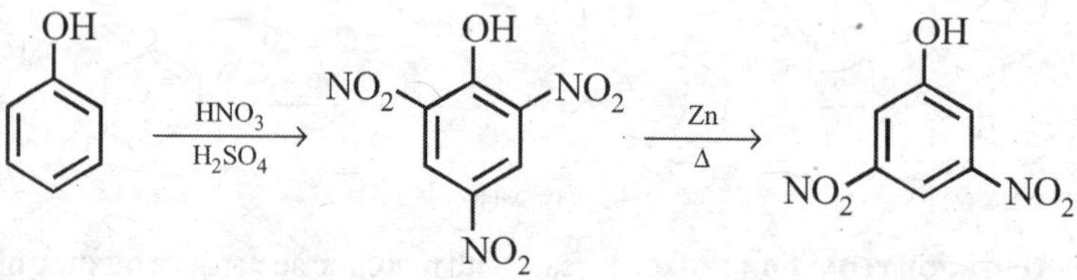

Type 3. Reasoning Type Questions

1. Alcohol is comparatively more soluble in water than hydrocarbons of comparable molecular masses. Explain this fact.

Ans. Alcohols can form H-bonds with water and can also break the H-bonds already existing between water molecules. Therefore, they are soluble in water

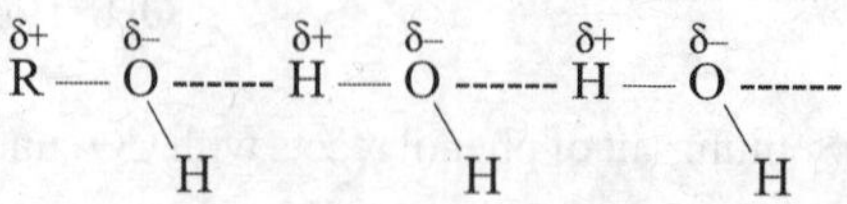

On the other hand, hydrocarbons can neither form H-bonds with water nor can break the H-bonds already existing between water molecules and hence are insoluble in water.

2. Explain why propanol has higher boiling point than of the hydrocarbon, butane ?

Ans. The molecules of butane are held together by weak van der Waals forces of attraction while those of propanol are held together by stronger intermolecular hydrogen bonding.

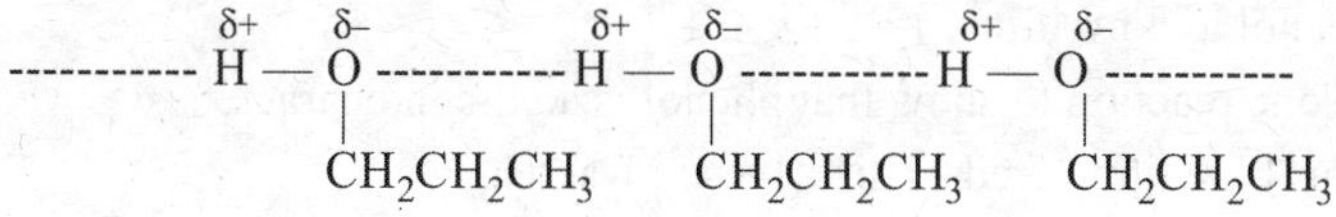

Therefore, the b.p. of propanol is much higher than that of butane.

3. Boiling point of phenol is greater than toluenes.

Ans. Phenol form intermolecular H-bonding but toluene does not show hydrogen bonding.

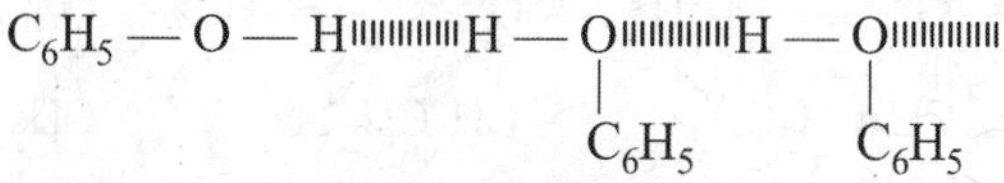

Therefore, boiling point of phenol is greater than toluene.

4. Otho-nitro phenol is less acidic than p-nitro phenol.

Ans. Ortho-nitro phenol is less acidic than p-nitro phenol due to nitramolecular H-bonding.

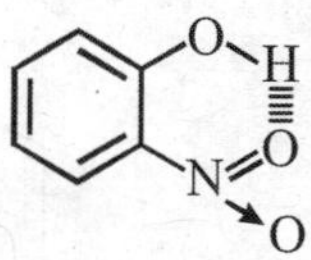

5. Ortho nitrophenol is more acidic than ortho-methoxy phenol.

Ans. This is because —NO_2 (nitro group) is electron withdrawing group and will increase the +ve charge on oxygen to make it more acidic. On the other hand, —OCH_3 group is electron releasing group and will decrease +ve charge on oxygen making it less acidic as O—H bond will not break easily.

Very Short Answer Type Questions

Q. 1. Phenol is acidic while alcohol is neutral when both contain hydroxyl group. Why ?

Ans. Phenyl group is elecron-withdrawing group and thus facilitates the release of H^+ forming phenoxide ion, which get highly stabilised by resonance. Alkyl group is electron-releasing and makes the O—H bond stronger in alcohol and alkoxide ion is not stabilised.

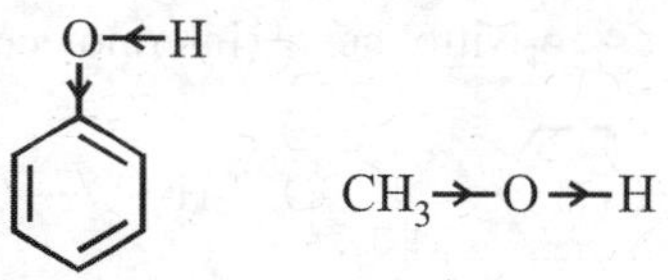

phenol (O—H bond weak) alcohol (O—H bond strong)

Q. 2. Name one reagent which is used for the distinction of primary, secondary and tertiary alcohols.

Ans. Lucas reagent (Anhyd. $ZnCl_2$ + Conc. HCl)

Q. 3. What is the order of dehydration of primary, secondary and tertiary alcohols?

Ans. Tertiary > Secondary > Primary.

Q. 4. What is the order of reactivity of HCl, HBr and HI with alcohols?

Ans. HI > HBr > HCl.

Q. 5. What is usually added to ethyl alcohol to make it unfit for drinking purposes?

Ans. Methanol and pyridine.

Q. 6. Give one reaction to show that phenol is acidic in character.

Ans. It turns blue litmus red or dissolves in NaOH.

Q. 7. Explain why propanol has higher boiling point than that of the hydrocarbon, butane?

Ans. The molecules of butane are held together by weak vander waals forces of attraction while those of propanol are held together by stronger intermolecular hydrogen bonding:

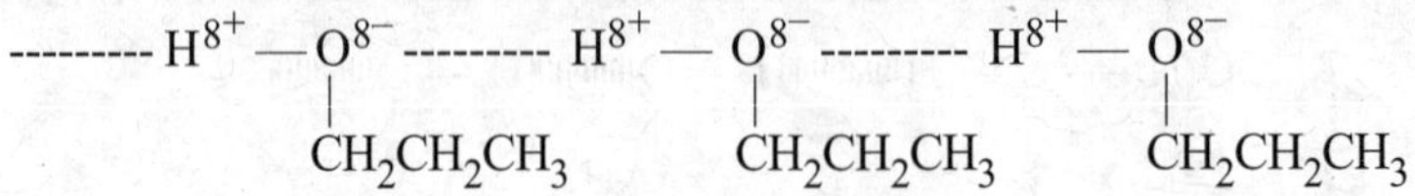

Therefore, the b.p. of propanol is much higher than that of butane.

Q. 8. Give the structures and IUPAC names of monohydric phenols of molecular formula C_7H_8O.

Ans. The three isomers are:—

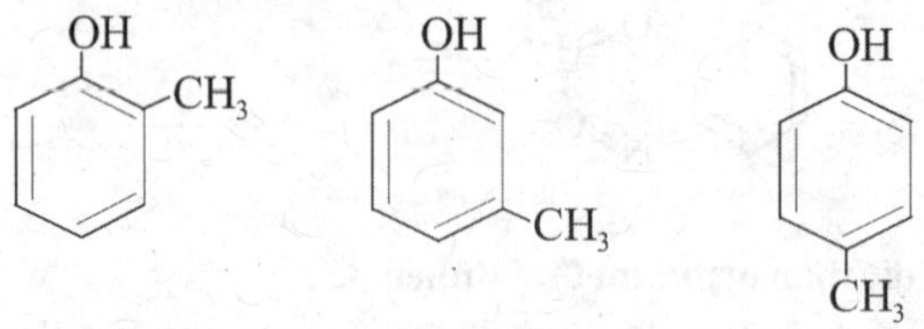

2-methylphenol or o-cresol   2-methylphenol or m-cresol   4-methylphenol or p-cresol

Q. 9. While separating a mixture of ortho and para-nitrophenols by steam distillation, name the isomer which will be steam volatile? Give reasons.

Ans. O-isomer is steam volatile due to chelation (interamolecular H-bonding) while P-isomer is not steam volatile due to association of molecules of intermolecular H-bonding.

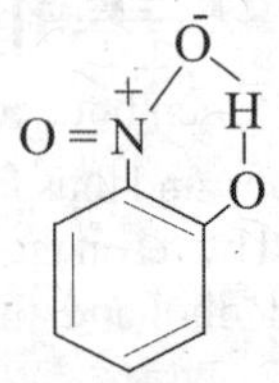

o-Nitrophenol (Intermolecular H-bonding)

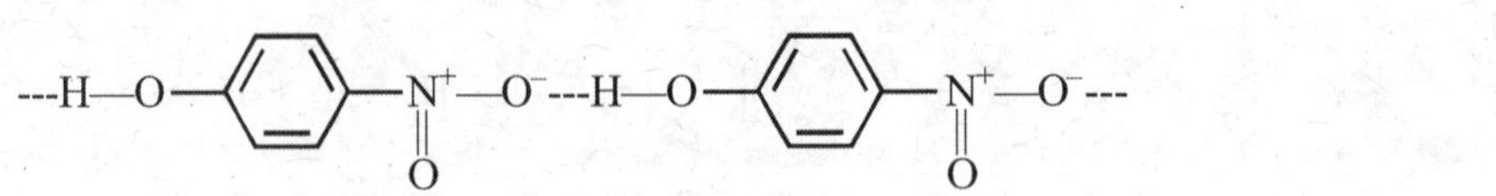

p-nitrophenol (Intramolecular H-bonding)

Q. 10. Write chemical reaction for the preparation of phenol from chlorobenzene.

Ans.

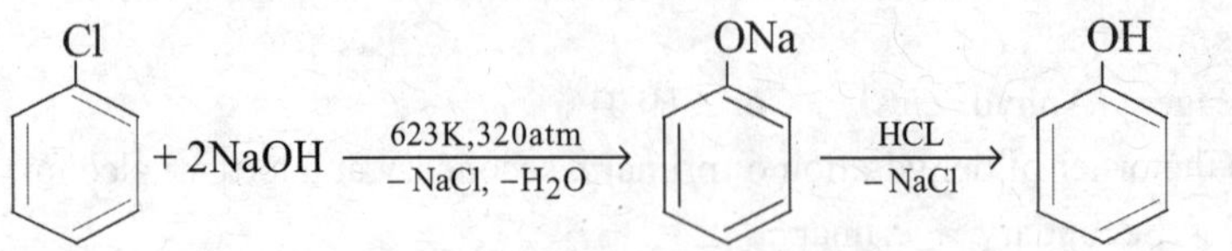

Chlorobenzene   Sod. Phenoxide   Phenol

Q. 11. You are given benzene, conc. H_2SO_4 and NaOH. Write the equations for the preparation of phenol using these reagents.

Ans. $\underset{\text{Benzene}}{C_6H_6} \xrightarrow[\text{(Sulphonation)}]{\text{Conc.}H_2SO_4,\Delta} \underset{\text{Benzene sulphonic acid}}{C_6H_5SO_3O} \xrightarrow[-Na_2SO_3]{\text{NaOH, fure 573 K}}$

$\underset{\text{Sod. Phenoxide}}{C_6H_5ONa} \xrightarrow[-NaCl]{\text{DilHCl}} \underset{\text{Phenol}}{C_6H_5OH}$

Q. 12. Give one reaction that shows the acidic nature of phenol. Compare its acidity with that of ethanol.

Ans. *Reaction with sodiumhydroxide—*

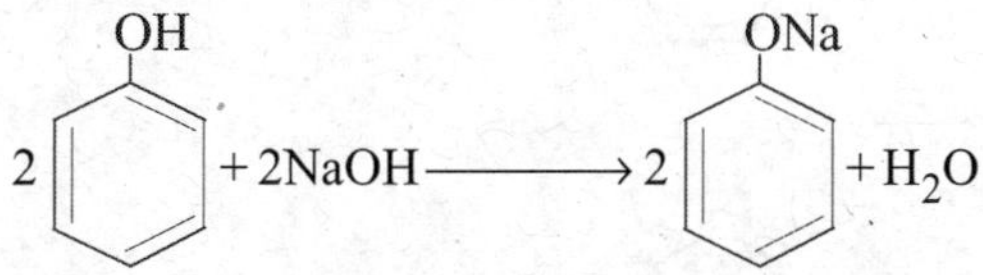

Phenol Sod. Phenoxidc

Phenol is more acidic than ethanol. This is due to the reason that the phenoxide ion left after the loss of a proton from phenol is stabilized by resonance while ethoxide ion is not.

Q. 13. How will you convert phenol to salicylic acid?

Ans.

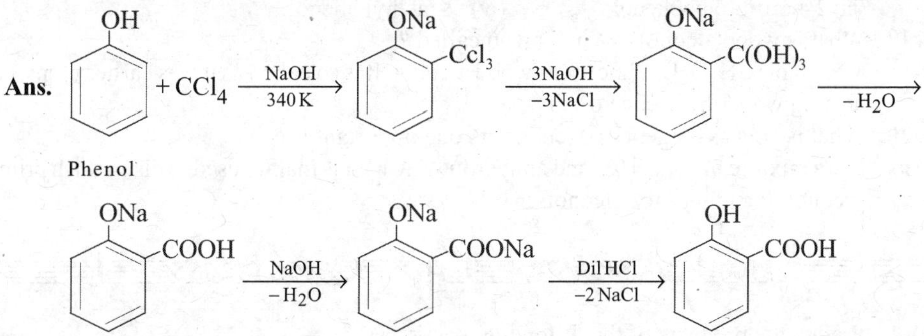

2-Hydroxybenzoic acid
(Salicylic acid)

Q. 14. What is dephenolisation?

Ans. When phenol is heated with Zn dust in alcohol, benzene is obtained. This reaction is called dephenolisation

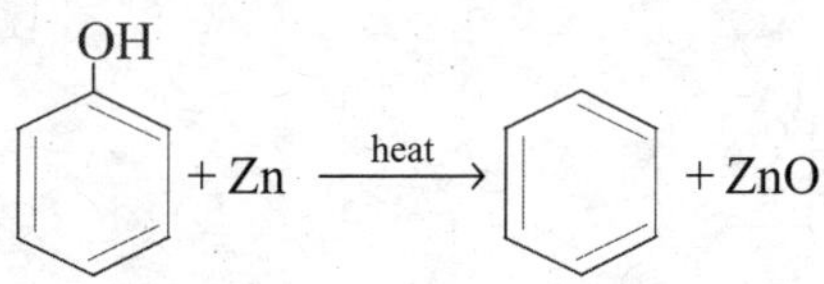

Phenol Benzene

Q. 15. Why are higher ethers insoluble in water?

Ans. Higher ethers are insoluble in water because due to the bigger size of the alkyl groups, the oxygen atom in ethers fails to form intermolecular H-bonds with water.

Q. 16. Write IUPAC name of following compound :

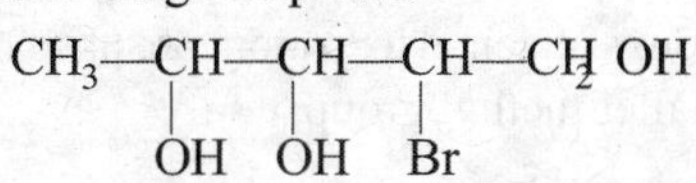

Ans. 2-Bromo-1, 3, 4-pentanetriol (or 2-bromo pentane-1,3,4-triol).

Q. 17. Write IUPAC names of the following :

(i) 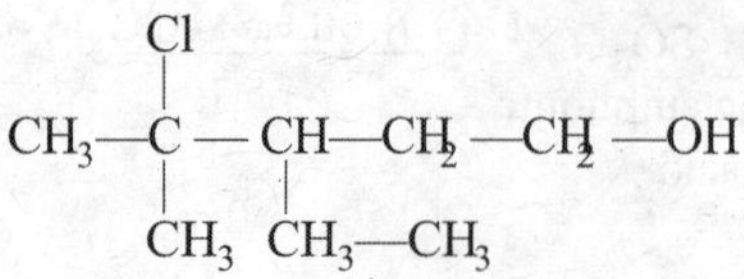 (ii) 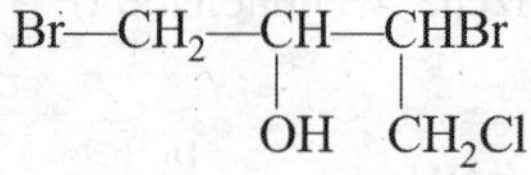

Ans. (i) 4-chloro-3-ethyl-4-methyl-1-pentanol

(ii) 1,3-dibromo-4-chloro-2-butanol.

Q. 18. Write IUPAC names of the following :

(i) 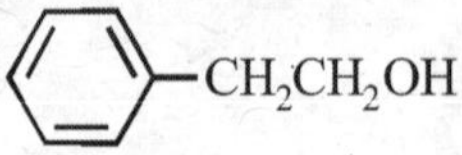 (ii) 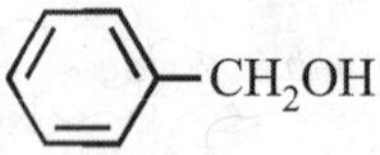

(iii) 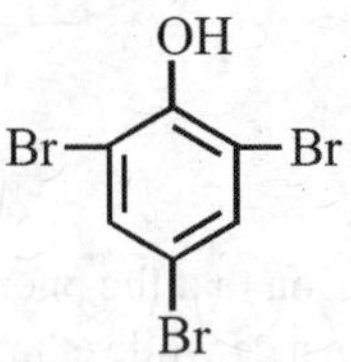 (iv) 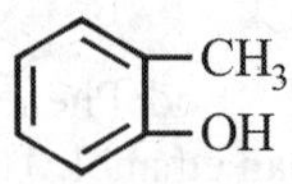

Ans. (i) 2-phenyl ethanol (ii) Phenyl methanol

(iii) 2,4,6-tribromophenol (iv) 2-methyl phenol

Q. 19. What is wood alcohol ? Why is it so called ?

Ans. Methanol (CH_3OH) is known as wood alcohol. It is so called as it was earlier prepared by heating wood in absence of air.

Q. 20. What is 'Lucas reagent' ? Mention its one important use.

Ans. It is a mixture of conc. HCl and anhydrous $ZnCl_2$. It is mainly used to distinguish primary, secondary and tertiary alcohols.

Short Answer Type Questions – I

Q. 1. Predict the products of the following reactions :

(i) $CH_3—CH_2—CH_2—O—CH_3 + HBr \longrightarrow$

(ii) 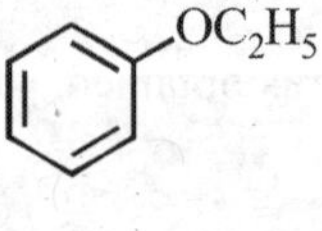 + $HBr \longrightarrow$

(iii) 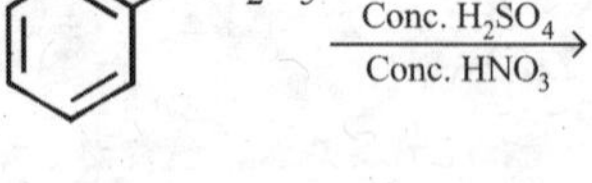

(iv) $(CH_3)_3C—OC_2H_5 \xrightarrow{HI}$

Ans. (i) $CH_3—CH_2—O—CH_3 + HBr \xrightarrow{373K} \underset{\text{Propan-1-ol}}{CH_3CH_2CH_2—OH} + \underset{\text{Bromomethane}}{CH_3Br}$

Both the alkyl groups attached to O atom are primary and, therefore, attack of Br^- ion occurs on the smaller methyl group.

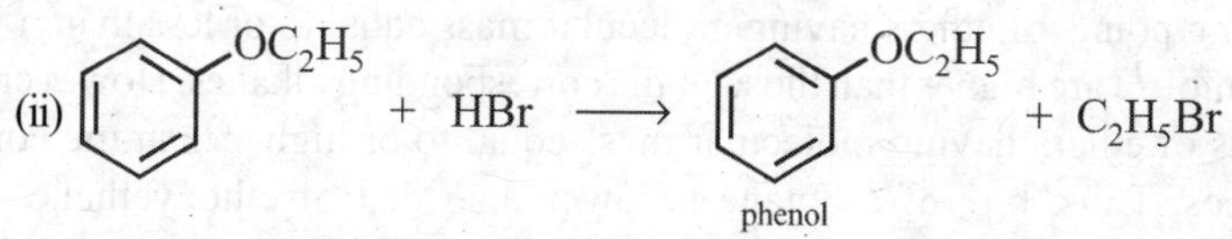

phenol

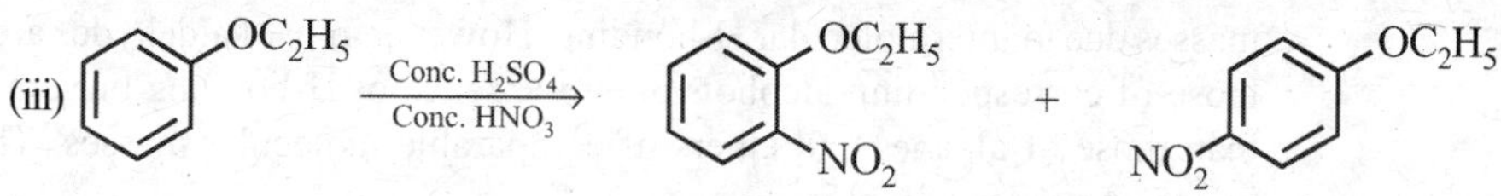

2-Nitro-1-ethoxybenzene (Minor) — 4-Nitro-1-ethoxybenzene (Major)

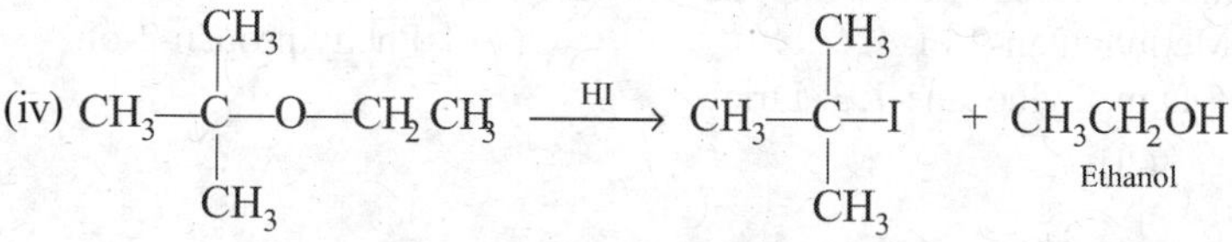

tert-butyl iodide

Q. 2. Give the structures and IUPAC names of products expected from the following reactions:
(*a*) Catalytic reduction of butanol.
(*b*) Hydration of propene in presence of concentrated sulphuric acid.
(*c*) Reaction of propanone with methylmagnesium bromide followed by hydrolysis.

Ans. (*a*) $\underset{\text{Butanal}}{CH_3CH_2CH_2CHO} \xrightarrow{H_2/Ni} \underset{\text{Butan-1-ol}}{CH_3CH_2CH_2CH_2OH}$

(*b*) $\underset{\text{Propene}}{CH_3CH=CH_2} \xrightarrow[H_2SO_4]{\text{Conc.}} \underset{\text{Isopropyl hydrogen sulphate}}{CH_3-\underset{OSO_3H}{\underset{|}{CH}}-CH_3} \xrightarrow[-H_2SO_4]{H_2O,\text{ boil}} \underset{\text{Propan-2-ol}}{CH_3-\underset{OH}{\underset{|}{CH}}-CH_3}$

(*c*) 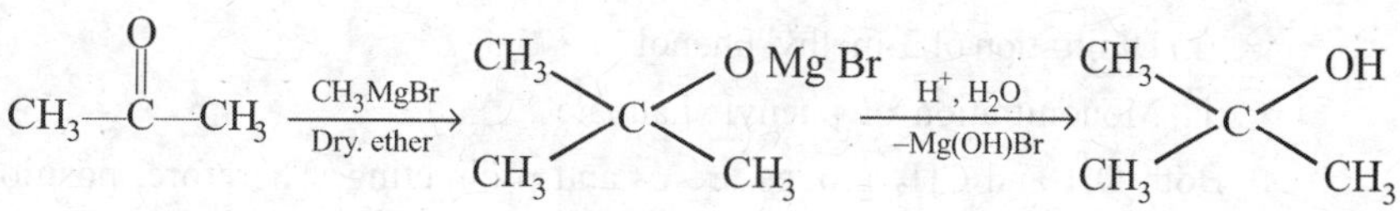

Propanone — Addition product — 2-methylpropon-2-ol

Q. 3. Arrange the folloiwng sets of compounds in order of their increasing boiling points :
(i) Pentan-1-ol, butan-1-ol, butan-2-ol, ethanol, propan-1-ol, methanol.
(ii) Pentan-1-ol, n-butane, pentanal, ehoxy ehtane.

Ans. Increasing order of boiling points :
(i) Methanol < ethanol < propan-1-ol < butan-2-ol < butan-1-ol < pentan-1-ol
(ii) *n*-Butane < ethoxy ethane < pentanal < pentan-1-ol.

Q. 4. Arrange the following compounds in increasing order of boiling points:
(*a*) Pentan-1-ol, butan-l-ol, butan-2-ol, ethanol, propan-1-ol, methanol.
(*b*) Pentan-1-ol, n-butana, pentanal, ethyoxyethane.

Ans. (*a*) Boiling points increase regularly as the molecular mass increases due to the corresponding increase in their vander waals forces of attraction. Thus, boiling points increase in the order.
Methanol < ethanol < propan-1-ol < butan-2-ol < butan-1-ol < pentan-1-ol.

(*b*) Boiling points of ethers having molecular mass equal to or less than n-butane (i.e., 58 g mol^{-1}) are higher than those of the corresponding alkanes. However, the boiling points of ethers having molecular mass equal to or higher than the corresponding alkanes. Thus, b.p. of n-butane is lower than that of ethoxyethane. The b.p. of alcohols are much higher than those of alkanes and ethers of comparable molecular masses due to intermolecular H-bonding. However, b.p. of aldehydes are lower than those of corresponding alcohols due to absence of H-bonding but are still higher than those of alkanes and ethers of comparable molecular masses. Thus, overall increasing order of b.p. is

n-butane < ethoxyethane < pentanal < pentan-1-ol.

Q. 5. Write the structures of the compounds whose IUPAC names are as follows:

(*i*) 2-Methylbutan-2-ol (*ii*) 1-Phenylpropan-2-ol

(*iii*) 3, 5-Dimethylhexane-1, 3, 5 triol

Ans. (*i*) 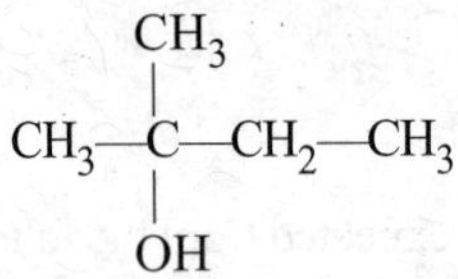

(*ii*) 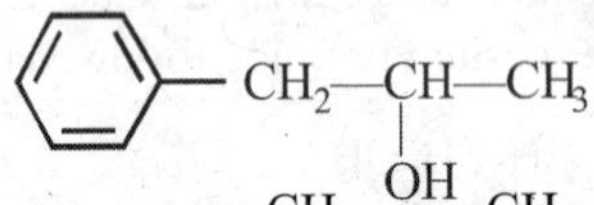

(*iii*) 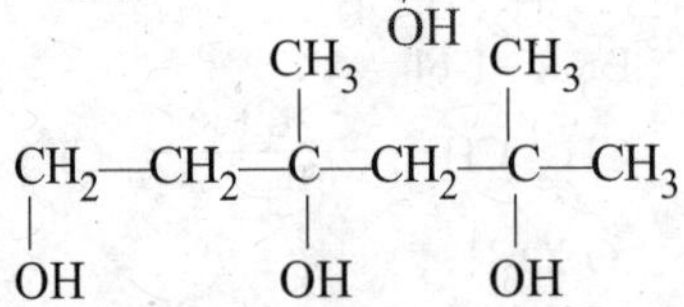

Q. 6. Write the structures of the major products expected from the following reactions :

(i) Mononitration of 3-methyl phenol

(ii) Dinitration of 3-methyl phenol

(iii) Mononitration of phenylethanoate

Ans. Both OH and CH_3 groups are o- and p-directing. Therefore, position 2,4 and 6 are activated. But due to stearic hindrance, substitution does not occur at position 2.

(i) 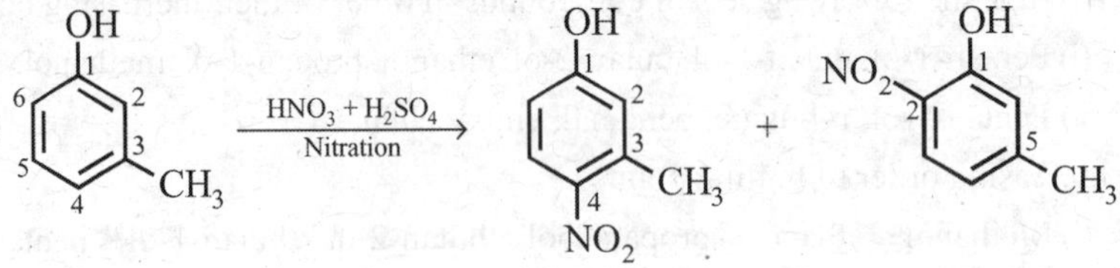

4-Nitro-3-methylphenol 2-Nitro-5-methylphenol

(ii) 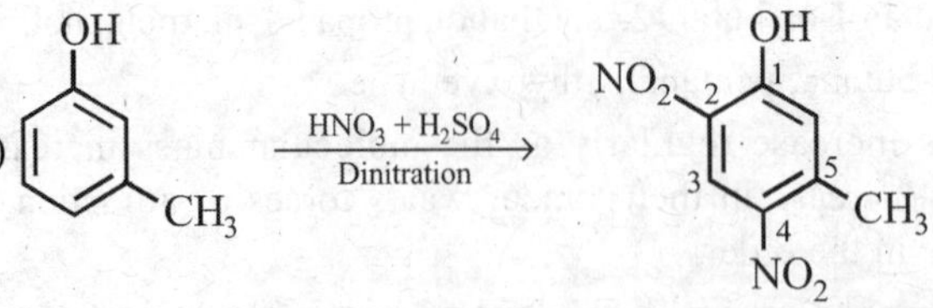

2,4-Dinitro-5-methylphenol

(iii) 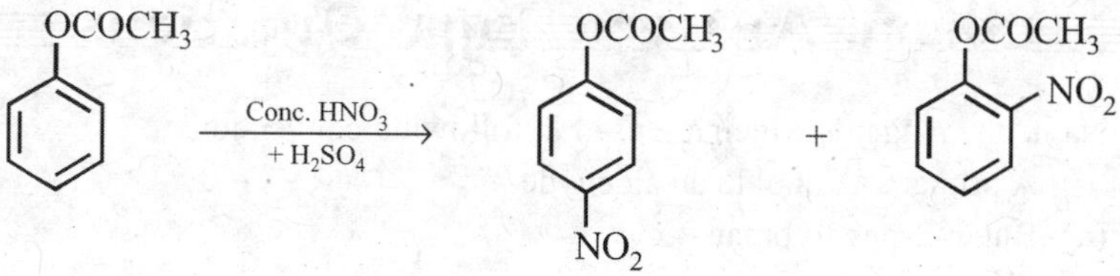

4-Nitrophenyl ethanoate (major) 2-Nitrophenyl ethanoate

Q.7. The following is not an appropriate reaction for the preparation of *t*-butyl ether :

$$C_2H_5ONa + CH_3-C(CH_3)_2-Cl \longrightarrow CH_3-C(CH_3)_2-OC_2H_5$$

(i) What would be the major product of the reaction ?

(ii) Write a suitable reaction for the preparation of tert-butyl ethyl ether.

Ans. (i) The major product of the given reaction is 2-methyl prop-1-ene. This is becaues sodium ethoxide is a strong nucleophile as well as a strong base. Therefore, elimination reaction predominates over substitution.

$$\text{(ii) } CH_3-C(CH_3)_2-\ddot{\underset{\cdot\cdot}{O}}^{-}\,Na^{+} + CH_3CH_2Cl \xrightarrow[-NaCl]{} CH_3-C(CH_3)_2-OCH_2CH_3$$

tert-butyl ethyl ether

Q. 8. Write all the possible isomers of C_4H_9OH and classify them as:

(*a*) Chain isomers (*b*) Position isomers

Ans. The possible isomers of C_4H_9OH are:

(*a*) Chain isomers:

(*i*) $CH_3-CH_2-CH_2-CH_2OH$ (*ii*) $CH_3-CH(CH_3)-CH_2OH$

(*b*) Position isomers:

(*i*) $CH_3-CH_2-CH_2-CH_2OH$ (*ii*) $CH_3-CH(OH)-CH_2CH_3$

Q. 9. How will you distinguish between 1-Phenyl-ethanol and 2-Phenylethanol?

Ans. By iodoform test-1-Phenylethanol contains the grouping —CHOH — CH_3 linked to carbon and hence gives iodoform test while 2-Phenyl ethanol does not contain the grouping —CHOH—CH_3 and hence does not give iodoform test.

$$C_6H_5-CHOH-CH_3 \xrightarrow{I_2/NaOH} CHI_3$$

1-Phenylethanol Iodoform

$$C_6H_5CH_2CH_2OH \xrightarrow{I_2/NaOH} \text{No reaction}$$

2-Phenylethanol

Short Answer Type Questions – II

Q. 1. Name the reagents which are used in following conversions:

(*i*) A primary alcohol to an aldehyde

(*ii*) Butan-2-one to butan 2-ol

(*iii*) Phenol to 2, 4, 6-tribromophenol

Ans. (*i*) Pyridinium chlorochromate convcerts 1° alcohols to aldehyde.

$$\underset{1^\circ \text{ alcohol}}{R-CH_2-CH_2-CHO} \xrightarrow[CH_2Cl_2]{C_6H_5NH^+CrO_3Cl^-} \underset{\text{Aldehyde}}{R-CH_2-CH_2-CHO}$$

(*ii*) Butan-2-one can be reduced to butan 2-ol by reagents such as Ni/H_2, Na/alcohol, $NaBH_4$ or $LiAlH_4$.

$$\underset{\text{Butan-2-one}}{CH_3-\overset{\overset{O}{\|}}{C}-CH_2CH_3} \xrightarrow{NaBH_4} \underset{\text{Butan-2-ol}}{CH_3-\overset{\overset{OH}{|}}{CH}-CH_2CH_3}$$

(*iii*) Phenol reacts with Br_2-H_2O to give 2, 4, 6-tri-bromophenol.

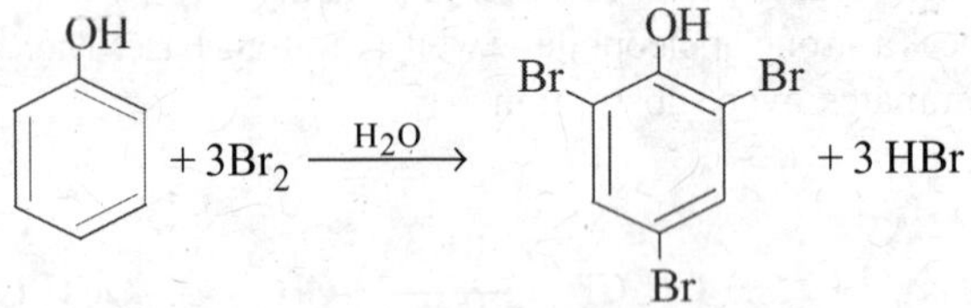

2, 4, 6-Tribromophenol
(white ppt.)

Q. 2. Give equations of the following reactions:—

(*i*) Oxidation of propan-1-ol with alkaline $KMnO_4$ solution.

(*ii*) Bromine in CS_2 with phenol.

(*iii*) Dilute nitric acid with phenol.

(*iv*) Treating phenol with chloroform in presence of aqueous NaOH.

Ans. (*i*) $CH_3CH_2CH_2OH + 2[O] \xrightarrow[\text{Oxidation}]{\text{Alk.}KMnO_4} \underset{\text{Propanoic acid}}{CH_3CH_2COOH} + H_2O$

(*ii*)

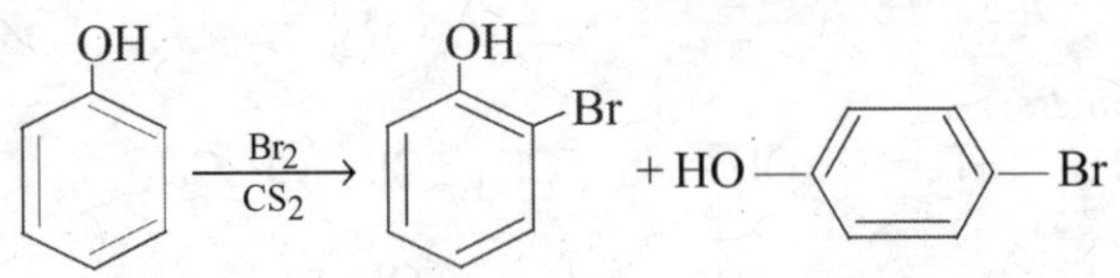

Phenol — o-Bromophenol (minor product) — p-Bromophenol (major product)

(*iii*)

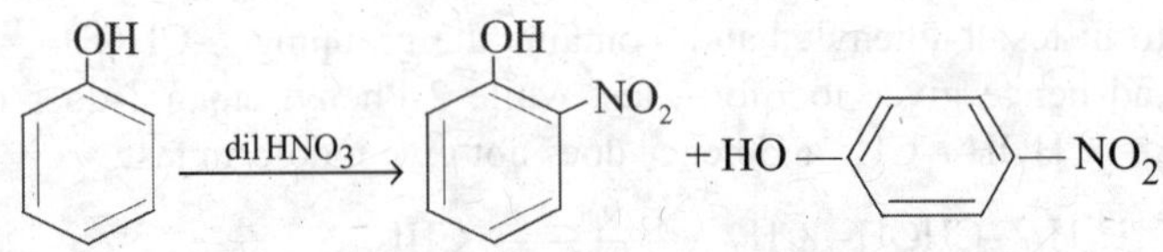

Phenol — o-Nitrophenol (major product) — p-Nitrophenol (minor product)

(iv) 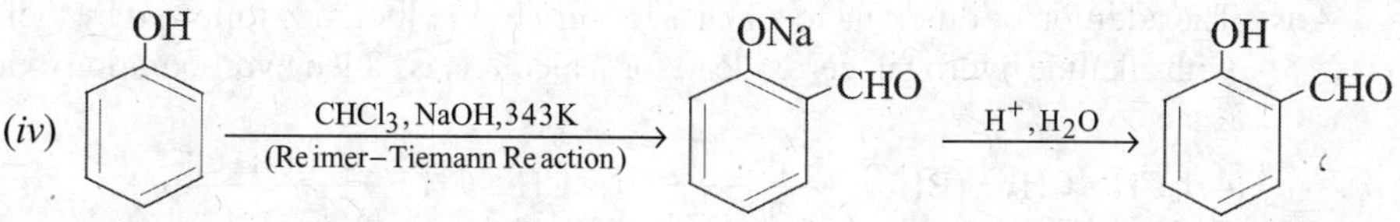

Phenol → Salicylaldehyde (major product)

Q. 3. (*i*) Draw the structures of all isomeric alcohols of molecular formula $C_5H_{12}O$ and give their IUPAC names.

(*ii*) Classify the isomers of alcohols in questions, as primary, secondary and tertiary alcohols.

Ans. Eight isomers are possible. These are:

(*a*) $CH_3—CH_2—CH_2—CH_2OH$

Pentan–1–ol (1°)

(*b*) $CH_3—CH_2—CH_2—\underset{}{\overset{OH}{\overset{|}{C}H}}—CH_3$

Pentan–2–ol (2°)

(*c*) $CH_3—CH_2—\overset{OH}{\overset{|}{C}H}—CH_2CH_3$

Pentan–3–ol (2°)

(*d*) $CH_3CH_2—\overset{CH_3}{\overset{|}{C}H}—CH_2OH$

2-methylbutan–1–ol (1°)

(*e*) $CH_3—\overset{CH_3}{\overset{|}{C}H}—CH_2—CH_2—OH$

3-Methylbutan–1–ol (1°)

(f) $CH_3—\underset{OH}{\underset{|}{\overset{CH_3}{\overset{|}{C}}}}—CH_2\ CH_3$

2-Methylbutane-2-ol (3°)

(*g*) $CH_3—\underset{CH_3}{\underset{|}{\overset{CH_3}{\overset{|}{C}}}}—CH_2OH$

2, 2-Dimethylpropan–1–ol (1°)

(*h*) $CH_3—\overset{CH_3}{\overset{|}{C}H}—\overset{OH}{\overset{|}{C}H}—CH_3$

3-Methylbutan–2–ol (2°)

Q. 4. What is meant by hydroboration-oxidation reaction? Illustrate with an example.

Ans. The addition of diborane to alkenes to form trialkylboranes followed by their oxidation with alkaline hydrogen peroxide to form alcohols is called hydroboration oxidation. For example—

$$\underset{\text{Propene}}{CH_3CH=CH_2} + \underset{\text{Diborane}}{(BH_3)_2} \xrightarrow[\text{ether}]{\text{Dry}} \underset{\quad\ \ \mathrm{H}\qquad \mathrm{BH_2}}{CH_3-\underset{|}{CH}-\underset{|}{CH_2}} \xrightarrow{CH_3CH=CH_2}$$

$$(CH_3CH_2CH_2)_2B-H \xrightarrow{CH_3CH=CH_2} \underset{\text{Tri-n-Propylborane}}{(CH_3CH_2CH_2)_3B}$$

$$\underset{\text{Tri-n-propylborane}}{(CH_3CH_2CH_2)_3B + 3H_2O_2} \xrightarrow{OH^-,\,H_2O} \underset{\text{Propan-2-ol}}{3CH_3CH_2OH} + \underset{\text{Boric acid}}{B(OH)_3}$$

Q. 5. Give structures of the products you would expect when each of the following alcohol reacts with

(*a*) $HCl-ZnCl_2$ (*b*) HBr

(*c*) $SOCl_2$

(*i*) Butan-1-ol (*ii*) 2-Methylbutan-2-ol.

Ans. (*a*) With $HCl-ZnCl_2$ (Lucas reagent)

$$\underset{\text{2-Methylbutan-2-ol (3°)}}{CH_3-\underset{OH}{\overset{CH_3}{C}}-CH_2CH_3} + \text{HCL (Conc.)} \xrightarrow[-H_2O]{\text{Anhyd. }ZnCl_2} \underset{\substack{\text{2-chloro-2-methylbutane}\\ \text{(white turbidity)}}}{CH_3-\underset{Cl}{\overset{CH_3}{C}}-CH_2CH_3}$$

$$\underset{\text{Butan-1-ol (1°)}}{CH_3CH_2CH_2CH_2-OH} + \text{HCl (Conc.)} \xrightarrow{\text{Anhyd. }ZnCl_2} \text{No reaction at room temp.}$$

(*b*) Both the alcohols react to produce the corresponding alkyl bromides.

$$\underset{\text{Butan-1-ol (1°)}}{CH_3CH_2CH_2CH_2OH} + HBr \xrightarrow{\Delta} \underset{\text{1-Bromobutane}}{CH_3CH_2CH_2CH_2Br} + H_2O$$

$$\underset{\text{2-Methylbutan-2-ol (3°)}}{CH_3-\underset{OH}{\overset{CH_3}{C}}-CH_2CH_3} + HBr \xrightarrow{\Delta} \underset{\text{2-Bromo-2-methylbutane}}{CH_3-\underset{Br}{\overset{CH_3}{C}}-CH_2CH_3} + H_2O$$

(*c*) Both the alcohols react to form the corresponding alkyl chlorides

$$\underset{\text{Butan-1-ol (1°)}}{CH_3CH_2CH_2CH_2OH} + SOCl_2 \xrightarrow{\Delta} \underset{\text{1-chlorobutane}}{CH_3CH_2CH_2CH_2Cl} + SO_2 + HCl$$

$$\underset{\text{2-Methylbutan-2-ol}}{CH_3-\underset{OH}{\overset{CH_3}{C}}-CH_2CH_3} + SOCl_2 \xrightarrow{\Delta} \underset{\text{2-Chloro-2-methylbutane}}{CH_3-\underset{Cl}{\overset{CH_3}{C}}-CH_2CH_3} + SO_2 + HCl$$

Q. 6. Give Lucas test to distinguish between 1°, 2° and 3° alcohols.

Ans. Tertiary alcohols react immediately with Lucas reagent (a solution of $ZnCl_2$ in conc. HCl) to produce an insoluble layer of the 3° alkyl chlorides. Secondary alcohols produce 2°-alkyl chlonides within five minutes whereas primary alcohols produce 1° alkyl chloride only on heating, e.g.

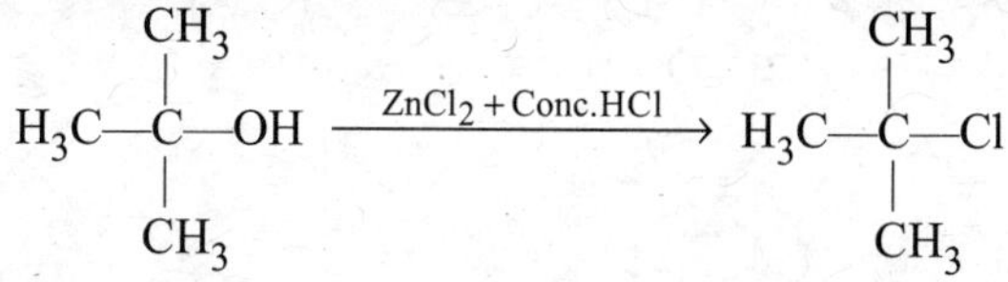

(3° alcohol)

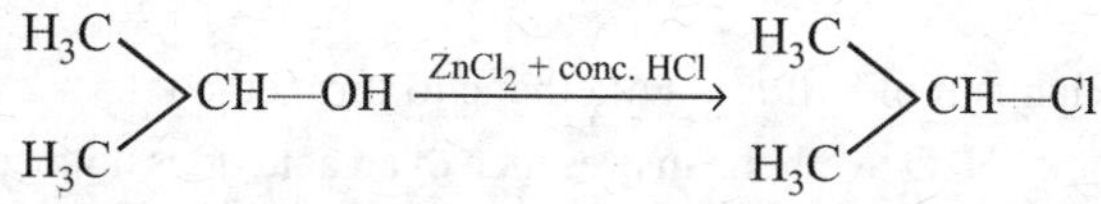

(2° alcohol)

$$CH_3CH_2CH_2CH_2OH \xrightarrow[\Delta]{ZnCl_2 + Conc.HCl} CH_3CH_2CH_2Cl$$

Butan-1-ol
(1°-alcohol)

Q. 7. (*a*) Why o-Nitrophenol has a lower boiling point and less solubility than p-Nitrophenol in water?

(*b*) Introduction of $—NO_2$ group in aromatic nucleus increases the acidity of phenols but introduction of $—CH_3$ group in the nucleus decreases the acidity of phenols. Explain giving reasons.

Ans. (*a*) It is because in o-Nitrophenol due to the presence of intra-molecular H-bonding, o-Nitrophenol exists in the form of individual molecules and hence has lower boiling point and lesser solubility in water. On the other hand, in p-Nitrophenol has the intermolecular H-bonding. Hence, p-Nitrophenol exists in the form of associated molecules. Hence, p-Nitrophenol has higher boiling point and more solubility in water than o-Nitrophenol.

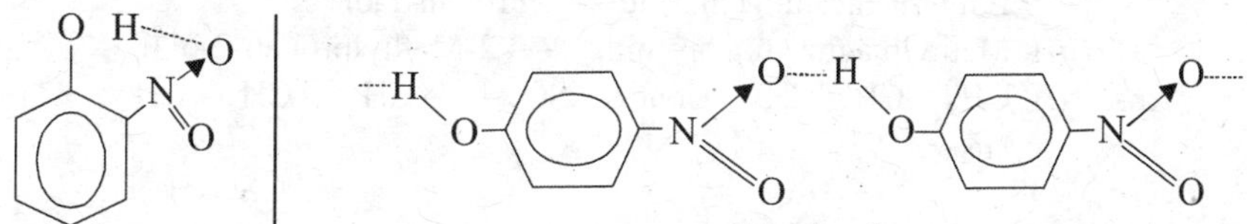

o-Nitrophenol | p-Nitrophenol

(*b*)

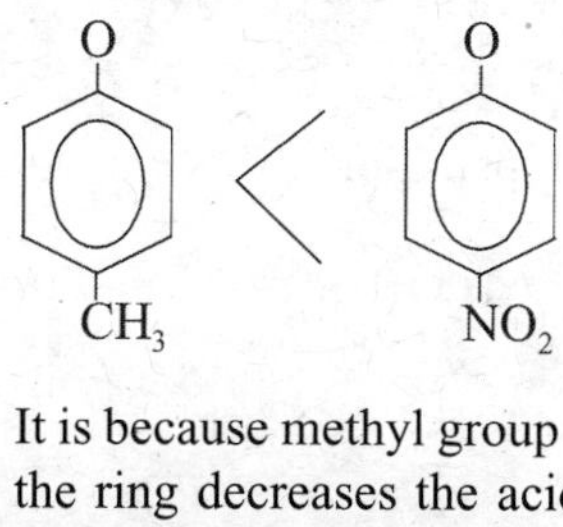

It is because methyl group $(—CH_3)$ is electron releasing, group whose presence on the ring decreases the acidic nature than phenol itself. On the other hand, nitro-group $(—NO_2)$ is electron withdrawing group whose presence on the benzene ring increases the acidic nature than phenol itself.

Q. 8. Which is a stronger acid, phenol or cresol? Explain.

Ans. Cresol is methylphenol. It has three positional isomers: o-Cresol, m-Cresol and p-Cresol. Due to +I effect of CH_3 group, electron density in the O—H bond increases. Therefore, it becomes difficult to break the O—H bond as compared to that in phenol and hence all cresols are less acidic than phenol or phenol is a stronger acid than cresols.

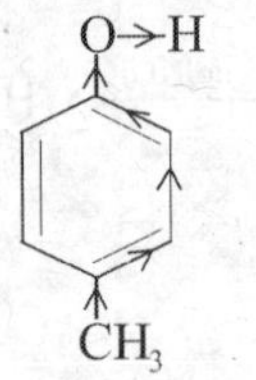

Q. 9. Write the mechanism of hydration of ethene to form ethanol.

Ans. Direct addition of H_2O to ethene in presence of an acid does not occur. Indirectly, ethene is first passed through conc. H_2SO_4, when ethyl hydrogen sulphate is formed.

$$H_2SO_4 \longrightarrow H^+ + O^-SO_2OH$$

$$\underset{\text{Ethene}}{CH_2=CH_2} + H^+ \longrightarrow \underset{\text{Ethyl carbocation}}{CH_3—C^+H_2} \xrightarrow[\text{Fart}]{-OSO_2OH} \underset{\text{Ethyl hydrogen sulphate}}{CH_3—CH_2—OSO_2OH}$$

Ethyl hydrogen sulphate when boiled with water undergoes hydrolysis to form ethanol.

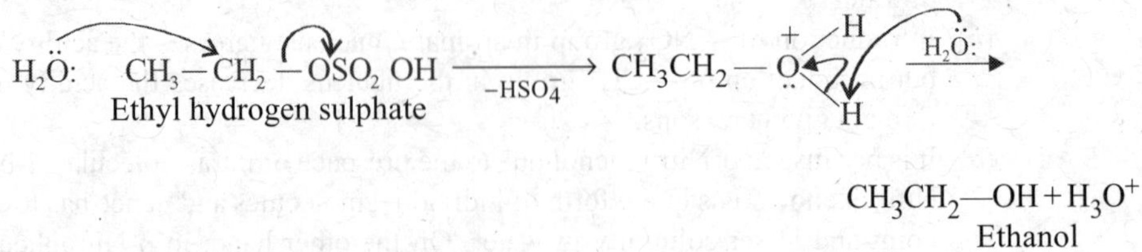

Q. 10. How are the following conversions carried out?

(*i*) Propene ⟶ Propan 2-ol

(*ii*) Benzyl chloride ⟶ Benzyl alcohol

(*iii*) Ethylmagnesium chloride ⟶ Propan-1-ol

(*iii*) Methylmagnesium bromide ⟶ 2-Methylpropan-2-ol

Ans. (*i*) $\underset{\text{Propene}}{CH_3—CH=CH_2} + \text{Conc. } H_2SO_4 \longrightarrow \underset{\text{Isopropyl hydrogen sulphate}}{CH_3—\underset{|}{\overset{}{CH}}(OSO_3H)—CH_3}$

$$CH_3—\underset{OSO_3H}{\underset{|}{CH}}—CH_3 + H_2O \xrightarrow{\text{Boiling}} \underset{\text{Propan-2-ol}}{CH_3—\underset{OH}{\underset{|}{CH}}—CH_3} + H_2SO_4$$

(*ii*)

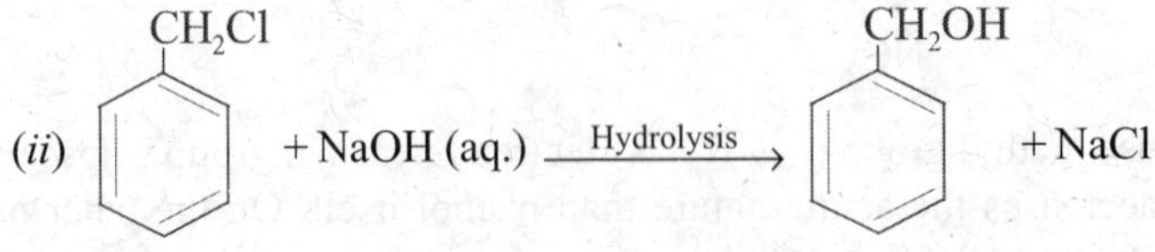

Benzyl chloride Benzyl alcohol

(*iii*)

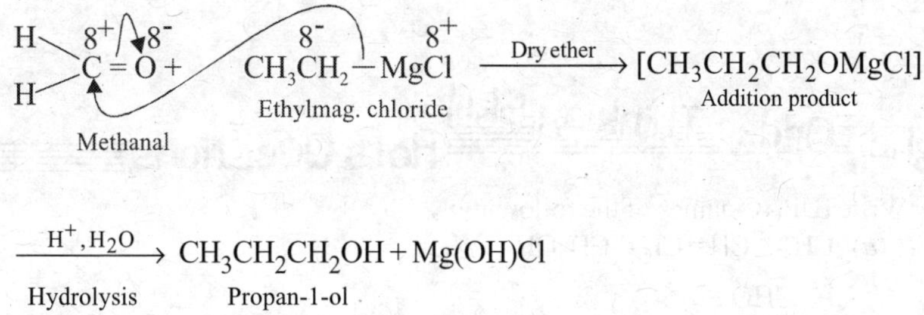

H
H
δ+ δ-
C = O +
Methanal
δ- δ+
CH_3CH_2—MgCl
Ethylmag. chloride
Dry ether
[$CH_3CH_2CH_2OMgCl$]
Addition product
H^+, H_2O
Hydrolysis
$CH_3CH_2CH_2OH$ + Mg(OH)Cl
Propan-1-ol

(*iv*)

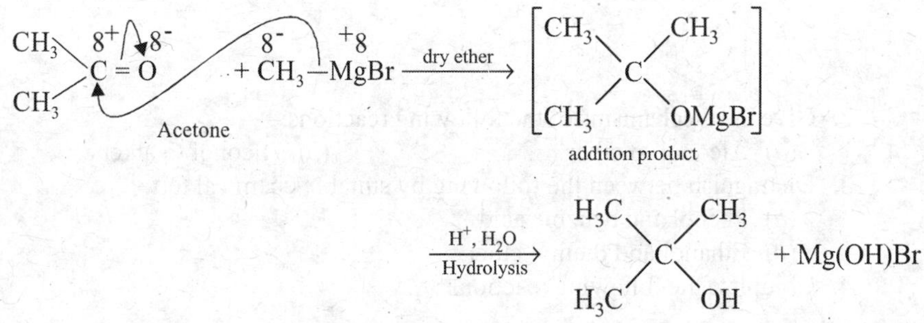

CH_3
CH_3
δ+ δ-
C = O
Acetone
δ- +δ
+ CH_3—MgBr
dry ether
CH_3 CH_3 C CH_3 OMgBr
addition product
H^+, H_2O
Hydrolysis
H_3C CH_3 C H_3C OH
+ Mg(OH)Br

Higher Order Thinking Skills Hots Questions

1. Write IUPAC names of the following:
   (*a*) $CH_3—CH=CH—CH_2OH$
   (*b*) 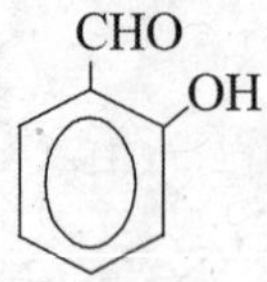

2. Give the mechanisms of the following reactions:—
   (*a*) Alcohol to ether (*b*) Alcohol to alkene
3. Distinguish between the following by suitable chemical tert:
   (*a*) Phenol and benzoic acid
   (*b*) Ethanol and diethyl ether
4. Complete the following reactions :
   (*a*) $C_2H_5OH + NH_3 \xrightarrow[\Delta]{Al_2O_3}$
   (*b*) $(CH_3)_3CCl + KOH\ (alc.) \longrightarrow$
   (*c*) 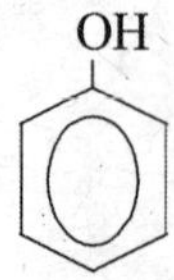 $+ Br_2\ (aq.) \longrightarrow$

5. Convert the following :
   (*a*) Phenol to aspirin
   (*b*) Phenol to oil of winter green.

❑❑❑

CHAPTER

12 ALDEHYDES, KETONES AND CARBOXYLIC ACIDS

Syllabus

- ***Aldehydes and Ketones :*** *Nomenclature, nature of carbonyl group, methods of preparation, physical and chemical properties and mechanism of nucleophilic addition, reactivity of alpha hydrogen in aldehydes; uses.*
- ***Carboxylic Acids :*** *Nomenclature, acidic nature, methods of preparation, physical and chemical properties; uses.*

Type 1. Name Reaction

1. **Aldol condensation :** Two molecules of aldehydes or ketones react in the presence of a dil acid or dil base. A new compound is formed. In aldol condensation, it is the H-atom at the α-carbon atom which takes part in the reaction.

$$\underset{\text{acetaldehyde 2 molecules}}{CH_3\underset{\underset{O}{\|}}{C}H + \overset{\alpha}{C}H_3CHO} \xrightarrow{NaOH} \underset{\text{3-hydroxy butanal (aldol)}}{CH_3\underset{\underset{OH}{|}}{C}H\,CH_2CHO}$$

$$\underset{\text{acetone (2 molecules)}}{(CH_3)_2\underset{\underset{O}{\|}}{C} + CH_3COCH_3} \xrightarrow{Ba(OH)_2} \underset{\text{4-hydroxy-4-methyl-pentan-2-one (diacetone alcohol)}}{(CH_3)_2\underset{\underset{OH}{|}}{C} - CH_2COCH_3}$$

2. **Benzoin condensation :** Benzaldehyde is heated with alocoholic solution of KCN. Two molecules of benzaldehyde condense to give benzoin.

$$\underset{\text{two molecules of benzaldehyde}}{C_6H_5\underset{\underset{O}{\|}}{C}H + \underset{\underset{O}{\|}}{C}HC_6H_5} \xrightarrow[\Delta]{KCN/C_2H_5OH} \underset{\text{benzoin}}{C_6H_5-\underset{\underset{O}{\|}}{C}-CHOH-C_6H_5}$$

3. **Cannizzaro reaction :** This reaction is given by those aldehydes which do not contain H-atom at the α-carbon.This aldehyde is treated with concentrated solution of NaOH. The aldehyde undergoes disproportionation. One molecule of aldehyde is reduced while the other is oxidised. Thus, an alcohol and sodium salt of an acid is obtained.

$$\underset{\text{methanal}}{2HCHO} + NaOH \longrightarrow \underset{\text{methanol}}{CH_3OH} + \underset{\text{sod.formate}}{HCOONa}$$

$$\underset{\text{benzaldehyde}}{2C_6H_5CHO} + NaOH \longrightarrow \underset{\text{benzylalcohol}}{C_6H_5CH_2OH} + \underset{\text{sod.benzoate}}{C_6H_5COONa}$$

$$\underset{\text{2, 2-dimethyl propanal}}{2CH_3-\overset{\overset{\large CH_3}{|}}{\underset{\underset{\large CH_3}{|}}{C}}-CHO} + NaOH \longrightarrow \underset{\text{2, 2-dimethyl propanol}}{CH_3-\overset{\overset{\large CH_3}{|}}{\underset{\underset{\large CH_3}{|}}{C}}-CH_2OH} + \underset{\text{sod. 2,2-dimethyl propanoate}}{CH_3-\overset{\overset{\large CH_3}{|}}{\underset{\underset{\large CH_3}{|}}{C}}-COONa}$$

If a molecule contains two —CHO groups, intermolecular cannizzaro reaction may occur. One —CHO group gets oxidised to —COOH group. The other —CHO group gets reduced to —CH_2OH group.

$$\underset{\text{Glyoxal}}{\begin{matrix} CHO \\ | \\ CHO \end{matrix}} + NaOH \longrightarrow \begin{matrix} CH_2OH \\ | \\ COONa \end{matrix} \xrightarrow{\text{dil. HCl}} \underset{\text{Glycollic acid}}{\begin{matrix} CH_2OH \\ | \\ COOH \end{matrix}}$$

4. **Etard reaction :** Toluene is oxidised by chromyl chloride. A brown complex is formed. This complex is decomposed with water to give benzaldehyde. Chromyl chloride is dissolved in CCl_4 or CS_2.

$$C_6H_5-CH_3 \xrightarrow{CrO_2Cl_2/CS_2} \underset{\text{brown complex}}{\left[C_6H_5-CH\begin{matrix} OCr(OH)Cl_2 \\ OCr(OH)Cl_2 \end{matrix}\right]} \xrightarrow{H_2O} C_6H_5CHO$$

5. **Esterification reaction :** Alcohols and carboxylic acids react together in the presence of dry HCl gas or H_2SO_4 as catalyst. An ester is formed and a molecule of water is given out. It is called **esterification.** The reaction is reversible. The reverse reaction is called **hydrolysis.** Dry HCl gas or conc. H_2SO_4 acts as catalyst for both the forward and backward reaction.

$$\underset{\text{carboxylic acid}}{R-CO\boxed{OH\ +\ H}}\underset{\text{alcohol}}{OR'} \xrightleftharpoons{\text{conc. } H_2SO_4} \underset{\text{ester}}{RCOOR'} + H_2O$$

$$CH_3CO\boxed{OH\ +\ H}OC_2H_5 \xrightleftharpoons{\text{conc. } H_2SO_4} \underset{\text{Ethyl acetate}}{CH_3COOC_2H_5} + H_2O$$

$$HCO\boxed{OH\ +\ H}OCH_3 \xrightleftharpoons{\text{conc. } H_2SO_4} \underset{\text{Methyl formate}}{HCOOCH_3} + H_2O$$

6. **Gattermann– Koch reaction :** This reaction is used to prepare aryl halides form diazonium salts. Diazonium salt is treated with Cu/HCl or Cu/HBr.

$$C_6H_5N_2^+Cl^- \xrightarrow[\Delta]{Cu/HCl} C_6H_5Cl + N_2$$

$$\underset{\text{Benzene diazonium chloride}}{C_6H_5N_2^+Cl^-} \xrightarrow[\Delta]{Cu/HCl} \underset{\text{bromo benzene}}{C_6H_5Br} + N_2$$

7. **Gattermann–Koch reaction :** This reaction is also called Gattermann-Koch aldehyde synthesis. When a mixture of CO and HCl gas is passed thorugh benzene at 323 K in the presence of

anhydrous $AlCl_3$ as catalyst and small amount of cuprous chloride (CuCl), benzaldehyde is formed. Mixture of CO and HCl is supposed to act as formyl chloride.

$$CO + HCl \longrightarrow \underset{\text{formyl chloride(unstable)}}{HCOCl}$$

$$C_6H_6 + HCOCl \xrightarrow{AlCl_3/CuCl} C_6H_5CHO + HCl$$

8. **Hell-Volhard Zelinsky reaction (HVZ reaction) :** Aliphatic carboxylic acids are treated with Cl_2/red P or Br_2/red P. The H-atoms at the α-carbon of carboxylic acids get successively replaced by the halogen atom. HCOOH does not have α-H-atom. It does not give HVZ reaction.

$$\overset{\alpha}{CH_3}COOH \xrightarrow[-HCl]{Cl_2/\text{red P}} \underset{\text{chloroacetic acid}}{ClCH_2COOH} \xrightarrow[-HCl]{Cl_2/P} \underset{\text{dichloro acetic acid}}{Cl_2CHCOOH} \xrightarrow[-HCl]{Cl_2/P} \underset{\text{trichloro acetic acid}}{Cl_3CCOOH}$$

9. **Perkin reaction :** Benzaldehyde is heated with sod. acetate and acetic anhydride. An unsaturated acid is formed.

$$C_6H_5CHO + \underset{\text{Aceticanhyd.}}{(CH_3CO)_2O} \xrightarrow{CH_3COONa} \underset{\text{Cinnamicacid}}{C_6H_5CH = CH — COOH} + CH_3COOH$$

10. **Rosenmund reduction :** Acid chlorides are reduced with H_2/Pd in boiling xylene to give aldehydes. Pd catalyst is supported on $BaSO_4$. Ketones cannot be prepared by this method.

$$RCOCl + H_2 \xrightarrow{Pd\text{-}BaSO_4} RCHO + HCl$$

$$\underset{\text{acetyl chloride}}{CH_3COCl} + H_2 \xrightarrow{Pd\text{-}BaSO_4} \underset{\text{acetaldehyde}}{CH_3CHO} + HCl$$

Type 2. Reasoning Type Questions

1. **Cyclohexanone forms cyanohydrin in good yield but 2, 2, 6-trimethylcyclohexanone does not.**

Ans.

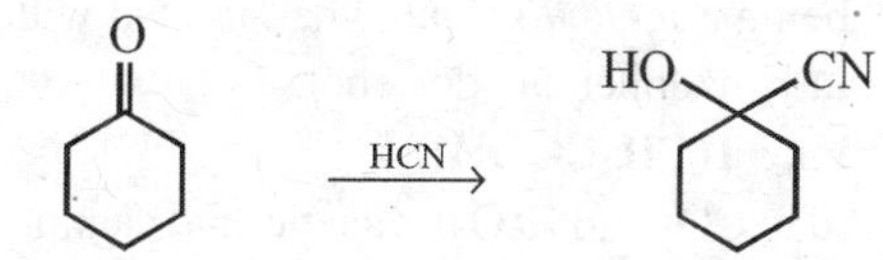

Cyclohexanone   Cyclohexanone cyanohydrin

Due to the presence of 3-methyl groups at the α-positions, the carbonyl group is sterically hindered and is not attacked by CN^-.

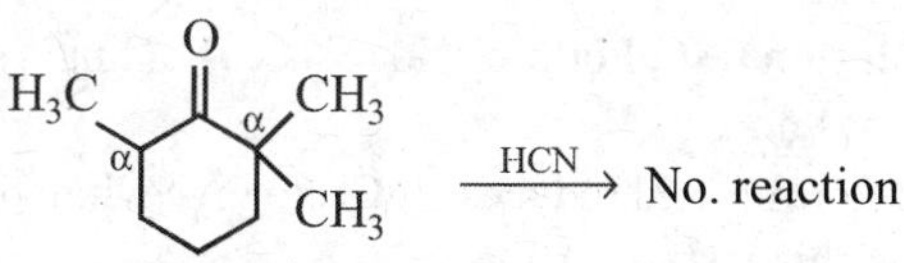

2,2,6-Trimethylcyclohexanone

2. **There are two NH_2 groups in semicarbazide. However, only one is involved in the formation of semicarbazones.**

Ans. Due to resonance, the NH_2 group attached to C = O group acquires + ve charge and does not acts as a nucleophile. The NH_2 group attached to — NH group is not involved in resonance. The electron pair on this $\ddot{N}H_2$ group is available for the nucleophilic attack on the carbonyl carbon atom of aldehydes and ketones.

$$H_2\ddot{N}-\overset{O}{\overset{\|}{C}}-\ddot{N}HNH_2 \longleftrightarrow H_2\ddot{N}-\overset{O}{\overset{\|}{C}}=\overset{+}{N}H-NH_2 \rightleftharpoons NH_2-\overset{OH}{\overset{|}{C}}=N-NH_2$$

3. **During the preparation of esters from a carboxylic acid and an alcohol in the presence of an acid catalyst, the water or the ester should be removed as soon as it is formed.**

Ans. Esterification is a reversible process.

$$R-COOH + R'OH \rightleftharpoons \underset{\text{ester}}{RCOOR'} + H_2O$$

On of the product ester or water should be removed from the reaction mixture to prevent the hydrolysis of the ester in backward direction.

Type 3. Distinguishing between Compounds

1. **Pentanone-2 ($CH_3COCH_2CH_2CH_3$) and pentanone-3 ($CH_3CH_2COCH_2CH_3$)**

These can be distinguished by the following tests :

(*i*) **Sodium bisulphate test :** 2-Pantanone being a *methyl ketone* when treated with a saturated solution of sodium bisulphite gives a white ppt. of 2-pentanone sodium bisulphite addition compound whereas 3-pentanone does not.

(*ii*) **Iodoform test :** 2-Pentanone being a methyl ketone when treated with NaOI (I_2/NaOH) gives yellow ppt. of iodoform but 3-pentanone does not.

2. **Benzaldehyde (C_6H_5CHO) and acetophenone ($C_6H_5COCH_3$)**

These two compounds can be distinguished by the following tests :

(*i*) **$AgNO_3$ test :** Benzaldehyde being an aldehyde reduces *Tollens' reagent* to give mirror test but acetophenone does not give this test.

(*ii*) **Idodoform test :** Acetophenone being a methyl ketone on treatment with I_2/NaOH (undergoes iodoform test to give yellow ppt. of iodoform but benzaldehyde does not.

3. **Acetophenone ($C_6H_5COCH_3$ and benzophenone ($C_6H_5COC_6H_5$)**

These can be distinguished by the iodoform test.

Iodoform test : Acetophenone being a *methyl ketone* when treated with NaOI (I_2/NaOH) gives yellow ppt. of iodoform but benzophenone does not.

4. **Formic acid (HCOOH) and acetic acid (CH_3COOH)**

Formic acid can be easily oxidized to CO_2 and H_2O but acetic acid cannot. Therefore, formic acid behaves as a reducing agent whereas acetic acid does not. These may be distinguished by the following tests :

(i) **Tollens' reagent test :** Formic acid reduces *Tollens' reagent* to metallic silver but acetic acid does not.

(ii) **Fehling's solution test :** Formic acid reduces Fehling's solution to red ppt. of Cu_2O but acetic acid does not.

(*iii*) **$HgCl_2$ test :** Formic acid reduces $HgCl_2$ to give white ppt. of Hg_2Cl_2 while acetic acid does not give this test.

(*iv*) **$KMnO_4$ test :** Formic acid decolourises the pink colour of acidified $KMnO_4$ solution while acetic acid does not give this test.

5. **Benzoic acid (C_6H_5COOH) and phenol (C_6H_5OH) :**

These may be distinguished as follows :

(*i*) **$NaHCO_3$ test :** Benzoic acid being a stronger acid than carbonic acid (H_2CO_3) decomposes $NaHCO_3$ to evolve CO_2 but phenol being a weaker acid than carbonic acid does not.

(*ii*) **$FeCl_3$ test :** Phenol gives a violet colouration with neutral $FeCl_3$ solution while benzoic acid gives buff coloured ppt. of ferric benzoate.

Type 4. Analytical Based Questions

Problem 1. An organic compound with the molecular formula $C_9H_{10}O$ forms 2,4-DNP derivative, reduces Tollen's reagent and undergoes Cannizzaro reaction. On vigorous oxidation, it gives 1,2-benzenedicarboxylic acid. Identify the compound.

Solution (a) Since the given compound forms a 2,4-DNP derivative and reduces Tollen's reagent, it must be an aldehyde.

(b) Since it undergoes Cannizzaro reaction, therefore, CHO group is directly attached to the benzene ring.

(c) Since on oxidation, it gives 1,2-benzenedicarboxylic acid; therefore, it must be *o*-ethylbenzaldehyde.

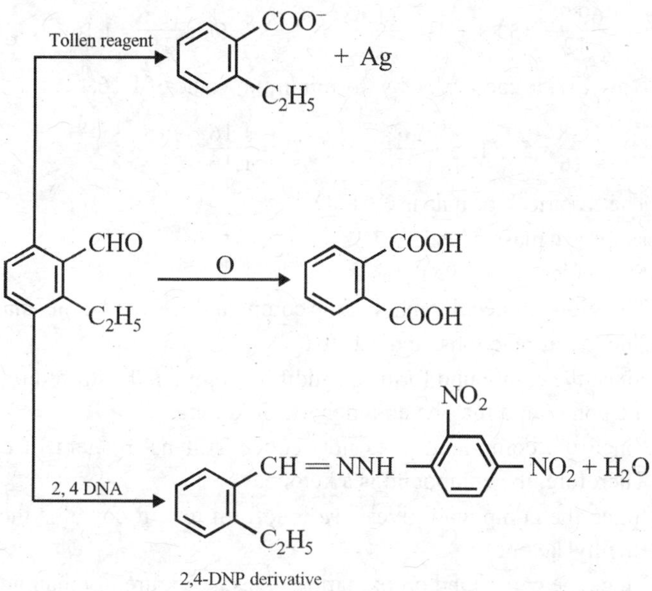

Problem 2. An organic compound (A) (molecular formula $C_8H_{16}O_2$) was hydrolysed with dilute sulphuric acid to give a carboxylic acid (B) and an alcohol (C). Oxidation of (C) with chromic acid produced (B). (C) on dehydration gives but-1-ene. Write equations for the reactions involved.

Solution (a) The compound (A) on hydrolysis gives a carboxylic acid (B) and alcohol (C). Therefore, compound A is an ester.

(b) The alcohol (C) on oxidation gives the same carboxylic acid (B). Therefore, the number of carbon atoms in compound (B) and compound (C) are equal.

(c) The compound (A) [an ester] contains 8C atoms. Therefore, the acid (B) and alcohol (C) should contain 4C atoms each.

(d) Alcohol (C) on dehydration gives but-1-ene; therefore, alcohol is butan-1-ol ($CH_3CH_2CH_2CH_2OH$).

(e) Alcohol (C) on oxidation gives the carboxylic acid (B). Therefore, carboxylic acid (B) is butanoic acid ($CH_3CH_2CH_2COOH$). Ester (A) is butyl butanoate.

$$\underset{\text{Butylbutanoate(A)}}{CH_3CH_2CH_2COOCH_2CH_2CH_2CH_3} \xrightarrow{H_3O^+} \underset{\text{Butanoic acid(B)}}{CH_3CH_2CH_2COOH} + \underset{\text{Butan-1-ol(C)}}{CH_3CH_2CH_2OH}$$

$$\underset{\text{But-1-ene}}{CH_3CH_2CH = CH_2} \xleftarrow[-H_2O]{\text{dehydration}} \underset{(C)}{CH_3CH_2CH_2CH_2OH} \xrightarrow{[O]} \underset{(B)}{CH_3CH_2CH_2COOH}$$

Problem 3. An organic compound contains 69.77% carbon, 11.63% hydrogen and rest oxygen. The molecular mass of the compund is 86. It does not reduce Tollens reagent but forms an addition compound with sodium hydrogen sulphite and gives positive iodoform test. On vigorous oxidation, it gives ethanoic and propanoic acid. Write the possible structure of the compound.

Solution : Let us calculate the molecular formula of the compound.

$\%\text{ of } O = 100 - 69.77 - 11.63 = 18.60$

Divide each element by its atomic mass.

$$C = \frac{69.77}{12} = 5.88, \quad H = \frac{11.63}{1} = 11.63, \quad O = \frac{18.6}{16} = 1.16$$

Now, divide each value by the minimum value of 1.16.

$$C = \frac{5.88}{1.16} = 5, \quad H = \frac{11.63}{1.16} = 10, \quad O = \frac{1.16}{1.16} = 1$$

The empirical formula is $C_5H_{10}O$.

Empirical mass $= 5 \times 12 + 10 \times 1 + 1 \times 16 = 86$.

Molecular mass given $= 86$

Therefore, molecular mass of the compound $= 86$ and molecular formula $C_5H_{10}O$.

The given reactions suggest that :

(i) Since the compound forms an addition compound with sodium hydrogen sulphite, the compound may be an aldehyde or ketone.

(ii) Since the compound does not reduce Tollens' reagent, it cannot be aldehyde. Therefore, the compound is a ketone.

(iii) Since the compound gives +*ve* iodoform test, it contains the group $CH_3 — CO$ (methyl ketone).

(iv) Since the compound on oxidation gives a mixture of ethanoic acid and propanoic acid, the compund is $CH_3COCH_2CH_2CH_3$. This formula explains all the reactions.

$$CH_3COOH + CH_3CH_2COOH \xleftarrow[K_2Cr_2O_7 + H_2SO_4]{[O]} CH_3COCH_2CH_2CH_3$$

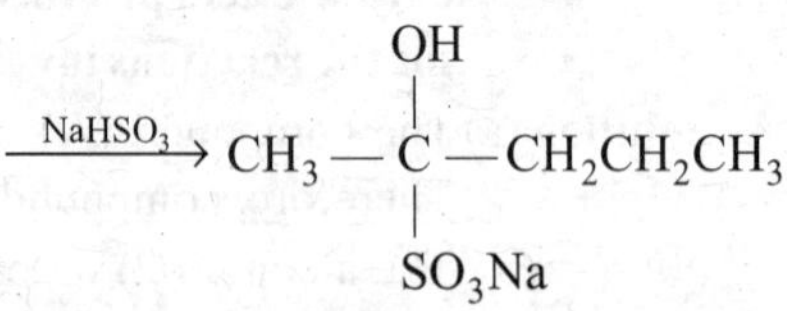

$$CH_3COCH_2CH_2CH_3 + 3I_2 + 4NaOH \longrightarrow CHI_3 + CH_3CH_2CH_2COONa + 3NaI + 3H_2O$$

Type 5. Conversion

1. Ethanal to lactic acid

$$CH_3—CHO \xrightarrow[HCN]{KON} CH_3CH(OH)CN \xrightarrow{\text{Hydrolysis}} CH_3—CH(OH)—COOH$$

2. Acetaldehyde to Acetone

$$CH_3—CHO \xrightarrow{\text{oxidation}} CH_3COOH \xrightarrow{Ca(OH)_2} (CH_3COO)_2Ca \xrightarrow{\text{heat}} CH_3COCH_3$$

3. Acetic acid to ethanol

$$CH_3COOH \xrightarrow{PCl_5} CH_3COCl \xrightarrow{Pd/BaSO_4} CH_3CHO$$

Very Short Answer Type Questions

Q. 1. Write IUPAC names of the following compounds:

(*i*) aspirin, 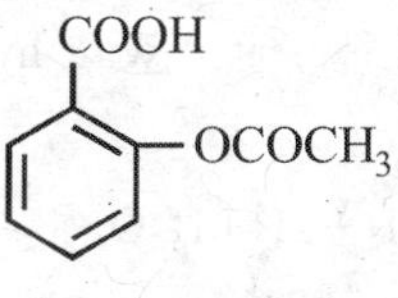

(*ii*) $CH_3—\underset{\underset{COOH}{|}}{CH}—CH_2—CHO$

Ans. (*i*) 2-Acetoxy benzoic acid (*ii*) 2-Methyl-4-oxo-butanoic acid

Q. 2. Name the reaction and the reagent used for the conversion of acid chlorides to the corresponding aldehydes.

Ans. Name–Rosenmund's reaction.

Reagent–H_2 in presence of Pd and partially poisoned by addition of sulphur or quinoline.

$$\underset{\text{Acid chloride}}{R—\overset{\overset{O}{||}}{C}—Cl} + H_2 \xrightarrow[+\text{ S or quinoline}]{Pd/BaSO_4} \underset{\text{Aldehyde}}{R—\overset{\overset{O}{||}}{C}—H} + HCl$$

Q. 3. What is Tollen's reagent?

Ans. Ammonical silver nitrate solution, $[Ag(NH_3)_2]^+ NO_3^-$.

Q. 4. Name one reagent used to distinguish acetaldehyde from acetone.

Ans. Tollen's reagent or Fehling's solution.

Q. 5. Arrange the following in order of their increasing reactivity towards HCN:

CH_3CHO, CH_3COCH_3, HCHO, $C_2H_5COCH_3$

Ans. $C_2H_5COCH_3 < CH_3COCH_3 < CH_3CHO < HCHO$.

Q. 6. Give the structure and IUPAC name of an aliphatic aldehyde having five carbon atoms which undergoes cannizzaro reaction.

Ans. 2, 2-Dimethylpropanal, $(CH_3)_3\,C—CHO$.

Q. 7. Name two methods which are commonly used to convert $a > c = 0$ group into a $> CH_2$ group.

Ans. Clemmensen reduction and wolff-Kishner reduction.

Q. 8. What product is obtained when acetophenone is treated with hydrazine hydrate and KOH at 453–473 K ?

Ans. $$\underset{\text{Acetophenone}}{C_6H_5COCH_3} \xrightarrow[453-473K]{NH_2NH_2,\, H_2O, KOH ethyleneglycol} \underset{\text{Ethylbenzene}}{C_6H_5CH_2CH_3}$$

Q. 9. Give the IUPAC name of the following:

(i) $CH_3-\underset{\displaystyle OH}{\underset{|}{CH}}-CH_2-OC_2H_5$ (ii) 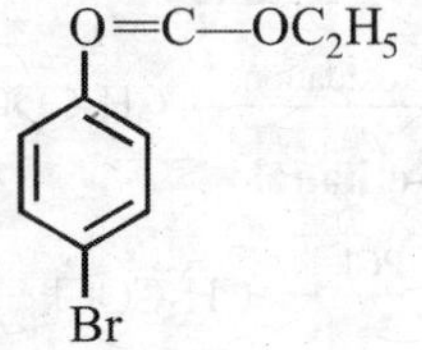

Ans. (i) 1-ethoxy-2-propanol (ii) Ethyl-4-bromobenzoate

Q. 10. Write the IUPAC name of $CH_3-\underset{\displaystyle CH_3}{\underset{|}{CH}}-\underset{\displaystyle O}{\underset{\|}{C}}-CH_2CH_3$

Ans. 2-Methylpentan-3-one.

Q. 11. Give the chemical reaction, when ethanol is heated with hydrogen iodide and red phosphorus under high pressure.

Ans. $CH_3CHO + 4\,HI \xrightarrow{\text{red.P,Pressure}} CH_3-CH_3 + 2I_2 + H_2O.$

Q. 12. Write the structural formula of 3-Phenylprop-2-enal.

Ans. $C_6H_5CH=CH-CHO.$

Q. 13. What is vinegar?

Ans. An 8–10% solution of acetic acid in water called vinegar.

Q. 14. How will you convert an acid into an ether without using an alcohol?

Ans. By using diazomethane.

$$\underset{\text{Carboxylic acid}}{RCOOH} + \underset{\text{Diazomethane}}{CH_2N_2} \xrightarrow{\text{Dry.ether}} \underset{\text{Methyl ether}}{RCOOCH_3} + N_2$$

Q. 15. Give the IUPAC name of the following compound.

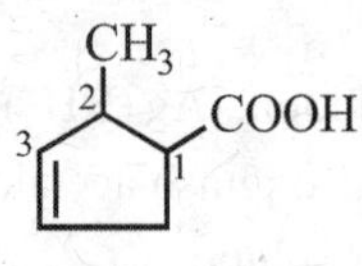

Ans. 2-Methylcyclopent-3 ene-1-carboxylic acid.

Q.16. Write IUPAC names of the following compounds :

(i) $CH_3COCH(C_2H_5)-CH_2CH_2Cl$, i.e. $CH_3CO\underset{\displaystyle C_2H_5}{\underset{|}{CH}}-CH_2CH_2Cl$ (ii) 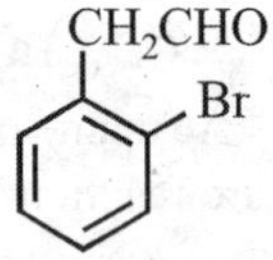

Ans. (i) 5-chloro-3-ethyl-2-pentanone (ii) 2-(2-bromophenyl) ethanal.

Q. 17. Write IUPAC names of following compounds :

(i) 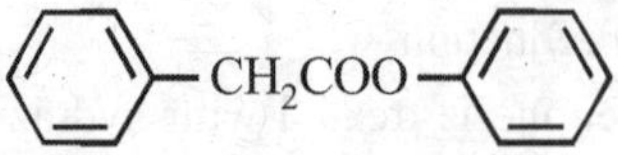 (ii) 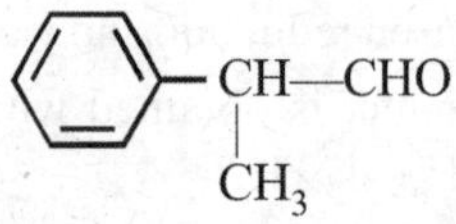

(iii) $CH_3-CO-CH-\underset{\displaystyle CH_3}{\underset{|}{CH_2}}-CH_2Cl$ (iv) $CH_3-CH_2-\underset{\displaystyle CH_3}{\underset{|}{CH}}-CH=CH_2$

Ans. (i) Phenyl-2-(phenyl) ethanoate (ii) 2-phenyl propanal
(iii) 5-chloro-3-methyl-2-pentanone (iv) 3-methyl-1-pentene

Q. 18. What is 'formaline' ? Mention its important use.

Ans. An aqueous solution of formaldehyde (40%) is known as formaline. It is used in preservation of biological specimens.

Q. 19. Arrange the following in order of increasing boiling points :
(i) propanone, (ii) propanal, (iii) propane, (iv) 1-propanol

Ans. The boiling point increases in the following order :
propane < propanal < propanone < 1-propanol.

Q. 20. Write the following in order of decreasing reactivity towards HCN :
(i) HCHO, (ii) CH_3COCH_3, (iii) CH_3CHO

Ans. $HCHO > CH_3CHO > CH_3COCH_3$
(It is because C═O group is most polar in HCHO and least polar in CH_3COCH_3 due to inductive effect).

Short Answer Type Questions

Q. 1. (i) Aldehydes are more reactive than ketones in nucleophilic addition reactions.
(ii) Acetic acid is weaker acid than chloro acetic acid.

Ans. (i) In aldehyde and ketones

reactively depend on magnitude of positive charge. This magnitude of +ve charge decrease by positive inductive effect.

$$\text{reactivity} \propto \frac{1}{\text{Magnitude of +ve charge}} \propto \frac{1}{+\text{I effect}}$$

ketones have more +I effect than aldehydes.

(ii) $\text{Acidic nature} \propto \frac{1}{+\text{I effect}}$ and $\propto -\text{I effect}$

due to –I effect Cl—CH_2COOH is more acidic than CH_3COOH.

Q. 2. Explain why acid chlorides are the most reactive acid derivatives while acid amides are the least reactive.

Ans. Among the different acid derivatives, acid chlorides are probably the most reactive chemically towards nucleophilic substitution reactions. This may be attributed to two factors. The chlorine atom has a strong electron withdrawing –I effect. At the same time, it has a weak-electron releasing resonance effect (+R effect).

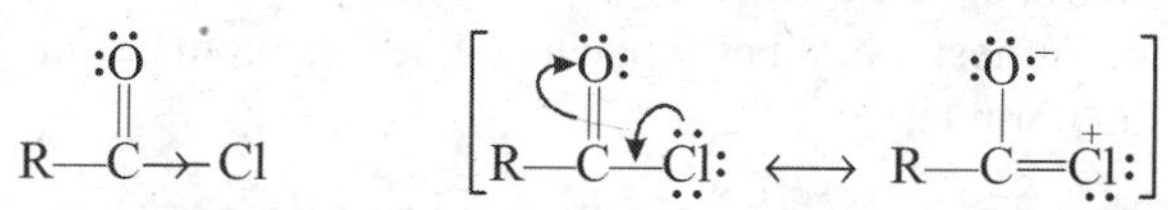

(Strong –I effect) (Weak +R effect)

As a result of the combined influence of both these effects, the acyl carbon atom becomes highly electron deficient in nature. The nucleophile attack can readily take place.
But in acid amides magnitude of –I effect of NH_2 group is quite weak consequently, the carbonyl carbon atom is not sufficiently electron deficient and the nucleophile attack

can not take place so easily.

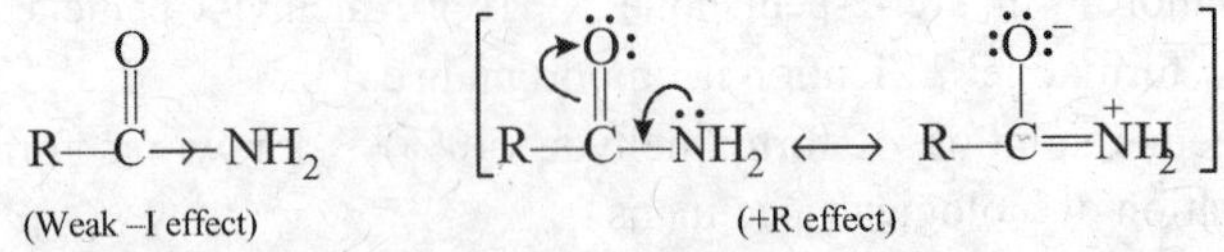

Q. 2. Give the mechanism of Hoffmann Bromamide reaction.

Ans. The reaction proceeds by the following mechanism.

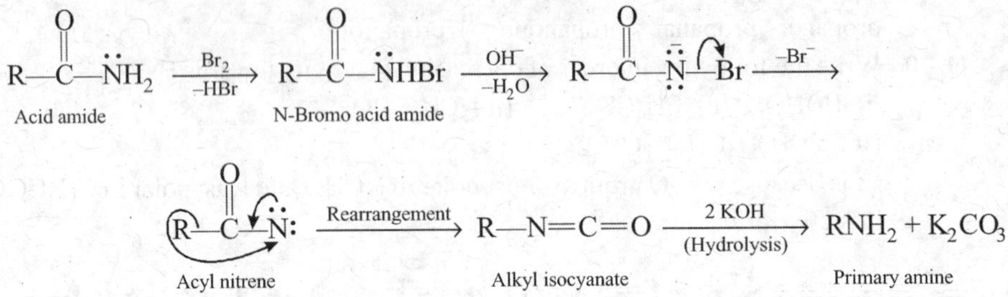

Q. 3. (*i*) How acetone obtained from ethanol ?

(*ii*) How will you convert acetone into 2-methyl-2-propanol ?

Or How is tert-butyl alcohol obtained from acetone ?

Ans. (*i*)

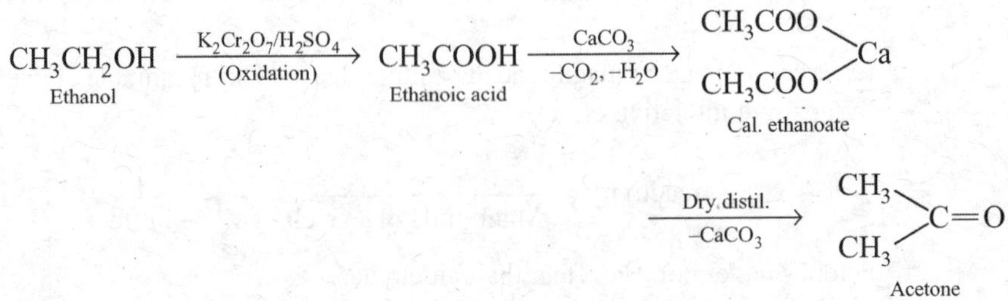

(*ii*) By reaction of acetone with CH_3MgBr followed by hydrolysis.

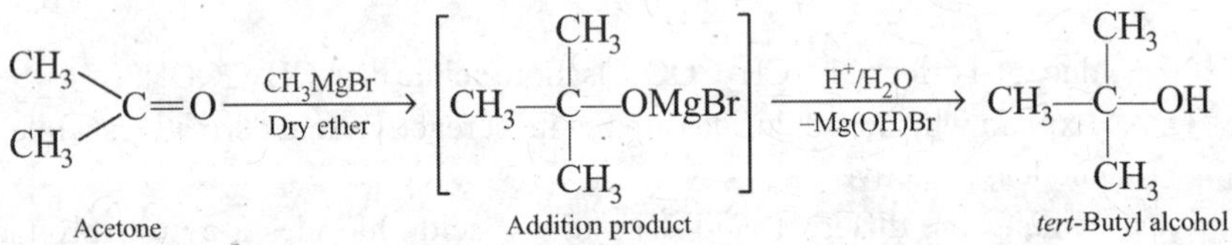

Q. 4. Which gives iodoform test out of acetophenone and benzophenone? Write the reaction involved.

Ans. Acetophenone ($C_6H_5COCH_3$) contains the group CH_3CO attached to carbon and hence gives iodoform test while benzophenone does not contain this group and hence does not give iodoform test.

$$\underset{\text{Acetophenone}}{C_6H_5COCH} + 3I_2 + 4NaOH \longrightarrow \underset{\text{Iodoform}}{CHI_3} + C_6H_5COONa + 3NaI + 3H_2O$$

$$\underset{\text{Benzophenone}}{C_6H_5COC_6H_5} \xrightarrow{I_2/NaOH} \text{No reaction}$$

Q. 5. Complete each synthesis by filling the missing starting materials, reagents or products. (X, Y and Z),

(*i*) $C_6H_5CHO + CH_3CH_2CHO \xrightarrow{NaOH} X$

(*ii*) $CH_3CH_2CH_2CH_2OH \xrightarrow{Y} CH_3CH_2CH_2COOH$

(*iii*) $CH_3(CH_2)_9\,COOC_2H_5 \xrightarrow{Z} CH_3(CH_2)_9CHO$

Ans. (*i*) $C_6H_5CHO + CH_3CH_2CHO \xrightarrow{NaOH} C_6H_5-\underset{OH}{\underset{|}{CH}}-\underset{CH_3}{\underset{|}{CH}}-CHO$
(X)

(*ii*) $CH_3CH_2CH_2CH_2OH \xrightarrow[\text{acidified}]{KMnO_4} CH_3CH_2CH_2COOH$

(*iii*) $CH_3(CH_2)_9\,COOC_2H_5 \xrightarrow{DIBALH/H_2O} CH_3(CH_2)_9CHO$

Long Answer Type Questions

Q. 1. Write the structures of the following compounds:

(*i*) α-Methoxypropionaldehyde
(*ii*) 3-Hydroxybutanal
(*iii*) 2-Hydroxycyclopentane carbaldehyde
(*iv*) 4-Oxopentanal
(*v*) Di-Sec-butyl ketone

Ans. (*i*) $CH_3-\overset{OCH_3}{\overset{|}{CH}}-\overset{O}{\overset{||}{C}}-H$

(*ii*) $CH_3-\overset{OH}{\overset{|}{CH}}-CH_2-\overset{O}{\overset{||}{C}}-H$

(*iii*) 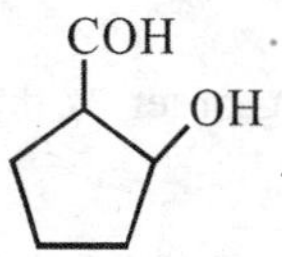

(*iv*) $CH_3-\overset{O}{\overset{||}{C}}-CH_2\,CH_2-\overset{O}{\overset{||}{C}}-H$

(*v*) $CH_3-CH_2-\overset{CH_3}{\overset{|}{CH}}-\overset{O}{\overset{||}{C}}-\overset{CH_3}{\overset{|}{CH}}-CH_2-CH_3$

Q. 2. Write the structures of products of the following reaction:

(i) 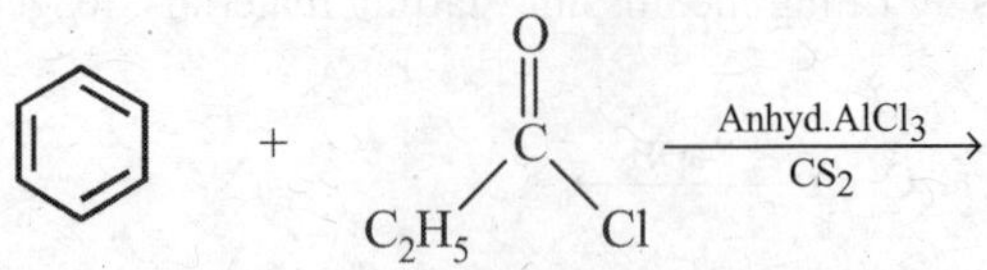

(ii) $(C_6H_5CH_2)_2Cd + 2CH_3COCl \longrightarrow$

(iii) $CH_3—C\equiv CH \xrightarrow{Hg^{2+},\ H_2SO_4}$

(iv) 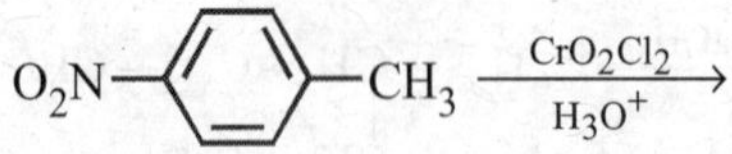

Ans. (i) 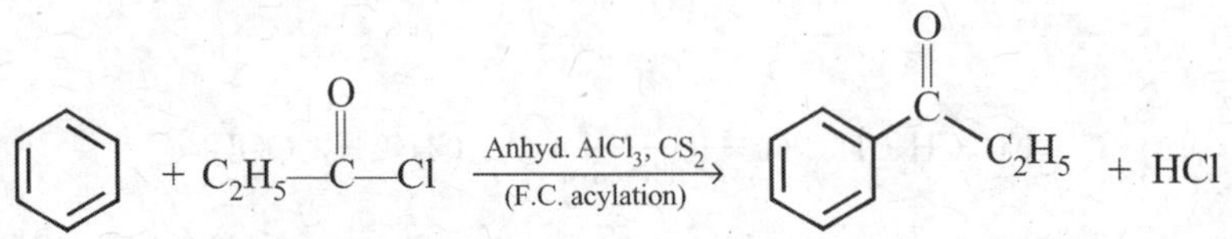

Benzene   Propanoyl chloride   Propiophenone

(ii) $(C_6H_5CH_2)_2\,Cd + 2CH_3—\overset{O}{\overset{\|}{C}}—Cl \xrightarrow{\text{Dry ether}} 2CH_3—\overset{O}{\overset{\|}{C}}—CH_2CH_5 + CdCl_2$

1-Phenylpropanone

(iii) $CH_3—C\equiv CH + H—OH \xrightarrow{Hg^2,\ \text{dil.}\,H_2SO_4} \left[CH_3—\overset{OH}{\overset{|}{C}}=CH_3\right] \xrightarrow{\text{Tautomerises}} CH_3—\overset{O}{\overset{\|}{C}}—CH_3$

Propanone

(iv) 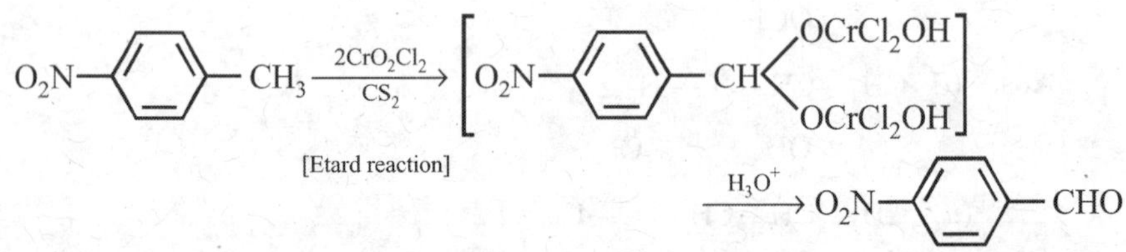

P-Nitrobenzaldehyde

Q. 3. Arrange the following carbonyl compounds in increasing order of their reactivity in nucleophilic addition reactions.

(i) Ethanol, Propanol, Propanone, Butanone.

(ii) Benzaldehyde, P-Tolualdehyde, P-Nitrobenzaldehyde Acetophenone.

Ans. (i) 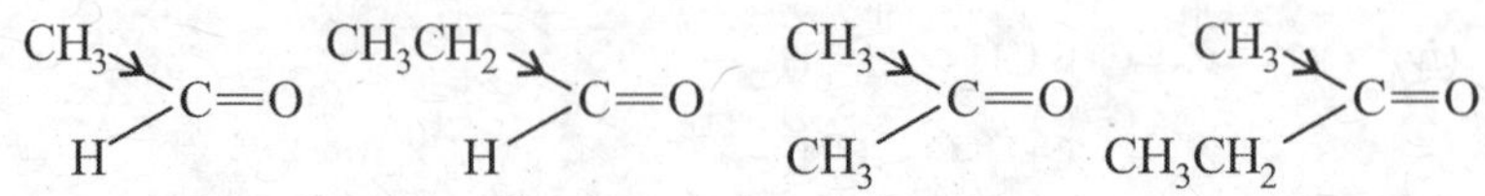

Ethanol   Propanol   Propanone   Butanone

As we move from ethanol to butanone, the +I–effect of the alkyl group increases. With the result, electron density on the carbon atom of the carbonyl group progressively increases, hence attack by the nucleophile becomes slower and slower.

Thus, the reactivity increases in the order:

Butanone < Propanone < Propanol < Ethanol

(*ii*) Acetophenone is a ketone, while all others are aldehydes; therefore, it is the least reactive. In P-tolualdehyde, there is a CH_3 group at the P-position to the carbonyl group, which increases the electron density on the carbon of the carbonyl group by hyperconjugation effect thereby making it less reactive than benzaldehyde.

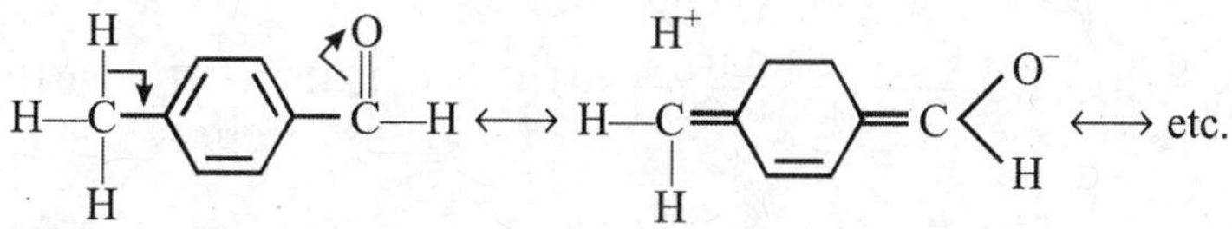

On the other hand, in p-nitrobenzaldehyde, the NO_2 group is a powerful electron withdrawing group. So it withdraws electrons, both by inductive and resonance effect thereby decreasing the electron-density on the carbon atom of the carbonyl group. This facilitates the attack of the nucleophile and hence makes it more reactive than benzaldehyde.

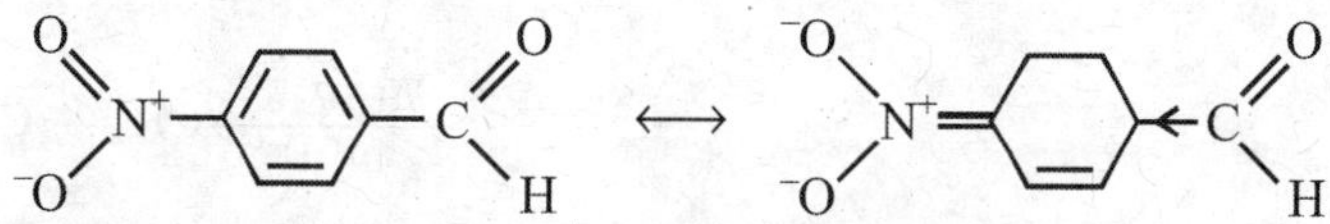

Therefore, the overall reactivity increases in the order:

Acetophenone < p-Tolualdehyde < Benzaldehyde < p-Nitrobenzaldehyde.

Q. 4. (*i*) Give the IUPAC names of the following compounds:

(*a*) $PhCH_2CH_2COOH$ (*b*) $(CH_3)_2C{=}CHCOOH$

(*c*) 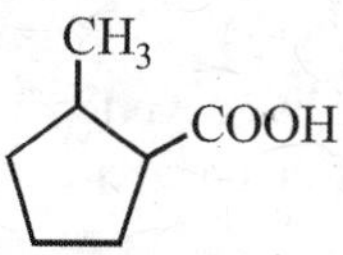

(*d*) 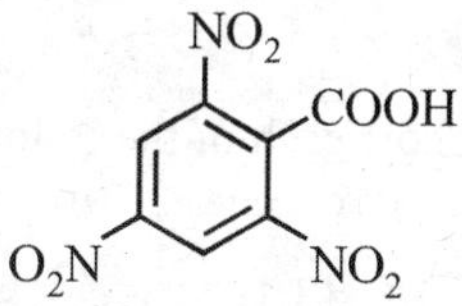

(*ii*) Draw structures of the following derivatives:

(*a*) The 2, 4-dinitrophenylhydrazone of benzaldehye

(*b*) Cyclopropanone oxime (*c*) Acetaldehydedimethyl acetal

(*d*) The ethylene Ketal of hexan-3-one

(*e*) The methyl hemiacetal of formaldehyde

Ans. (*i*) (*a*) 3-Phenylpropanoic acid (*b*) 3-Methylbut-2-enoic acid

(*c*) 2-Methylcyclohexane carboxylic acid (*d*) 2, 4, 6-Trinitrobenzoic acid

(*ii*) (*a*) 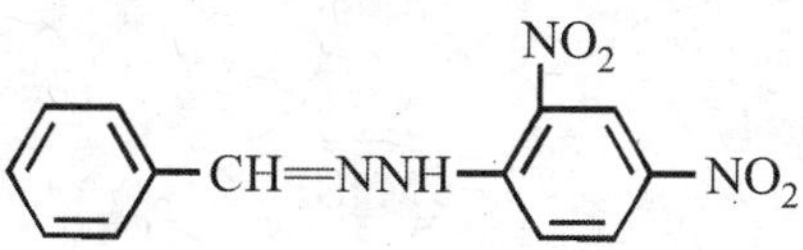

(*b*) 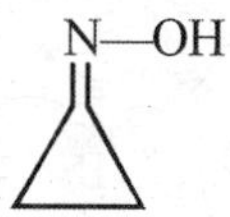

(*c*) 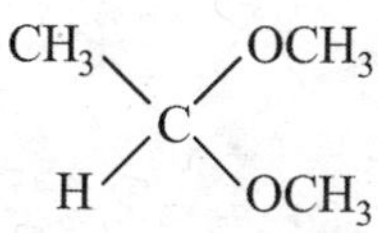

(*d*) 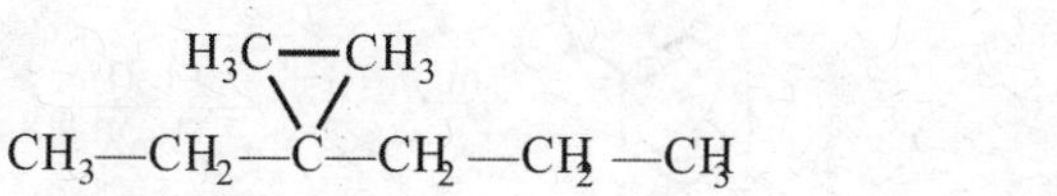

(e) 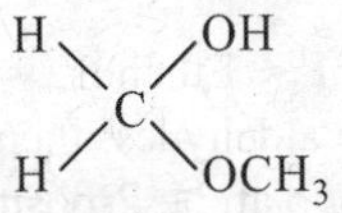

Q. 5. How will you convert ethanol into following compounds?

(*i*) Butane-1, 3-diol (*ii*) But-2-enal (*iii*) But-2-enoic acid

Ans. (*i*)

$$\underset{\text{Ethanol}}{2CH_3CHO} \xrightarrow[\text{(Aldol condensation)}]{\text{Dil.NaOH}} \underset{\text{3-Hydroxybutanal}}{\overset{4}{H_3C} - \overset{3}{CHOH} - \overset{1}{CH_2} - \overset{1}{CHO}}$$

$$\xrightarrow[\text{(Reduction)}]{NaBH_4} \underset{\text{Butane-1,3-diol}}{CH_3 - CHOH - CH_2CH_2OH}$$

(*ii*)

$$\underset{\text{Ethanol}}{2CH_3CHO} \xrightarrow[\text{(Aldol condensation)}]{\text{Dil.NaOH}} \underset{\text{3-Hydroxybutanal}}{\overset{4}{H_3C} - \overset{3}{CHOH} - \overset{1}{CH_2} - \overset{1}{CHO}}$$

$$\xrightarrow[-H_2O]{H_3O^+/\Delta} \underset{\text{But-2-enal}}{CH_3 - CH = CH - CHO}$$

(*iii*)

$$\underset{\text{Ethanol}}{CH_3CHO} \xrightarrow[\text{(Aldol condensation)}]{\text{Dil.NaOH}} CH_3CH = CHCHO \xrightarrow[\text{Tollens' reagent}]{[Ag(NH_2)_2]^+OH^-}$$

$$\underset{\text{But-2-enoic acid}}{CH_3CH = CHCO_2H}$$

Q. 6. Show how each of the following compounds could be converted benzoic acid.

(*i*) Ethylbenzene (*ii*) Acetophenone (*iii*) Bromobenzene (*iv*) Styrene

Ans. (*i*)

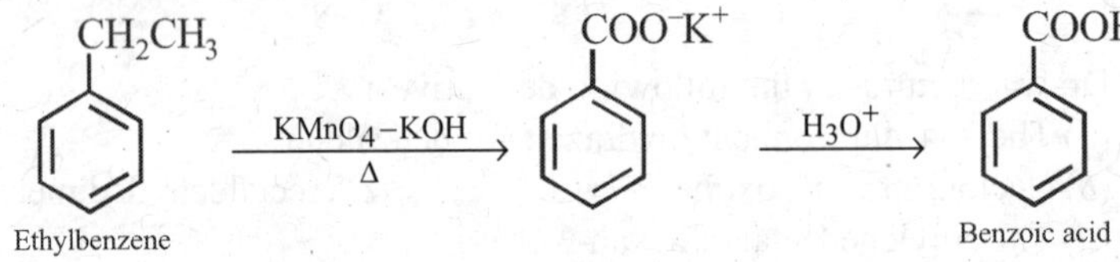

(*ii*)

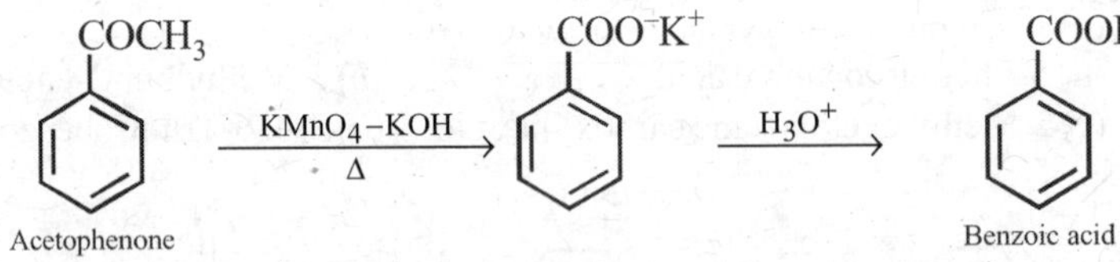

(*iii*)

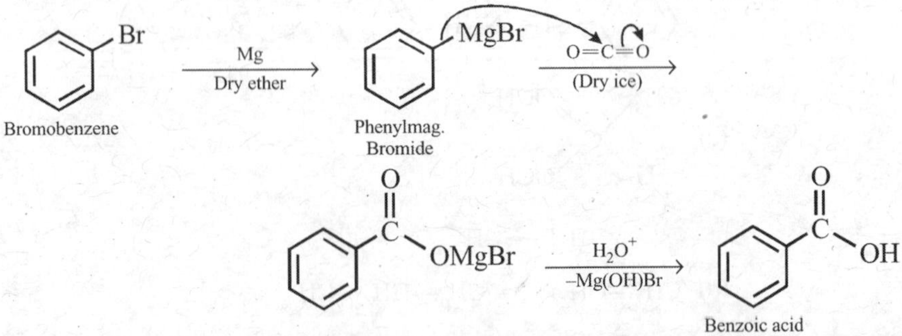

(iv)

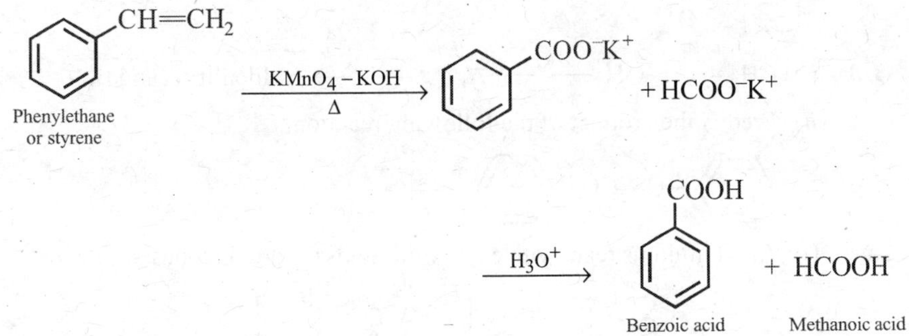

Q. 7. Which acid of each pair show here would you expect to be stronger?

(*i*) CH_3CO_2H or FCH_2CO_2H (*ii*) FCH_2CO_2H or $ClCH_2CO_2H$

(*iii*)

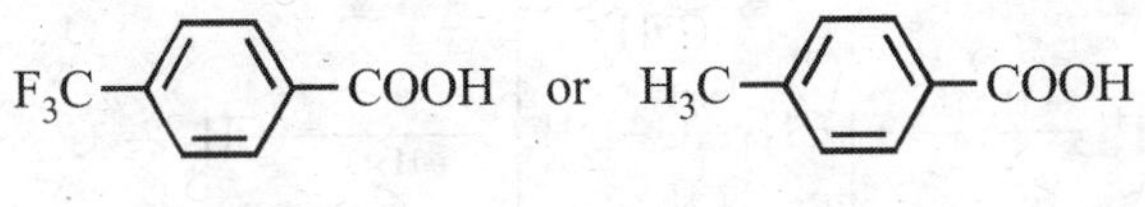

Ans. (*i*)

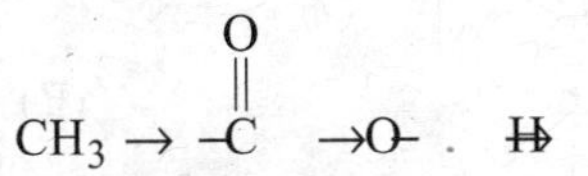

+ I effect of CH_3 group increases the electron density in the O—H bond thereby making the release of a proton difficult

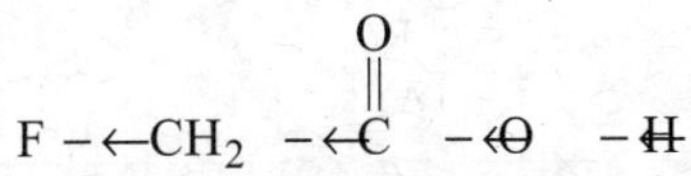

—I effect of F decreases the electron density in the O—H bond thereby making the release of a proton easier.

Thus, due to lesser electron density in the O—H bond and greater stability of FCH_2COO^- ion over CH_3COO^- ion, FCH_2COOH is a stronger acid than CH_3COOH.

(*ii*) Due to much stronger —I effect of F over Cl, the FCH_2COO^- ion is much more stable than $ClCH_2COO^-$ ion and hence FCH_2COOH is a stronger acid than $ClCH_2COOH$.

(*iii*)

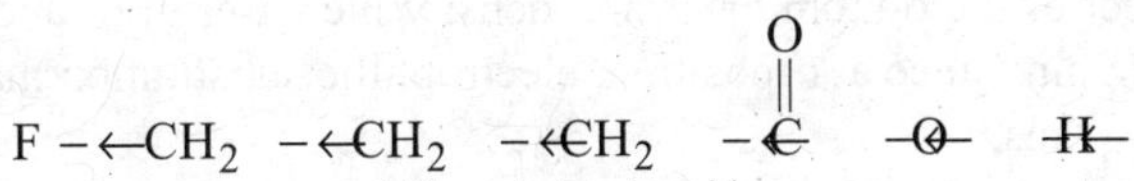

4-Fluorobutanoic acid

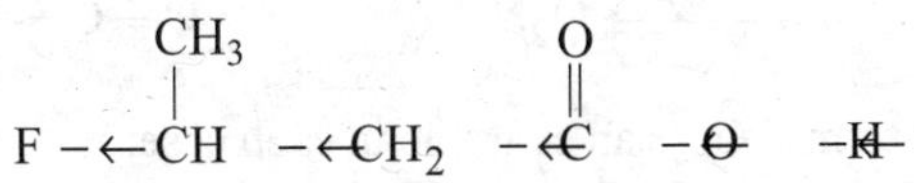

3-Fluarobutanoic acid

Inductive effect decreases with distance therefore, –I effect of F is stronger in 3-fluorobutanoic acid than 4-fluorobutanoic acid.

(*iv*)

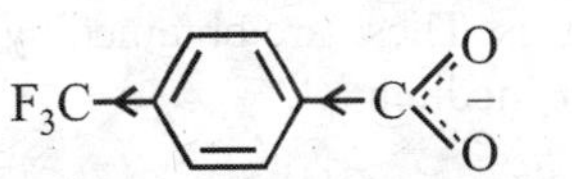

CF_3 has a strong –I-effect it stabilizes the carboxylate ion by disperring the –ve charge.

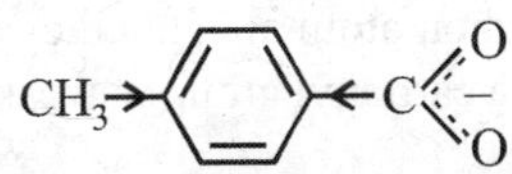

CH_3 has a weak +I-effect. It stabilizes the carboxylate ion by intensifying ion by intensifying the –ve charge.

Therefore, due to greater stability of $F_3C—C_6H_4—COO^-$ ion over $CH_3—C_6H_4COO^-$ ion, $F_3C—C_6H_4—COOH$ is much stronger acid than $H_3C—C_6H_4—COOH$.

Q. 8. (*i*) $CH_3-\overset{O}{\overset{\|}{C}}-OH \xrightarrow{2RLi} A,\ A \xrightarrow{H_3O^+} B$. Identify A and B.

(*ii*) Predict the product of the following reaction.

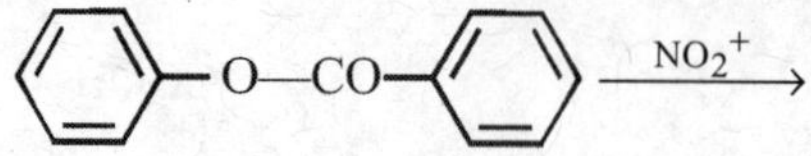

Ans. (*i*) Alkyl lithiums react with carboxylic acids to form ketones.

$$CH_3-\overset{O}{\overset{\|}{C}}-OH \xrightarrow[-RH]{R-Li} \left[CH_3-\overset{O}{\overset{\|}{C}}-O^-Li^+\right] \xrightarrow{R-Li}$$

$$\underset{(A)}{CH_3-\overset{O^-Li^+}{\overset{|}{\underset{R}{\underset{|}{C}}}}-O^-Li^+} \xrightarrow{H_3O^+} \underset{\text{unstable}}{\left[CH_3-\overset{OH}{\overset{|}{\underset{R}{\underset{|}{C}}}}-OH\right]} \xrightarrow{-H_2O} \underset{(B)}{CH_3-\overset{O}{\overset{\|}{C}}-R}$$

(*ii*) Due to the presence of lone pairs of electrons on oxygen, it has +R–effect while C=O group has –R–effect.

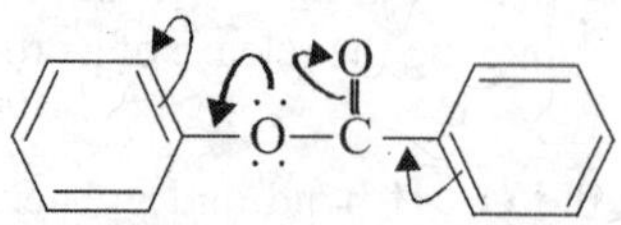

+R-effect —R-effect

As a result, electron-density is more in the ring attached to o-atom than in the ring attached to C=O group. In other words, when NO_2^+ will attack the ring attached to oxygen. +R effect of the o-atom electron –density increases at o- and p-position. But, due to steric hindrance at o-position, electrophilic substitution mainly occurs at the p-position, thus,

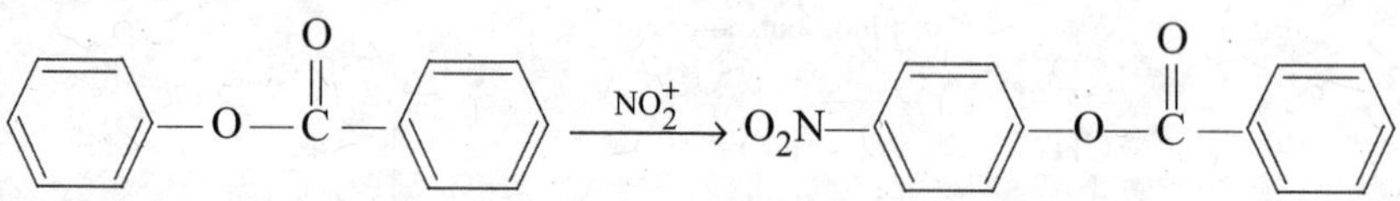

Q. 9. What is meant by the following terms? Give an example in each case:

(*i*) Cyanohydrin (*ii*) Hemiacetal (*iii*) 2, 4-DNP-derivative
(*iv*) Ketal (*v*) Aldol (*vi*) Acetal
(*vii*) Schiff's base

Ans. (*i*) **Cyanohydrins**—The compounds containing hydroxyl and cyano groups on the same carbon atom are called cyanohydrins. These are obtained by the addition of HCN to a carbonyl group in weakly basic medium:

e.g., $$\underset{\text{Acetaldehyde}}{CH_3CHO} + HCN \xrightarrow{pHg} \underset{\substack{\text{Acetaldehyde}\\ \text{(cynohydsin)}}}{\overset{H_3C\quad\ OH}{\underset{H\quad\ \ CN}{\ C\ }}}$$

(*ii*) **Hemiacetal**—Gem-alkoxy alcohols are called hemiacetals. These are obtained by the addition of one molecule of monohydric alcohol to an aldehyde in the presence of dry HCl gas.

e.g.;

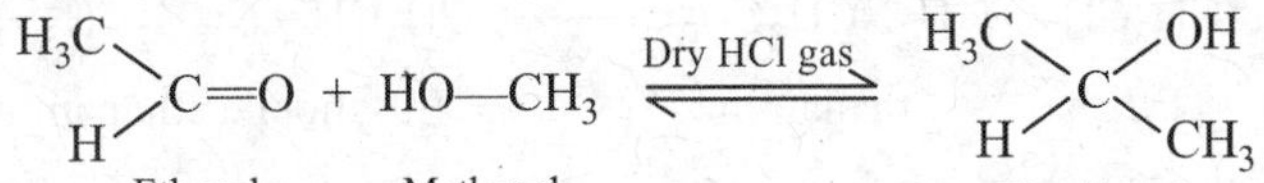

Ethanal Methanol Hemiacetal

(iii) **2, 4-DNP-derivative**—2, 4–DNP derivative are produced when aldehydes or ketones react with 2, 4-dinitrophenyl hydrazine in weakly acidic medium

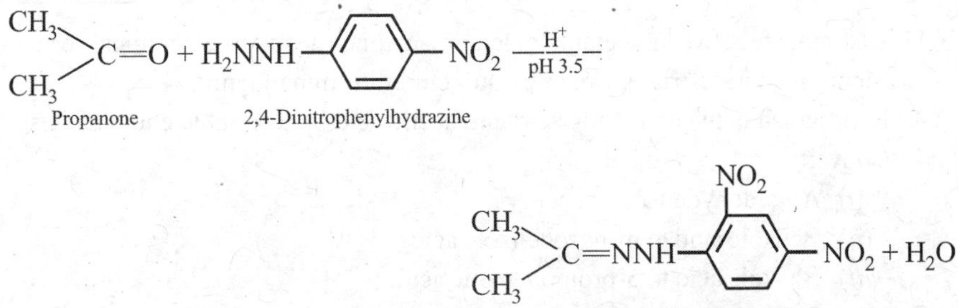

Propanone 2,4-Dinitrophenylhydrazine

Propanone 2,4-dinitrophenyl-hydrozone (2,4-DNP)

(iv) **Ketal**—Gem-dialkoxy alkanes are called ketals. In these compounds, the two alkoxy groups are present on the same carbon within the chain. These are produced by the reaction of ketones with ethylene glycol in the presence of dry HCl gas:

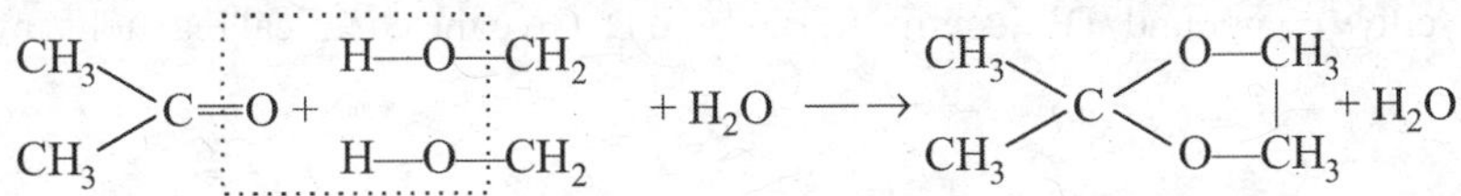

Acetone Acetone ethylene ketal

(v) **Aldol** : Aldols are β-hydroxyaldehydes or ketones which are produced by the condensation of two molecules of aldehydes or ketones containing α-hydrogen atoms in the presence of a dilute aqueous base:

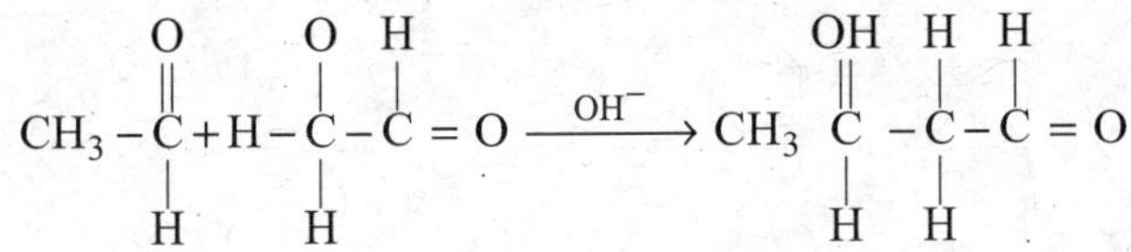

Acetaldehyde 3-Hydroxy butanol (aldol)

(vi) **Acetal**—These are diolkoxy compounds in which two alkoxy groups are present on the terminal carbon atom. These are produced by the action of an aldehyde with two equivalents of a monohydric alcohol in the present of dry HCL gas.

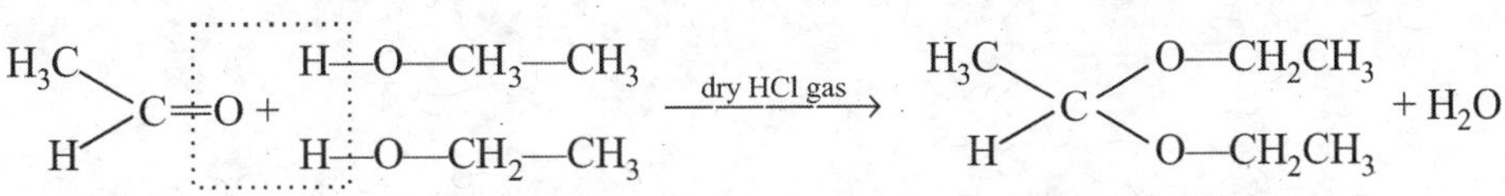

Ethanal Ethanol Acetaldehyde diethyl-acetal

(vii) **Schiff's bases**—Aldehydes and ketones react with primary aliphatic or aromatic amines to form azomethines which are also called Schiff's bases.

$$R{-}CH{=}O + H_2N{-}R' \xrightarrow[\text{Heat}]{H^+} R{-}CH{=}N{-}R' + H_2O$$

Aldehyde Schiff's base

e.g., $CH_3CH_2O + H_2NCH_2CH_3 \xrightarrow[\Delta]{H^+} CH_3CH{=}NCH_2CH_3 + H_2O$

Ethanal Ethanamine Ethylidene ethanamine

Higher Order Thinking Skills — Hots Questions

1. Distinguish between acetaldehyde and acetone by suitable chemical test.
2. Mention an industrial product manufactured from methanol.
3. Distinguish between formic acid and acetic acid by a suitable chemical test.
4. Convert:
   (*i*) An aldehyde to an acetal.
   (*ii*) Benzoic acid to m-nitrobenzoic acid.
   (*iii*) Benzoic acid to 3-bromobenzoic acid.
   (*iv*) Acetylene to acetic acid
   (*v*) Toluene to benzene
5. An organic compound 'A' C_8H_6 on treatment with dilute H_2SO_4 containing mercuric sulphate gives compound 'B' which can also be obtained from a reaction of benzene with acid chloride in presence of $AlCl_3$? 'B' on treatment with I_2 in aq. KOH gives 'C' and a yellow compound 'D'. Identify A, B, C and D. Give the chemical reactions involved.

❑❑❑

CHAPTER 13 ORGANIC COMPOUNDS CONTAINING NITROGEN

Syllabus

- ***Amines :*** *Nomenclature, classification, structure, methods of preparation, physical and chemical properties, uses, identification of primary, secondary and tertiary amines.*
- ***Cyanides and Isocyanides****—will be mentioned at relevant places in context.*
- ***Diazonium states :*** *Preparatin, chemical reactions and importance in synthetic organic chemistry.*

Type 1 — Name reactions

1. **Carbylamine reaction (or isocyanide test) :** Aliphatic and aromatic primary amines when warmed with chloroform and an alcoholic solution of KOH, form isocyanide or carbylamine which have very unpleasant or foul smell.

$$\underset{\text{1°-amine}}{R - NH_2} + CHCl_3 + 3KOH\,(\text{alc.}) \xrightarrow{\text{Warm}} \underset{\text{Alkyl isocyanide}}{R - NC} + 3KCl + 3H_2O$$

$$\underset{\text{Aniline}}{C_6H_5NH_2} + \underset{\text{Chloroform}}{CHCl_3} + 3KOH\,(\text{alc.}) \xrightarrow{\text{Warm}} \underset{\text{Alkyl isocyanide}}{C_6H_5NC} + 3KCl + 3H_2O$$

Secondary and tertiary amines do not give this test.

2. **Gabril phthalimide synthesis :** Aliphatic primary amine or aryl alkyl primary amine is prepared by this method.

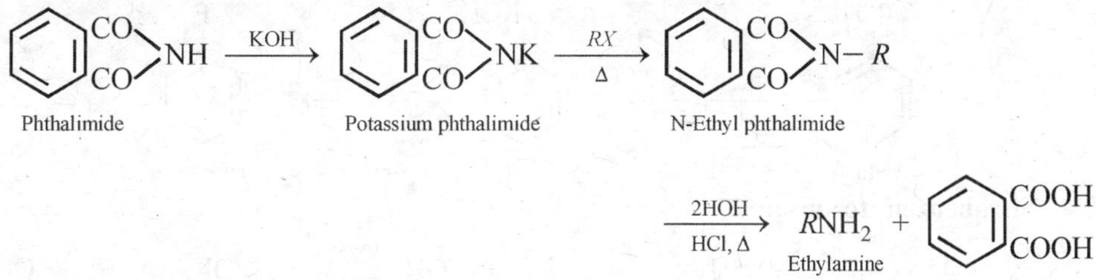

3. **Hoffmann Degradation of Acid Amides :** Acid amide reacts with Br_2 + NaOH or KOH [alkaline hypohalite (NaOBr or KOBr)] give, primary amines containing one carbon atom less than the amide.

$$\underset{\text{Amide}}{RCONH_2} + Br_2 + 4KOH \longrightarrow \underset{\text{1° amine}}{RNH_2} + 2KBr + 2H_2O + K_2CO_3$$

$$\underset{\text{Acid amide}}{R{-}CONH_2} \xrightarrow{\text{KOBr}} \underset{\text{N-Bromoamide}}{R{-}CONH{-}Br} \longrightarrow \underset{\text{Alkyl isocynate}}{R{-}N{=}C{=}O} \xrightarrow[-K_2CO_3]{2KOH} \underset{\text{Primary amine}}{R{-}NH_2}$$

Intermediates

4. **Hoffmann mustard oil reaction :** This reaction is given by aliphatic primary amine. In this aliphatic primary reacts with carbon disulphide gives alkyldithiocarbamic acid which on

heating with $HgCl_2$ gives alkyl isothiocyanate (mustard oil smell) and black ppt. or HgS.

$$\underset{\text{Primary amine}}{RNH_2} \xrightarrow[\text{Heat}]{S=C=S} \underset{\text{Alkyl dithiocarbamic acid}}{S=C\begin{smallmatrix}\diagup NHR \\ \diagdown SH\end{smallmatrix}} \xrightarrow{HgCl_2} \underset{\substack{\text{Alkyl isothiocyanate} \\ \text{(Mustard oil smell)}}}{RNC=S} + \underset{\text{Black ppt.}}{HgS}$$

5. **Diazonium coupling reaction :** They react with highly reactive aromatic compounds (phenols and amines) to yield azo compounds. This electrophilic aromatic substitution is called a diazo coupling reaction.

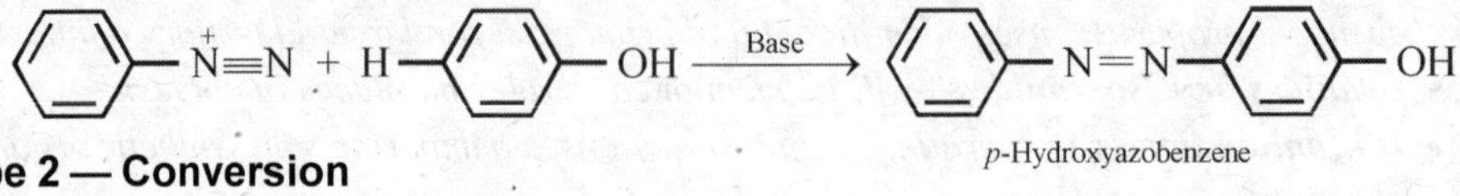

Type 2 — Conversion

1. **Aniline to benzaldehyde**

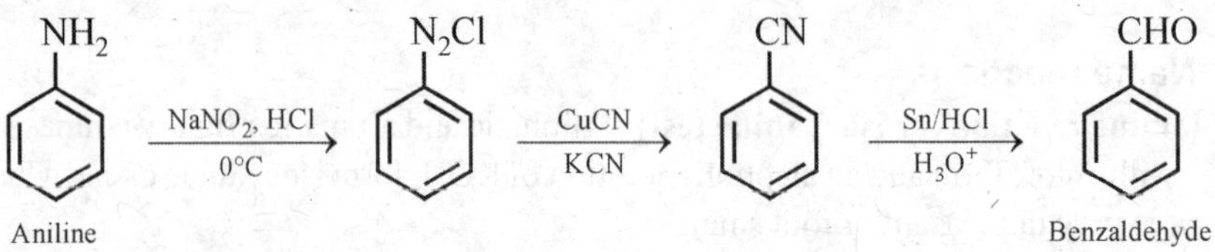

2. **Aniline to phenyl hydrazine**

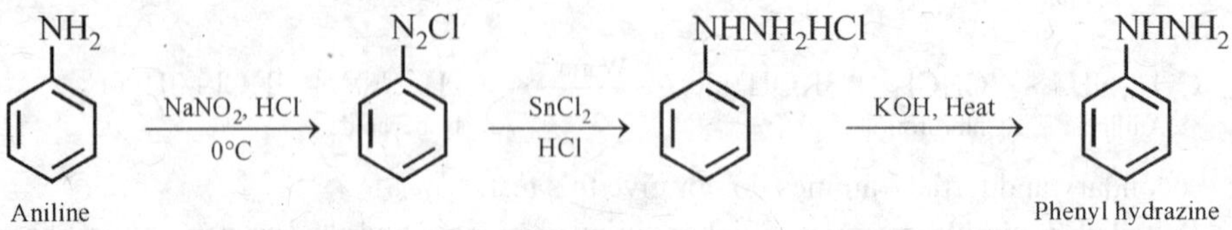

3. **Aniline to fluorobenzene**

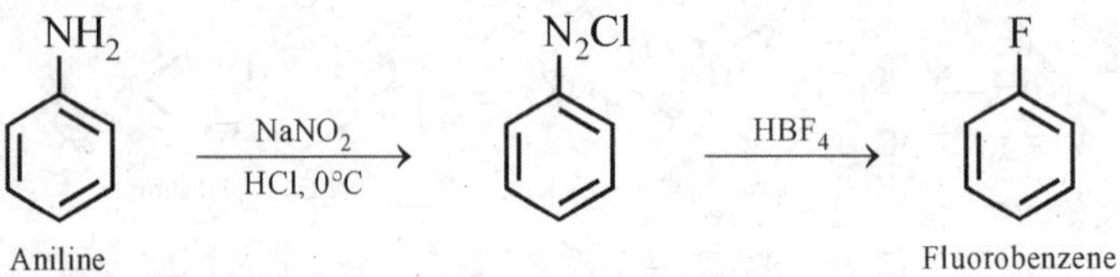

4. **Nitrobenzene to anisole**

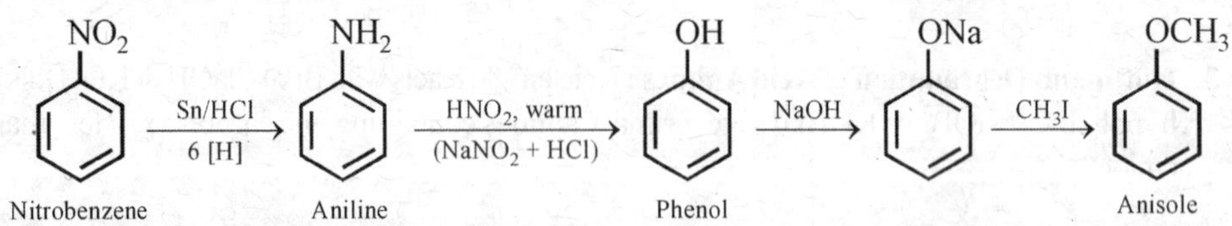

5. **Nitrobenzene to benzyl alcohol**

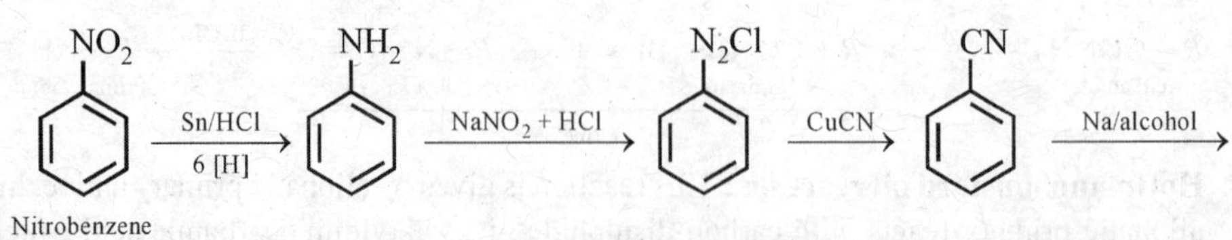

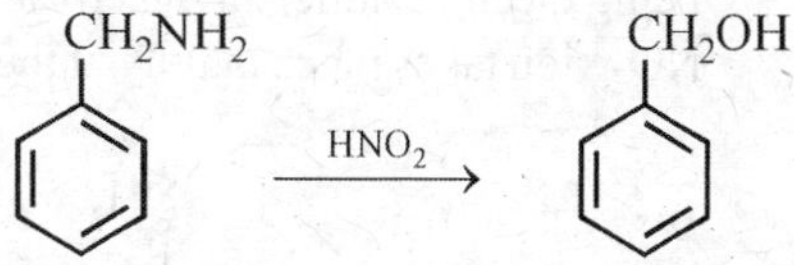

Benzyl alcohol

6. **Benzoic acid to aniline**

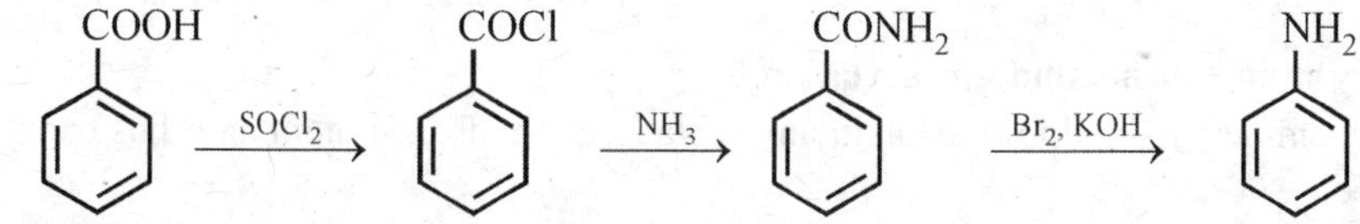

Benzoic acid — Aniline

7. **Aniline to benzylamine**

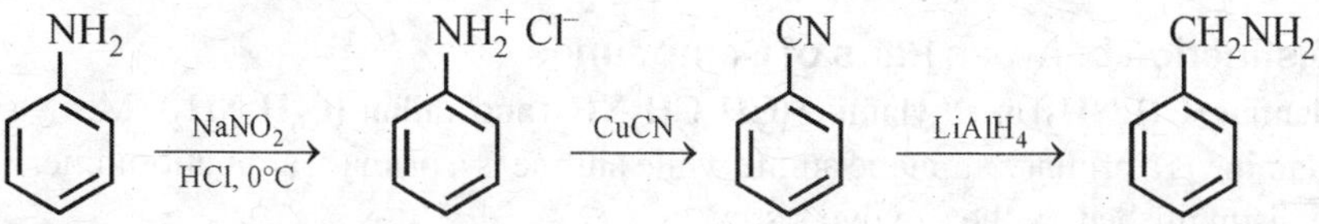

Aniline — Benzylamine

8. **Methyl amine to ethyl amine**

$$CH_3-CH_2 \xrightarrow{HNO_2} CH_3-OH \xrightarrow{PCl_5} CH_3Cl \xrightarrow{KCN} CH_3CN$$

$$\xrightarrow{LiAlH_4} CH_3-CH_2-NH_2$$

9. **Ethyl amine to methyl amine**

$$CH_3-CH_2-NH_2 \xrightarrow{K} CH_3-CH_2-OH \xrightarrow{\text{oxidation}} CH_3COOH \xrightarrow{N_3H} CH_3NH_2$$

Type 3

1. **Why do we acetylate aniline before carrying halogenation and nitration?**

Amino group ($-NH_2$) is a highly activating due to its conjugation with the π-electron pairs of the ring. The ortho and parapositions become centres of highly electron density. The halogenation is not selective and a trisubstituted product is formed. Because of the activated state of aniline, nitric acid employed for nitration causes its partial oxidation to give a black mass and only a very small percentage of the nitro derivative. The purpose of acetylating aniline before subjecting to halogenation or nitration is to decrease its activation.

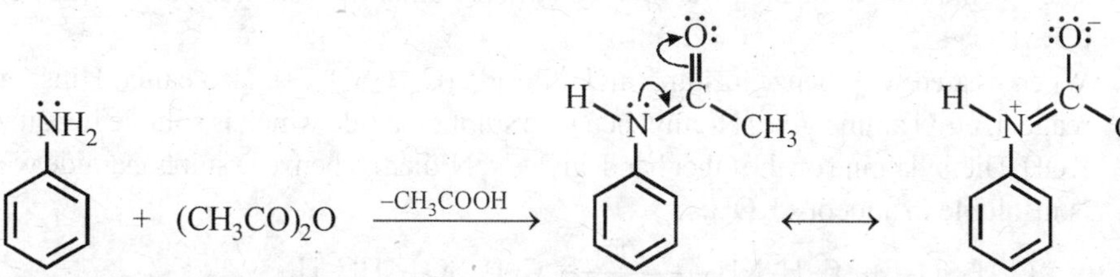

Aniline — Acetic anhydride — acetanilide

2. **Under strongly acidic conditions, the nitration of aniline give mainly *m*-nitroaniline. Discuss.**

Under strongly acidic conditions, NH_2 also gets protonated to form anilinium cation which being electron deficient deactivates the ortho and para position. The electrophile attack by NO_2^+ ion takes place mainly at the meta position to give *m*-nitroderivative.

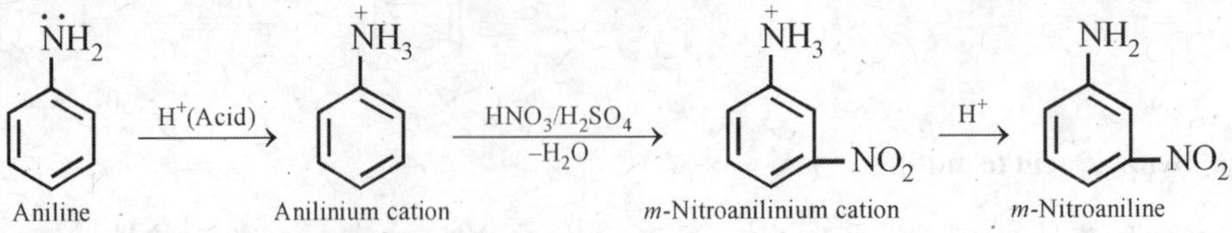

3. **Tertiary amines do not undergo acylation.**
   Tertiary amines, R_3N, do not contain any replaceable hydrogen atom and thus cannot be acylated.
4. **Methyl amine is stronger base than ammonia.**
   Methyl group being electron repelling increases electron density at nitrogen atom. This results in increasing tendency to lose electron pair and show more basic character.

Type 4—Distinction between Pairs of Compounds

1. **Methylamine (CH_3NH_2) or ethylamine ($CH_3CH_2NH_2$) and aniline ($C_6H_5NH_2$) :** Methylamine or ethylamine is a primary aliphatic amine while aniline is a primary aromatic amine. These may be distinguished by the azo dye test :
   Azo dye test : Primary amine with HNO_2 ($NaNO_2$ + dil. HCl) at 273–278 K followed by treatment with an alkaline solution of 2-naphthol (β-naphthol(when a brilliant orange or red coloured dye is obtained.
   Aliphatic primary amines such as methylamine, ethylamine etc. under these condition give a brisk evolution of N_2 gas with the formation of primary alcohols, i.e., the *solution remains clear*.

$$CH_3NH_2 + HONO \xrightarrow{273-278K} CH_3OH + N_2\uparrow + H_2O$$

2. **Ethyl cyanide (C_2H_5CN) and ethyl isocyanide (C_2H_5NC) or RCN and RNC :** These may be distinguished by the hydrolysis test :
   Hydrolysis test : Ethyl cyanide on hydrolysis with aqueous mineral acid gives propionic acid which does not reduce Tollens' reagent while ethyl isocyanide on similar hydrolysis gives formic acid (along with ethylamine) which reduces Tollens' reagent to give a shining silver mirror.
3. **Ethylamine and Diethylamine**
   (i) Ethyl amine being a primaryt amine gives positive isocyanide (carbylamine) test with KOH + $CHCl_3$. No such test is shown by diethylamine.
   (ii) These primary and secondary amines can be convaniently distinguished by Hinsberg's test.
   When treated with benzene sulphonyl chloride ($C_6H_5SO_2Cl$), also called Hinsberg's reagent, ethyl amine gives N-ethyl benzene sulphonamide which is soluble in aqueous KOH. Diethylamine on the other hand, gives N, N-diethyl benzene sulphonamide which is insoluble in aqueous KOH.

$$C_6H_5SO_2Cl + \underset{\text{ethyl amine}}{C_2H_5NH_2} \xrightarrow{-HCl} \underset{\text{(soluble in aq. KOH)}}{C_6H_5SO_2NHC_2H_5}$$

$$C_6H_5SO_2Cl + (C_2H_5)_2NH \xrightarrow{-HCl} \underset{\text{(insoluble in aq. KOH)}}{C_6H_5SO_2N(C_2H_5)_2}$$

Very Short Answer Type Questions

Q. 1. Give the common and IUPAC name of

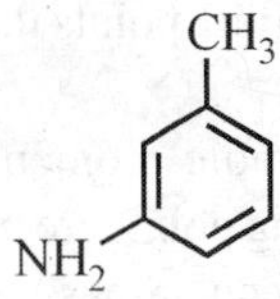

Ans. Common : M-Toluidine

IUPAC : 3-Methylaniline or 3-Methylbenzenamine.

Q. 2. What reaction is used for the preparation of pure aliphatic and aralkyl primary amines?

Ans. Garbriel Phthalimide reaction.

Q. 3. Give an example of Zwitter ion.

Ans. 

Sulphanilic acid

Q. 4. Why do amines act as nucleophiles?

Ans. Due to the presence of a lone pair of electrons on the N-atom, amines can easily donate this lone pair to a carbon species and hence act as nucleophiles.

Q. 5. How will you convert aniline into nitrobenzene without the intermediacy of benzene?

Ans. $C_6H_5NH_2 \xrightarrow[273-278\,K]{HNO_2\,/\,HBF_4} C_6H_5N_2^+BF_4^- \xrightarrow[\Delta]{NaNO_2\,/\,C_4} C_6H_5NO_2.$

Q. 6. Write the chemical reaction for the reduction of nitroethane by $LiAlH_4$.

Ans. $\underset{\text{Nitroethane}}{CH_3CH_2-NO_2} \xrightarrow[\text{(ii) } H_3O^+]{\text{(i) } LiAlH_4\,/\,\text{ether}} \underset{\text{Ethanamine}}{CH_3CH_2NH_2}$

Q. 7. The diazonium ion acts as an electrophile. Explain.

Ans. Being electron deficient species, diazonium ion (ArN_2^+) acts as an electrophile.

Q. 8. Explain mendius reaction.

Ans. When an alkyl cyanide is reduced with sodium and alcohol, 1° amine is produced. This reaction is called mendius reaction. For example,

$$R-C\equiv N+4[H] \xrightarrow{Na\,/\,alc.} \underset{1^\circ\text{ amine}}{R-CH_2-NH_2}$$

$$CH_3-C\equiv N+4[H] \xrightarrow{Na\,/\,alc.} CH_3-CH_2-NH_2$$

Q. 9. What for are quaternary ammonium salts widely used?

Ans. Quaternary ammonium salts are used as detergents.

Q. 10. Write IUPAC name of the following compound.

Ans. 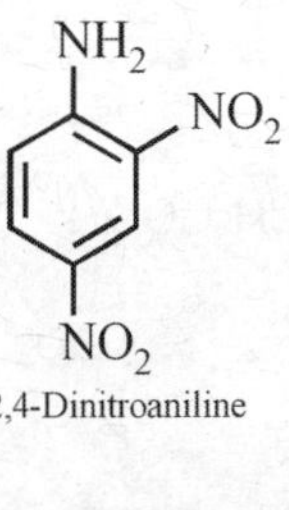

2,4-Dinitroaniline

Q. 11. Direct nitration of aniline is not carried out. Explain why?

Ans. Nitric acid being a strong oxidising agent oxidiser most of aniline to form tarry oxidation products.

Q. 12. Nitro compounds have higher boiling points than hydrocarbons having almost the same molecular mass.

Ans. Nitro compounds have high dipole moments and thus have strong dipole-dipole interaction. Therefore, their boiling points are much higher as compared to hydrocarbons or other compounds of same molecular mass.

Q. 13. Which is more basic : CH_3NH_2 or $(CH_3)_3N$?

Ans. CH_3NH_2 is more basic than $(CH_3)_3$ N due to greater stability of conjugate acid $CH_3{}^+NH_3$ over $(CH_3)_3$ NH due to H-bonding.

Q. 14. Arrange the following in the order of their increasing basicity : P-toluidine, N, N-dimethyl-p-toluidine, p-nitro aniline, aniline.

Ans. P-nitroaniline < aniline < p-toluidine < N, N-dimethyl-p-toluidine.

Q. 15. Classify the following amine as primary, secondary and tertiary:

(i) 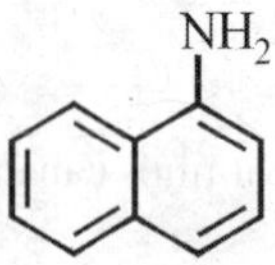

(ii) 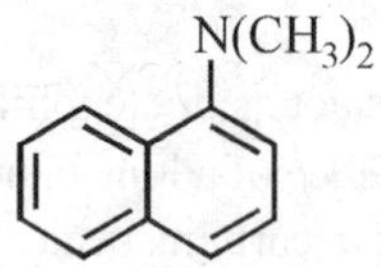

(iii) $(C_2H_5)_2$ CH NH_2 *(iv)* $(C_2H_5)_2$ NH

Ans. *(i)* 1° *(ii)* 3° *(iii)* 1° *(iv)* 2°

Q. 16. Which is more basic : aniline or p-toluidine ?

Ans. Due to electron repelling nature of methyl group, it tends to increase the electron density at N atom in toluidine and as a result of this toluidine is more basic.

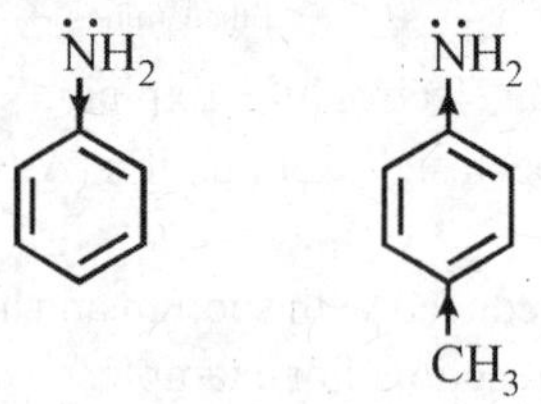

Q. 17. Aniline is primary amine but it cannot be prepared by Gabriel synthesis. Why ?

Ans. Aniline is aromatic primary amine and it cannot be prepared by Gabriel synthesis by treating aryl halide (Ar—X) with potassium salt of pthalimide. It is due to low reactivity of arylhalide as C—C bond in aryl halide is very strong and N-aryl pthalimide is not formed.

Q.18. How is acetanilide obtained from aniline ?

Ans. By acetylation of aniline with CH_3COCl or acetic anhydride.

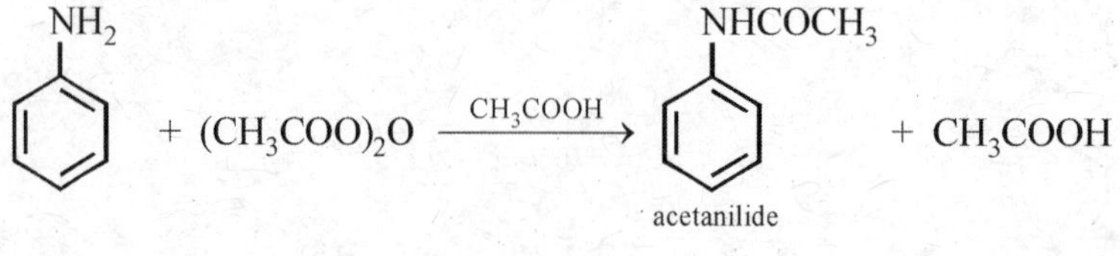

Short Answer Type Questions - I

Q. 1. Write chemical equation for the following conversions :

(*i*) CH_3CH_2Cl into $CH_3CH_2CH_2NH_2$

(*ii*) $C_6H_5CH_2Cl$ to $C_6H_5CH_2CH_2NH_2$

Ans. (*i*)
$$\underset{\text{Chloroethane}}{CH_3CH_2{-}Cl} \xrightarrow[-KCl]{KCN(alc.),\Delta} \underset{\text{Propanenitrile}}{CH_3CH_2{-}C{\equiv}N} \xrightarrow[\text{(Reduction)}]{LiAlH_4/Ether} \underset{\text{Propan-1-amine}}{CH_3CH_2CH_2{-}NH_2}$$

(*ii*)
$$\underset{\text{Benzyle chloride}}{C_6H_5CH_2Cl} \xrightarrow[-NaCl]{NaCN(alc.)\Delta} \underset{\text{Benzyl cyanide}}{C_6H_5CH_2CN} \xrightarrow[\text{(Reduction)}]{H_2/Ni} \underset{\text{2-Phenylethanamine}}{C_6H_5CH_2CH_2NH_2}$$

Q. 2. Write structures and IUPAC names of

(*i*) the amide which gives propanamine by Hofmann bromamide reaction.

(*ii*) the amine produced by the Hofmann degradation of benzamide.

Ans. (*i*)
$$\underset{\text{Butanamide}}{CH_3-CH_2-CH_2-\overset{\overset{\displaystyle O}{\|}}{C}-NH_2}$$

The complete reaction is :

$$\underset{\text{Butanamide}}{CH_3CH_2CH_2CONH_2} + Br_2 + 4KOH \xrightarrow{\Delta} \underset{\text{Propanamide}}{CH_3CH_2CH_2NH_2} + 2KBr + K_2CO_3 + 2H_2O$$

(*ii*)

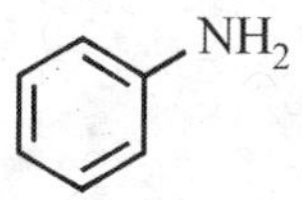

Aniline or Bezenamine

The complete reaction is :

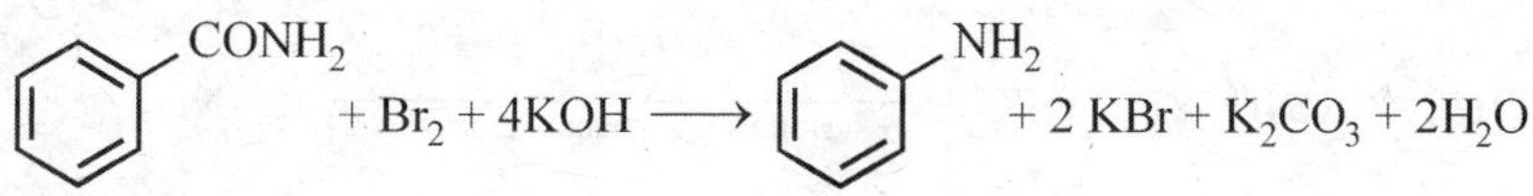

Benzamide Aniline

Q. 3. How will you convert:

(*i*) Benzene into aniline

(*ii*) Benzene into N, N-dimethylaniline

Ans. (*i*)

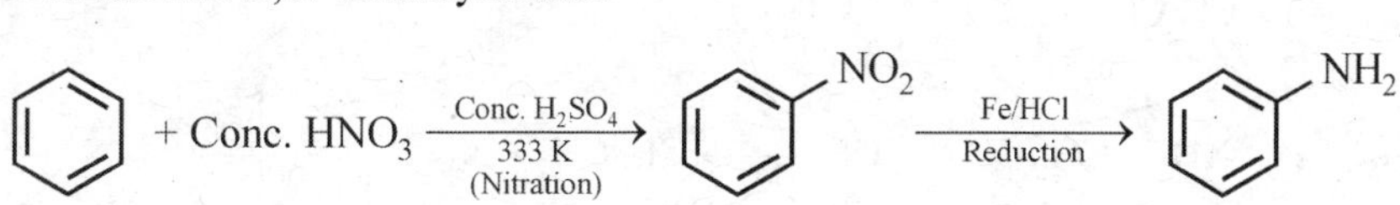

Benzene Nitro-benzene Aniline

(*ii*)

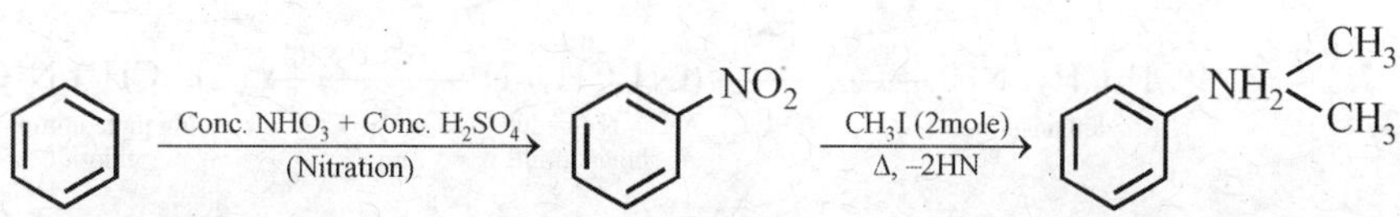

N, N-Dimethylaniline

Q. 4. How is aniline prepared on large scale? How will you convert it into

(*i*) Acetanilide,

(*ii*) Benzalaniline ?

Ans. From Nitro benzene –

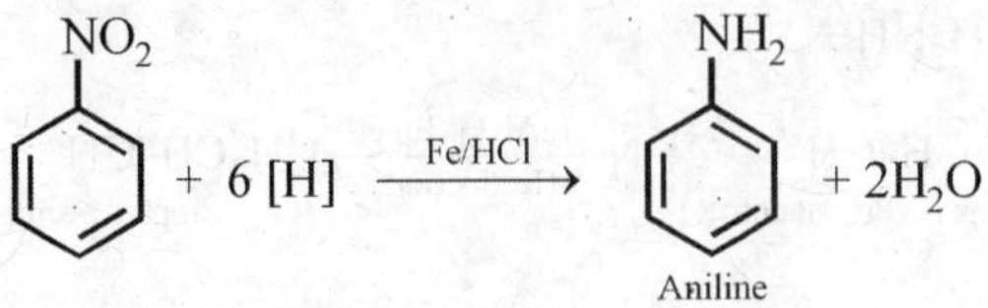

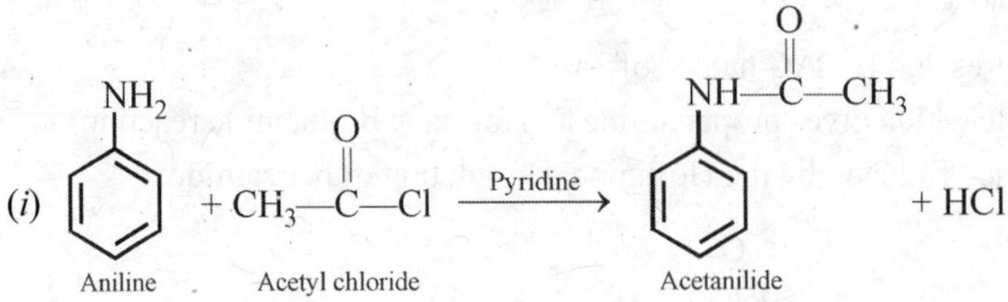

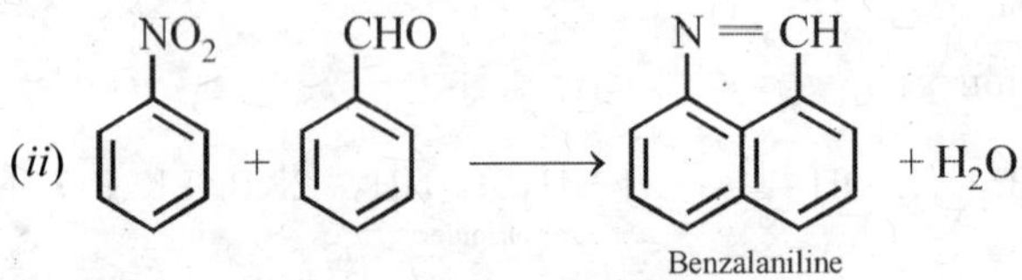

Q. 5. Complete and name the following reactions:

(*a*) $RNH_2 + CHCl_3 + 3KOH \longrightarrow$

(*b*) $RCONH_2 + Br_2 + 4KOH \longrightarrow$

Ans. (*a*) $\underset{1^\circ \text{ Amine}}{RNH_2} + \underset{\text{Chloroform}}{CHCl_3} + 3KOH \xrightarrow[\text{(Carbylamine reaction)}]{\Delta} \underset{\text{Alkyl isocyanide}}{R-N{=}C} + 3KCl + 3H_2O$

(*b*) $RCONH_2 + Br_2 + 4KOH \xrightarrow[\text{(Hofmann bromamide reaction)}]{\Delta} R{-}NH_2 + K_2CO_3 + 2KBr + 2H_2O$

Q. 6. Write chemical equations for the following reactions:

(*i*) Reaction of ethanolic NH_3 with C_2H_5Cl

(*ii*) Ammonolysis of benzyl chloride and reaction of amine so formed with two moles of CH_3Cl.

Ans. (*i*) $\ddot{N}H_3 + CH_3CH_2{-}Cl \xrightarrow{-HCl} \underset{\text{Ethanamine}}{CH_3CH_2{-}\ddot{N}H_2} \xrightarrow[-HCl]{CH_3CH_2{-}Cl}$

$\underset{\text{N-Ethylethanamine}}{(CH_3CH_2)_2\ddot{N}H} \xrightarrow{CH_3CH_2{-}Cl} \underset{\text{N, N-Diethyl ethanamine}}{(CH_3CH_2)_3\ddot{N}} \xrightarrow[-HCl]{CH_3CH_2{-}Cl} \underset{\text{Tetraethyleommonium chloride}}{(CH_3CH_2)_4N^+Cl^-}$

(*ii*) $\ddot{N}H_3 + C_6H_5CH_2—Cl \xrightarrow[-NH_4Cl]{NH_3} C_6H_5CH_2\ddot{N}H_2 \xrightarrow[-HCl]{CH_3—Cl}$

Benzyl chloride — Benzylamine

(*iii*) $C_6H_5CH_2\ddot{N}HCH_3 \xrightarrow[-HCl]{CH_3—Cl} C_6H_5CH_2—N\begin{matrix} CH_3 \\ CH_3 \end{matrix}$

Q. 7. Write chemical equations for the following conversions:

(*i*) CH_3CH_2Cl into $CH_3CH_2CH_2NH_2$

(*ii*) $C_6H_5CH_2Cl$ to $C_6H_5CH_2CH_2NH_2$

Ans. (*i*) $CH_3CH_2—Cl \xrightarrow[\Delta, -KCl]{KCN(alc.)} CH_3CH_2—C\equiv N \xrightarrow[(Reduction)]{LiAlH_4/Ether} CH_3CH_2CH_2—NH_2$

Propan-1-amine

(*ii*) $C_6H_5CH_2Cl \xrightarrow[-NaCl]{NaCN(alc.),\Delta} C_6H_5CH_2CN \xrightarrow[(Reduction)]{H_2/Ni} C_6H_5CH_2CH_2NH_2$

Chlorophenylmethane (Benzyl chloride) — Phenylthanenitrile (Benzyl cyanide) — 2-Phenylethanamine

Q. 8. Arrange the following in decreasing order of their basic strength:

$C_6H_5NH_2$, $C_2H_5NH_2$, $(C_2H_5)_2NH$, NH_3.

Ans. Due to +I effect of the alkyl groups $(C_2H_5)_2NH$ is a stronger base than $C_2H_5NH_2$ and both of these are stronger bases than NH_3.

However, due to delocalization of lone pair of electrons present on nitrogen over the benzene ring, $C_6H_5NH_2$ is weaker base than aliphatic amines and ammonia.

Thus, basic strength cf the given amines decreases in the order:

$$(C_2H_5)_2NH > C_2H_5NH_2 > NH_3 > C_6H_5NH_2.$$

Q. 9. What is Hoffmann's degradation? Mention its use.

Ans. The method of preparing a primary amine from an acid amide is known as Hoffmann's degradation.

$$\underset{1°\text{ Aminde}}{R—CONH_2} + Br_2 + 4KOH \longrightarrow \underset{1°\text{ Amine}}{R—NH_2} + K_2CO_3 + 2KBr + 2H_2O$$

Use—This reaction is used to step down a homologous series.

Q. 10. Convert:

(*i*) 3-Methylaniline into 3-nitrotoluene

(*ii*) Aniline in to 1, 3, 5-tribromoaniline

Ans. (*i*)

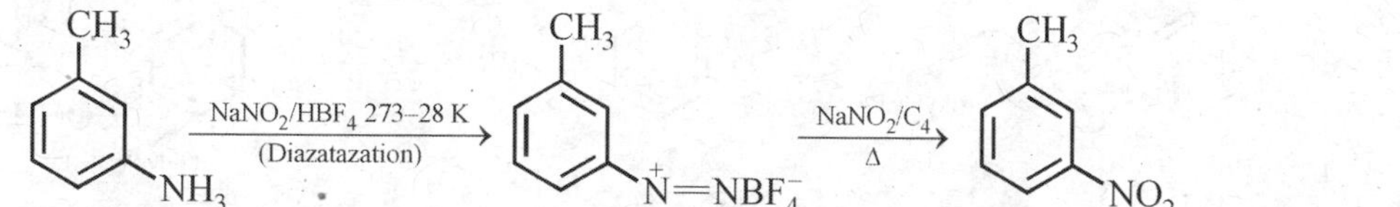

3-Methylaniline — 3-Methylbenzene diazonium fluoroborate — 3-Nitrotoluene

(*ii*)

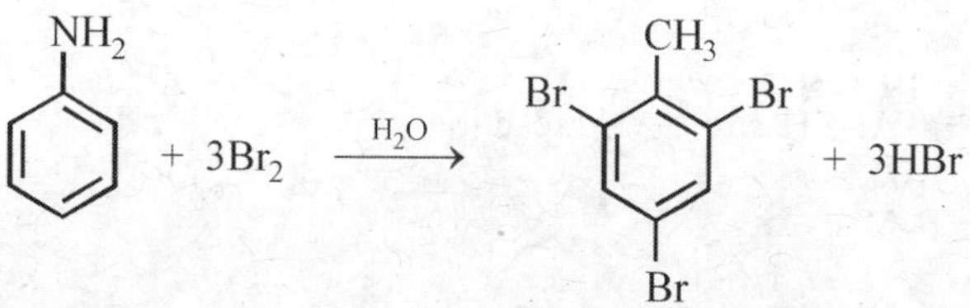

Aniline — 2,4,6-Tribromoaniline

Short Answer Type Questions - II

Q. 1. Give the structures of A, B and C in the following reactions:

(*i*) $CH_3CH_2I \xrightarrow{NaCN} A \xrightarrow[\text{Partial hydralysis}]{OH^-} B \xrightarrow{NaOH + Br_2} C$

(*ii*) $C_6H_5N_2Cl \xrightarrow{CuCN} A \xrightarrow{H_2O/H^+} B \xrightarrow[\Delta]{NH_3} C$

(*iii*) $CH_3CH_2Br \xrightarrow{KCN} A \xrightarrow{LiAlH_4} B \xrightarrow[0°C]{HNO_2} C$

Ans. (*i*)

$$\underset{\text{Iodoethane}}{CH_3CH_2I} \xrightarrow[-NaI]{NaCH} \underset{\substack{\text{Propanenitrile}\\(A)}}{CH_3CH_2CN} \xrightarrow[\text{(Partial Hydrolysis)}]{OH^-} \underset{\substack{\text{Ethanomide}\\(B)}}{CH_3-\overset{\overset{O}{\|}}{C}-CH_2}$$

$$\xrightarrow[\text{(Hofmann bromamide reaction)}]{NaOH + Br_2} \underset{\text{Methanamine (C)}}{CH_3-NH_2}$$

(*ii*)

$$\underset{\text{Benzenediazonium}}{C_6H_5N_2Cl} \xrightarrow[\text{(Sandmeyer reaction)}]{C_4CN} C_6H_5CN \xrightarrow[\text{Hydrolysis}]{H_2O/H^+} \underset{\text{Benzoic acid (B)}}{C_6II_5COOH}$$

$$\xrightarrow{NH_3} [C_6H_5COONH_4] \xrightarrow[-H_2O]{\Delta} \underset{\text{Benzamide (C)}}{C_6H_5CONH_2}$$

(*iii*)

$$CH_3CH_2Br \xrightarrow{KCN} \underset{\substack{\text{Propane nitrile}\\(A)}}{CH_3CH_2CN} \xrightarrow[\text{Reduction}]{LiAlH_4} \underset{\substack{\text{Propan-1-Amine}\\(B)}}{CH_3CH_2CH_2NH_2}$$

$$\xrightarrow[\text{(Diazotisation)}]{HNO_2, 0°C} [CH_3CH_2CH_2\overset{+}{N} \equiv NCl^-] \xrightarrow[-N_2, -HCl]{H_2O} \underset{\text{Propanol (C)}}{CH_3CH_2CH_2OH}$$

Q. 2. Why aromatic primary amines cannot be prepared by Gabriel Phthalimide synthesis?

Ans. Arylhalides do not undergo nucleophilic substitution reactions easily; therefore, arylamines, i.e. aromatic primary amines cannot be prepared by Gabriel Phthalimide reaction

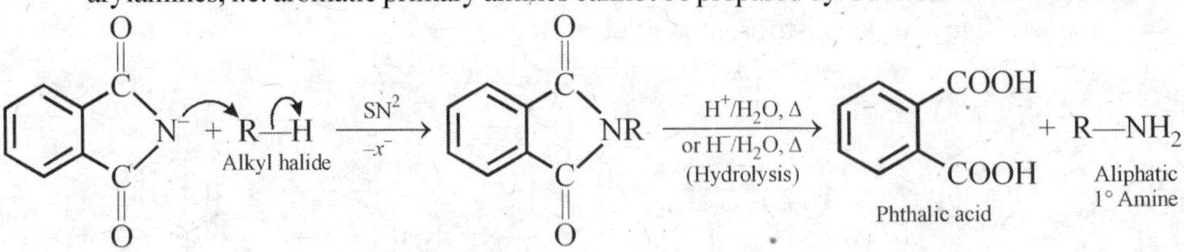

Phthalimide anion (Nucleophile) N-Alkylphthalimide

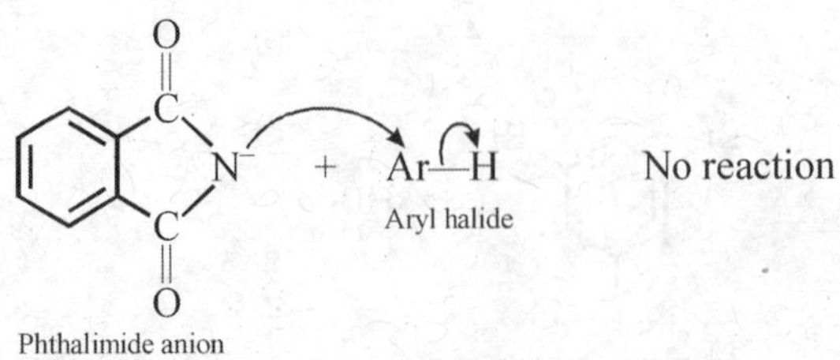

Phthalimide anion (Nucleophile)

Q. 3. How do aromatic and aliphatic primary amines react with nitrous acid?

Ans. (1) Aromatic primary amines react with HNO_2 at 273–278 K to form aromatic diazonium salts.

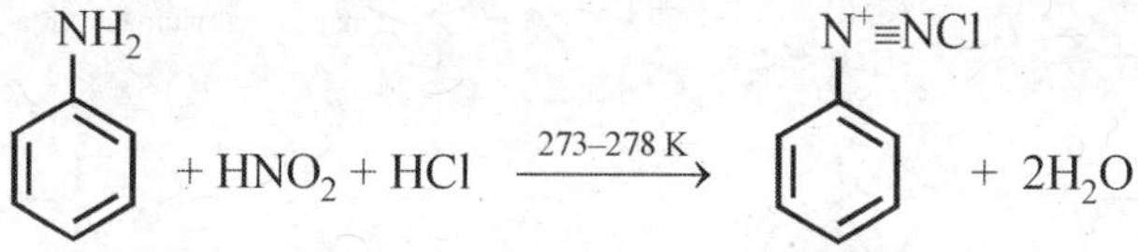

Aniline

(2) Aliphatic primary amines also react with HNO_2 to 273–278K to form aliphatic diazonium salts. However, these are unstable even at low temperature and therefore, decompose readily to form alcohols and N_2 is evolved.

$$\underset{\text{Ethylamine}}{CH_3CH_2NH_2} + HNO_2 + HCl \xrightarrow[(-2H_2O)]{273\text{–}278\,K} \underset{\substack{\text{Ethanediazonium Chloride} \\ \text{((unstable)}}}{[CH_3CH_2 - N^+ \equiv N]Cl^-}$$

$$\xrightarrow{H_2O} \underset{\text{Ethanol}}{CH_3CH_2OH} + N_2 + HCl$$

Q. 4. Give one chemical tert to distinguish between the following pairs of compounds:

(*i*) Methylamine and dimethylamine

(*ii*) Secondary and tertiary amines

(*iii*) Ethylamine and aniline

Ans. (*i*) These can be distinguished by carbylamine tert. When heated with alcoholic solution of KOH and chloroform, methylamine gives foul smell of methyl isocyanide

$$\underset{\text{Methyllamine}}{CH_3NH_2} + CHCl_3 + \underset{\text{alc.}}{3KOH} \longrightarrow \underset{\substack{\text{Methyl isocyanide} \\ \text{(foul smell)}}}{CH_3NC} + 3KCl + 3H_2O$$

Dimethylamine does not give this test.

$$\underset{\text{Dimethylamine}}{(CH_3)_2NH} \xrightarrow[\Delta]{CHCl_3,\,KOH} \text{No reaction}$$

(*ii*) A secondary amine forms N, N-dialkylbenzene-sulphonamide which due to the absence of acidic hydrogen on N-atom does not dissolve in KOH.

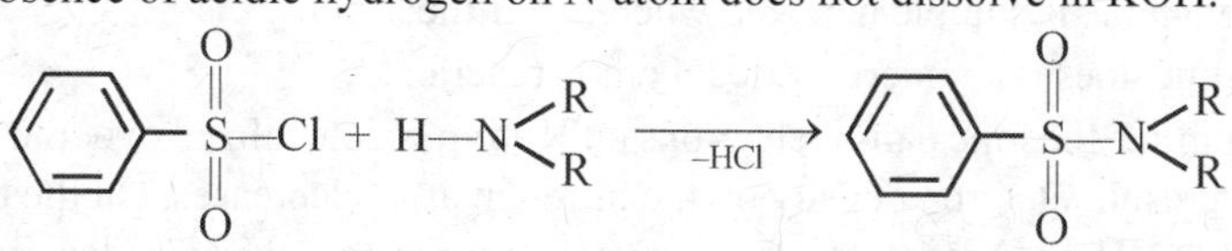

Benzenesulphonyl chloride | 2° Amine | N,N-Dialkyl benzenesulphonamide (Insoluble in KOH

The tertiary amine under these conditions does not react at all since it does not contain a replaceble hydrogen on the nitrogen atom.

(*iii*) **Ethylamine**—These can be distinguished by azo dye test. Ethylamine does not form dye. It will give brick effervescence due to the evolution of N_2 but solution remains clear.

Aniline—(Azo dye test)

Dissolve the compound in conc. HCl and add ice-cold solution of HNO_2 ($NaNO_2$ + dil HCl) and then treat it with an alkaline solution of 2-naphthol. Appearance of brilliant orange or red indicates aniline.

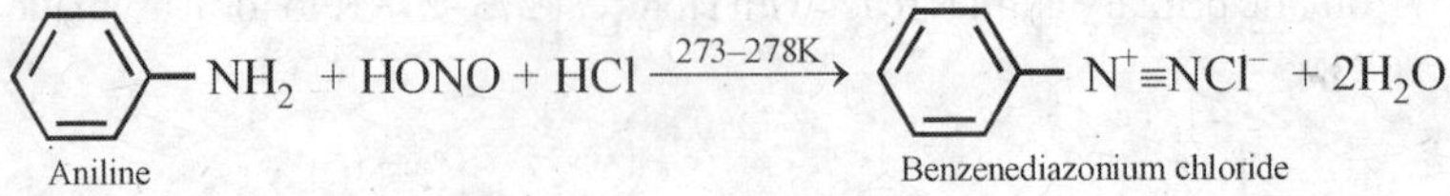

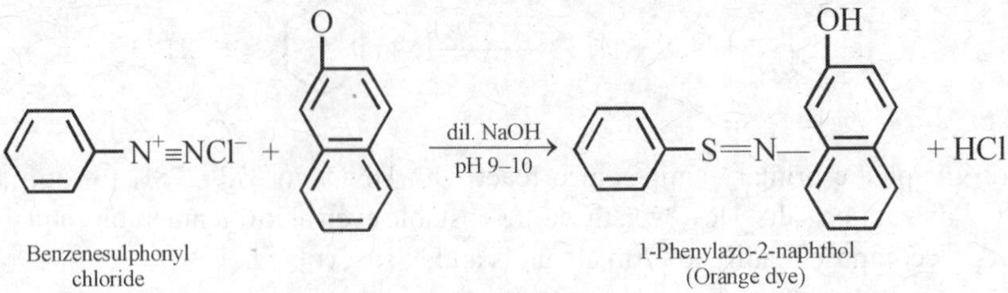

Q. 5. An aromatic compound 'A' on treatment with aqueous ammonia and heating forms compound B which on heating with Br, and KOH forms a compound 'C' of molecular formula C_6H_7N. Write the structures and IUPAC names of compounds A, B and C.

Ans. (*i*) Since the compound C of molecular formula C_6H_7N is formed from B on treatment with Br_2 and KOH; therefore, the compound 'B' must be an amide and 'C' must be an amine. The only aromatic amine having molecular formula C_6H_7N is $C_6H_5NH_2$.

(*ii*) Since 'C' is aniline, the amide form which is formed by must be benzamide ($C_6H_5CONH_2$).

$$\underset{\text{Aniline (C)}}{C_6H_5NH_2} \xleftarrow{Br_2,\,KOH} \underset{\text{Benzamide (B)}}{C_6H_5CONH_2}$$

Thus, B is benzamide.

(*iii*) Since B is formed from A with aqueous ammonia and heating, therefore, compound 'A' must be benzoic acid.

$$\underset{\text{Benzoic acid (A)}}{C_6H_5COOH} \xrightarrow[\text{Heat}]{\text{aq. }NH_3} \underset{\text{Benzamide (B)}}{C_6H_5CONH_2}$$

Thus, A = C_6H_5COOH, B = $C_6H_5CONH_2$, C = $C_6H_5NH_2$.

Q. 6. Account for the following:

(*i*) pKb of aniline is more than that of methylamine.

(*ii*) Ethylamine is soluble in water, whereas aniline is not.

(*iii*) Aniline does not undergo Friedel crafts reaction.

Ans. (*i*) In aniline, the lone pair of electrons on N atom is delocalized over the benzene ring. As a result, electron density on the nitrogen atom decreases. On the other hand, in $CH_3—NH_2$ +I effect of CH_3 group increases the electron density of N-atom. Therefore, aniline is less basic than methylamine and hence pKb of aniline is higher than that of methylamine.

(*ii*) Ethylamine dissolves in water due to intermolecular hydrogen bonding as shown below:

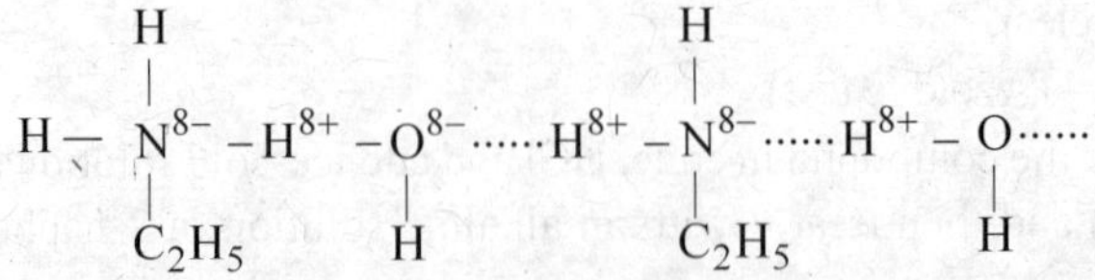

However, because of large hydrophobic part (i.e. hydrocarbon part/of aniline, the extent of hydrogen bonding is less and therefore, aniline is insoluble in water.

(*iii*) Aniline being a Lewis base reacts with Lewis acid such as $AlCl_3$ to form a salt.

$$\underset{\text{Lewis base}}{C_5H_5NH_2} + \underset{\text{Lewis acid}}{AlCl_3} \longrightarrow \underset{\text{Salt}}{C_6H_5N^+H_2AlCl_3^-}$$

As a result, N of aniline acquires +ve charge and hence it acts as a strong deactivating group for electrophilic substitution reaction. Hence, aniline does not undergo Friedel crafts reaction.

Q. 7. How will you convert 4-nitrotoluene to 2-bromobenzoic acid?

Ans.

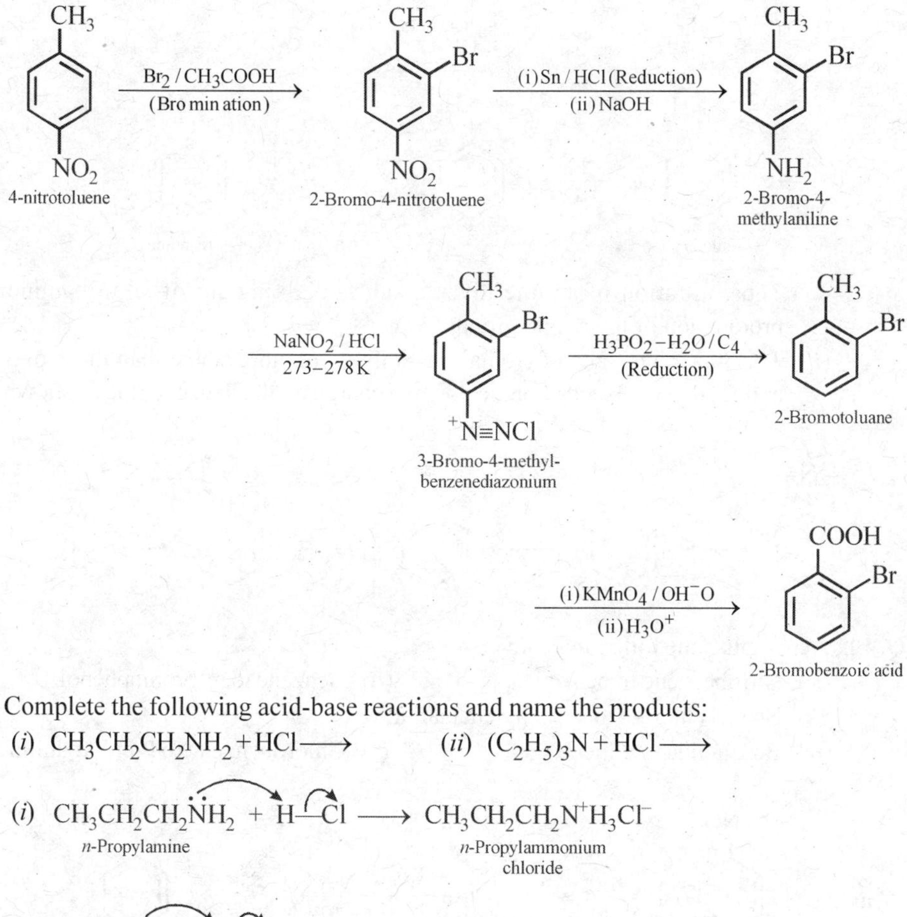

Q. 8. Complete the following acid-base reactions and name the products:

(*i*) $CH_3CH_2CH_2NH_2 + HCl \longrightarrow$ (*ii*) $(C_2H_5)_3N + HCl \longrightarrow$

Ans. (*i*) $\underset{n\text{-Propylamine}}{CH_3CH_2CH_2\ddot{N}H_2} + H{-}Cl \longrightarrow \underset{n\text{-Propylammonium chloride}}{CH_3CH_2CH_2N^+H_3Cl^-}$

(*ii*) $\underset{\text{Triethylamine}}{(C_2H_5)_3\ddot{N}} + H{-}Cl \longrightarrow \underset{\text{Triethylammonium chloride}}{(C_2H_5)_3N^+HCl^-}$

Q. 9. Account for the following:

(*i*) Although amino group is O, p-directing in aromatic substitution reaction, anline on nitration gives a substantial amount of m-nitroaniline.

(*ii*) Diazonium salts of aromatic amines are more stable than those of aliphatic amines.

Ans. (*i*) Nitration is usually carried out with mixture of conc. HNO_3 + Conc. H_2SO_4. In presence of these acids, most of aniline gets protonated to form anilinium ion. Therefore, in presence of acides, the reaction mixture consists of aniline and anilinium

ion. $-NH_2$ group in aniline is O, P-directing and activating while the N^+H_3 group in anilinium ion is m-directing and deactivating.
Whereas nitration of aniline (due to steric hindrance at O-position) mainly gives p-nitroaniline, the nitration of anilinium ion gives m-nitroaniline.

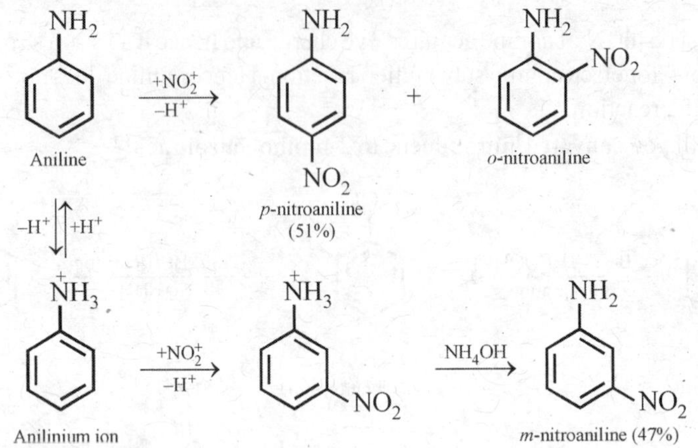

Thus, nitration of aniline gives a substantial amount of *m*-nitroanline due to protonation of the amino group.

(*ii*) The diazonium salts of aromaestic amines are more stable than those of aliphatic amines due to dispersal of the positive charge on the benzene ring as shown below:

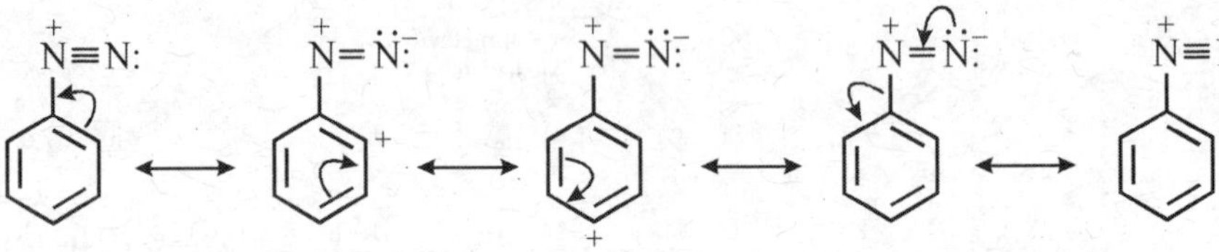

Q. 10. Accomplish the following conversions:

(*i*) Nitrobenzene to benzoic acid (*ii*) Benzene to m-bromophenol

(*iii*) Benzyl chloride to 2-Phenylethanamide

(*iv*) Benzamide to toluene (*v*) Chlorobenzene to P-chloroaniline

Ans. (*i*)

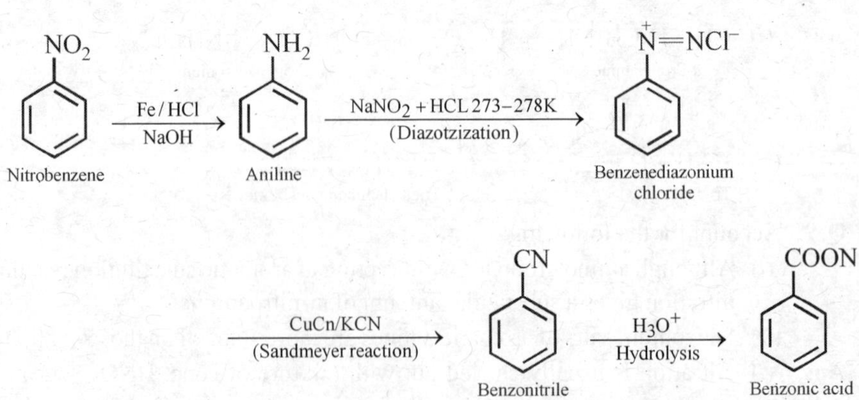

(ii)

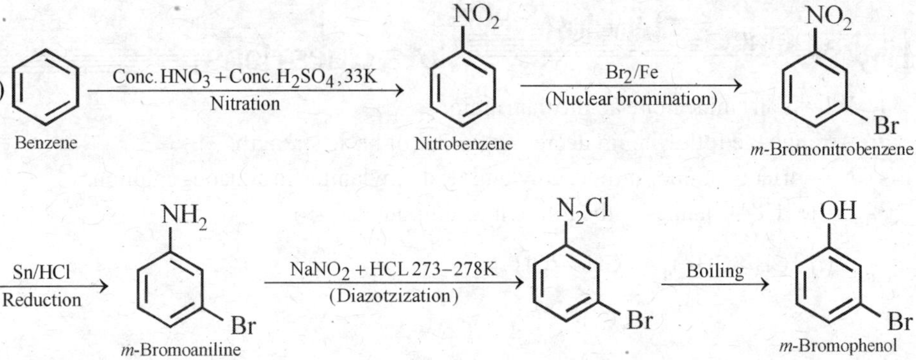
NO2
NO2
Conc. HNO3 + Conc. H2SO4, 33K
Nitration
Br2/Fe
(Nuclear bromination)
Br
Benzene
Nitrobenzene
m-Bromonitrobenzene
NH2
N2Cl
OH
Sn/HCl
Reduction
NaNO2 + HCL 273–278K
(Diazotzization)
Boiling
Br
Br
Br
m-Bromoaniline
m-Bromophenol

(iii)

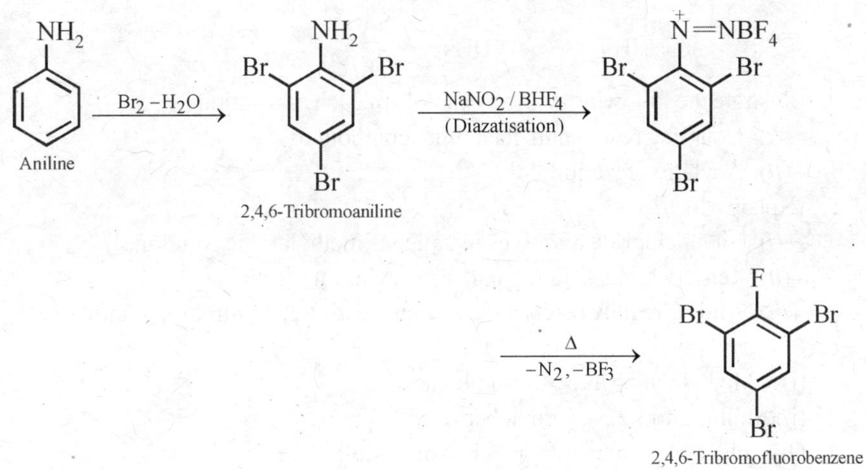
NH2
NH2
N=NBF4
Br
Br
Br
Br
Br2 –H2O
NaNO2 / BHF4
(Diazatisation)
Aniline
Br
Br
2,4,6-Tribromoaniline
F
Br
Br
Δ
–N2, –BF3
Br
2,4,6-Tribromofluorobenzene

(iv)

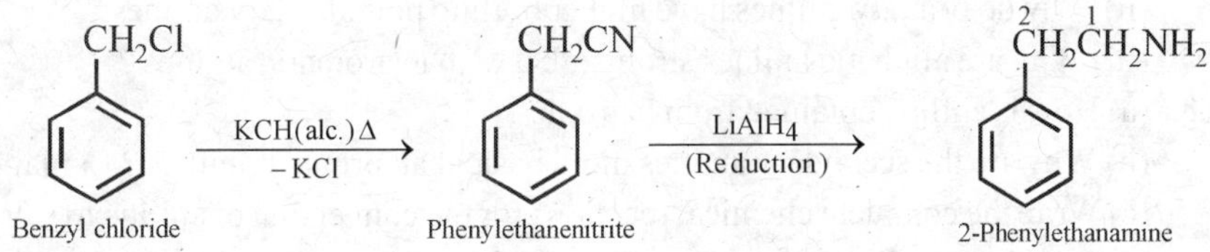
CH2Cl
CH2CN
2 1
CH2CH2NH2
KCH(alc.) Δ
– KCl
LiAlH4
(Reduction)
Benzyl chloride
Phenylethanenitrite
2-Phenylethanamine

(v)

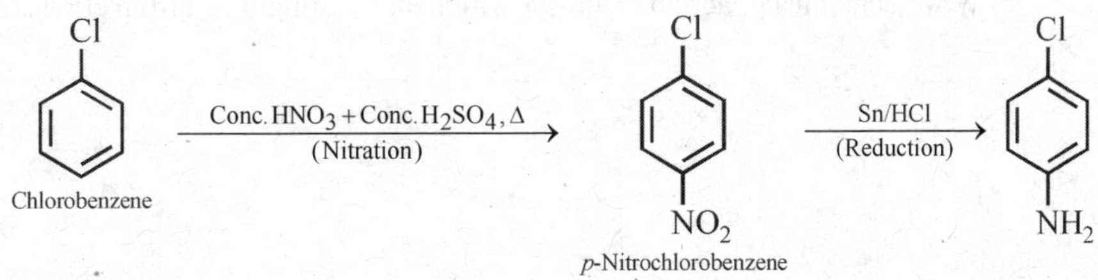
Cl
Cl
Cl
Conc. HNO3 + Conc. H2SO4, Δ
(Nitration)
Sn/HCl
(Reduction)
Chlorobenzene
NO2
NH2
p-Nitrochlorobenzene

Higher Order Thinking Skills Hots Questions

1. Why is an amide more acidic than amine?

2. Arrange the following in decreasing order of basic strength:
NH_3, triethylamine, aniline, ethylamine, diethylamine in aqueous solution.

3. Write IUPAC names of the following compounds:

(*i*) $CH_3(CH_2)_4—\underset{\underset{CH_3}{|}}{CH}—CH_2NH_2$

(*ii*) $CH_3—\underset{\underset{NH_2}{|}}{CH}—CH_2—\underset{\underset{NH_2}{|}}{CH}—CH_3$

4. Illustrate the following with an example of each of reaction:
(*i*) Coupling reaction in diazonium compounds
(*ii*) Acylation reaction

5. Explain why:
(*i*) Silver chloride dissolves in aqueous methylamine solution.
(*ii*) Tertiary amines do not undergo acylation reaction.
(*iii*) Aniline readily reacts with bromine to give 2, 4, 6-trobromoaniline.

6. Convert :
(i) 3-Methylaniline into 3-nitrotoluene
(ii) Aniline into 1,3,5-tribromobenzene.

7. Give plausible explanation for each of the following :
(i) Why are amines less acidic than alcohols of comparable molecular masses ?
(ii) Why do primary amines have higher boiling point tertiary amines ?
(iii) Why are aliphatic amines stronger bases than aromatic amines ?

8. (a) How is aniline obtained from benzene ?
(b) Why are the secondary amines more basic than primary amines ? Explain.
(c) Write the complete chemical reactions for the conversion of aniline to sulphanilic acid.
(d) Mention two important uses of sulphanilic acid.
(e) Write a chemical reaction of aniline which may distinguish it from ethylamine.

❑❑❑

CHAPTER

14 BIOMOLECULES

Syllabus

- ***Carbohydrates :*** *Classification (aldoses and ketoses), monosaccharides (glucose and fructose), oligosaccharides (sucrose, lactose, maltose), polysaccharides (starch, cellulose, glycogen); importance.*
- ***Proteins :*** *Elementary idea of α-amino acids, peptide bond, polypeptides, proteins, structure of proteins—primary, secondary, tertiary structure and quaternary structures (qualitative idea only), denaturation of proteins.*
- ***Vitamins :*** *Classification and functions.*
- ***Nucleic Acids :*** *DNA and RNA.*

1. Cyclic Structure of Glucose :

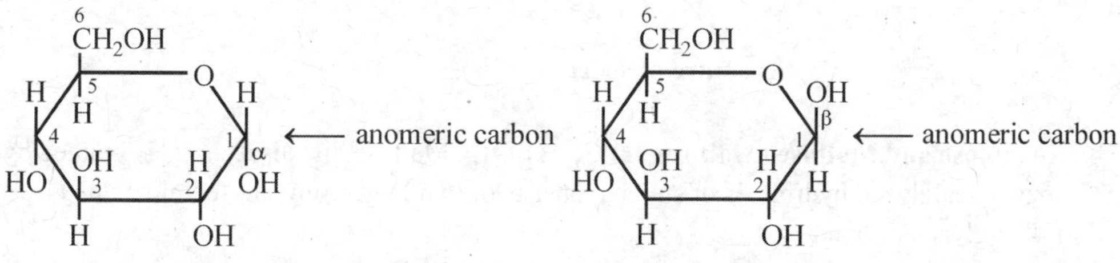

α-D Glucose β-D Glucose

2. Cyclic Structure of Fructose : On cyclization, the carbonyl carbon turns into a new stereocenter. As a consequence, hemiacetal formation leads to two new compounds, two diastereomers differing in the configuration of the hemiacetal group. If that configuration is *S*, the sugar is labeled α; when it is *R*, the sugar is called β.

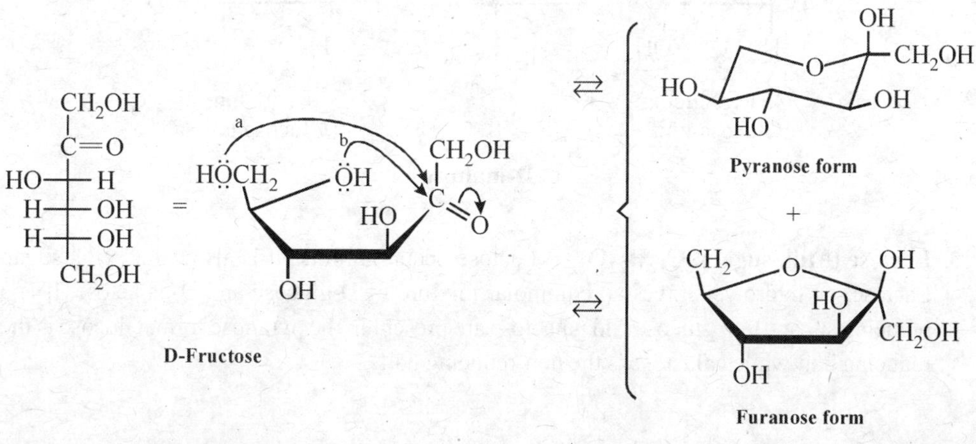

3. **Sucrose :** Sucrose is a disaccharides that yields 1 equivalent of glucose and 1 equivalent of fructose on hydrolysis. This 1 : 1 mixture of glucose and fructose is often referred to as *invert sugar* because the sign of optical rotation changes (inverts) during the hydrolysis from sucrose ($[\alpha]_D = +66.5°$) to a glucose/fructose mixture ($[\alpha]_D \approx -22.0°$).
Sucrose is not a reducing sugar and does not exhibit mutarotation. These observations imply that sucrose is not a hemiacetal and suggest that glucose and fructose must both be glycosides.

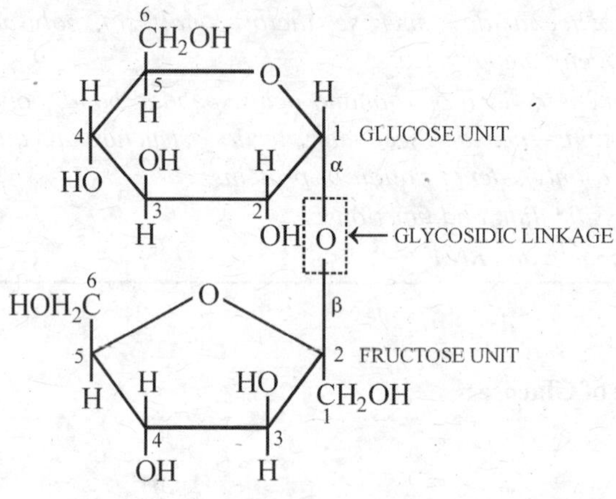

Structure of sucrose

4. **Cellobiose and Maltose (Malt sugar) $C_{12}H_{22}O_{11}$:** Maltose, the disaccharide obtained by enzyme-catalyzed hydrolysis of starch, consists of two D-glucopyranose units joined by a 1,4'-α-glycoside bond.

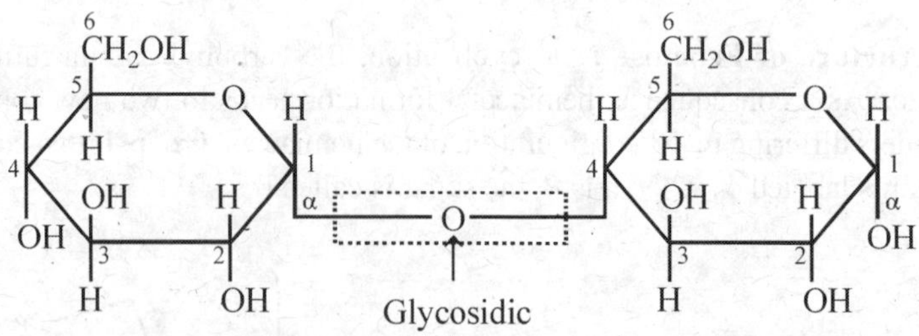

α-D-maltose

5. **Lactose (Milk sugar), $C_{12}H_{22}O_{11}$:** Lactose occurs in milk. It is also called milk sugar. Lactose, on hydrolysis gives an equimolar mixture of D-glucose and D-galactose. It is a reducing sugar. Both glucose and galactose are present in the pyranose form. Glucose is the reducing half while galactose is the non-reducing half.

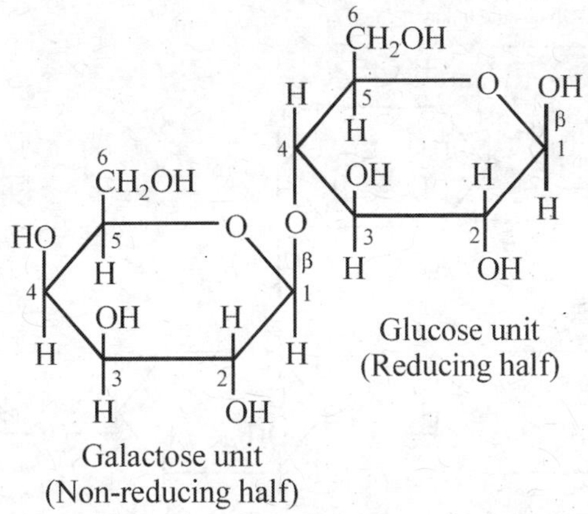

β-D-lactose

6. **Starch, Amylum $(C_6H_{10}O_5)_n$:** Starch contains two component—(i) amylose (water soluble), (ii) amylopectin (water insoluble).

   (i) ***Amylose :*** Amylose is the water soluble component. It gives blue colour with iodine. It is a linear polymer of α-D-glucose. The different α-glucose molecules are linked by glycosidic linkage between C-1 of one glucose molecule and C-4 of another glucose molecule. Amylose can have 200-1000 units of D-glucose.

   Amylose is a linear polymer of α-D-glucose. In amylose C_1 of one glucose unit attach to C_4 of other glucose unit by through α-glycosidic linkage.

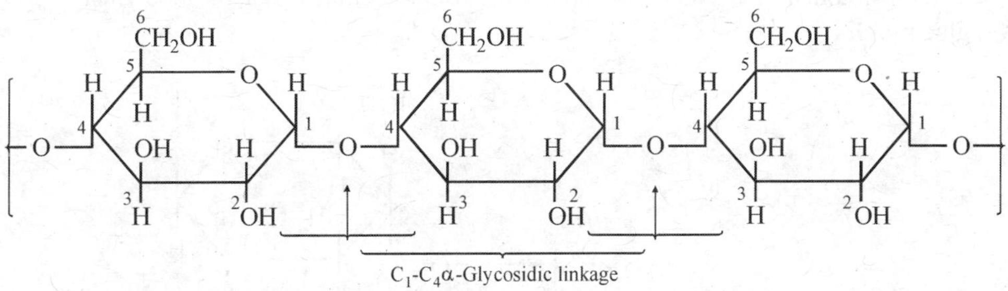

Structure of amylose

   (ii) ***Amylopectin :*** Amylopectin is insoluble in water. It is a highly branched polymer. The branched chain contains 25-30 glucose units. In the main chain, different glucose units are linked together by glycosidic linkage between C-1 and C-4 atoms of the glucose molecules. Branching occurs through the glycosidic linkage between the C-1 of one glucose unit and C-6 of another glucose unit of another chain. Branching also occurs through C-1 and C-3 glycosidic bonds.

   Enzyme amylase is present in saliva. Starch gets hydrolysed by the enzyme amylase into maltose. The end product of hydrolysis of starch is glucose which is an essential nutrient.

   Amylopectin is water in soluble component and does not give blue colour with iodine solution.

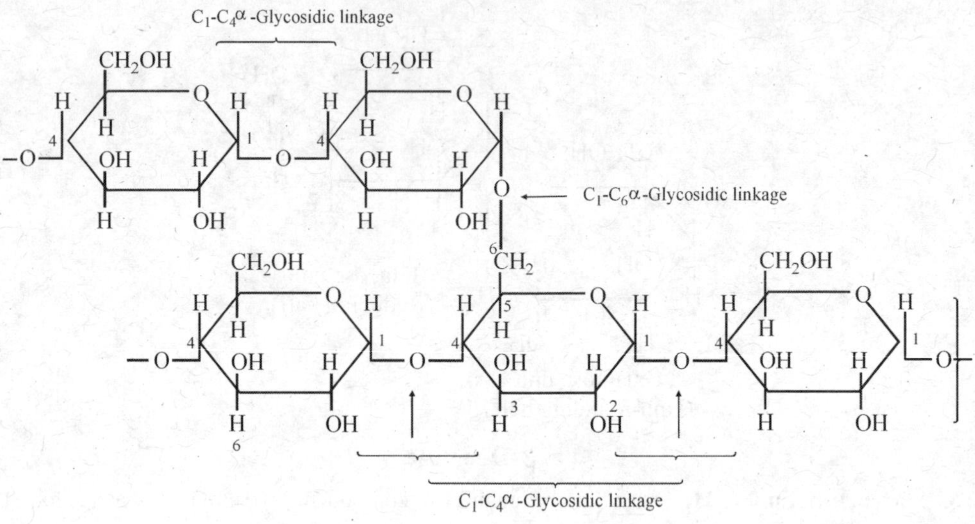

Structure of amylopectin

7. **Cellulose ($C_6H_{10}O_5$) :** It is a linear polymer of β-D-glucose. Different glucose units are linked together through glycosidic linkage between C-1 of one glucose unit and C-4 of other glucose unit. The chains are arranged to form bundles and are held together by hydrogen bonds. It can be woven into fibres. Cellulose is a colourless amorphous solid. It does not reduce Tollen's reagent or Fehling's solution. It is non-reducing and does not reduce fehling solution or tollen's reagent. It does not form osazone. Cellulose is a linear polymer of β-D-glucose.

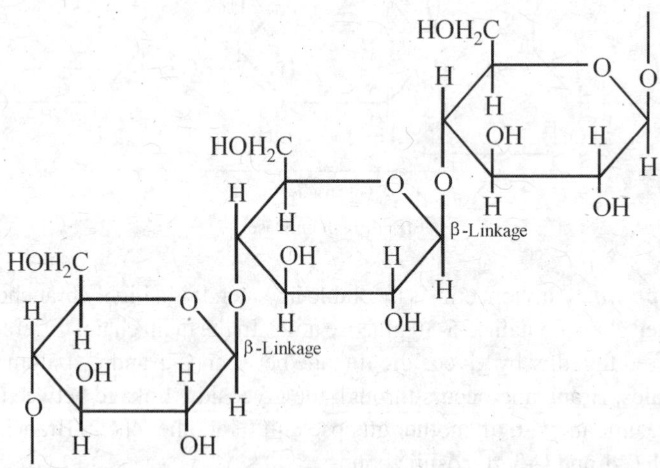

Structure of cellulose

Cellulose is used as a food material by animals such as cattles, sheep etc. The cellulolytic bacteria present in the stomach (rumen) of ruminant mammals break down cellulose with the help of enzyme cellulose. It is then digested and converted into glucose cannot be used as food material by humans.

Very Short Answer Type Questions

Q. 1. Name the enzymes present in the saliva of human beings.

Ans. Amylases.

Q. 2. Deficiency of which vitamin causes scurvy?

Ans. Vitamin C.

Q. 3. Name one reducing and one non-reducing disaccharide.

Ans. Reducing— Maltose or lactose.

Non-reducing— Sucrose.

Q. 4. What is invert sugar?

Ans. An equimolar mixture of glucose and fructose, obtained by hydrolysis of sucrose in presence of an acid such as dil. HCl or the enzyme invertase or sucrase, is called invert sugar.

Q. 5. Which biomolecules act as catalysts?

Ans. Globular proteins (enzymes).

Q. 6. Define genetic code.

Ans. The relation between nucleotide triplets and the amino acids is called genetic code.

Q. 7. What are the building blocks of proteins?

Ans. α— amino acids are the building blocks of proteins.

Q. 8. What are enzymes? How many types of enzymes have been identified so far?

Ans. Enzymes are biocatalysts. These are globular proteins. About 3000 enzymes have been identified so far.

Q. 9. What is denaturation of proteins?

Ans. On heating or on treatment with mineral acids, electrolytes etc., the water soluble globular proteins undergo coagulation resulting in the loss of biological activity to give water insoluble fibrous proteins. This process is called denaturation of proteins.

Q. 10. What is meant by inversion of sugar?

Ans. Sucrose is dextrorotatory but on hydrolysis it gives an equimolar mixture of D(+) –glucose and D(–) fructose which is laevorotary. This change of specific rotation from dextrorotation of laevorotation is called inversion of sugar.

Q. 11. What is isoelectric point?

Ans. The pH at which there is no net migration of the amino acid under the influence of an applied electric field is called isoelectric point. For example, the isoelectric point of glycine is 6.1.

Q. 12. Name the purines present in DNA?

Ans. Adenine (A), Guanine (G), Cytosine (C) and Tymine (T).

Q. 13. What is a peptide bond?

Ans. The covalent bond NH—CO formed between $—NH_2$ group of one amino acid and —COOH of the other with elimination of a molecule of H_2O is called a peptide bond.

Q. 14. Sketch the zwitterion form of aminoacetic acid.

Ans. $H_3N^+—CH_2—COO^-$.

Q. 15. Mention the two classes of nitrogen containing base found in nucleotides.

Ans. The two types of bases are : (i) Purines (ii) Pyrimidines.

Q. 16. α-amino acids have relatively higher melting point than corresponding halo acids. Explain.

Ans. The α-amino acids exist as zwiter ions, $H_3\overset{+}{N}—\underset{\underset{R}{|}}{C}H—COO^-$. Therefore, due to strong intermolecular dipolar attractions or electrostatic attractions, the melting points of α-amino acids are much higher than those of correxponding halo acids which are covalent compounds and have only weak intermolecular hydrogen bonding in them.

Q. 17. What is hypervitaminoses and avitaminoses?

Ans. Excess intake of vitamins A and B causes hypervitaminoses. Multiple deficiencies caused by lack of more than one vitamins is called avitaminoses.

Q. 18. Name the vitamins in each case whose deficiency causes :

(i) night blindness (ii) poor coagulation of the blood.

Ans. (i) Vitamin A (ii) Vitamin K.

Q. 19. Except for vitamin B_{12}, all other vitamins of group B, should bne supplied regularly in diet. Why ?

Ans. Vitamin-B_{12} does not occur in plants but is exclusively snythesized by the microorganisms present in the body. Therefore, it may not be supplied regularly in diet, white all other vitamins of group B should be supplied regularly in diet.

Q. 20. What are nucleosides ? Give examples.

Ans. Nucleosides are formed by the combination of nitrogeneous bases (purines and pyrimidines) and sugar (ribose or deoxyribose). For example,

Adenosine : Adenine + Ribose
Guanosine : Guanine + Ribose
Cytodine : Cytosine + Ribose
Deoxythymidine : Thymine + Deoxribose

Q. 21. Name the three different type of RNA.

Ans. *m* RNA, *r* RNA and *t* RNA.

Q. 22. Name the bonding in α-helix structure of protein.

Ans. H-bonding.

Short Answer Type Questions - I

Q. 1. (*a*) What are reducing and non-reducing sugars?

(*b*) Pyorrhoea is caused by deficiency of which vitamin?

Ans. (*a*) **Reducing sugars**— The carbohydrates which contain aldehydic or ketonic group in the hemiacetal or hemiketal form the reduce Tollen's reagent or Fehling's solution are called reducing sugars.

Non-reducing sugars— The carbohydrates which do not reduce Tollen's reagent or Fehling's solution are called non-reducing sugars.

(*b*) Pyorrhoea is caused by the deficiency of vitamin C.

Q. 2. Give two differences between starch and cellulose.

Ans. Starch	Cellulose
1. It is a main storage polysaccharide of plants.	1. It is a major structural polysaccharide of plants and constitutes of the bulk of cell wall.
2. It is polymer of α-D glucose units.	2. It is polymer of β-glucose units.

Q. 3. What are anomers? How many anomers of glucose are known? Name them.

Ans. Isomers which differ in stereochemistry at C_1 in cyclic structure are called anomers. The two anomers of glucose are α-D glucose and β-D-glucose.

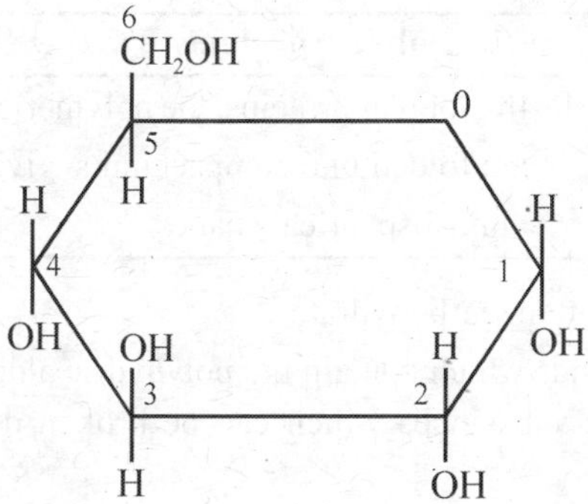

α-D-Glucose

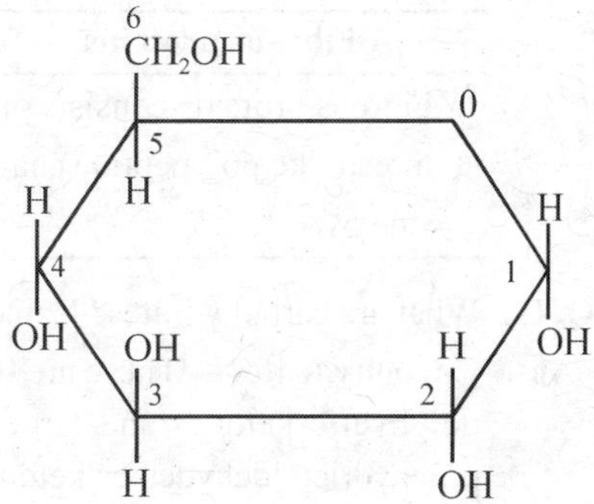

β-D-glucose

Q. 4. What are the expected products of hydrolysis is of lactose?

Ans. Lactose is a diassacharide. On hydrolysis, it gives two molecules of monosaccharides, *i.e., one* molecule of each D-(+)-glucose and D-(+) galactose.

$$\underset{\text{Lactose}}{C_{12}H_{22}O_{11}} + H_2O \xrightarrow[\text{or Lactase}]{H_3O^+} \underset{\text{D-(+)-Glucose}}{C_6H_{12}O_6} + \underset{\text{D-(+)-Galactose}}{C_6H_{12}O_6}$$

Q. 5. Glucose or sucrose are soluble in water but cyclohexane or benzene (simple six membered ring compounds) are insoluble in water. Explain.

Ans. Glucose or sucrose are soluble in water because it (Glucose) contains five and sucrose contains eight –OH group. These –OH group form H-bonds with water. Due to presence of H-bonding, glucose and sucrose are soluble in water.

In contrast cyclohexane (benzene) are insoluble in water because these compounds do not contain –OH groups and do not form H-bonds with water.

Q. 6. Where does the water present in the egg go after boiling the egg?

Ans. When the egg is boiled, the proteins first undergo denaturation and then coagulation, and the water present in the egg gets absorbed/absorbed in the coagulated proteins through H-bonding.

Q. 7. What products would be formed when a nucleotide form DNA containing thymine is hydrolysed?

Ans. Besides thymine, the two other products are: 2 deoxy-D-ribose and phosphoric acid.

Q. 8. Give two differences between peptides and proteins.

Ans. Peptides	Proteins
1. Peptides are compounds formed by the condensation of two or more same bonds.	1. Proteins are long polymers of amino acids linked by peptide (–CO–NH) bonds.
2. They have molecular weight up to 10,000.	2. They have molecular weight more than 10,000.

Q. 9. What are proteins? State a difference between globular and fibrous proteins?

Ans. Proteins are the polymers of α-amino acids, having high molecular mass more than 10,000.

Fibrous proteins	Globular proteins
1. Fibrous proteins consists of linear thread like polypeptide chains lying side by side.	1. In globular proteins, the polymeric chains are folded into compact units giving almost spherical shapes.

Q. 10. What are carbohydrates? Name four important carbohydrates.

Ans. **Carbohydrates**— These are the compounds which contain the polyhydric aldehydes, polyhydric ketones and large polymeric substances which can be broken down to polyhydric aldehydes or ketones

Name four carbohydrates—

1. Glucose ($C_6H_{12}O_6$)
2. Fructose ($C_6H_{12}O_6$)
3. Sucrose ($C_{12}H_{22}O_{11}$)
4. Ribose ($C_5H_0O_5$)

Q. 11. Classify the following into monosaccharides and disaccharides.

Ribose, 2-deoxyribose, maltose, galactose, fructose and lactose.

Ans. 1. **Monosaccharides**— Ribose, 2-deoxyribose, galactose, fructose.

2. **Disaccharides**— Maltose and lactose.

Q. 12. Name the deficiency diseases caused due to lack of vitamin A, C, E, B_1, B_{12}, B_6 and K.

Ans. A lack of one or more vitamins leads to characteristic deficiency symptoms in an individual human being. Multiple deficiencies caused by lack of more than one vitamin are more common in human beings. This condition of vitamin deficiency is known as 'avitaminoses'. Deficiency diseases caused due to lack of a particular vitamin are as follows :

Name of Vitamins	Deficiency disease
Vitamin A	Xerophthalmia i.e., hardenging of cornea of eye.
Vitamin C	Scurvy
Vitamin E	Sterility
Vitamin B_1	Beri-beri (a disease of nervous system)
Vitamin B_{12}	Pernicious anaemia
Vitamin B_6	Severe dermatitis, convulsions.
Vitamin K	Homorrhagic conditions

Short Answer Type Questions – II

Q. 1. What do you understand by the term glycoside linkage?

Ans. The oxygen linkage through which two monosaccharides are joined together by the loss of a water molecule to form a molecule of disaccharide is called the glycoridic linkage. The glycosidic linkage in maltose is shown below:

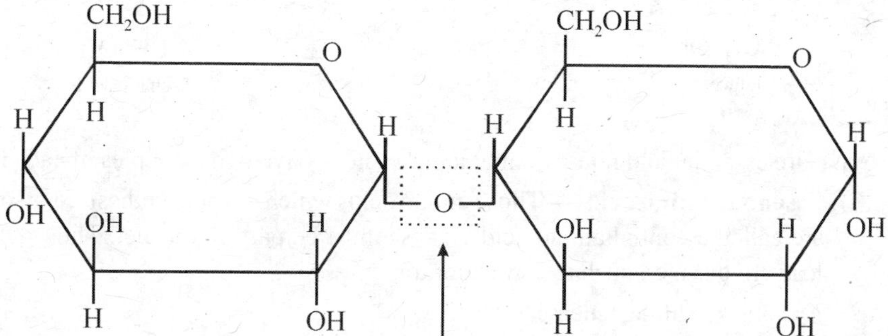

α-D-Glucose β-D-Glucose

Glycosidic linkage

Q. 2. What happens when D-glucose is treated with the following reagents?

(*i*) HI (*ii*) Bromine water (*iii*) HNO_3

Ans. (*i*)

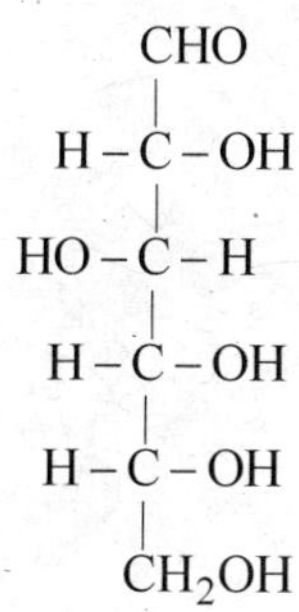

$\xrightarrow[\text{Reduction}]{\text{HI}} \underset{n\text{-Hexane}}{CH_3(CH_2)_4CH_3} + \underset{\text{2-Iodohexane}}{CH_3—CH_2—CH_2—CHI—CH_3}$

(*ii*)

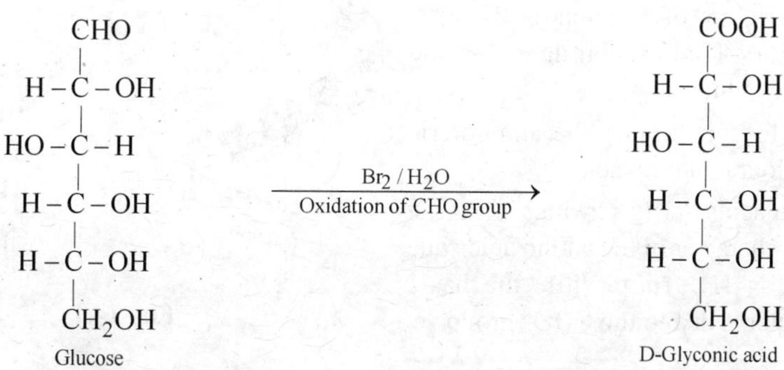

Glucose D-Glyconic acid

(iii)

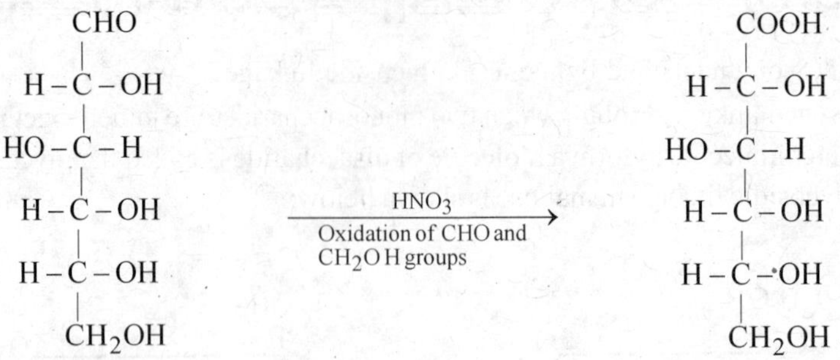

Glucose → D-Saccharic acid

Q. 3. What are essential and non-essential amino acids? Give two examples of each type.

Ans. (*i*) **Essential amino acids**— Those amino acids which are not synthesised by our body are called essential amino acids. These must be part of our diet. Their deficiency leads to diseases such as Kwashiorkor.

Examples : valine, leucine.

(*ii*) **Non-essential amino acids**— They are synthesised by our body. They are also called dispersable amino acids.

Examples : glycine, alanine.

Q. 4. Enumerate the reactions of D-glucose which cannot be explained by its open chain structure.

Ans. (1) Open chain of glucose does not undergo certain characteristic reactions of aldehydes. For example—

(*i*) Glucose does not respond to Schiff's reagent test.

(*ii*) Open chain of glucose does not form $NaHSO_3$ addition product, aldehyde-ammonia adduct, 2,4-DNP derivative.

Q. 5. What type of bonding helps in stabilising the α-helix structure of proteins?

Ans. The α-helix structure of proteins is stabilized by intra molecular H-bonding between C = O of one amino acid residue and the N–H of the fourth amino acid residue in the chain.

Q. 6. How do you explain the amphoteric behaviour of amino acids?

Ans. Amino acids exist as zwitter ions. The acidic character of the amino acids due to the N^+H_3 group while the basic character is due to the COO^- group.

Fig. 14.1

$$H_2N-\underset{\underset{R}{|}}{CH}-COOH \longrightarrow H_3N^+-\underset{\underset{R}{|}}{CH}-CCO^-$$

Zwitter ion

In zwitter ionic form, α amino acids show amphoteric behaviour as they react with both acids and bases.

Q. 7. Explain mutarotation. Give its mechanism in case of D-glucose.

Ans. The process of spontaneous gradual change in specific rotation of an optically active compound is called mutarotation. For example, a freshly prepared solution of glucose has a specific rotation + 111° and when this solution is kept for some time, the specific rotation falls to +52.5° and remians constant at the value. On the other hand, a fresh solution of β-D-glucose has a specific rotation of 19.2° which changes to +52.5° when allowed to stand for some time.

Mechanism: The two forms of glucose, known as 'anomers' of glucose, differ from each other in stereochemistry at C–1.

By analogy to the formation of two methyl glucosides, glucose exists in two forms—α-D-glucose and β-D-glucose.

$$\underset{\text{glucose}}{\alpha\text{-D-}(+)} \rightleftharpoons \text{Equilibrium mixture } +52.5^\circ \rightleftharpoons \underset{\text{glucose}}{\beta\text{-D-}(+)}$$

Q. 8. How are vitamins classified? Name the vitamin responsible for coagulation of blood.

Ans. Vitamins are classified into two groups depending upon their solubility in water or fat.

(*i*) **Water soluble vitamins**— These include vitamin-B-complex (B_1, B_2, B_5, *i.e.*, nicotinic acid, B_6, B_{12}) and vitamin C.

(*ii*) **Fat soluble vitamins**— These include vitamins, *A*, *D*, *E* and *K* which are stored in liver and adipose (fat storing tissues)

"Biotin, *i.e.*, vitamin H is neither soluble in water nor in fat.

Vitamin K is responsible for coagulation of blood.

Q. 9. What are nucleic acids? Mention their two important functions.

Ans. Nucleic acids are biomolecules which are found in the nuclei of all living cells in form of nucleoproteins or chromosomes.

Nucleic acids are of two types:—

(*i*) Deoxyribonucleic acid (DNA).

(*ii*) Ribonucleic acid (RNA).

The two important functions—

(*i*) DNA is responsible for transmission of hereditary effects from one generation to another.

(*ii*) DNA and RNA are responsible for synthesis of all proteins needed for the growth and maintenance of our body.

Q. 10. How do you explain the absence of aldehyde group in the pentaacetate of D-glucose?

Ans. The cyclic hemiacetal form of glucose contains an OH group at C-1 which gets hydrolysed in aqueous solution to produce the open chain aldehydic form which then reacts with NH_2OH to form the corresponding oxime. Thus, glucose contains an aldehydic group. In contrast, when glucose is reacted with acetic anhydride, the OH group at C–1, along with the four other OH groups at C–2, C–3, C–4 and C–6 form a pentaacetate. Since the pentaacetate of glucose does not contain a free OH group at C-1, it can not get hydrolysed in aqueous to produce the open chain aldehydic form and hence glucose pentaacetate does not react with NH_2OH to form glucose group.

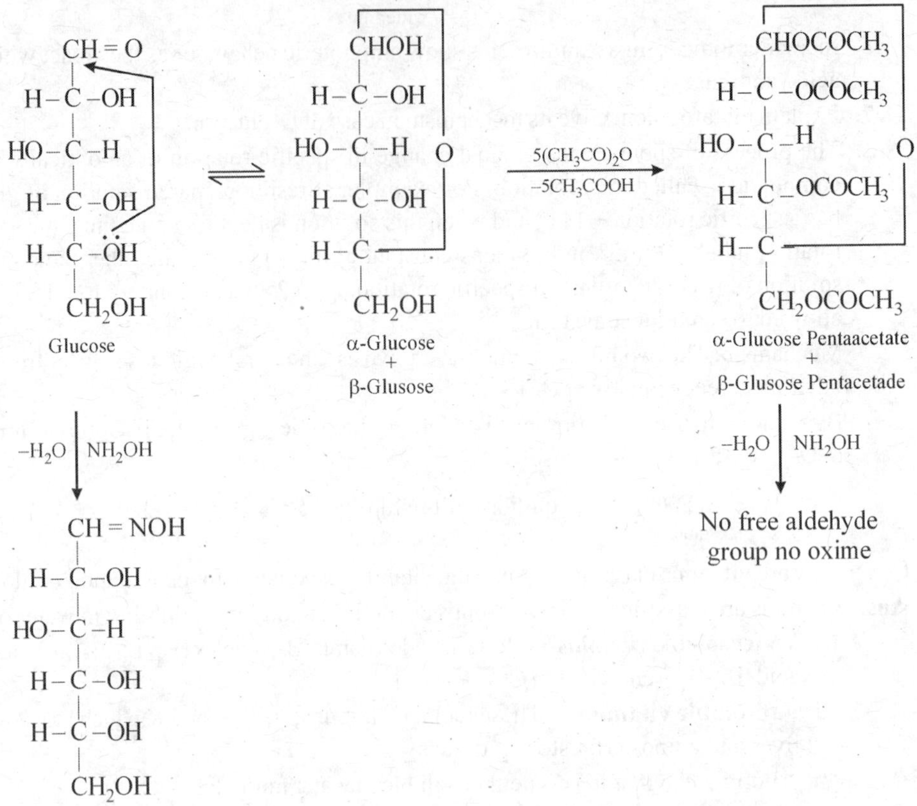

Long Answer Type Questions

1. Why vitamins are essential to us ? Give the role of various vitamins in our body.

Ans. Vitamins are required for the normal metabolic process and for the life, growth and good health of human beings and animals. These carry out various physiological actions and stimulate the growth of the cells.

(i) ***Vitamin A :*** Renitol, carotene derivative, soluble in fats and oil but insoluble in water. Destroyed in cooking.

Source : Milk, butter, ghee, egg yolk.

Deficiency disease : Night blindness, xeropthalamia. Retarded growth lower resistance to infection.

(ii) ***Vitamin B_1 :*** Thiamine, soluble in water destroyed by heat above)°C.

Source : Milk, vegetables, yeast, unpolished rice, liver, nuts.

Deficiency disease : Beri-Beri, loss of apetitie.

(iii) ***Vitamin B_2 :*** Ribiflavin, water soluble, resistance to heat.

Source : Milk, vegetables, unpolished rice, liver nuts, egg.

Deficiency disease : Soring of tongue cracked lips, premature aging.

(iv) ***Vitamin B_6 :*** Pyridoxine, soluble in water and alcohol.

Source : Cereal grains, yeast, egg, meat.

Deficiency disease : Nervous disturbance, convulsions.

(*v*) ***Vitamin B_{12} :*** Cobalamin, water soluble, containing cobalt.

Source : Occurs only in animals and microorganisms but not in plants, liver.

Deficiency disease : Bad form of anaemia.

(*vi*) ***Vitamin C :*** Ascorbic acid, water soluble, destroyed by cooking and by ari. Reducing agent.

Source : Citrus fruts, organes, lemons, grapes, tomatoes, cabbage, amala, leafy vegetable, sprouted seeds.

Deficiency disease : Scurvy, pyorrhoes (in teeth) anaemia, pain in joints, bone fragility.

(*vii*) ***Vitamin D :*** Soluble in fats and oils, insoluble in water.

Source : Milk, egg, liver, meat.

Deficiency disease : Rickets, deformation of bones and teeth.

(*viii*) ***Vitamin E :*** α-toco-phenol, coluble in fats and oils, insoluble in water.

Source : Cotton seed oil, milk, ghee, egg, wheat gram.

Deficiency disease : Homolytic anaemia, degeneration changes in muscles.

(*ix*) ***Vitamin K :*** Soluble in fats, insoluble in water.

Source : Leafy vegetables, fish, oils, meat, alfa-alfa.

Deficiency disease : Haemorrage clotting of blood.

Higher Order Thinking Skills Hots Questions

1. Glucose forms an oxime but glucose pentaacetate does not. Explain.

2. What is the importance of amino acids to us?

3. Why are carbohydrate, optically active?

4. The melting point and solubility of amino acids are generally higher than that of corresponding haloacids. Explain.

5. State the difference between the following pairs:

(*i*) α-helix and β-pleated sheet structure.

(*ii*) Primary and secondary structures of proteins.

(*iii*) Enzymes and co-enzymes.

❑❑❑

CHAPTER

15 POLYMERS

Syllabus

- *Classification—natural and synthetic, methods of polymerization (addition and condensation), copolymerization. Some important polymers: natural and synthetic like polythene, nylon, polyesters, bakelite, rubber.*

1. **Homopolymers :** A polymer may have indentical monomers or monomers of different structures, and accordingly they are called homopolymers and copolymers.

   Examples of Homopolymers : Nylon 6, polybutadiene, teflon (polytetrafluoroethylene), cellulose, starch, polypropene, polyvinyl chloride (PVC), polyisoprene, neoprene (polychloroprene), polyacrylonitrile (PAN).

2. **Copolymers :** Polymers whose repeating structural units are derived from two or more types of monomer units are called copolymers.

   Examples of Copolymers : Buna-S, polyester, alkyd resins, bakelite, melamine-formaldehyde polymer.

3. **Additional Polymers :** Additional polymers are formed by the repeated addition of a large number of same or different monomers.

   Examples of Additional Polymers : *cis*-Polyisopene (natural rubber), Polyvinyl chloride (PVC), Polytetrafluoroethylene (PTEE) or Teflon, Polybutadiene.

4. **Condensation polymers :**

   Example : Polyurethane, Melamine-form-aidehyde resin, Bakelite, Terylene or Dacron, Cellulose, Starch (amylose, and amylopectin) and glycogen, Nylon-6.

5. **Elastomers :** Polymers in which the intermolecular forces of attraction between the polymer chains are the weakest are called elastomers.

   Examples : Buna-N, neoprene, SBR or Buna-S.

6. **Low density polythene and High density polythene :**

   (i) Low density polythene (LDP) or Low density polyethylene (LDPE) :

   - It is produced by heating ethylene to 400-600K under a pressure of 1000-2000 atmospheres and in presence of a trace of oxygen or peroxide.
   - No solvent can dissolve low density polyethylene at room temperature. But it is soluble in many solvents at high temperatures like toluene, carbon tetrachloiede, xylene, trichloroethylene.
   - It is used as a packaging material, as insulation for electrical wires and cables.

   (ii) High density polythene (HDP) or High density polyethylene (HDPE) :

   - It is manufactured by coordination polymerization of ethene.
   - In this method, ethene (in a hydrocarbon solvent) is heated to 333-343 K under a pressure of 6-7 atmospheres in presence of a catalyst consisting of triethylaluminium and titanium trichloride or tetrachloride (Ziegler–Natta catalyst).

$$nCH_2 = CH_2 \xrightarrow[333-343K,\ 6-7\ atm.]{(CH_3CH_2)_3Al + TiCl_4} \left(CH_2 - CH_2 \right)_n$$

Ethene — High density Polythene (HDP)

- High density polyethylene is much stiffer than low density polyethylene and has a higher tensile strength and hardness.
- Chemically, it is more resistant than low density polyethylene and ahs significantly lower gas permeability.

7. **Polytetrafluoroethene (PTFE) or Teflon :** Teflon is prepared by heating tretrafloroethene in presence of a free radical or persulphate catalyst at high pressures. They have crowding chains of $-CF_2-CF_2-$ in the polymeric molecule.

$$nF_2C = CF_2 \xrightarrow[\text{High pressure}]{\text{Catalyst}} \left[F_2C - CF_2 \right]_n$$

Tetrafluoroethene — Polytetrafluoroethene or Teflon

Teflon is flexible and inert to solvents and to boiling acids even to aqua regia and is stable upto 598K.

Taflon has widely been used in pump packings, shaft bearing, and for cable insulation, insulation for motors, generators, transformer coils and capacitors.

8. **Nylon 6, 6 :**
   - It is manufactured by the condensation polymerization of adipic acid and hexamethylenediamine.

$$\left.\begin{array}{c} nHO - \overset{O}{\overset{\|}{C}} - (CH_2)_4 - \overset{O}{\overset{\|}{C}} - OH \\ \text{Adipic acid} \\ + \\ nH_2N - (CH_2)_6 - NH_2 \\ \text{Hexamethylenediamine} \end{array}\right] \longrightarrow \text{salt} \xrightarrow[\substack{\text{Polymerization} \\ -(2n-1)\,H_2O}]{\substack{553K, \\ \text{High pressure}}}$$

$$\left[\overset{O}{\overset{\|}{C}} - (CH_2)_4 - \overset{O}{\overset{\|}{C}} - NH - (CH_2)_6 - NH \right]_n$$

Nylon 6, 6

   - It is called nylon-66 (read as nylon six, six) since both adipic acid and hexamethylenediamine contain six carbon atoms each.
   - Nylon is strong, tough, elastic and can be readily dyed.
   - Nylon has a low affinity for direct cotton, sulphur and vat dyes.

9. **Nylon 6, 10 :**
   - It is obtained by the condensation of hexamethylenediamine (containing six carbon atoms) and sebacic acid [HOOC $(CH_2)_8$ COOH], a dibasic acid containing ten carbon atoms.

$$\left.\begin{matrix} nH_2N-(CH_2)_6-NH_2 \\ \text{Hexamethylenediamine} \\ + \\ nHOOC-(CH_2)_8-COOH \\ \text{Sebacic acid} \end{matrix}\right| \xrightarrow[-(2n-1)\,H_2O]{\Delta,\ \text{Polymerization}} \left[-HN-(CH_2)_6-NH-\overset{\overset{\displaystyle O}{\|}}{C}-(CH_2)_8-\overset{\overset{\displaystyle O}{\|}}{C}- \right]_n$$

Nylon 6, 10

- Nylon 6, 10 is not much used as textile fibre, but is used to manufacture articles like brushes and bristles.

10. Nylon 6 or Perlon :

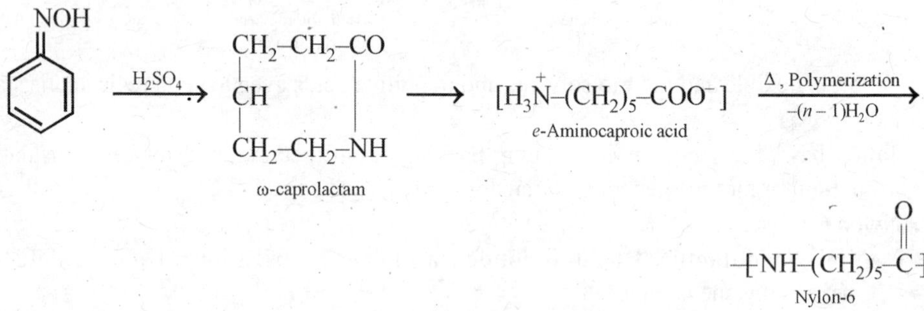

When caprolactam is heated with a trace of water, it hydrolyses to ∈-aminocaproic acid which upon continued heating undergoes polymerization to give nylon-6.

11. Polyesters :

- Polymers which have ester linkages are called polyesters.
- Terylene or Dacron is the best known example of polysters.

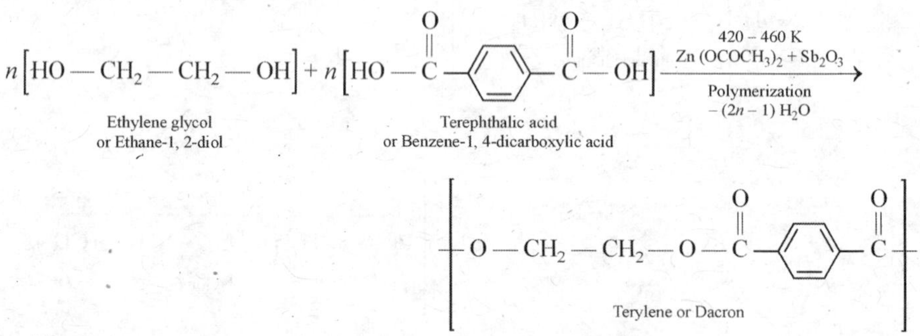

12. Natural Rubber :

- Natural rubber is a linear 1, 4-addition polymer of isoprene (*i.e.*, 2-methyl-1, 3-butadiene)

$$n CH_2=\overset{\overset{\displaystyle CH_3}{|}}{C}-CH=CH_2 \xrightarrow{\text{Polymerization}} \left[CH_2-\overset{\overset{\displaystyle CH_3}{|}}{C}=CH-CH_2 \right]_n$$

Isoprene (2-Methyl-1,3-butadiene)   Polyisoprene

- Natural rubber is *cis*-polysoprene. Synthetic rubber (gutta percha) obtained by free radical polymerization of isoprene has all trans-configuration.

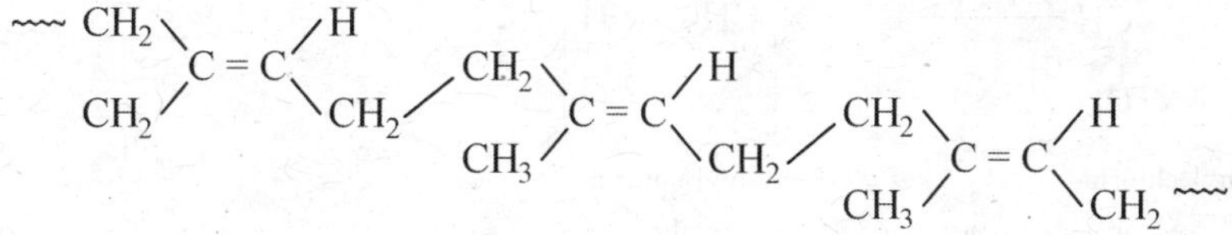

trans-Polyisoprene
(Gutta-Percha)

Gutta percha is used in the manufacture of golf ball covers, submarine cables, adhesives and tissues for surgical purposes.

13. Synthetic Rubbers

Neoprene : It is a polymer of chloroprene (2-chloro-1, 3-butadiene) and is also called polychloroprene.

$$CH_2 = CH - C \equiv CH + HCl \xrightarrow[\text{addition.}]{\text{Mark}} \underset{\text{Chloroprene}}{CH_2 = CH - \overset{\overset{\large Cl}{|}}{C} = CH_2}$$

14. Terylene or Dactron : Terylene is the British name for Dacron and can be prepared from terephthalic acid and ethylene glycol, ether by direct esterification or by catalysed ester inter change.

$$\underset{\text{Terephthalic acid}}{nHO_2C.C_6H_4CO_2H} + \underset{\text{Ethylene glycol}}{nHOCH_2CH_2OH} \xrightarrow{-H_2O} .....(-COC_6H_4CO - OCH_2CH_2O)_n....$$

Terylene or Dacron is used for preparing fabric, such as suitings and shirtings, for making sweeters.

Very Short Answer Type Questions

Q. 1. What is Buna-S ?

Ans. It is a copolymer of butadiene and styrene.

Q. 2. Name a synthetic polymer which is an amide.

Ans. Nylon 6 or Nylon 6,6.

Q. 3. Name the monomer of natural rubber.

Ans. Monomer of natural rubber is : isoprene, $CH_2 = \overset{\overset{\large CH_3}{|}}{C} - CH = CH_2$

Q. 4. What is a plasticizer?

Ans. The organic compounds which when added to plastics make them soft and workable are called plasticizers. For example, cresyl triphosphate.

Q. 5. What are the monomers of SBR?

Ans. Styrene (25%), $C_6H_5CH = CH_2$ and 1,3 butadine (75%) $CH_2=CH-CH=CH_2$.

Q. 6. Write chemical equation for the preparation of polymer.

Ans. $$\underset{\substack{\text{Ethene}\\\text{(Monomer)}}}{nCH_2 = CH_2} \xrightarrow{\text{Polymerzation}} \underset{\substack{\text{Polythene}\\\text{(Polymer)}}}{-[CH_2 - CH_2]_n}$$

Q. 7. Write chemical equation for the preparation of polyvinyl chloride.

Ans. $$n\mathrm{CH_2=\underset{\underset{Cl}{|}}{CH}} \xrightarrow{\text{Polymerisation}} \left[\mathrm{CH_2-\underset{\underset{Cl}{|}}{CH}}\right]_n$$

Vinyl chloride Polyvinyl chloride

Q. 8. Define homopolymer. Give an example.

Ans. These are polymers in which the repeating structural units are derived from only one type of monomer, *e.g.* polythene.

Q. 9. What are addition polymers?

Ans. These are the polymers in which monomers combine without the elimination of simple molecular.

Q. 10. What are condensation polymers?

Ans. The polymers in which monomers combine with the ion of simple molecules are called condensation polymers.

Q. 11. What are thermoplastics?

Ans. Polymers which can be repeatedly softened on heating and hardened on cooling and can be used again and again without any change in their chemical composition and mechanical strength are called thermoplastics.

For example— polythene, teflon, nylon etc.

Q. 12. Enlist one use of melamine.

Ans. For making unbreakable plastic crockery.

Q. 13. What does PMMA stand for? How is it prepared?

Ans. PMMA stands for polymethyl methacrylate. It is prepared by the polymerisation of methyl methacrylate.

$$n\mathrm{CH_2=\overset{\overset{CH_3}{|}}{C}-COOCH_3} \xrightarrow{\text{Polymerisation}} \left[\mathrm{CH_2-\underset{\underset{COOCH_3}{|}}{\overset{\overset{CH_3}{|}}{C}}-}\right]_n$$

PMMA

Q. 14. Name a polymer which is used for making (i) non-stick wares (ii) non-breakable crockery.

Ans. (*i*) Teflon (also known as PTFE) (*ii*) Melamine-formaldehyde resin.

Q. 15. Classify the following as addition and condensation polymers :

Terylene, Bakelite, Polyvinyl chloride, Polythene.

Ans. Addition polymers— Polyvinyl chloride, polythene.

Condensation polymers— Terylene, Bakelite.

Q. 16. Which of the following is a natural polymer :

nylon-66, nylon-6, polyester, cellulose, PVC

Ans. Cellulose is a natural polymer.

Q. 17. Arrange the following in the order of increasing intermolecular forces :

thermoplastics, elastomers, synthetic fibres.

Ans. Elastomers < Thermoplastics < Synthetic fibers.

Q. 18. Which is a better material for making PVC pipes — a thermoset plastic or a thermoplastic ?

Ans. Thermoplastic.

Q. 19. Name the monomer of 'Orlon'.

Ans. Monomer of orlon is acrylonitrile (or vinyl cyanide), $H_2C=CH-CN$.

Short Answer Type Questions - I

Q. 1. Explain the difference between Buna-N and Buna-S.

Ans. Both are copolymers. Whereas Buna-N is a copolymer of 1, 3—butadiene and acrylonitrile, Buna-5 is a copolymer of 1, 3—butadiene and styrene.

Q. 2. Arrange the following polymers in increasing order of their intermolecular forces.

(*i*) Nylon 6, 6, Buna-S, Polythene.

(*ii*) Nylon 6, Neoprene, Polyvinyl chloride.

Ans. Elastomers or rubbers have the weakest intermolecular forces of attraction followed by plastics while fibres have the strongest forces of attraction. Thus, the increasing intermolecular forces of attraction follows the order: Elastomer < Plastic < Fibre, *i.e.,*

(*i*) Buna-S, Polythene, Nylon 6, 6.

(*ii*) Neoprene, Polyvinyl chloride, Nylon 6.

Q. 3. What is the difference between elastomers and fibres? Illustrate with an example of each.

Ans. *Differences between elastomers and fibres—*

S.No.	*Elastomers*	*Fibres*
1.	Polymers in which the intermolecular forces of attraction between the polymer chains are the weakest are called elastomers.	1. Polymers in which the intermolecular forces of attraction are the strongest are called fibres.
2.	Amorphous in structure.	2. Crystalline in structure.
3.	Low tensile strength.	3. High tensile strength.
4.	Flexible.	4. Rigid and strong.
5.	Examples— Buna-S, styrene, Buna-N.	5. Examples— Cotton, cellulose, silk, wool, polyester.

Q. 4. What are biodegradable polymers? Give two examples.

Ans. Polymers which are degraded by microorganisms within a suitable period so that the polymer and its degraded products do not cause any serious effect on environment are called biodegradable polymers. *e.g.* PHBV, Nylon-6.

Q. 5. Write the monomers used for getting the following polymers.

(*i*) Polyvinvl chloride (*ii*) Teflon (*iii*) Bakelite

Ans. (*i*) The monomer of polyvinyl chloride is vinyl chloride, ($CH_2 = CH—Cl$).

(*ii*) The monomer of teflon is tetrafluoroethene, $CF_2 = CF_2$.

(*iii*) The monomers of bakelite are formaldehyde (HCHO) and phenol, (C_6H_5OH).

Q. 6. State two properties of thermosetting polymers and thermoplastic polymers.

Ans. (*i*) Thermosetting polymers do not soften on heating and burn if heating is continued for a long period. They are generally insoluble in organic solvents because of three-dimensional cross-linkages in their structures.

(*ii*) Thermoplastics often melt on heating. They can be remoulded, recast and reshaped on heating. They are soluble in organic solvents.

Q. 7. Distinguish between the terms 'homopolymer' and 'copolymer' and give an example of each.

Ans. (*i*) *Homopolymer* — Homoplymers are those polymers which are obtained by polymerisation of a single monomeric chemical species. For example—

$$\underset{\text{(Monomer)}}{\underset{\text{Ethene}}{nCH_2 = CH_2}} \xrightarrow{\text{Polymerisation}} \underset{\text{(Homopolymer)}}{\underset{\text{Polythene}}{[CH_2-CH_2]_n}}$$

(*ii*) *Copolymer*— Copolymers are the polymers which are obtained by polymerisation of two or more than two different monomeric chemical species. The copolymer can be made by chain growth polymerisation as well as step growth polymerisation, *e.g.* Buna-S.

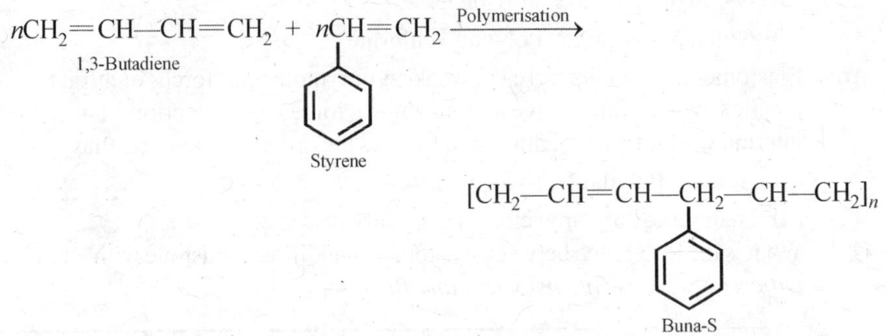

Q. 8. How is dacron prepared? Which film is used in making magnetic recording tapes?

Ans. Dacron is prepared by the condensation polymerisation of ethylene glycol and terephthalic acid.

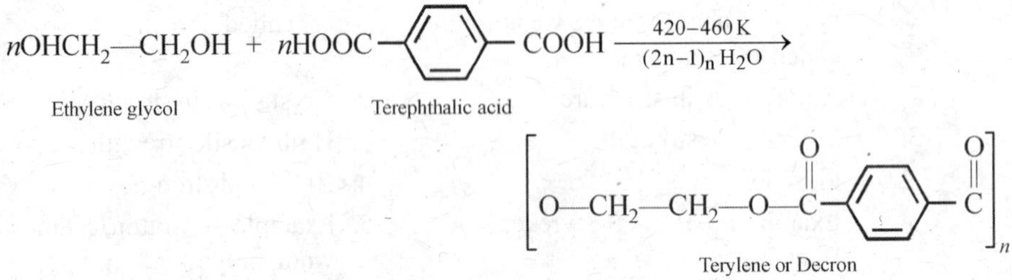

Dacron film is used for making magnetic recording tapes.

Q. 9. Explain the terms polymer and monomer.

Ans. *Polymers*— Polymers are high molecular mass (10^3–10^7u) substances consisting of a very large number of simple repeating structural units joined together through covalent bonds in a linear fashion. *e.g.*, polythene, bakelite etc.

Monomers— Simple and reactive molecules, from which the polymers are prepared either by addition or condensation are called monomers. *e.g.*, ethene, vinyl chloride, phenol etc.

Q. 10. (*a*) What is the role of benzoyl peroxide in polymerization of ethene?

(*b*) Is $[CH_2—CH(C_6H_5)]_n$ a homopolymer or a copolymer?

Ans. (*a*) Benzoyl peroxide acts as a radical initiator in the polymerization of ethene.

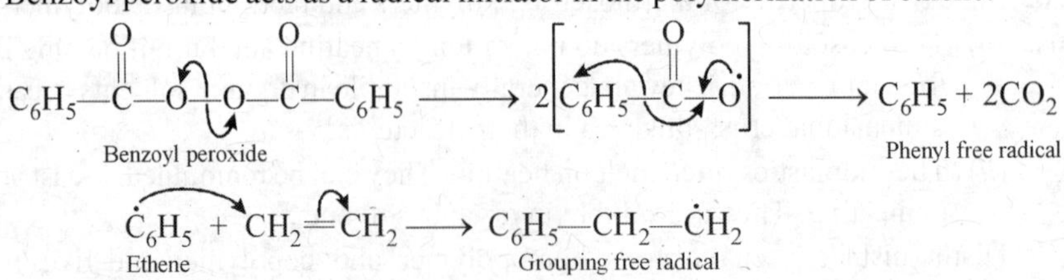

(*b*) The repeating structural unit of the given polymer contains only one type of monomer unit, *i.e.* styrene, $C_6H_5CH=CH_2$; therefore it is a homopolymer.

Short Answer Type Questions – II

Q. 1. Write the names of monomers of the following polymers.

(*i*) $\left[\begin{matrix} \text{H} & & \text{H} & \text{O} & & \text{O} \\ | & & | & \| & & \| \\ \text{N} & -(\text{CH}_2)_6- & \text{N} & -\text{C}- & (\text{CH}_2)_4- & \text{C} \end{matrix}\right]_n$

(*ii*) $\left[\begin{matrix} \text{O} & & \text{H} \\ \| & & | \\ \text{C} & -(\text{CH}_2)_5- & \text{N} \end{matrix}\right]_n$ (*iii*) $[CF_2—CF_2]_n$

Ans. (*i*) Hexamethylenediamine, $H_2N—(CH_2)_6—NH_2$
Adipic acid, $HOOC—(CH_2)_4—COOH$.

(*ii*) Caprolactom, 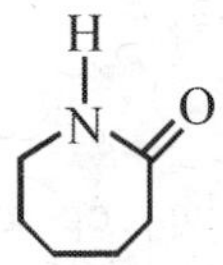

(*iii*) Tetrafluoroethene, $F_2C{=}CF_2$.

Q. 2. In which classes, the polymers are classified on the basis of molecular forces?

Ans. On the basis of intermolecular forces of attraction operating between the different polymer chains, polymers are classified into the following classes:

1. Elastomers. 2. Fibres. 3. Thermoplastics. 4. Thermosetting plastics.

Q. 3. How does the presence of double bonds in rubber molecules influence their structure and reactivity?

Ans. Natural rubber is cis-polyisoprene and is obtained by 1, 4-polymerization of isoprene units.

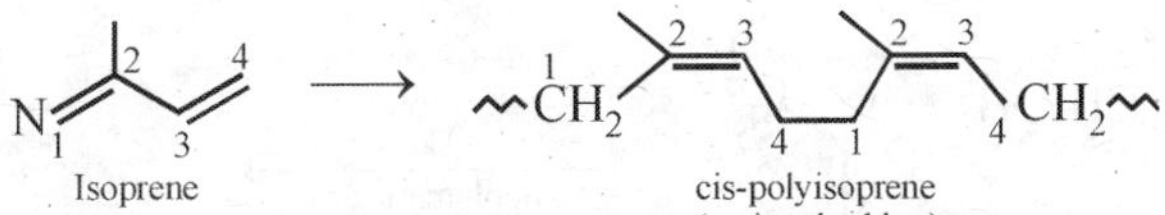

In this polymer, double bonds are located between C_2 and C_3 of each isoprene unit. These cis-double bonds do not allow the polymer chains to come closer for effective interactions and hence intermolecular forces are quite weak. As a result, natural rubber, *i.e.*, cis-polyisoprene has a randomly called structure and hence shows elasticity.

Q. 4. Discuss the main purpose of vulcanization of rubber.

Ans. *Main purpose of vulcanization of rubber—*

(*i*) Natural rubber is soft and sticky, but after vulcanization it becomes hard.

(*ii*) The vulcanized rubber has excellent elasticity over a larger range of temperature, has low water absorption tendency, is resistant to the action of organic solvents and oxidising agents.

Q. 5. Identify the monomer in the following polymeric structures:

(*i*) $\left[\begin{matrix} \text{O} & & \text{O} & \\ \| & & \| & \\ \text{C} & -(\text{CH}_2)_8- & \text{C} & -\text{NH}-(\text{CH}_2)_6-\text{NH} \end{matrix}\right]_n$

(ii) 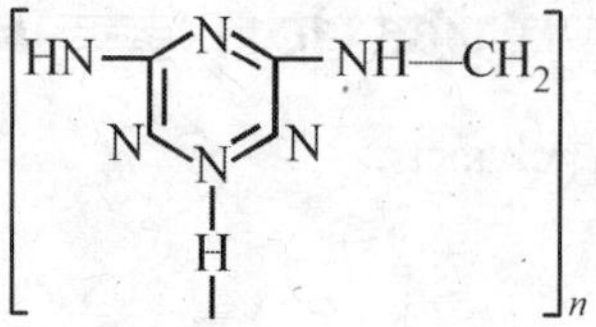

Ans. Monomers are :

(i) $HOOC—(CH_2)_8—COOH$ and $H_2N—(CH_2)_6—NH_2$

Sebacic acid   Hexamethylenediamine

(ii) 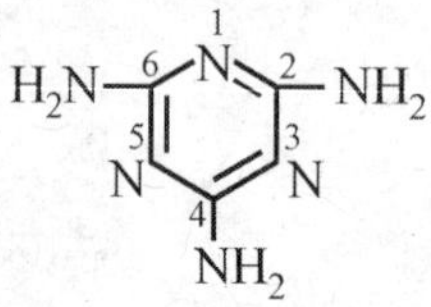 and 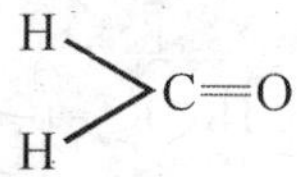

2,5,6-Triamino-1,3,5-triazine

Q. 6. Differentiate the following of polymers based on the property mentioned against each.

(i) Novolac and bakelite (structure).

(ii) Buna-S and terylene (intermolecular forces of attraction).

Ans. (i) Novolac is a linear but bakelite is a cross-linked polymer of phenol and formaldehyde.

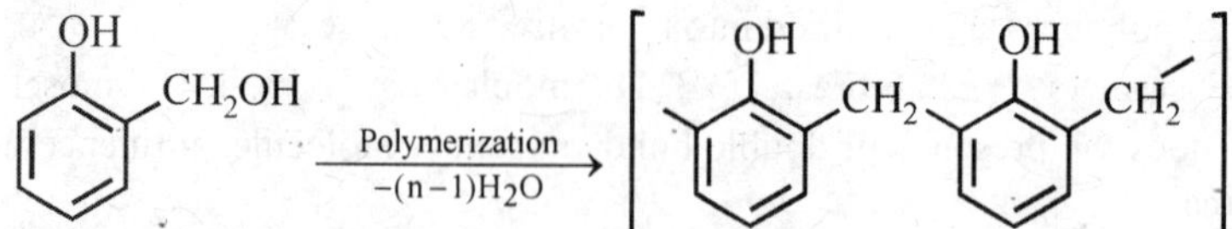

o-Hydroxymethlphenol

Novolac (Linear Polymer)

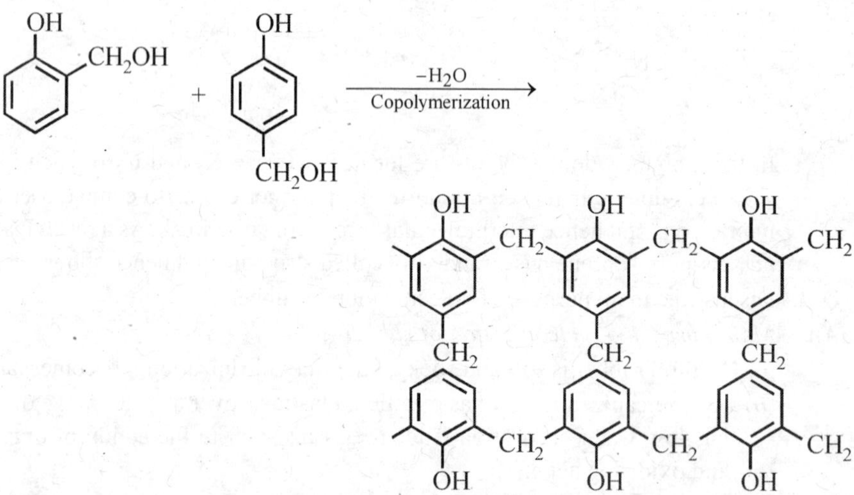

Bakelite (cross-linked polymer)

(ii) Terylene contains ester functional group which are polar in nature. Therefore, the intermolecular forces of attraction involved in terylene are strong dipole-dipole interactions.

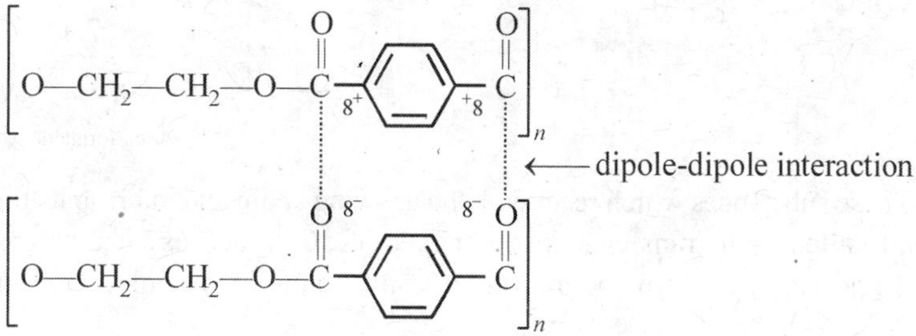

Terylene polymer chains

Buna-S, does not have polar functional group. It has only non-polar hydrocarbon chains and hence has only vander waals forces of attraction.

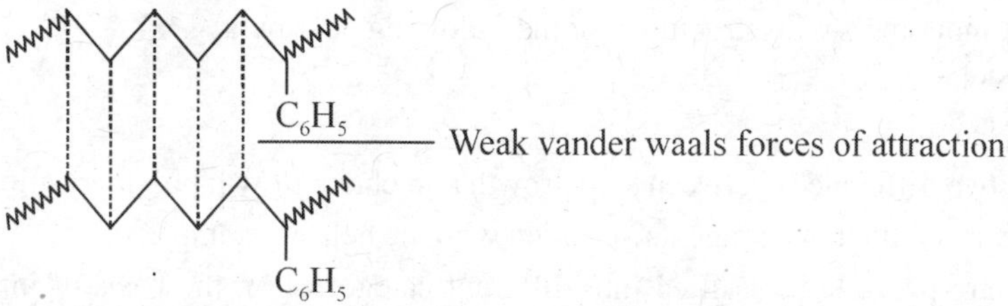

Buna-S Polymer Chains

Q. 7. How are polymers classified on the basis of structure?

Ans. On the basis of structure, the polymers are classified as follows:

(*i*) Linear polymers such as high density polythene (HDP), PVC, nylons, polyester etc.

(*ii*) Brached polymers such as low density polythene (LDP), amylopectin, glycogen etc.

(*iii*) Cross-linked polymers such as bakelite, melamine-formaldehyde polymer etc.

Q. 8. What is latex? Explain.

Ans. It is a colloidal dispersion of negatively charged particle of rubber about 1-2μ in a diameter and looks like milk. The average composition of latex is:

water = 60%, rubber hydrocarbon = 35%, proteins, enzymes and nucleic acid = 3%, fatty acids and water = 1% and inorganic salts = 0.5%.

Q. 9. Give reasons :

(*a*) PVC is a hard plastic and polyethylene is a soft wax like plastic.

(*b*) Thermosetting plastic can not be reused and reshaped.

(*c*) Rayon is superior to cotton for use as bandage.

Ans. (*a*) It is because dipole-dipole interaction is absent in polyethylene.

(*b*) It is because there are cross linkages in thermosetting plastics.

(*c*) It is because there exists strong hydrogen bonding in rayon molecules which makes it superior to cotton.

Q. 10. (*a*) Give an equation for the preparation of urea-formaldehyde resin.

(*b*) What do you mean by chain transfer agents? Give an example.

Ans. (*a*) $$\underset{\text{Urea}}{H_2N{-}\overset{O}{\overset{\|}{C}}{-}NH_2} + \underset{\text{Formaldehyde}}{2HCHO} \xrightarrow{\text{Heat}} HO{-}CH_2CH_2NH{-}\overset{O}{\overset{\|}{C}}{-}NH{-}CH_2OH$$

$$\longrightarrow \left[CH_2 - NH - \overset{\overset{O}{||}}{C} - NH - CH_2 \right]_n$$

Urea-formaldehyde resin

(*b*) Those substances which react with the growing chain and interrup its further growth are called chain transfer agents. For example, CCl_4 acts as a chain transfer agent in the polymerisation of styrene, and it results to produce a polymer of low mass.

Higher Order Thinking Skills Hots Questions

Q. 1. Give monomers of glyptal.

Q. 2. Write monomers with structures for the following polymers.

(*i*) Nylon-6, 6

(*ii*) Neoprene

Q. 3. Give two differences between step growth and chain growth polymerisation.

Q. 4. What are chain transfer agents? Explain with the help of example.

Q. 5. How are polymers classified into different categories on the basis of intermolecular forces? Give one example of a polymer of each of these categories.

❑❑❑

CHAPTER

16 CHEMISTRY IN EVERYDAY LIFE

Syllabus

- ***Chemicals in medicines :*** *Analgesics, tranquilizers, antiseptics, disinfectants, antimicrobials, antifertility drugs, antacids, antihistamines.*
- ***Chemicals in food :*** *Preservatives, artificial sweetening agents.*
- ***Cleansing agents :*** *Soaps and detergents, cleansing action.*

1. **Antacids :** Substances which remove the excess acid and raise the pH to appropriate level in stomach are called *antacids*.

   Omeprazole and lansoprazole are also marketed as antacids. These prevent formation of acid in the stomach.
2. **Tranquillizers :** The chemical substances used for the treatment of stress, fatigue, mild and severe mental diseases are called tranquillizers.

   Examples : The most common one is non-adrenaline which induces a feeling of well-being and helps in changing mood.

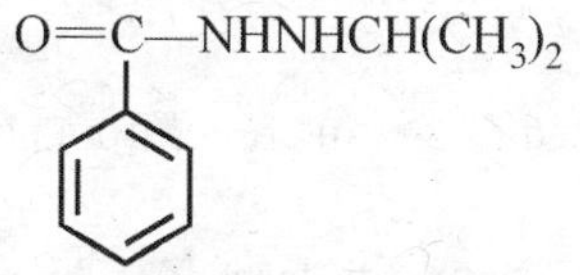

Iproniazid

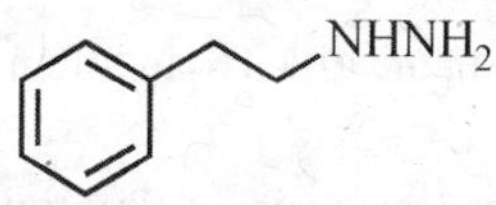

Phenelzine (Nardil)

3. **Antihistamines :** These drugs are also called as *anti-allergic drugs* and are used to treat allergy. Diphenylhydramine, chlorpheniramine, promethazine, brompheniramine (Dimetapp) and terfenadine (seldane).
4. **Antipyretics :** These are drugs which bring down the body temperature in high fever. They lead to perspiration and thereby cooling the body. Examples are aspirin, phenacetin, paracetamol (4-acetamidophenol), analgin, novalgin.
5. **Chemotherapy :** It reefers to treatment of diseases by use of chemicals.
6. **Anaesthetics :** The chemical substances which produce general or local insensibility to pains and other sensations.
7. **Antibiotics :** The substances which are metabolic products produced by microorganisms and can inhibit the growth or even destroy other microorganisms.
8. **Antimalarials :** The substances which are used for treatments of malaria.
9. **Antiseptics :** The chemical substances which kill or prevent the growth of microorganisms.
10. **Analgesics :** The substances used to relieve pains.
11. **Disinfectant :** The chemical substances which are used to kill microorganisms but cannot be applied on living tissues.
12. **Germicide :** The chemical substances which destroy microorganisms especially germs of disease. *Example :* mercurochrome, phenol, DDT etc.

13. **Narcotics :** Those substances which produce complete insensibility or sleep. These are habit forming drugs. *Example :* LSD, heroin, morphine etc.
14. **Sulpha drugs :** These are sulphur containing organic substances which have great antibacterial power and are used as medicines in form of substitute of antibiotics for patients who are allergic to antibiotics. *Example :* sulphadiazine, sulphathiazole etc.
15. **Preservatives :** Chemical substances which are used to protect food against bacteria, yeasts and moulds are called preservatives. *Examples :*
    (*i*) ***Sodium benzoate :*** The most commonly used preservative is sodium benzoate. It is used in soft drinks and acidic foods.
    (*ii*) ***Sodium metabisulphite ($Na_2S_2O_6$) :*** Sodium or potassium metabisulphite is used as a preservative for food products such as jams, squashes, pickles, etc.
16. **Artificial sweetners :** These are the chemical compounds which give sweetening effect to the food, enhance its odour and flavour, and prove to be a life saver for diabetics. These are also of great value to people who needs to control intake of calories.
    The most common example of artificial sweetner is 'Saccharine' which is approximately 300 times more sweet than cane sugar. Other example are : Aspartame (methyl ester), alitame, nitro aniline, dulcin, dihydrochal cones (DHC) etc.
    Sucralose is predicted to be a very good substitute of saccharine. Aspartame is unstable at cooking temperature and its use is limited to cold foods and soft drinks.

Very Short Answer Type Questions

Q. 1. What type of drug is chloramphenical?
Ans. Antibiotic
Q. 2. What is the name given to medicines need for getting relief from pain?
Ans. Analgesic
Q. 3. Name a broad spectrum antibiotic and state two diseases for which it is prescribed?
Ans. Chloramphenicol.
It is used for treatment of typhoid fever and pneumonia.
Q. 4. Name the medicine which can act both as an analgesic as well as antipyretic.
Ans. Aspirin
Q. 5. Give one important use of each of the following in pharmacy.
Ans. (i) Equanil (ii) Morphine
(*i*) Equanil is a tranquilliser. It is used for removing depression and hypertension.
(*ii*) Morphine is an alkaloid. It is used as an analgesic.
Q. 6. Why is bithional added to soap?
Ans. Bithional acts as an antiseptic agent and reduces the odours produced by bacterial decomposition of organic matter on the skin.
Q. 7. Name an antacid which prevents the formation of acid in the stomach.
Ans. Cimetidine or Ranitidine
Q. 8. What type of detergents are used for dish washing?
Ans. Non-ionic
Q. 9. Write the structure of a medicine which is used for prevention of heart attacks.
Ans. Aspirin

Q. 10. Give one example of an artificial sweetenar used by diabetic patients.

Ans. Saccharin is taken an artificial sweetener by diabetic patients.

Q. 11. Name the macromolecules which are chosen as drug targets.

Ans. Macromolecules such as proteins, nucleic acids, carbohydrates and lipids are called drug targets.

Q. 12. Name a substance which can be used as an antiseptic as well as disinfectant.

Ans. 0.2% solution of Phenol-Antiseptic

1% solution of Phenol-Disinfectant.

Q. 13. Name the sweetening agent used in the preparation of sweets for a diabetic patient.

Ans. Saccharin, Aspartame.

Q. 14. Why is use of aspartame limited to cold foods and drinks?

Ans. It decomposes at baking.

Q. 15. Name an alkaloid which is used for treatment of hypertension.

Ans. Reserpine.

Q.16. Give two examples of analgesics and antipyretics.

Ans. *Analgesics* : Butazolidine, Aspirin, Novalgin.

Antipyretics : Aspirin, paracetamol.

Q.17. Which substance can act both analgesic as well as antipyretic ?

Ans. Aspirin can act both as antipyretic as well as analgesic.

Q.18. What are the constituents of detol ?

Ans. The constituents of dettol are chloroxylenol and terpineol dissolved in a suitable solvent.

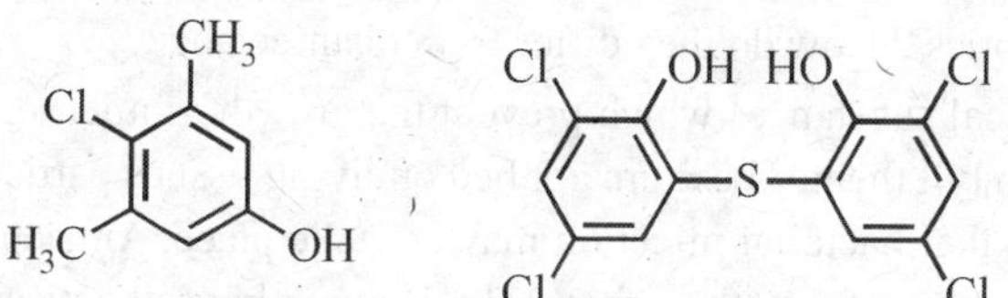

Chloroxylenol   Bithional

Q.19. Why is bithional added to soap ?

Ans. Bithional is added to soap to impart antiseptic properties.

Short Answer Type Questions – I

Q. 1. Sleeping pills are recommended by doctors to the patients suffering from sleeplessness but it is not advisable to take its doses without consultation with the doctor. Why?

Ans. Most of drugs taken in doses higher than recommended may produce harmful effects and, act as poison and cause even death. Therefore, a doctor must always be consulted before taking the drug.

Q. 2. With reference to which classification has the statement, "ranitidine is an antacid", been given?

Ans. This statement refers to the classification of drugs according to pharmacological effect because any drug which will be used to neutralize the excess acid present in the stomach will be called an antacid.

Q. 3. Define the term chemotherapy.

Ans. The branch of chemistry which deals with the treatment of diseases using chemicals is called chemotherapy.

Q. 4. Which forces are involved in holding the drugs to the active site of enzymes?

Ans. Hydrogen bonding, ionic bonding, dipole-dipole interactions or vander Walls interactions.

Q. 5. What is meant by the term broad spectrum antibiotics? Explain.

Ans. Broad spectrum antibiotics are effective against several different types of harmful bacteria. For example, tetracycline, chloramphenicol, ofloxacin etc.

Q. 6. What is tincture of iodine? What is its use?

Ans. 2-3% solution of iodine in alcohol and water is called tincture of iodine. It is a powerful antiseptic. It is applied on wounds.

Q. 7. What are food preservatives?

Ans. Chemical substances which are used to protect food against bacteria, yeasts and moulds are called preservatives. For example, sodium benzoate, sodium metabisulphite etc.

Q. 8. How are synthetic detergents better than soaps?

Ans. These can be used in hard water as well in acidic solution because the sulphonic acid and their calcium and magnesium salts are soluble in water but the fatty acid and their calcium and magnesium salts are insoluble.

Q. 9. Why do soaps not work in hard water?

Ans. Hard water contains calcium and magnesium salts. Therefore, in hard water soaps get precipitated as calcium and magnesium soaps which being insoluble stick to the clothes as gummy mass.

Q.10. What is the role of antiseptics ? How do they differ from disinfectants ?

Ans. Antiseptics are the chemical substances which prevent the growth of microorganisms causing infection and also kill them. These are applied on living tissues particularly in open wounds and cuts so that bacterial infection may not take place. Antiseptics also constitute certain deodorants and breath purifier. The commonly used antiseptics are phenol, dettol, iodoform. Gentian violet and Methylene blue.

Disinfectant can also behave in the same way as antiseptics. However, these are harmful to the living tissues and are therefore, used to disinfect floors, toilets instruments etc.

Q.11. What are analgesics ? How do differ from antipyretics ?

Ans. Analgesics are the substances which are given to relieve body pains. These may be both narcotics (habit forming) non-narcotics (not habit forming). Antipyretics are the substances used to bring body temperature in case of fever.

Q.12. Why should not aspirin be taken empty stomach ?

Ans. Aspirin, i.e., acetyl salicylic acid when taken at empty stomach may undergo hydrolysis to give salicylic acid. The acid can cause ulcers which are quite painful and may even bleede in some cases.

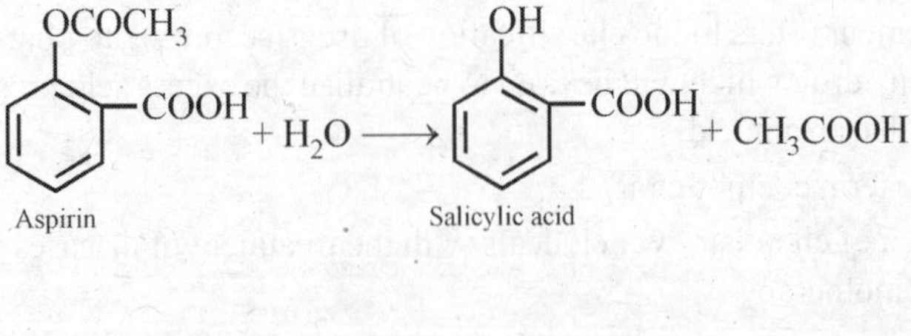

Short Answer Type Questions - II

Q. 1. What are soaps? What are hard and soft soaps? Give the limitations of soaps.

Ans. *Soaps* — Soaps are sodium and potassium salts of higher fatty acids.

Hard soaps — These are sodium salts of higher fatty acids.

Soft soaps — These are potassium salts of higher fatty acids. Soaps can't be used as cleaning agents in hard water and in acidic medium.

Q. 2. What are surfactants? Give the difference between soaps and detergents with example.

Ans. *Surfactants*:— These are the substances which concentrate on the surface of solution or interface and reduce the surface tension of solution. They remove the dirt by emulsifying greasy dirt.

Soaps	*Detergents*
1. These are sodium or potassium salts of higher fatty acids. *e.g.* $C_{17}H_{35}COONa$, sodium stearate.	1. These are sodium alkyl sulphate or sodium benzene sulphate or quartrnary ammonium salts. *e.g.* $C_{11}H_{23}CH_2OSO_3^-Na^{-1}$ sodium laurylsulphate.

Importance—Detergents used as cleansing agent in acidic medium as well as in hard water whereas soaps can't be used.

Q. 3. Give one important use of each of the following:

(*i*) Bithional (*ii*) Chloramphenicol

(*iii*) Streptomycin (*iv*) Paracetamol

Ans. (*i*) *Bithional*— It is an antiseptic and in added to medicated soaps to reduce the odour produced by bacterial decomposition of organic matter on the skin.

(*ii*) *Chloramphenicol*— It is broad spectrum antibiotic and can be used for curing typhoid, acute fever, dysentery, pneumonia etc.

(*iii*) *Streptomycin*— It is an antibiotic used for the treatment of tuberculosis, meningitis, pneumonia, local infection etc.

(*iv*) *Paracetamol*— It is used to lower the temperature of the body in high fever and as analgesic to relieve pain.

Q. 4. Explain the following with suitable examples :

(*i*) Tranquillizers (*ii*) Anaesthetics

Ans. (*i*) *Tranquillizers*— These are substances used to relieve mental diseases, and the same reduce tension, anxiety and act on higher centres of nervous system. The same are the constituents of sleeping pills, *e.g.* derivatives of barbituric acid, equanil, luminal and methednine etc.

(*ii*) *Anaesthetics*— These are substances which produce general or local insensibility to pains and other sensations. Cocanine, inovacaine are local anaesthetics chloroform, diethyl and vinyl ethers etc.

Q. 5. What are antibiotics? Name any two antibiotics which are specific for certain diseases.

Ans. *Antibiotics*— These are the chemical substances produced by micro-organisms (bacteria, fungi and moulds) which can inhibit the growth or even destroy other micro-organisms. Two antibiotics are

(*i*) Penicillin (*ii*) Stretptomycin

Q. 6. Explain the following with examples:

(*a*) Antipyretics (*b*) Analgesics

Ans. (*a*) *Antipyretics*— These are the substances used to lower the temperature of the body in high fever. Most common antipyretics are

(*i*) Aspirin (*ii*) Paracetamol (*iii*) Phenacetin

(*b*) *Analgesics*— These are the medicines used to relieve pains. Aspirin and some other antipyretics are also used as analgesics. Certain narcotics are also used as analgesics. For example, morphine, codeine, heroin, marijuana. These are known to be habit forming.

Q. 7. What are biodegradable and non-biodegradable detergents? Give one example of each.

Ans. *Biodegradable detergents*— Detergents having straight hydrocarbon chains are easily decomposed by microorganisms are called biodegradable detergents. *e.g.*— sodium lauryl sulphate, sodium p-dodecyl benzene sulphonate.

Non-biodegradable— The detergents having branched hydrocarbon chains are not easily decomposed by microorganisms and are called non-biodegradable detergents. e.g., sodium-4-(1, 3, 5, 7-tetramethyloctyl) benzene sulphonate.

Q. 8. Why the medicines should not be taken without consulting doctors?

Ans. The drugs or medicines have side effects also. In addition to normal desired therapeutic effect, drugs may also cause other effects which may be beneficial or harmful. These side effects arise because the drug may bind to more than one type of receptor. Therefore, the doctor must be consulted to choose the right drug which has maximum affinity for a particular receptor site to have the desired effect. The doctor will also advise for the correct doses because more drugs like opiates in higher doses may act as poisons leading to serious problems and even may cause death.

Q. 9. Explain the following terms with suitable examples.

(a) Cationic detergents (b) Anionic detergents (c) Neutral detergents

Ans. (*a*) *Cationic detergents*— These are quaternary ammonium salts. For example, cetyltrimethylammonium chloride.

$$[CH_3(CH_2)_{15}N^+(CH_3)_3]Cl^-$$

Cetyltrimethylammonium chloride

(*b*) *Anionic detergents*— These are also called because a large part of their molecules are anions. These are of two types.

(*i*) *Sodium alkyl sulphates*— *e.g.* $C_{11}H_{23}CH_2OSO_3Na$

(Sodium lauryl sulphate)

(*ii*) *Sodium alkylbenzenes sulphonates*— The most widely used domestic detergent is sodium 4(1–dodecyl) benzenesulphonate (SDS)

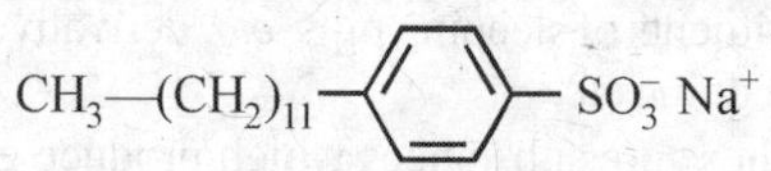

Sodium 4-(1-dopdecyl) benzenesulphonate

(*c*) *Neutral or Non-ionic detergents*— These are esters of high molecular man alcohols with fatty acids. For example, polyethylene glycol stearate.

$$CH_3(CH_2)_{16}COO(CH_2CH_2O)_nCH_2CH_2O$$

Polyethylene glycol stearate

Q.10. What are antihistamines? Give two examples. Explain how do they act on the human body?

Ans. *Antihistamines*— These drugs are also called as anti-allergic drugs and are used to treat allergy, *e.g. skin* rashes, since the allergic reactions are caused due to liberation of histamine in the body. That is why these drugs are called antihistamines. Other than skin rashes these drugs are useful for conjuctivitis (eye disease/and rhinitis).

e.g. Diphenylhydramine, chlorpheniramine, promethazine, brompheniramine and terfenadine.

Mode of action— Histamines interact with the binding sites of receptor in the body to produce allergy. Antihistamine compete with histamines for these binding sites of receptor and thus do not allow histamine to produce allergy. Thus, antihistamine are drugs which interfere with the natural action of histamine by competing for histamine binding sites of receptor.

Q. 11. How do tranquilizers act ? Give two examples.

Ans. Tranquilizers are the substances which are given to the patients suffering from anxiety and mental tension. They can act on the nervous system and reduce tension. These can even result in sleep and are the constituents of many sleeping pills. Tranquilizers are quite effective in case of patients of mental depression. Equanil and luminal are the commonly used tranquilizers.

Q.12. How can phenol behave both as antiseptic as well as disinfectant ?

Ans. In some cases, the dilute solution of certain substances can act as antiseptics while the concentrated solutions may behave as disinfectants. For 0.2 per cent solution of phenol is an antiseptic and nearly 1.0 per cent which is more concentrated can act as disinfectant.

Higher Order Thinking Skills Hots Questions

1. Give an examples of sulpha drug.
2. State an example each and function of the following :
   (*i*) Tranquilizers
   (*ii*) Wide spectrum antibiotics
3. "Ranitidine is an antacid". Explain the statement.
4. Give two example of artificial sweeteners. What are their advantages over natural sweeteners?
5. Label the hydrophilic and hydrophobic parts in the following compounds.
   (*a*) $CH_3(CH_2)_{10}CH_2OSO_3^-Na^+$
   (*b*) $CH_3(CH_2)_{15}N^+(CH_3)_3Br^-$
   (*c*) C_9H_{19}— 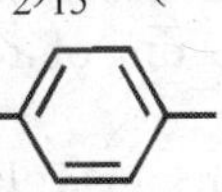 —$O(CH_2CH_2O)_n$—CH_2CH_2OH
6. Describe the following with examples :
   (a) Preservatives
   (b) Biodegradable detergents
7. Write the formula of paracetamol. What is it used for in medicine ?
8. Name the drug used in :
   (i) typhoid
   (ii) tuberculosis
   (iii) pneumonia.

❑❑❑

MOCK TEST PAPER I

Time Allowed : 3 Hours **[Maximum Marks 70]**

General Instructions—

(i) All questions are compulsory.
(ii) Question No. 1 to 8 are very short answer type questions and carry 1 mark each.
(iii) Question No. 9 to 18 are short answer type questions and carry 2 mark each.
(iv) Question No. 19 to 27 are also short answer type questions and carry 3 mark each.
(v) Question No. 28 to 30 are long answer type questions and carry 5 mark each.
(vi) Use log tables if necessary use of calculators is not allowed.

1. Why is ferric chloride preferred over potassium chloride in case of a cut leading to bleeding?
2. What is the coordination number in a rock salt type structure?
3. How do you account for the miscibility of ethoxyethane with water?
4. Give the IUPAC name of the organic compound.

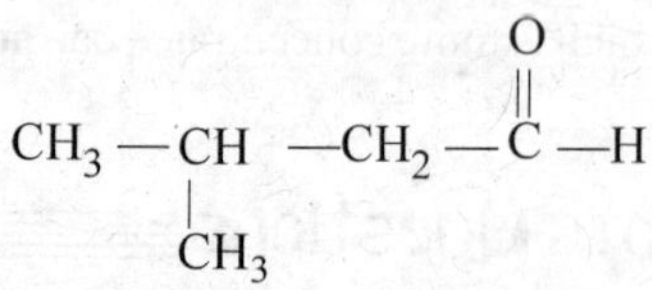

5. Name the monomers of Nylon 6, 6 polymer.
6. Give one example of an artificial sweetener used by the diabetic patients.
7. Direct nitration of aniline is not carried out. Explain why?
8. What type of linkage holds together the monomers of D.N.A.?
9. Name an element with which silicon can be doped to give an n-type semiconductor.
10. If NaCl is doped with 10^{-3} mole% of $SrCl_2$, what is the concentration of cation vacancies?

OR

If the radius of the octahedral void is *r* and radius of the atoms in close packing is *R*, derive relation between *r* and R.

11. With the help of a neat diagram indicate why the solution of a non-volatile solute should freeze at a temperature lower than the freezing point of the pure solvent.
12. Write the chemical equation for all the steps involved in the rusting of iron. Give any one method to prevent rusting of iron.
13. A solution of $[Ni(H_2O)_6]^{2+}$ is green but a solution of $[Ni(CN)_4]^{2-}$ is colourless. Explain.
14. A mixed oxide of iron and chromium $FeOCr_2O_3$ is fused with sodium carbonate in the presence of air to form a yellow coloured compound (A). On acidification the compound (A) forms an orange coloured compound (B), which is a strong oxidising agent. Identify:
    (*i*) the compound (A) and (B).
    (*ii*) write balanced chemical equation for each step.
15. An optically, active compound having molecular formula $C_1H_{15}Br$ reacts with aqueous KOH to give a racemic mixture of products. Write the mechanism involved for this reaction.
16. Write the formula of main product in the following chemical reactions:

(*a*) $CH_3CH_2CH_2Cl + NaI \xrightarrow[\text{heat}]{\text{acetone}}$

(*b*) $(CH_3)_2\,C\text{—}Br + KOH \xrightarrow[\text{heat}]{\text{ethanol}}$

(c) $C_6H_5ONa + C_2H_5Cl(g) \longrightarrow$

(d) $CH_3CH_2CH = CH_2 + HBr \xrightarrow{\text{Peroxide}}$

17. Differentiate the following pair of polymers based on the property mentioned against each:
    (i) Novolac and Bakelite (structure)
    (ii) Bun-S and Terylene (intermolecular formes of attraction)
18. How are synthetic detergents betten than soaps?
19. Heptane and octane form ideal solution. At 373K, the vapour pressures of the two liquid components are 105.2 KPa and 46.8 KPa respectively. What will be the vapour pressure of a mixture of 26.0 g of heptane and 35.0 g of octane?
20. The following chemical reaction is occurring in an electrochemical cell

$$Mg(S) + ZAg^+ \ (0.0001\ M) \longrightarrow Mg^{2+}\ (0.10\ M) + 2Ag$$

The E° electrode values are

$$Mg^{2+}/mg = -2.36\ V$$
$$Ag^+/Ag = 0.81\ V$$

For this cell calculate/write:

(a) (i) E° value for the electrode $2Ag^+/2\ Ag$
(ii) Standard cell potential E° cell.

(b) Cell Potential (E) cell.

(c) (i) Symbolic representation of the above cell.
(ii) Will the above cell reaction be spontaneous?

21. At elevated temperature. HI decomposes according to the chemical equation:

$$2HI\ (g) \longrightarrow H_2(g) + I_2(g) \text{ at } 443°C.$$

The rate of the reaction increases with concentration of HI, as shown in the following table:

	1	2	3
[HI]/mol L^{-1}	0.005	0.01	0.02
Rate/mol $L^{-1}S^{-1}$	7.5×10^{-4}	3.0×10^{-3}	1.2×10^{-2}

(a) Determine the (i) order of reaction and (ii) write the rate expression.
(b) Calculate the rate constant and give its units.

22. Account for the following facts:
    (a) the reduction of a metal oxide is earlier if the metal formed is in liquid state at the temperature of reduction.
    (b) the reduction of Cr_2O_3 with Al is thermodynamically feasible, yet it does not occur at room temperature.
    (c) Pine oil is used in froth floatation method.
23. Explain the following facts:
    (a) Tanition metals act as catalyats.
    (b) Chromium group elements have the highest melting points in their respective series.
    (c) Transition metals form coloured complexes.
24. (a) Give a chemical test to distinguish between the following pairs of compounds

(i) 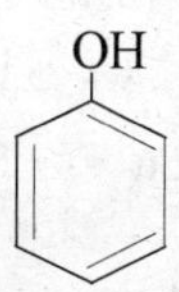 and 

(ii) $CH_3-\underset{\underset{OH}{|}}{CH}-CH_3$ and 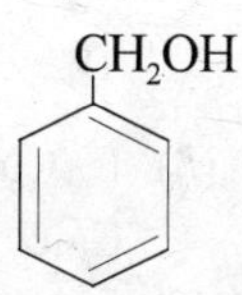

(b) Why is Phenol more acidic than ethanol?

25. Write short notes on the following:
   (*i*) Carbylamine reaction
   (*ii*) Diazatisation
   (*iii*) Hofmann's bromamide reaction
26. An optically active compound having molecular formula $C_6H_{12}O_6$ is found in two isomeric forms (A) and (B) in nature when (A) and (B) are dissolved in water, these show the following equilibrium.

$$\text{(A)} \rightleftharpoons \text{Equilibrium mixture} \rightleftharpoons \text{(B)}$$
$$[a]_D = 111° \qquad 55.2° \qquad 19.2°$$

   (*i*) What are such isomers called?
   (*ii*) Can they be called enantiomers? Justify your answer.
   (*iii*) Draw the cyclic structure of isomer (A).

OR

   (*a*) Arrange the following in order of increasing basic strength:
   Aniline, Ethylamine, Ethane, Phenol.
   (*b*) Complete the following reactions giving structure of two products formed:

   (*i*) $CH_3CH_2NH_2 \xrightarrow[\text{Heat}]{(CH_3CO)_2O}$

   (*ii*) $CH_3CONHC_6H_5 \xrightarrow{Br_2/Fe}$
27. (*a*) How will you distinguish between:
   (*i*) Propan-1-ol and Propan-2-ol?
   (*ii*) Methylamine (CH_3NH_2) and Dimethylamine [$(CH_3)_2NH$]?
   (*b*) Propose the mechanism of the following reaction:

$$CH_3CH_2Br + CH_3O^- \longrightarrow CH_3CH_2OCH_3 + Br^-$$
28. (*a*) Define standard electrode potential. How is it related to free energy change and equilibrium constant?
   How is standard electrode potential of an electrode is determined and how to decide the sign of electrode potential? Calculate the electrode potential of hydrogen electrode in neutral solution.
   (*b*) Explain the effect of:
   (*i*) temperature
   (*ii*) surface area
   (*iii*) nature of reactants on the rate of reaction.

OR

   (*a*) The following initial rate data were obtained at 300 K for the reaction:
   $2A + B \longrightarrow C + D$

	[A]/mol L^{-1}	[B]/mol L^{-1}	Rate/mole L^{-1} S^{-1}
I	0.2	0.1	6.0×10^{-2}
II	0.4	0.1	2.4×10^{-1}
III	0.2	0.2	1.2×10^{-1}

   (*b*) E° Cu^+/Cu = + 0.52 V   E° Cu^{2+}/Cu^+ = + 0.16 V.
   Calculate E° Cu^{2+}/Cu^+.
29. A translucent white waxy solid (A) on heating in an inert atmosphere is converted to its allotropic form (B). Allotrope (A) on reaction with very dilute aqueous KOH liberates a

highly poisonous gas (C) having rotten fish smell with excess of chlorine forms (D) which hydrolyses to compound (E). Identify compounds (A) to (E).

OR

Complete and balance the following chemical equations:

(*i*) $F_2 + H_2O \text{ (cold)} \longrightarrow$ (*ii*) $BrO_3^- + F_2 + OH^- \longrightarrow$

(*iii*) $Li + N_2 \text{ (cold)} \longrightarrow$ (*iv*) $Ca_3P_2 + H_2O \longrightarrow$

(*v*) $CuO + NH_3 \xrightarrow{\Delta}$

30. Identify the unknown organic compounds (A) to (E) in the following series of chemical reactions:

(*i*) 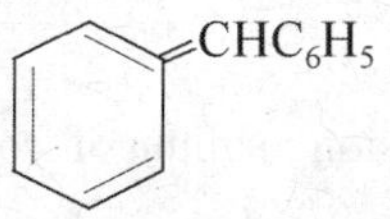 $\xrightarrow[\text{(ii) Zn / H}_2\text{O}]{\text{(i) O}_3}$ (A) + (B)

(*ii*) (A) + (B) $\xrightarrow{\text{dil. NaOH}}$ (A) + (D)

(*iii*) (C) $\xrightarrow[\text{(ii) Zn / H}_2\text{O}]{\text{(i) O}_3}$ (A) + (D)

(*iv*) (D) $\xrightarrow[\Delta]{H_2 / Ni}$ (E)

OR

Organic compound (A) has the molecular formula $C_5H_{10}O$. It does not reduce Fehling's solution but forms a bisulphite compound. It also gives positive iodoform test. What are possible structures of (A)? Explain your reasoning which helped to arrive at the structures.

❑❑❑

MOCK TEST PAPER II

Time Allowed : 3 Hours **[Maximum Marks 70]**

General Instructions—As given in Mock Test Paper I.

1. Give IUPAC name of the following organic compound.

$$\begin{array}{lll} CH_3—CH = \underset{\displaystyle |\atop \displaystyle CH_3}{C} & —\underset{\displaystyle |\atop \displaystyle Br}{CH}—Br \end{array}$$

2. What are the physical states of dispersed phase and dispersion medium of froth?
3. What is meant by specific rotation?
4. Write the structure of 4 methylpent-3-en-zone.
5. A cubic solid is made of two elements x and y. Atoms y are at the corners of the cube and x at the body centre. What is the formula of the compound.
6. What is the van't Hoff factor for a compound which undergoes tetramerization in an organic solvent?
7. Give formula of (*i*) Haematite, (*ii*) Magnetite.
8. Predict the shape of ClF, on the basis of VSEPR theory.
9. H_2S, a toxic gas with rotten egg like smell, is used for the qualitative analysis. If the solubility of H_2S in water at STP is 0.195 m, calculate Henry's law constant.
10. In a reaction, $ZA \longrightarrow$ Products, the concentration of A decreases from 0.5 mal L^{-1} to 0.4 mol L^{-1} in 10 minutes. Calculate the rate during this interval.
11. Free energies of formation ($\Delta_f G$) of MgO (S) and CO(g) at 1273 K and 2273 K are given below:

    $\Delta_f G$ [MgO(S)] = – 941 KJ/mol at 1273 K

    $\Delta_f G$ [MgO(S)] = – 314 KJ/mol at 2275 K

    $\Delta_f G$ [CO(g)] = – 439 KJ/mol at 1273 K

    $\Delta_f G$ [Co(g)] = – 628 KJ/mol at 2273 K

    On the basis of above data, predict the temperature at which carbon can be used as reducing agent for MgO(S).
12. How do you explain the absence of aldehyde group in the pentacetate of D-glucose?
13. (*a*) What changes occur in the nature of egg proteins on boiling?

    (*b*) Name the type of bonding which stabilizes α-helix structure in proteins.
14. Describe the mechanism of the formation of diethyl ether from ethanol in the presence of concentrated sulphuric acid.
15. Complete and name of the following reactions:

    (*a*) $CH_3CH_2NH_2 \xrightarrow{HCl}$ (*b*) 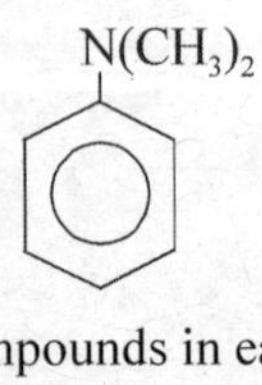 $\xrightarrow{HNO_2}$
16. Give chemical terts to distinguish between compounds in each of the following pairs:

    (*i*) Phenol and Benzyl alcohol

    (*ii*) Butan 2-ol and 2-methyl propan 2-ol
17. Account for the following:

    (*i*) Aniline is weaker base than methylamine.

(*ii*) Aryl cyanides cannot be formed by the reaction of arylhalides and sodium cyanide.

OR

How will you convert:

(*i*) Nitrobenzyne to Phenol (*ii*) Aniline to chlorobenzene.

18. Give reasons for the following:
    (*a*) At higher altitudes, people suffer from a disease called anoxia. In this disease, they become weak and cannot think clearly.
    (*b*) When mercuric iodide is added to an aqueous solution of KI, the freezing point is raised.
19. An element Crystallises in fcc structure. Its density is 7.2 g cm^{-3}, 208 g of this element has 4.283×10^{24} atoms. Calculate the edge length of the unit cell.
20. Write the names of monomers of the following polymers and classify them as addition or condensation polymers:
    (*a*) Teflon (*b*) Bakelite (*c*) Natural Rubber
21. (*a*) Give the IUPAC name of : $[CrCl_2(H_2O)_4]$ Cl.
    (*b*) Give the number of unpaired electrons in the following complex ions:
    $[Fe\ F_6]^{4-}$ and $[Fe\ (CN)_6]^4$.
    (*c*) Name the isomerism exhibited by the following pair of coordination compounds:
    $[Co(NH_3)_5\ Br]\ SO_4$ and $[Co\ (NH_3)_5\ SO_4]$ Br.
22. (*a*) Which will absorb more gas, a lump of charcoal or its powder and why?
    (*b*) Describe the preparation of the following colloidal solution. Name the method used in each care:
    (*i*) Silver sol (*ii*) Sulphor sol
    (*c*) State the principle of electrodialysis.
23. Account for the following:
    (*a*) Chlorine water has both oxidizing and bleaching properties.
    (*b*) H_3PO_2 and H_3PO_3 act as a good reducing agents while H_3PO_4 does not.
    (*c*) On addition of ozone gas to KI solution, violet vapours are obtained.
24. (*a*) Define rate constant:
    (*b*) Calculate the ratio of rate constants at 290 K and 300 K for the first order reaction with half-life periods 20 and 12 minutes at these temperature.
25. (*a*) Which of the following two compounds would react faster by SN^2 pathway:
    1-bromobutane or 2-bromobutane and why?
    (*b*) Allyl chloride is more reactive than *n*-propyl chloride towards nucleophilic substitution reaction. Explain why.
    (*c*) Haloalkanes react with KCN to give alkyl cyanide as main product while with AgCN they form isocyanide as main product. Give reasons.
26. (*a*) Arrange the hydrides of group 15 in increasing order of basic strength.
    (*b*) Why does Xe form compounds whereas Ne does not?
    (*c*) Arrange hydrogen halides in increasing order of their boiling points.

    OR

    Write balanced ionic equation for what happens when:
    (*i*) Acidified potassium permanganate solution is treated with an oxalate ion in solution.
    (*ii*) An iodide ion is treated with an acidified dichromate ion in solution.
27. Define the following and give one example of each:
    (*i*) Ardihutamines (*ii*) Antacids
28. (*a*) An organic compound 'A' with molecular formula $C_5H_8O_2$ is reduced to *n*-pentane on treatment with Zn-Hg/HCl. 'A' forms a dioxime with hydroxylamine and gives a positive iodoform tert and Tollen's tert. Identify the compound A and deduce its structure.

(*b*) Write the chemical equations for the following conversions:

(*i*) Ethylbenzene to benzene (*ii*) Acetaldehyde to butane-1, 3-diol

(*iii*) Acetone to propene

OR

(*a*) A compound 'A' with molecular formula $C_5H_{10}O$ gave a positive 2,4-DNP tert but a negative Tollen's reagent tert. It was oxidised to carboxylic acid 'B' with molecular formula $C_6H_6O_2$ when treated with alkaline $KMnO_4$ under vigorous condition sodium salt of 'B' gave a hydrocarbon. 'C' on Kobe's electrolytic reduction. Identify A, B and C write and chemical equations for the reaction.

(*b*) Complete the following reactions by identifying A, B and C.

(*i*) $A + H_2(g)\ (CH_3)_2\ CH—CHO$

(*ii*) $CH_3—\overset{\overset{CH_3}{|}}{\underset{\underset{CH_3}{|}}{C}}—\underset{\underset{O}{\|}}{C}—CH_3 + NaOI \longrightarrow B + C$

29. (a) (*i*) Represent the galvanic cell in which the reaction

$Zn(S) + 2Ag^+ (aq) \longrightarrow Zn^{2+} (aq) + 2\,Ag(S)$

takes place.

(*ii*) Which electrode is negatively charged?

(*iii*) Write reactions taking place at each electrode.

(*a*) Calculate the number of coulombs required for the oxidation of 1 mole of water to oxygen as per equation:

$2H_2O \longrightarrow 4H^+ + O_2 + 4e^-$

[Given 1F = 96,500 C mol^{-1}]

OR

(*a*) Define the terms specific conductance and molar conductivity for solutions of electrolytes.

(*b*) Write the cell formulation and calculate the standard cell potential of the galvanic cell in operation of which the following reaction takes place:

$2Cr(S) + 3Cd^{2+} (aq) \longrightarrow 2Cr^{3+} (aq) + 3Cd(S)$

(*c*) Calculate $\Delta rG°$ for the above reaction.

(Given : $E°Cr^{3+}/Cr = -0.74$ V;

$E°Cr^{2+}/Cd = -0.40$ V; 1F = 96500 C mol^{-1}.

30. (*a*) A blackish brown coloured solid 'A' when fused with alkali metal hydroxides in presence of air, produces a dark green coloured compound 'B', which on electrolytic oxidation in alkaline medium gives a dark purple coloured compound C. Identify A, B and C and write the reactions involved.

(*b*) What happens when an acidic solution of the green compound (B) is allowed to stand for some time? Give the equation involved. What is this type of reaction called?

OR

(1) Give examples and suggest reasons for the following features of the transition metal chemistry:

(*a*) The lowest oxide of transition metal is basic the highest is amphoteric acidic.

(*b*) A transition metal exhibits higher oxidation states in oxides and fluorides.

(*c*) The highest oxidation state is exhibited in oxoanions of a metal.

(2) What are alloys? Name an important alloy which contains some of the lanthanoid metals. Mention its uses.

❑❑❑

MOCK TEST PAPER III

Time Allowed : 3 Hours **[Maximum Marks 70]**

General Instructions—As given in Mock Test Paper I.

1. Name the type of point out defect that occurs in a crystal of zinc sulphide.
2. The rate constant of a reaction is 2×10^{-2} L mol^{-1} S^{-1}. What is the order of the reaction?
3. Give the IUPAC name of the following compound.

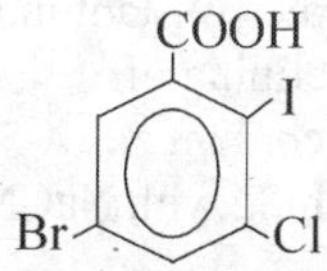

4. How many octahedral voids are there in 1 mole of a compound having cubic close packed structure?
5. What is the molecularity of the reaction?

   $A + H_2O \longrightarrow B$

   rate α [A]
6. An alkyl halide having molecular formula C_4H_9Cl is optically active. What is its structure?
7. In the ring tert for identification of nitrate ion, what is the formula of the compound responsible for the brown ring formed at the interface of two liquids?
8. Write the formula and IUPAC name of aspirin. Why should it not be taken on an empty stomach?
9. The length of the unit cell edge of a body centred metal crystal is 352 Pm. Calculate the radius of an atom of a metal.
10. The e.m.f. of the cell Zn/ Zn_2 + (0.1 m) 11Ccl^{2+}/Cd has been found to be 0.3305 V at 298 K. Calculate the value of M1 given

    E° Zn^{2+}/Zn = –0.76 V

    E° cd2+/cd = –0.40V
11. What are emulrious? How are they classified? State an application of emulrification.
12. Give four differences between physical and chemical adsorption?
13. (*a*) What is the covalence of nitrogen in N_2O_5?

    (*b*) Explain why both N and Bi do not form pentahalides while phosphorus does?

    OR

    When conc. H_2SO_4 was added into an unknown salt present in a test tube, a brown gas(A) was evolved. This gas intensified when copper turnings were also added in to this test-tube. On cooling, the gas (A) changed into a colourless gas (B).

    (*a*) Identify the gases A and B.

    (*b*) Write the equations for the reactions involved.
14. Write the structure of the main product of each of the following:

    (*i*) Action of excess of Br_2-water on phenol.

    (*ii*) Action of alkaline $KMnO_4$ solution on ethene.
15. Explain with the help of suitable example.

    (*i*) Sandmeyer's reaction

    (*ii*) coupling reaction
16. (*i*) Why does chlorine water lose its yellow colour on standing?

(*ii*) What happens when Cl_2 reacts with cold dilute solution of sodium hydroxide? Write equation only.

17. (*i*) Give a chemical test to distinguish between acetophenone and benzophenone.
    (*ii*) Why do tertiary halide undergo elimination faster with strong nucleophilic?
18. Give mechanisms of preparation of ethoxyethane from ethanol.
19. (*i*) Explain the principle of cathodic protection of iron against rusting.
    (*ii*) Define molar conductivity. How does vary with temperature? Why does molar conductance of weak electrolyte increases appreciably on dilution?
20. (*i*) A first order reaction is 15% completed in 20 minutes. How long will it take to complete 60%?
    (*ii*) What is the significance of rate constant in rate law?
21. (*a*) Name the method used for refining of
    (*i*) Nickel (*ii*) Zirconium
    (*b*) The extraction of Au by leaching with NaCN involves both oxidation and reduction. Justify giving equations.
22. (*a*) How is SO_2 an air pollutant?
    (*b*) Write the reaction of F_2 with water.
    (*c*) Give the disproportionation reaction of H_3PO_3.
23. Give the electronic configuration of the
    (*a*) d-orbitals of $[Ti(H_2O)_6]^{3+}$ ion in an octahedral crystal field?
    (*b*) Why is this complex coloured? Explain on the basis of distribution of electrons in the d-orbitals.
    (*c*) How does the colour change on heating $[Ti(H_2O)_6]^{3+}$ ion?
24. Convert:
    (*i*) chloroform to chloropicrin
    (*ii*) Acetone to iodoform.
    (*iii*) Toleune to p-nitrobenzoic acid.
25. Define the following and give one example of each:
    (*a*) Isoelectric acid
    (*b*) mutarotation
    (*c*) Enzymes
26. (*a*) What is the chain growth polymer? Identify which of the following are chain growth polymers and which are step growth polymers.
    Teflon, Nylon, Polyester, PVC.
    (*b*) What is monomer of nylon-6? Is it addition or condensation polymer?
27. Classify synthetic detergents giving an example in each case.

    OR

    What are antihirtamines? Give two examples. Explain how they act on the human body.
28. (*a*) What type of deviation (positive or negative) from ideal behaviour will be shown by the solution of cyclohexane and ethanol? Give suitable reason.
    (*b*) Assuming the Raoult's law is followed, what would be the vapour pressure of the solution formed when 40 g of sugar (molar mass = 342 g mol^{-1}) is dissolved in 360 ml of water at 25°C.
    [Vapor pressure of water is 20 mm Hg and density of water is 1 gml^{-1}]
    (*c*) Define ebullioscopic constant.

    OR

    (*a*) What are isotonic solutions? Give one example.
    (*b*) Determine the amount of $CaCl_2$ ($\alpha = 73.5\%$) dissolved in 2.5 L of water such that its osmotic pressure is 7.50 atm at 27°C.

(*c*) How is molar mass of solute related to elevation in boiling point of the solution? Derive the relationship.

29. (a) What happens when pH of a solution of dichromate is raised?

(b) Draw the structure of dichromate ($Cr_2O_7^{2-}$) ion.

(c) Give reasons.

(*i*) Ni(II) compounds are thermodynamically more solute than Rt(II) compounds.

(*ii*) The second and third elements have very similar atomic radii.

(*iii*) Transition metals can form alloys.

OR

(*a*) In the titration of $FeSO_4$ with $KMnO_4$ in the acidic medium, why is dil H_2SO_4 used instead of dil HCl?

(*b*) Give reasons.

(*i*) Among transition metals, the highest oxidation state is ehibited in oxoanious of a metal.

(*ii*) Ce^{4+} is used as an oxidising agent in volumetric analysis.

(*iii*) Zn^{2+} salts are white while Cu^{2+} salts are blue.

30. A compound 'A' with molecular formula $C_5H_{10}O$ gave a positive 2, 4 DNP test but a negative tollen's reagent test. It was oxidised to carboxylic acid 'B' with molecular formula $C_3H_6O_2$ when treated with alkaline $KMnO_4$ under vigorous oxidation. Sodium salt of 'B' give a hydrocarbon 'C' on Kolbe's electrolyte method. Identify A, B, C and unite the reactions involved.

OR

A Compound 'X' (C_2H_4O) on oxidation gives 'Y' ($C_2H_4O_2$). 'X' undergoes haloform reaction. On treatment with HCN 'X' forms a product 'Z' which on hyrolysis gives Z-hydroxypropanoic acid.

(*i*) Write down structures of 'X' and 'Y'.

(*ii*) Name the product when 'X' reacts with dil NaOH.

(*iii*) Write down the equations for the reactions involved.

❑❑❑

Sample Question Paper - I
CHEMISTRY
CLASS - XII

Time Allowed : 3 Hrs **Maximum Marks : 70**

General Instructions:

1. All questions are compulsory
2. Question no. 1-8 are very short answer questions and carry 1 mark each.
3. Question no. 9-18 are short answer questions and carry 2 marks each.
4. Question no. 19-27 are also short answer questions and carry 3 marks each.
5. Question no. 28-30 are long answer questions and carry 5 marks each
6. Use log tables if necessary, use of calculators is not allowed.

1. Why $LiC\ell$ acquires pink colour when heated in Li vapours?

2. Write the product obtained at anode on electrolysis of concentrated sulphuric acid using platinum electrodes.

3. For the reaction

   $N_2(g) + 3H_2(g) \rightarrow 2NH_3(g)$

   If $\Delta [NH_3] / \Delta t = 4 \times 10^{-8}$ mol L^{-1} s^{-1}, what is the value of $-\Delta [H_2] / \Delta t$.?

4. Which of the following is most effective electrolyte in the coagulation of $Fe_2O_3.H_2O/Fe^{3+}$ sol?

   $KC\ell$, $AlCl_3$, $MgCl_2$, $K_4[Fe(CN)_6]$

5. Write the overall reaction taking place in the process used for the electrolysis of Alumina by Hall- Heroult process.

6. Which Xenon compound is isostructural with $IC\ell_4^-$?

7. What happens to the colour of coordination compound $[Ti(H_2O)_6]$ Cl_3 when heated gradually?

8. Write the structure of phenyl isopentylether.

9. (i) For a weak electrolyte molar conductance in dilute solution increases sharply as its concentration in solution is decreased. Give reason.

   (ii) Write overall cell reaction for lead storage battery when the battery is being charged.

10. Sucrose decomposes in acid solution into glucose and fructose according to the first order rate law with $t_{1/2}$ = 3hrs. Calculate the fraction of sucrose which remains after 8hrs.

OR

The rate constants of a reaction at 500K and 700K are 0.02 s^{-1} and 0.07 s^{-1} respectively. Calculate value of activation energy for the reaction [Given R=8.314$JK^{-1}Ml^{-1}$].

11. For a chemical reaction variation in concentration,

In[R] Vs time (min) plot is shown below:

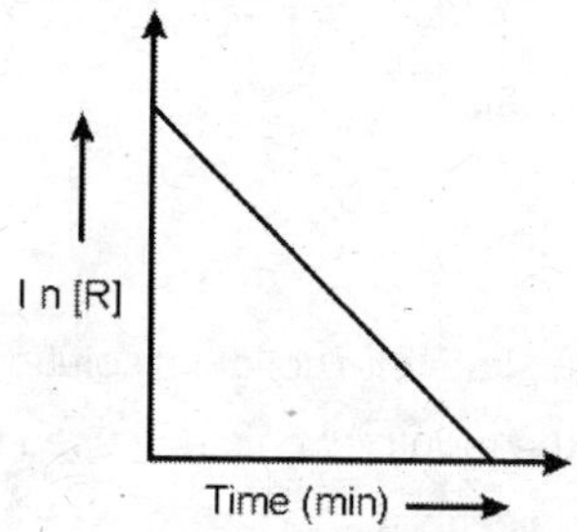

(i) What is the order of the reaction?

(ii) What are units of rate constant, k for the reaction?

(iii) If initial concentration of the reactant is half of the original concentration how will $t_{1/2}$ change?

(iv) Draw the plot of log $[R]_0$ / [R] VS time(s).

12. (i) Draw the structure of phosphinic acid (H_3PO_2)

(ii) Write a chemical reaction for its use as reducing agent.

13. (a) Suggest a quantitative method for estimation of the gas which protects us from U.V. rays of the sun.

(b) Nitrogen oxides emitted from the exhaust system of supersonic jet aeroplanes slowly deplete the concentration of ozone layer in upper atmosphere. Comment.

14. (a) Give the electronic configuration of the d-orbitals of Ti in $[Ti(H_2O)_6]^{3+}$ ion and explain why this complex is coloured? [At.No. of Ti = 22]

(b) Write IUPAC name of $[Cr(NH_3)_3(H_2O)_3]Cl_3$

15. Show the mechanism of acylation of ethanamine and write the IUPAC name of the product formed.

16. Write a chemical equation each to represent

(a) Gatterman reaction

(b) Carbylamine reaction

17. Sodium crystallizes in a bcc unit cell. Calculate the approximate number of unit cells in 9.2g of sodium? (Atomic Mass of Na =23u)

18. What is a semiconductor? Describe the two main types of semiconductors.

19. a) Calculate the charge in coloumbs required for oxidation of 2 moles of water to oxygen? [Given IF = 96, 500 C mol^{-1}]

b) Zinc/silver oxide cell is used in hearing aids and electric watches. The following reactions occur:

$Zn(s) \rightarrow Zn^{2+}(aq) + 2e^-$ $\quad$ $E^0 Zn^{2+} / Zn = -0.76v$

$Ag_2O + H_2O + 2e^- \rightarrow 2Ag + 2OH^-$ $\quad$ $E^0 Ag^+ / Ag = 0.344v$

Calculate (i) standard potential of the cell

(ii) standard Gibbs energy

20. Give reasons for the following observations:

(a) Peptizing agent is added to convert precipitate into colloidal solution.

(b) Cottrell's smoke precipitator is fitted at the mouth of chimney used in factories.

(c) Colloidal gold is used for intramuscular injection.

21. (a) Extraction of Au by leaching with NaCN involves both oxidation and reduction. Justify by giving equations for the reactions involved.

(b) Why is the froth flotation method selected for the concentration of sulphide ores?

OR

Outline the principle of the method used for refining of

(a) Nickel

(b) Zirconium

(c) Tin

22. Write balanced chemical equations for the following reactions:-

(a) Thermal decomposition of ammonium dichromate.

(b) Reaction of Cl_2 with cold and dilute NaOH.

(c) When Phosphine is passed through mercuric chloride solution.

23. Account for following:

(a) Chloromethane reacts with KCN to form ethanenitrile as main product and with AgCN to form methyl isocyanide as chief product.

(b) Use of DDT was banned in United States in 1973.

(c) Benzylic halides show high reactivity towards SN1 reaction.

24. (a) Give one reaction of D-glucose which can not be explained by its open chain structure.

(b) Give one example each for essential and non-essential amino acids.

(c) Differentiate between keratin and insulin.

25. (a) Identify aliphatic biodegradable polyester which is used in packaging and orthopedic devices.

(i) Write its full form.

(ii) Give the structures of monomers from which it is formed.

(iii) Show the formation of polymer.

b) Write the name and structure of the monomer of nylon-6

26. (a) Justify the following:

(i) Sleeping pills are recommended to patients suffering from sleeplessness but it is not advisable to take them without consulting the doctor.

(ii) Why do we require artificial sweetening agents?

(b) Write the composition of Dettol.

27. (a) Give chemical tests to distinguish between:

(i) Isopropyl alcohol and n-propylalcohol

(ii) Phenol and alcohol

(iii) Methyl ethanoate and Ethyl ethanoate

28. (a) Menthol is a crystalline substance with peppermint taste. A 6.2% solution of menthol in cyclohexane freezes at -1.95°C. Determine the formula mass of menthol. The freezing point and molal depression constant of cyclohexane are 6.5 °C and 20.2 K m^{-1}, respectively.

(b) State Henry's Law and mention its two important applications.

(c) Which of the following has higher boiling point and why?

0.1 M NaCl or 0.1 M Glucose

OR

(a) Define Azeotropes and explain briefly minimum boiling azeotrope by taking suitable example.

(b) The vapour pressures of pure liquids A and B are 450 mm and 700 mm of Hg respectively at 350K. Calculate the composition of liquid mixture if total vapor pressure is 600 mm of Hg. Also find the composition of the mixture in vapour phase.

Q.29: (a) (i) Which is stronger reducing agent Cr^{2+} or Fe^{2+} and why?

(ii) Explain why Cu^+ ion is not stable in aqueous solutions.

(iii) Explain why Ce^{4+} is a strong oxidizing agent.

(b) Describe the oxidizing property of $KMnO_4$ in neutral or faintly alkaline medium for its reaction with iodide ions and thiosulphate ions.

OR

(a) Account for the following:

(i) Oxidizing power in the series $VO^{2+} < Cr_2O_7^{2-} < MnO_4^-$

(ii) Actinoid contraction is greater from element to element than lanthanoid contraction.

(iii) Oxoanions of a metal show higher oxidation state.

(b) What is Misch metal? Give its one use.

30. (a) An organic compound (A) which has characteristic odour, On treatment with NaOH it forms two compounds (B) and (C). Compound (B) has molecular formula C_7H_8O which on oxidation gives back (A). The compound (C) is a sodium salt of an acid. When (C) is treated with soda lime it yields an aromatic hydrocarbon (D). Deduce the structures of (A), (B), (C) and (D). Write the sequence of reactions involved.

(b) Arrange the following in the increasing order of the property: indicated:

(i) Benzoic acid, 4-Nitro benzoic acid, 3,5-dinitrobenzoic acid, 4-Methoxybenzoic acid **(acid strength)**

(ii) Acetaldehyde, Acetone, Di-tertbutylketone, Methyltert-butyl ketone **(Reactivity towards HCN).**

OR

(a) Complete each synthesis by filling the missing starting materials, reagents or products. (X,Y and Z)

(i) $C_6H_5CHO + CH_3CH_2CHO \xrightarrow{NaOH} X$

(ii) $CH_3CH_2CH_2CH_2OH \xrightarrow{Y} CH_3CH_2CH_2COOH$

(iii) $CH_3(CH_2)_9COOC_2H_5 \xrightarrow{Z} CH_3(CH_2)_9CHO$

(b) How will you bring about the following conversions in not more than two steps?

(i) Toulene to Benzaldehyde

(ii) Ethylcyanide to 1-Phenylpropanone.

Sample Question Paper - I
MARKING SCHEME
CHEMISTRY

Time Allowed : 3 Hrs **Maximum Marks : 70**

1. Because on heating electrons are trapped at the anionic sites forming F-centres which absorb energy from visible light and radiate pink colour. 1

2. $S_2O_8^{2-}(aq)$ 1

3. 6×10^{-8} $molL^{-1}s^{-1}$ 1

4. $K_4[Fe(CN)_6]$ 1

5. $2Al_2O_3 + 3C \rightarrow 4Al + 3CO_2$ 1

6. XeF_4 1

7. Its colour becomes lighter on heating. 1

8. $C_6H_5-O-CH_2-CH_2-\underset{\displaystyle CH_3}{\underset{|}{C}H}-CH_3$ 1

9. (i) Because with dilution, there is increase in degree of dissociation and consequently the number of ions in total volume of solution increases and hence molar conductivity increases sharply.

   (ii) $2PbSO_4(s) + 2H_2O(\ell) \rightarrow Pb(s) + PbO_2(s) + 4H^+(aq) + 2SO_4^{2-}(aq)$ 1

10. $k = \frac{0.693}{t_{1/2}}$ 1

$$k = \frac{0.693}{3\ hr} = 0.231 hr^{-1}$$

$$0.231 hr^{-1} = \frac{2.303}{8\ hr} \log\frac{[A]_0}{[A]}$$

$$\frac{[A]}{[A]_0} = 0.158$$ 1

OR

(b) $\log \frac{k_2}{k_1} = \frac{Ea}{2.303 R} \left[\frac{T_2 - T_1}{T_1 - T_2} \right]$ ½

$\log \frac{0.07}{0.02} = \frac{Ea}{2.303 \times 8.314} \left[\frac{700 - 500}{700 \times 500} K^{-1} \right]$

$JK^{-1} mol^{-1}$

$0.5441 = \frac{Ea}{2.303 \times 8.314} \left[\frac{200}{700 \times 500} K^{-1} \right]$ ½

$JK^{-1} mol^{-1}$

Ea = 18231 J mol^{-1}

= 18.231 kJ mol-1 1

11. (i) Ist order

(ii) min^{-1}

(iii) t½ remain same as it is independent of $[R]_0$

(iv)

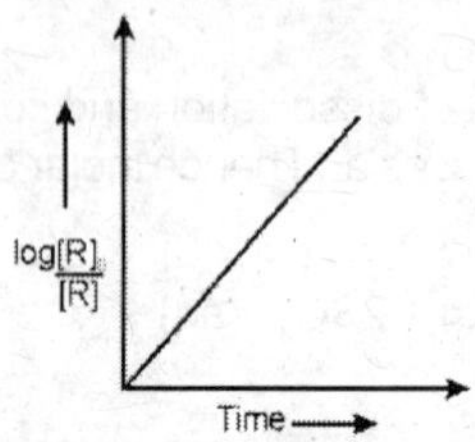

½ x4=2

12. Phosphinic acid (H_3PO_2)

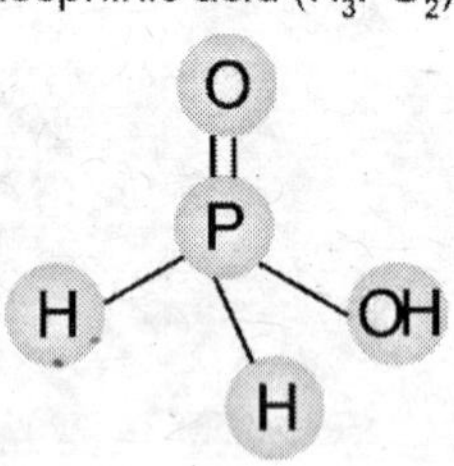

1

Evidence

$H_3PO_2 + 4 AgNO_3 + 2H_2O \rightarrow 4Ag + 4HNO_3 + H_3PO_4$ 1

H_3PO_2 reduces Ag^+ to Ag which shows its reducing nature.

13. (a) $O_3 + 2I^- + H_2O \rightarrow O_2 + I_2 + 2OH^-$ 1

I_2 liberated is then titrated against sodium thiosulphate solution and amount of O_3 can be estimated.

(b) $NO(g) + O_3(g) \rightarrow NO_2(g) + O_2(g)$ 1

'NO' combines rapidly with O_3 forming oxygen and thus is slowly depleting the concentration of the ozone. 1

14. (a) $Ti^{3+} = 3d^1 4s^0$

Due to d-d transition, complex is coloured. 1

(b) Triamminetriaquachromium (III) chloride 1

15. Mechanism

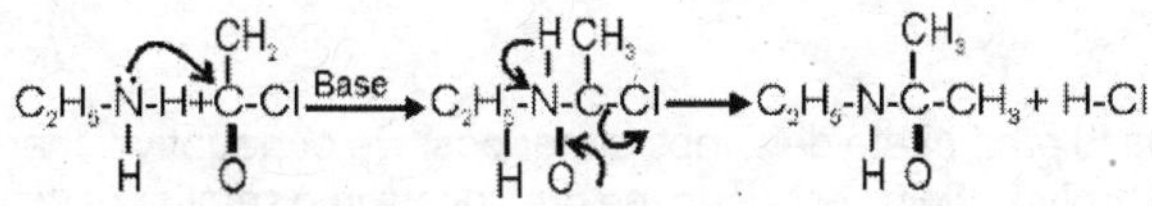

1

IUPAC name N-Ethylethanamide 1

16. (a) Gatterman Reaction for introduction of chlorine or bromine in the benzene ring. 1

$$ArN_2X \xrightarrow{Cu/HCl} ArCl + N_2 + Cux$$

$$ArN_2X \xrightarrow{Cu/HBr} ArBr + N_2 + Cux$$

(b) Carbylamine Reaction to test for presence of primary amines. 1

$$\text{Ar/R-NH}_2 + CHCl_3 + 3\,KOH\,(alc) \rightarrow \underset{\text{Isocyanide (Foul Smelling)}}{\text{Ar/R-NC}} + 3KCl + 3H_2O$$

17. (a) no. of atoms per unit cell for bcc(z) = 2

no. of atoms in 9.2 g of Na

$$= \frac{9.2\ g}{23\ gmol^{-1}} \times 6.022 \times 10^{23} \text{ atoms mol}^{-1}$$ ½

No. of Na atoms = $2.408\ 8 \times 10^{23}$ 1

No. of unit cells $\dfrac{2.4088 \times 10^{23} \text{atoms}}{2 \text{atoms unit cell}^{-1}} = 1.2044 \times 10^{23}$ ½

18. Semiconductor is a solid with conductivity in the intermediate range form 10^{-6} to 10^4 $Ohm^{-1}\ m^{-1}$. 1

(i) n-type Semiconductor : They have excess of electrons e.g Ge doped with As. ½

(ii) p- type Semiconductor : They have electron vacancy or hole eg Si doped with B. ½

19. (a) $2H_2O \rightarrow 4H^+ + O_2 + 4e^-$ ½

Therefore Q = 4F

$= 4 \times 96500\ C\ mol^{-1}$

$= 386000\ C\ mol^{-1}$ ½

(b) Zn is oxidized and Ag_2O is reduced to Ag

$\overset{o}{E}cell = \overset{o}{E}Cathode - \overset{o}{E}anode = [0.344 - (-0.76)]\ V$

$= 1.104\ V$ 1

$\Delta G^{\circ} = nF\overset{o}{E}cell$

$= -2 \times 96500\ C\ mol^{-1} \times 1.104\ V$

$= -2.13 \times 10^5\ J\ mol^{-1}$ 1

20. (a) Addition of peptizing agents to precipitate develops either positive or negative charge by adsorbing ions of the electrolyte; which break up the precipitate into smaller particles of the size of a colloid.

(b) The precipitator containing plates having a charge opposite to that carried by smoke particles which lose their charge and get precipitated and smoke is thus, free form carbon and dust particles after passing through chimney.

(c) Because of larger surface area of colloidal gold and easy assimilation with the blood which is colloidal. 1x3 =3

21. (a) Oxidation of Au

$4Au(s) + 8CN^-(aq) + 2H_2O + O_2(g) \rightarrow 4[Au(CN)_2]^- + 4OH^-$ 1

Reduction of Au^+ tu Au 1

$2[Au(CN)_2]^- + Zn \rightarrow [Zn(CN)_4]2^- + 2Au$

(b) Because sulphide ores are preferentially wetted by oil and impurities by water. 1

OR

(a) Nickel : Mond's Process : Impure nickel on reaction with carbon monoxide forms tetracarbonyl nickel which decomposes to form pure nickel and carbon monoxide.

(b) Zircorium : Vam-Ankel Method : Impure metal Z_r is heated with I_2 to get $Z_r I_4$ which is heated strongly at 2075K to get pure Z_r.

(c) Tin : Liquation: Impure metal is heated at the top of sloping furnace so that tin melts but impurity does not. Molten tin flows down and pure tin so formed is collected. 1 X 3=3

22. (i) $(NH4)_2 Cr_2O_7 \xrightarrow{\Delta} N_2(g) + Cr_2O_3 + 4H_2O$

(ii) $2NaOH + Cl_2 \rightarrow NaCl + NaClO + H_2O$

(cold and dilute)

(iii) $3HgCl_2 + 2PH_3 \rightarrow Hg_3P_2 + 6HCl$ 1x3 = 3

23. (a) Because with KCN, C act as a nucleophile due to ionic nature of K-C bond whereas with AgCN, N act as a nucleophile due to covalent nature of Ag-C bond.

(b) Due to chemical stability of DDT and its fat solubility it is not metabolized very rapidly by animals and hence is banned in US.

(c) Due to high stability of benzyl carbocation through Resonance. 1x3=3

24. (a) Despite having the presence of aldehyde group, glucose does not give 2,4 DNP test/schiff's test/ does not form the hydrogen sulphite additon product with $NaHSO_3$

(b) Essential aminoacid-valine; non-essential amino acid = glycine

(c) keratin is a fibrous protein whereas insulin is a globular protein. 1x3=3

25. (a) PHBV

(i) Poly β - Hydroxybutyrate-co - β -Hydroxyvalerate

(ii) CH_3- $CH(OH)CH_2COOH$ and CH_3-CH_2-$CH(OH)CH_2COOH$

(iii)

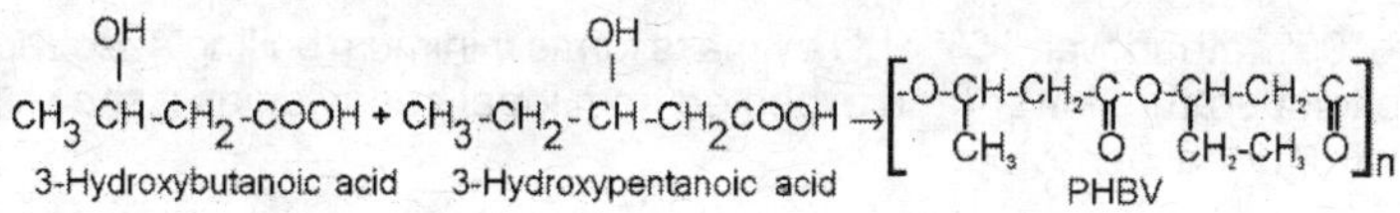

½ X4=2

(b) (iii) Nylon-6:Caprolactam

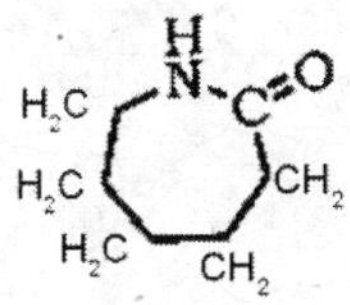

1

26. (a)

(i) Because most of the drugs act as poison in higher doses and may lead to death.

(ii) To control calorie intake and as a substitute of sugar for diabetics.

(b) Chloroxylenol and terpineol 1x3=3

27. (a)

(i) Isopropyl alcohol and n-propyl alcohol

On adding $NaOH/I_2$ or NaOI and heating, Isopropyl alcohol forms yellow ppt of iodoform(CHI_3) whereas n-propyl alcohol does not. (or any other suitable test)

(ii) Phenol and alcohol

On adding neutral $FeCl_3$ solution, Phenol forms red-violet complex whereas alcohol does not.

(or any other suitable test)

(iii) methyl ethanoate and ethyl ethanoateIodoform test:- On hydrolysis, ethylethanoate gives ethanol which on heating with NaOI gives yellow ppt. of CHI_3 whereas Methyl Ethanoate on hydrolysis gives Methanol which does not form Iodoform with NaOI.

1x3=3

28. (a) $\Delta T_f = K_f m = \frac{W_B}{M_B} \times \frac{1000g}{W_A}$ ½

$$8.45\,K = 20.2\,K\,kg\,Mol^{-1} \times \frac{6.2g}{M_B} \times \frac{1000g}{93.8\,kg}$$ ½

$M_B = 158$ g mol-1 1

(b) **Henry's Law :** The Solubility of gas in a liquid is directly proportional to the pressure of the gas. 1

Applications : 1. Solubility of CO_2 is increased at high pressure. ½

2. Mixture of He and O_2 are used by deep sea divers because He is less soluble than nitrogen ½

(c) 0.1 M NaCl, Because it dissociates in solution and furnishes greater number of particles per unit while glucose does not dissociate. 1

OR

(a) Azeotropes : is a liquid mixture which boils at constant temperature without undergoing change in composition .

Ex- A mixture of 95% ethanol and 5% H_2O by mass forms minimum boiling Azeotropes i.e it boils at a temperature lower than expected from ideal behavior, as it shows positive deviation from ideal behaviour. 1+1

(b) $p^{\circ}_B = 450$ mm Hg $p^{\circ}_B = 700$ mm Hg

$p = p^{\circ}_A X_A + p^{\circ}_B X_B$ 1

$600 = 450\,(X_A) + 700\,(1 - X_A)$

On solving

$X_A = 0.4$ ½ + ½

$X_B = 0.6$

in vapour phase

$p_A = 0.4 \times 450$ mm $= 180$ mm Hg : $p_B = 0.6 \times 700$ mm $= 420$ mm Hg

$$X_A = \frac{180mm}{600mm} = 0.3$$

$$: \quad X_B = \frac{420mm}{600mm} = 0.7$$ 1

29. (a)

(i) Cr^{2+} is stronger reducing agent than Fe^{2+} due to its change from d^4 to stable d^3 configuration incase of Cr^{2+} to Cr^{3+} than d^6 to d^5 in Fe^{2+} to Fe^{3+}Change.

(ii) Because Cu+ in aqueous solution undergoes disproportionation to more stable Cu^{2+} and Cu.

(iii) Because Ce is more stable in +3 oxidation state. 1x3=3

(b) $2MnO_4^- + I^- + H_2O \rightarrow 2MnO_2 + IO_3^- + 2OH^-$

$8MnO_4^- + 3S_2O_3^{2-} + H_2O \rightarrow 8MnO_2 + 6SO_4^{2-} + 2OH^-$ 1+1

OR

(a) (i) This is due to the increasing stability of the lower species to which they are reduced.

(ii) Due to poor shielding effect of 5f electrons of actinoids than 4f electron of anthanoids.

(iii) Due to high electronegativity and multiple bond formation with metal by oxygen. 1x3=3

(b) Misch metal is an alloy of a Lanthanoids metal and iron and traces of S,Ca, C and Al. It is used in making bullets and lighter flint (any one)

30. $\underset{(A)}{C_6H_5CHO} \xrightarrow{NaOH} \underset{(B)}{C_6H_5CH_2OH} + \underset{(C)}{C_6H_5COONa}$ 1

$C_6H_5COONa \text{ (C)} \xrightarrow{NaOH/CaO} \underset{(D)}{C_6H_6}$

(A) C_6H_5CHO

(B) $C_6H_5CH_2OH$

(C) C_6H_5COONa

(D) C_6H_6 ½x4=2

(b) (i) 4- methoxybenzoic acid < Benzoic acid < 4-nitrobenzoic acid < 3,5- dinitrobenzoic acid.

(ii) Di tertbutylketone < methyl t-butylketone < Acetone < Acetaldehyde 1+1

OR

(a) (i) $C_6H_5CHO + CH_3CH_2CHO \xrightarrow{NaOH} C_6H_5CH(OH)CH(CH_3)CHO$

(ii) $CH_3CH_2CH_2CH_2OH \xrightarrow{KMnO_4} CH_3CH_2CH_2COOH$

(iii) $CH_3(CH_2)_9\,COOC_2H_5 \xrightarrow{DIBAL\text{-}H\,/H_2O} CH_3(CH_2)_9\,CHO$ 1X3=3

(b) Toluene to Benzaldehyde

$C_6H_5\text{-}CH_3 \xrightarrow{Cl_2/hv} C_6H_5\text{-}CHCl_2 \xrightarrow[373K]{H_2O} C_6H_5\text{-}CHO$

(ii) EthylCyanide to 1- PhenylPropanone

$CH_3CH_2CN \xrightarrow{PhMgBr} PhC{=}(N\,MgBr)CH_2CH_3 \xrightarrow{H_2O} PhCOCH_2CH_3$ 1+1

Sample Question Paper - II
CHEMISTRY
CLASS - XII

Time Allowed : 3 Hrs **Maximum Marks : 70**

General Instructions:

1. *All questions are compulsory.*
2. *Question No. 1 to 8 are very short questions carrying one mark each.*
3. *Question No. 9 to 18 are short answer questions carrying 2 marks each.*
4. *Question No. 19 to 27 are also short answer questions carrying 3 marks each.*
5. *Question No. 28 to 30 are long answer questions carrying 5 marks each.*
6. *Use log table if necessary. Log tables will be provided on demand. Calculator is not allowed in exam hall.*

Q.1 Write the products obtained when benzyl phenylether is heated with HI.

Q.2 Name the type of potential difference produced between the fixed charged layer and diffused layer having opposite charges around the colloidal particle.

Q.3 Write the IUPAC name of the compound

$CH_2(Cl)COCH(CH_3)CONH_2$

Q.4 Which of the following compounds has a lone pair of electrons at the central atom?

$H_2S_2O_8$, $H_2S_2O_7$, H_2SO_3, H_2SO_4

Q.5 What type of linkage holds together the monomers of DNA?

Q.6 Complete the following reaction :

$$CH3 - CH = CH_2 \xrightarrow[\text{peroxide}]{\text{HBr}} X \xrightarrow[\text{Acetone}]{\text{NaI}} Y$$

Q.7 Write a non-exothermic reaction taking place in the blast furnace during extraction of iron.

Q.8 Iodoform has antiseptic properties. Give one reason to support this.

Q.9 Write the names associated with the following reactions

(a) $RCONH_2 + Br_2 + 4NaOH \rightarrow RNH_2 + Na_2CO_3 + 2\,NaBr + 2H_2O$

(b) $ArN_2^+x^- \xrightarrow{CuCN/KCN} ArCN + N_2$

(c) $R\text{-}NH_2 + CHCl_3 + 3KOH \xrightarrow{\text{Heat}} R\text{-}NC + 3KCl + 3H_2O$

(d) $ArN_2^+x^- \xrightarrow{Cu/HCl} ArCl + N_2 + CuX$

10. KF has ccp structure. Calculate the radius of unit cell if the side of the cube or edge length is 400pm. How many F ions and octahederal voids are there in this unit cell?

11. Give reason

(a) Why is Frenkel defect found in AgCl?

(b) What is the difference between Phosphorus doped and Gallium doped semi conductors?

12. Describe the construction of a H_2-O_2 fuel cell and the reactions taking place in it.

OR

Define the terms given below:

(a) Conductivity (b) Molar Conductivity

What are their units?

13. State Raoult's law for a solution containing volatile liquids. Explain with suitable example the concept of maximum boiling azeotropes.

14. Give chemical reactions in support of the following observations.

(a) Sulphuric acid has low volatility

(b) Iodide ions can be oxidized by oxygen in acidic medium.

15. Propose mechanism of the reaction taking place when

(a) (-) - 2-Bromooctane reacts with sodium hydroxide to form (+)-octane-2-ol.

(b) 2-Bromo pentane is heated with (alc.) KOH to form alkenes.

16. What is a flux? What is the role of flux in the metallurgy of Iron and Copper?

17. The sum of first and second ionization enthalpies and third and fourth ionization enthalpies of nickel and platinum are:

	IE_1+IE_2 (MJmol$_{-1}$)	IE_3+IE_4 (MJmol^{-1})
Ni	2.49	8.80
Pt	2.66	6.70

Based on the above information, answer the following:

(a) Which is the most common oxidation state for Ni and Pt? why?

(b) Out of the two, name the metal which can easily form compounds in +4 oxidation state and why?

18. Describe a chemical test in each case to distinguish between the following pairs of compounds

(a) Aniline and N-ethyl aniline.

(b) N-Methyl propane-2-amine and N-Ethyl-N-methyl ethanamine.

19. Give reason

(a) Why does an alkaline medium inhibit the rusting of iron?

(b) Why does a dry cell become dead after a long time even if it has not been used?

(c) Why is Zinc better than Tin in protecting iron from corrosion?

20. Write :

(a) Reaction involved in the preparation of a biodegradable polyester.

(b) Monomer unit of synthetic rubber (neoprene).

(c) One use of Nylon-6,6

21. (a) Write the Zwitter ion structure of glycine.

(b) What is meant by inversion of sugar?

(c) Name the Vitamin in each case whose deficiency causes

(i) Night Blindness

(ii) Poor coagulation of blood.

22. Write chemical equations for the following reactions :

(a) Oxidation of nitrite ion by MnO_4^- in acidic medium.

(b) Acidification of potassium Chromate solution.

(c) Disproportionation of Manganese(VI) in acidic solution.

OR

Account for the following

(a) Europium (II) is more stable than cerium(II).

(b) Transition metals have high enthalpies of atomization.

(c) Actinoid ions are generally coloured.

23. Give plausible explanation for each of the following:

(a) Ortho-nitrophenol is more acidic than ortho-methoxyphenol.

(b) Alcohols are easily protonated in comparison to phenols.

(c) The relative ease of dehydration of alcohols is tertiary > secondary > primary.

24. On dissolving 19.5 g of CH_2FCOOH in 500 g of water, a depression of 1°C in freezing point of water is observed. Calculate the Van't Hoff factor and dissociation constant of fluoro acetic acid. Given, $K_f = 1.86$ K kg mol^{-1}

25. (a) Name one substance which can act as both:-

(i) Analgesic and antipyretic.

(ii) Antiseptic and disinfectant.

(b) Explain the following terms with suitable example of each :

(i) Broad spectrum antibiotics.

(ii) Anionic detergents.

26. (a) Heat of adsorption is greater for chemisorptions than physisorption. Why?

(b) What is colloidion?

(c) Differentiate between peptization and coagulation.

27. (a) State the hybridization & magnetic behaviour of $[C_r(CO)_6]$.

(b) What are the various factors affecting crystal field splitting energy?

(c) Which of the two is more stable and why?

$K_4[Fe(CN)_6]$ OR $K_3[Fe(CN)_6]$.

28. (a) An orange solid A on heating gives a colourless gas B. The gas B in dry condition is passed over heated Ca to give a solid C . The solid C further reacts with water to produce gas D which forms a blue coloured compound E on reaction with Copper sulphate solution. Identify A,B,C,D,E and give the sequence of reactions involved.

(b) Arrange the following in order of property indicated for each set:

(i) HCl, HI, HBr, HF – Decreasing thermal stabilty.

(ii) Xe, He, Kr, Rn, Ne – Decreasing order of electron gain enthalpy.

OR

(a) Give Reasons:

(i) Solid $PC\ell_5$ is an ionic compound.

(ii) Most of the reactions of fluorine are exothermic.

(iii) Ozone is thermodynamically unstable.

(b) Draw the structures of the following

(i) XeOF4 (ii) $H_4P_2O_7$

29. (a) A compound A on oxidation gives $B(C_2H_4O_2)$. A reacts with dil. NaOH and on subsquent heating forms C. C on catalytic hydrogenation gives D. Identify A,B,C,D and write down the reactions involved.

(b) Write chemical equations to carry out the following conversions :-

(i) Benzene to Benzylalcohol.

(ii) Propane nitrile to 1-phenylpropanone.

OR

(a) An organic compound X undergoes acid hydrolysis to form two compounds Y and Z. Y reacts with Sodium carbonate to form A. A is heated with Soda lime to form B (CH_4). Y on reduction with $LiA\ell H_4$ forms Z. Identify X,Y,Z,A,B and write the reactions involved.

(b) Account for the following:-

(i) Benzoic acid does not undergo Friedel-Craft reaction.

(ii) pKa value of chloro acetic acid is lower than pKa value of acetic acid.

30. (a) For the reaction

$$C_{12}H_{22}O_{11} + H_2O \xrightarrow{H^+} C_6H_{12}O_6 \quad + \quad C_6H_{12}O_6$$

write:

(i) Rate of reaction expression,

(ii) rate law equation,

(ii) molecularity,

(iii) order of reaction

(b) The following data were obtained during the first order thermal decomposition of SO_2Cl_2 at constant volume.

$$SO_2Cl_2\ (g) \rightarrow SO_2\ (g) + Cl_2\ (g)$$

Experiment	Time/s	Total pressure/atm
1	0	0.5
2	100	0.6

Calculate the rate of reaction when total pressure is 0.65 atm.

OR

(a) Illustrate graphically the effect of catalyst on activation energy.

(b) Catalysts have no effect on the equilibrium constant. Why?

(c) The decomposition of A into product has value of k as $4.5 \times 10^3\ s^{-1}$ at 10°C and activation energy is 60 kJ mol^{-1}. Calculate the temperature at which the value of k W (J) be $1.5 \times 10^4\ s^{-1}$

MARKING SCHEME OF CHEMISTRY SAMPLE PAPER-II

A.1 Phenol and benzyl iodide 1

A.2 Zeta potential 1

A.3 4-Chloro-2-methyl-3-oxo butanamide 1

A.4 H_2SO_3 1

A.5 Phosphodiester linkage 1

A.6 $X = CH_3\text{-}CH_2\text{-}CH_2\text{-}Br$ ½ + ½

$Y = CH_3\text{-}CH_2\text{-}CH_2\text{-}I$

A.7 $CaCO_3 \longrightarrow CaO + CO_2$ 1

A.8 Iodoform has antiseptic properties due to free liberated iodine. 1

A.9 (a) Hoffmann Bromide Degradation

(b) Sandmeyer's reaction

(c) Carbylamine reaction

(d) Gattermann Reaction (½ x 4=2)

A.10 For ccp Lattice

$$r = \frac{\sqrt{2}a}{4}$$ ½

$$r = \frac{1.414 \times 400 \text{ pm}}{4}$$

r = 141.4 pm 1

There are four F^- ions and octahedral voids. ½

A.11 (a) Due to smaller size of Ag^+ cation.

(b) Silicon doped with Phosphorus gives n-type whereas Silicon doped with Gallium are p-type semi conductors. 1+1

A.12 Fuel cell consists of porous carbon electrodes containing catalysts (finely divided platinum or palladium metal) incorporated in them. Conc. Aqueous KOH/ NaOH solution is placed between the electrodes act as electrolyte. H_2 and oxygen are bubbled through porous electrodes into the electrolytic solution. (1)

At Anode : $2H_2(g) + 4OH^-(aq) \longrightarrow 4H_2O(l) + 4e^-$ (½)

At Cathode : $O_2(g) + 2H_2O(l) + 4e \longrightarrow 4OH^-(aq)$ (½)

(a) Inverse of resistivity is called conductivity/conductance of one centimeter cube of the solution of the electrolyte.

S I.Unit is Sm^{-1} (1)

(b) Molar conductivity : The conductance of the solution of an electrolyte containing one mole of electrolyte kept between two electrodes of a conductivity cell at unit distance. (1)

S I Unit Sm^2mol^{-1}

A.13 Roult's Law : For a solution of volatile liquids, the partial pressure of each component in a solution is directly proportional to its mole fraction. (½)

The solution showing large negative deviation from Raoult's law are maximum boiling azeotrops. e.g. mixture of chloroform and acetone.

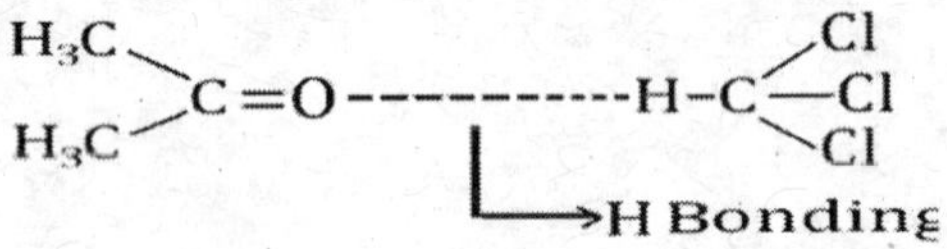

(½)

Hydrogen bonding formation decreases escaping tendency of a molecule i.e. exerts low V.P which leads to high B.P. (1)

A.14 (a) $2MX + H_2SO_4 \longrightarrow 2HX + M_2SO_4$ (1)

$(X = F, Cl, NO_3)$

(b) $4I^- + 4H^+ + O_2 \longrightarrow 2I_2 + 2H_2O$

A.15 (a)

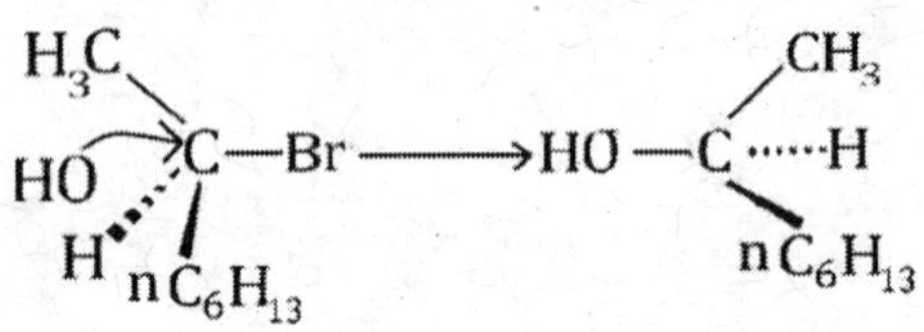

(1)

(b)

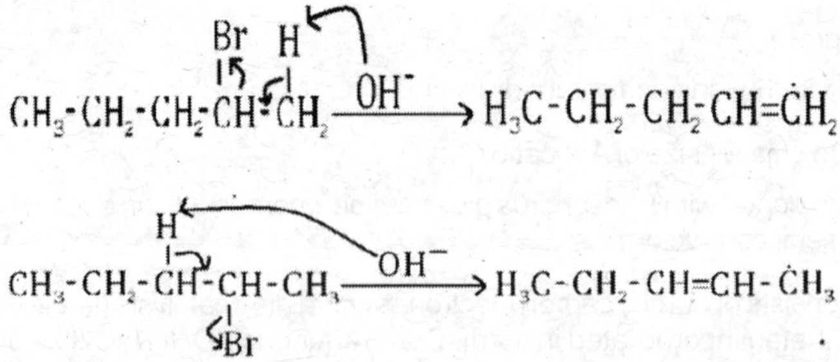

(1)

major

A16. Flux is a substance that combines with gangue (which may still be present in roasted or the calcined ore) to form slag. (1)

$FeO + SiO_2 \longrightarrow FeSiO_3$ (½)

In the blast furnace CaO(flux) removes silica presention in the Ore. (½)

$CaO + SiO_2 + CaSiO_3$

A.17 (a) Ni = + 2 Pt = + 4 because these have lower ionization enthalpy. (1)

(b) Pt, The sum of first four Ionization enthalpies for Pt is lower than of Ni. (1)

A.18 (a) Aniline is a primary amine. Therefore it gives carbyamine test, i.e., when heated with an alcoholic solution of KOH and $CHCl_3$, it gives offensive smell of phenyl isocyanide.

But N-ethyl aniline is a secondary amine and hence does not give carbylamines test. (1)

(b) N-methylpropane-2 amine is a secondary amine,on adding Hinsberg's reagent compound formed is soluble in aqueous NaOH.But N-ethyl-N-methylethamine does not react with Hinsberg's reagent.(or any other suitable test) (1)

A.19 (a) Rusting of Iron takes place in presence of H^+. Alkaline medium will neutralize H^+ and will inhibit rusting.

(b) This is because the acidic $NH_4C\ell$ corrodes the Zinc container.

(c) Zinc protects better because reduction potential of $Zinc^{2+}$ is lower but that of Tin^{2+} is higher than that of $iron^{2+}$. (1x3=3)

A.20 (a) $CH_3\text{-}CH(OH)\text{-}CH_2\text{-}COOH + CH_3\text{-}CH(OH)\text{-}CH_2\text{-}CH_2\text{-}COOH \longrightarrow$

3- Hydroxybutanoic acid **3- Hydroxypentanoic acid**

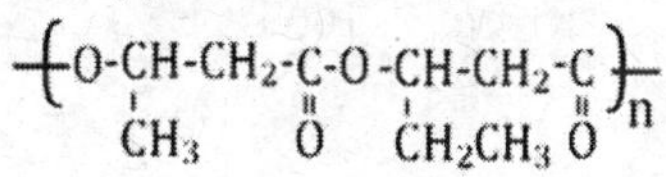

PHVB

(b) $CH_2{=}C(Cl){-}CH{=}CH_2$

2-chloro- 1, 3- butadiene

(c) For making sheets/ bristles for brushes/In Textile industry. (1x3=3)

A.21 (a) $C\text{-}CH(:NH_2)\text{-}C(=O)\text{-}O\text{-}H \rightleftharpoons H\text{-}CH(:\overset{+}{N}H_3)\text{-}C(=O)\text{-}O^-$

(Zwitter Ion) (1)

(b) The change of specific rotation of sugar from dextrorotation to laevorotation is called inversion of sugar. (1)

(c) (i) Vitamin A (ii) Vitamin K (½ + ½)

A.22 (a) $5NO_2^- + 2MnO_4^- + 6H^+ \longrightarrow 2Mn^{2+} + 3H_2O + 5NO_3^-$

(b) $2K_2CrO_4 + 2H^+ \longrightarrow K_2Cr_2O_7 + 2K^+ + H_2O$

(c) $3MnO_4^{2-} + 4H^+ \longrightarrow 2MnO_4^- + MnO_2 + 2H_2O$

OR

(a) Europium(II) has stable electronic configuration i.e $[Xe]4f^7 5d^0 6s^0$. (1)

(b) Due to large number of unpaired electrons in their atoms, stronger interatomic interaction & hence stronger bonding between their atoms is found. (1)

(c) Unpaired electrons present in their Ions undergo f-f transitions. (1)

A.23 (a) Due to strong -R and -I effect of $-NO_2$ group, electron density in the OH bond decreases

(b) In alcohols lone pair of electrons on oxygen is available for proton due to absence of resonance.

OR

Lone pair of electrons at oxygen are not available for donation due to resonance in phenols.

(c) Due to order of stability of carbocations, $3^o > 2^o > 1^o$

OR

Tertiary alcohols form more substituted alkenes.

A.24 Given $\omega_A = 19.5g$, $\omega_B = 500g$, $Kf = 1.86 KKg\ mol^{-1}$

$(Tf)obs = 1^oC$

$$\Delta Tf = \frac{Kf \times \omega_B \times 1000}{M_B \times M_A}$$ (½)

$$MB = \frac{Kf . \omega_B \times 1000}{\Delta Tf \times M_A}$$

$$= \frac{1.86\ K\ kg\ mol^{-1} \times 19.5\ g \times 1000\ g}{1.0\ K \times 500\ kg} = 72.54\ gmol^{-1}$$ (½)

Molecular mass of CH_2FCOOH= 12+2+19+32+1 = 78 g mol^{-1}

i = normal molecular mass/observed molecular mass = 78/72.54 (½)

= 1.0753 (½)

$$CH_2FCOOH \rightleftharpoons CH_2FCOO^- + H^+$$

C mol L^{-1} 0   0

$C(1-\alpha)$ $C\alpha$ $C\alpha$

$\alpha = i - 1 = 1.0753 - 1 = 0.0753$ (½)

$$Ka = \frac{[CH_2FCOO^-][H^+]}{[CH_2FCOOH]} = \frac{C\alpha}{C(1-\alpha)} = \frac{C\alpha^2}{1-\alpha}$$

$$C = \frac{19.5 \times 1000}{78 \quad 500} = 0'5M$$

$Ka = C\alpha^2$

$Ka = 0.5X(0.0753)^2$

$Ka = 3.07 \text{ X } 10^{-3}$ (1)

A.25 (a) (i) Aspirin (½)

(ii) Phenol (½)

(b) Antibiotics which kill or inhibit the growth of wide range of gram positive and gram negative bacteria. e.g., Chloramphenicol . (1)

(c) Sodium salts of sulphonated long chain alcohols or hydrocarbons are anionic detergents. e.g., Sodium lauryl sulphate. (1)

A.26 (a) Due to the formation of chemical bonds between adsorbate and Adsorbent. (1)

(b) 4% solution of nitro cellulose in a mixture of alcohol and ether. (1)

(c) Peptization: process of converting a precipitate into colloidal sol by adding an electrolyte. But coagulation is the settling of colloidal particles. (1)

A.27 (a) d^2sp^3 , diamagnetic (1)

(b) Factors : (i) Field produced by the ligand. (½)

(ii) Charge on the metal ions. (½)

(c) $K_4[Fe(CN)_6]$ is more stable due to higher charge or smaller size of metal ion. (1)

A.28 (a) $\underset{(A)}{(NH_4)_2Cr_2O_7} \longrightarrow \underset{(B)}{N_2(g)} + 4H_2O(l) + Cr_2O_3(s)$ (1)

$3Ca + N_2 \xrightarrow{Heat} \underset{(C)}{Ca_3N_2}$ $\quad \underset{(C)}{Ca_3N_2} + 6H_2O \longrightarrow \underset{(D)}{NH_3(g)} + Ca(OH)_2$ (1)

$\underset{(Blue)}{Cu^{2+}(aq) + 4NH_3(aq)} \rightleftharpoons \underset{\text{Deep blue (E)}}{[Cu(NH_3)_4]^{2+}(aq)}$ (1)

(b) (i) HF > HCl > HBr > HI (1)

(ii) Ne > Kr > Xe > Rn > He (1)

OR

(a) (i) It exists as$[PCl_4]^+ [PCl_6]^-$ (1)

(ii) Due to low bond dissociation enthalpy of fluorine and strong bond formation with other elements. (1)

(iii) Decomposition of Ozone$[2O_3 \longrightarrow 3O_2]$

results in

ΔH=negative

ΔS =positive

According to Gibb's equation $\Delta G = \Delta H - T\Delta S$, reactions with negative ΔG value are spontaneous (1)

(b) (i)

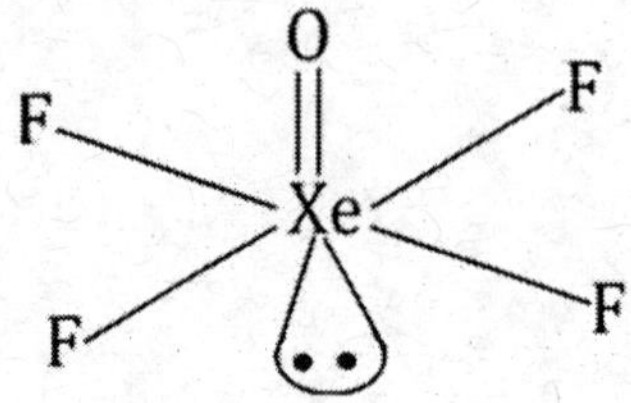

(1)

(ii)

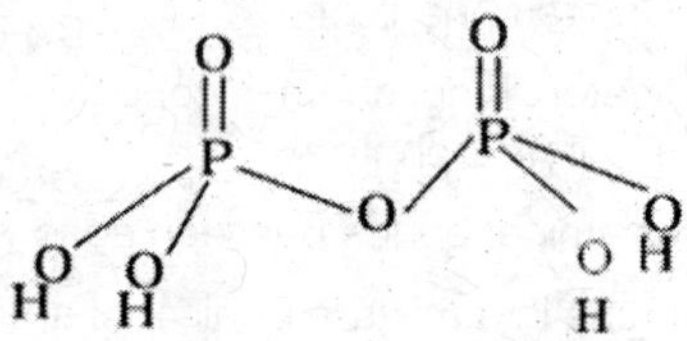

(1)

A.29 (a) $CH_3-\overset{O}{\overset{\|}{C}}-H$ (A) oxidation $CH_2-\overset{O}{\overset{\|}{C}}-OH$ (1)

(1)

$CH_3OHO + CH_3CHO \xrightarrow{NaOH(aq)} CH_3-\underset{OH}{CH}-CH_2-CHO$

(A) (A)

$CH_3\underset{OH}{CH}-CH_2CHO \xrightarrow{Heat} CH_3CH=CH.CHO$ (1)

(C)

(1)

$CH_3-CH=CH.CHO$ $H_2/N_2CH_3-CH_2-CH_2-CHO$

(C) (D)

(b) (i)

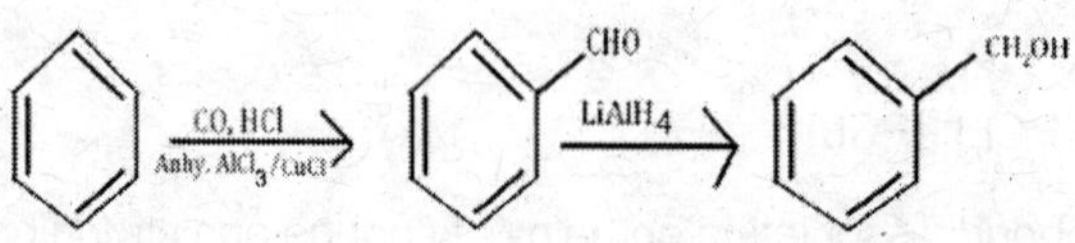

(1)

Benzene Benzylalcohol

(ii)

$$CH_3CH_2C\equiv N + C_6H_5MgBr \xrightarrow{ether} CH_3CH_2\text{-}C(=NMgBr)C_6H_5 \xrightarrow{H_3O^+} C_2H_5C(=O)C_6H_5$$ (1)

Propane nitrile

1- Phenylpropanone

OR

a) $CH_3COOC_2H_5 \xrightarrow{H_3O^+} CH_3COOH + C_2H_5OH$ (1)

(X) (Y) (Z)

$$CH_3COOH + Na_2CO_3 \longrightarrow \underset{(A)}{CH_3COONa} \xrightarrow[\text{Heat}]{NaOH \ \& \ CaO} \underset{(B)}{CH_4}$$

(1)

$$CH_3COOH \xrightarrow{LiAlH4} CH_3CH_2OH_{(z)}$$

(b) (i) – COOH group is deactivating and combines with Aluminium chloride(catalyst) during the reaction. (1)

(ii) Due to - I effect of chlorine atom in chloroacetic acid larger number of H^+Ions are released in its aqueous solution.Therefore It has lower PKa value. (1)

A.30 (a) 1. Rate equation

$$Rate = \frac{d[C_{12}H_{22}O_{11}]}{dt} = -\frac{d[H_2O]}{dt} = \frac{d[C_6H_{12}O6]}{dt} = \frac{d[C_6H_{12}O_6]}{dt}$$ (½)

Rate law equation:

$$Rate = K\,[C_{12}H_{22}O_{11}]$$ (½)

Molecularity ⟶ 2 (½)

Order ⟶ first order (½)

(b) As the reaction is of first order therefore

$$k = \frac{2.303}{t}\log\frac{P^o}{2P_o - P_T}$$ (½)

When t = 100s

k = (2.303)/100 log(0.5) 2 x 0.5 x 0.6

k = (2.303)/100 log1.25

$= (2.303)/100\ (.0969)$

$= -2.2316 \times 10^{-3}\ sec^{-1}$ (½)

When

$P_o = 0.65$ atm i.e $P_o + P = .65$ atm

$P = 0.65 - P^o = 0.65 - 0.50 = .15$ atm (½)

Therefore the pressure of SO_2Cl_2 at time t (PSO_2Cl_2)

$= P_o - P = (0.50 - .15)$ atm $= 0.35$ atm (½)

Rate at that time $= K \times PSO_2Cl_2 = 2.2316 \times 10^{-3} \times 0.35$

$= 7.8 \times 10^{-5}$ atm sec^{-1} (1)

OR

(a)

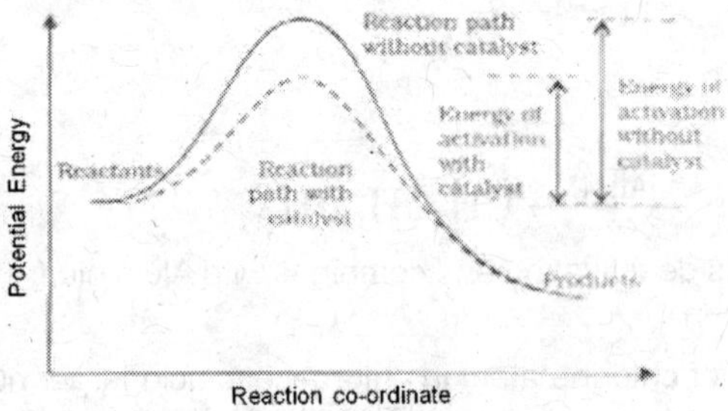

Effe (2)

(b) Because catalyst catalyses the forward as well as backward reaction to the same extent. (1)

Given

$K = 4.5 \times 10^3\ s^{-1}$, $T_1 = 283$ K

$K = 1.5 \times 10^4\ s^{-1}$, $T_2 = ?$, Ea = 60 Kj mol^{-1}

$$\log \frac{K_2}{K_1} = \frac{Ea}{2.303R}\left[\frac{T_2 - T_1}{T_1 . T_2}\right]$$

$$\text{Log}\ (1.5 \times 10^4)\ (4.5 \times 10^3) = 60000/(2.303 \times 8.314) \left[\frac{T_2 - T_1}{T_1 T_2}\right]$$ (½)

Log 3.333 = 3133.63 [$(T_2 - 283)/(283T)$] (½)

$T_2 = 283/0.9528$

$= 297K = (297-273)^{\circ}C$

$= 24^{\circ}C$ (1)

Sample Question Paper - III
CHEMISTRY
CLASS - XII

Time Allowed : 3 Hrs **Maximum Marks : 70**

General Instructions:

1. All questions are compulsory.
2. Question No. 1 to 8 are very short questions carrying one mark each.
3. Question No. 9 to 18 are short answer questions carrying 2 marks each.
4. Question No. 19 to 27 are also short answer questions carrying 3 marks each.
5. Question No. 28 to 30 are long answer questions carrying 5 marks each.
6. Use of calculators is not allowed. Use the log tables wherever necessary.

Q.1 A and B liquids on mixing produce a warm solution. Which type of deviation from Raoult's law is there? 1

Q.2 Why is Ferric Chloride preferred over Potassium Chloride in case of a cut leading to bleeding? 1

Q.3 Among Octahedral and Tetrahedral crystal fields, in which case the magnitude of crystal field splitting is larger?

Q.4 Why is ortho-nitrophenol more acidic than ortho-methoxyphenol?

Q.5 Write two important uses of Formalin.

Q.6 Why do amines act as nucleophiles?

Q.7 Why can't aluminium be reduced by carbon?

Q.8 What are the ultimate products of digesion of proteins? 1

Q.9 Gold (atomic mass =197u, atomic radius = 0.144nm) crystallizes in a face centered unit cell. Determine the density of gold, [$N_A = 6.022 \times 10^{23}\ mol^{-1}$] 2

Q.10 Classify each of the following as being either a p-type or an n-type semi-conductor. Give reason.

(a) Si doped with In

(b) Si doped with P.

Q.11 Determine the molarity of an antifreeze solution containing 250g water mixed with 222g ethylene glycol ($C_2H_6O_2$). The density of this solution is 1.07g/ml. 2

Q.12 An aqueous solution containing urea was found to have boiling point more than the normal boiling point of water (373.13 K).When the same solution was cooled it was found that its freezing point is less than the normal freezing point of water (273.13K).Explain these observations. 2

Q.13 Consider the decomposition of hydrogen peroxide in alkaline medium which is catalysed by iodide ions.

$$2H_2O_2 \xrightarrow{OH^-} 2H_2O+O_2$$

This reaction takes place in two steps as given below

<u>Step - I</u> $H_2O_2 + I^- \rightarrow H_2O + IO^-$ (slow)

<u>Step -II</u> $H_2O_2 + IO^- \longrightarrow H_2O + I^- + O_2$ (fast)

(a) Write the rate law expression and determine the order of reaction w.r.t. H_2O_2.

(b) What is the molecularity of each individual step? 2

Q.14 (a) What is the role of depressant in froth floatation process?

(b) Out of C and CO which is a better reducing agent for FeO

(i) In the lower part of blast furnace (Higher temperature) 2

(ii) In the upper part of blast furnace (Lower temperature) 2

Q.15 Complete the following reactions:-

(a) $(NH_4)_2Cr_2O_7 \xrightarrow{heat}$

(b) $I^- + O_3 + H_2O \longrightarrow$

Q.16 Using valence bond theory , predict the geometry and magnetic character of $[NiCl_4]^{2-}$. Atomic no of Ni is 28.

Q.17 (a) Write the structure of following compound

1-Bromo-4 -sec-butyl- 2- methylbenzene

(b) How will you bring about the conversion:

Methyl bromide to methyl iodide 2

Q.18 Explain-

(a) Grignard reagents should be prepared under anhydrous conditions.

(b) $C_6H_5CHClCH_3$ is hydrolysed more easily with KOH than $C_6H_5CH_2Cl$ 2

OR

Arrange the following compounds in the decreasing order of reactivity towards SN^2 displacement reaction and give reasons in support of your answer.

a) C_2H_5Br, C_2H_5I, C_2H_5Cl

b) $(CH_3)_3CBr$, $CH_3CH_2CHBrCH_3$, $CH_3CH_2CH_2CH_2Br$ 2

Q.19 Draw the structures of the following:

(a) $H_2S_2O_8$

(b) XeO_3

(c) $HOClO_2$

Q.20 In a hydrolysis reaction, 5g ethyl acetate is hydrolyzed in presence of dilute HCl in 300 minutes. If the reaction is of first order and the initial concentration of ethyl acetate is 22g/L, calculate the rate constant of the reaction. 2

Q.21 (a) Give reasons for the following:

(i) Glucose does not give 2, 4- DNP test and Schiff's test.

(ii) Amino acids have high melting points and are soluble in water. 2

(c) What is meant by the secondary structure of proteins ? 1

Q.22 (a) Give an example of a synthetic rubber and mention its main advantage.

(b) Write the structures of the monomers of Dacron.

(c) Arrange the following polymers in the increasing order of tensile strength.

Nylon6, Buna-S, Polythene 3

Q.23 Give one example for each of the following:

(a) An artificial sweetner whose use is limited to cold drinks.

(b) A non ionic detergent.

(c) A pain reliever used for relief from severe pain like post-operative pain or pain due to terminal cancer. 3

Q.24 (a) Give chemical tests to distinguish between the following compounds (One test in each case).

(i) Aniline and ethylamine

(ii) Methylamine and dimethylamine 2

(b) How will you convert aniline to sulphanilic acid? 1

OR

An aromatic compound (A) on treatment with ammonia followed by heating forms compound (B), which on heating with Br_2 and KOH forms a compound (C) having molecular formula C_6H_7N. Give the structures of A, B and C and write the reactions involved. 3

Q.25 (a) Give the mechanism of the following reaction:

$$2CH_3CH_2OH \xrightarrow[413K]{dil H_2SO_4} CH_3CH_2OCH_2CH_3$$

Does this reaction follow S_N1 or S_N2 pathway? 2

(b) Describe hydroboration oxidation reaction with the help of an example. 1

Q.26 Give reasons:-

(a) Interhalogen compounds are more reactive than halogens.

(b) PCl_5 is known but NCl_5 is not known.

(c) Amongst all noble gases only xenon is known to form compounds with oxygen and fluorine. 3

Q.27 (a) Give one main difference between lyophillic and lyophobic colloids. 1

(b) Explain:-

(i) Sky appears blue in colour. 2

(ii) A freshly formed precipitate of ferric hydroxide can be converted to a colloidal sol by shaking it with a small quantity of ferric chloride. 3

Q.28 (a) Two electrolytic cells containing silver nitrate solution and dilute sulphuric acid solution were connected in series. A steady current of 2.5 amp was passed through them till 1.078g of silver was deposited. [Ag = 107.8g mol^{-1}, IF = 96, 500 C]

(i) How much electricity was consumed?

(ii) What was the weight of oxygen gas liberated? 3

(b) Give reason:-

(i) Rusting of iron pipe can be prevented by joining it with a piece of magnesium.

(ii) Conductivity of an electrolyte solution decreases with the decrease in concentration. 2

OR

(a) What is a fuel cell? What is its main advantage? 1

(b) What are the reactions occurring at the cathode and anode of a Lachlanche cell? 1

(c) In the button cell widely used for watches and other devices, the following reaction takes place:

$$Zn(s) + Ag_2O(s) + H_2O(l) \longrightarrow Zn^{2+}(aq) + 2Ag(s) + 2OH^-(aq)$$

Give the cell representation and determine the value of Kc for the above reaction using the following data:

$$Ag_2O(s) + H_2O(l) + 2e^- \longrightarrow 2Ag(s) + 2OH^-(aq) \quad (E^0 = 0.344V)$$

$$Zn^{2+}(aq) + 2e^- \longrightarrow Zn(s) \quad (E^0 = -0.76V)$$

3

Q.29 Explain the following:

(a) Actinoids show large number of oxidation states.

(b) The transition metals form a large number of complex compounds.

(c) Chromium is a typical hard metal while mercury is a liquid.

(d) MnO is basic while Mn_2O_7 is acidic in nature.

(e) Silver is a transition metal but zinc is not.

OR

(a) Give two consequences of lanthanoid contraction. 1

(b) Complete the following reactions:

(i) $MnO_4^- + S_2O_3^{2-} + H_2O \longrightarrow$

(ii) $Cr_2O_7^{2-} + Sn^{2+} + H^+ \longrightarrow$ 2

(c) Which of the following has maximum number of unpaired electrons?

Ti^{3+}, V^{3+}, Fe^{2+}, Mg^{2+} 1

(d) Based on the data, arrange Fe^{2+}, Mn^{2+} and Cr^{2+} in the increasing order of stability of +2 oxidation state

$E^0_{Cr^{3+}/Cr^{2+}} = -0.4\ V$ $E^0_{Mn^{3+}/Mn^{2+}} = 1.5V$ $E^0_{Fe^{3+}/Fe^{2+}} = 0.8V$

Q.30 (a) Identify A, B and C in the following reaction

$$CH \equiv CH \xrightarrow[HgSO_4]{dil.\ H_2SO_4} A \xrightarrow{dil.NaOH} B \xrightarrow{heat} C \text{———}$$ 3

(b) Give reasons:

(i) p-Nitro benzoic acid has higher K_a value than benzoic acid.

(ii) Acetone is highly soluble in water but benzophenone is not. 2

OR

(a) An organic compound(A) has molecular formula ($C_5H_{10}O$). It does not reduce Tollen's reagent but forms an orange precipitate with 2,4 - DNP reagent. It forms a carboxylic acid(B)with molecular formula ($C_3H_6O_2$) when treated with alkaline $KMnO_4$, yellow precipate on treatment with NaOH and I_2. Under vigorous conditions. On oxidation it gives ethanoic acid and propanoic acid. Sodium salt of (B) gave a hydrocarbon (C) in Kolbe,s Electrolytic Reduction. Identify (A), (B) and (C) and write the reactions involved. 3

(b) Predict the products formed in the following cases :

(i) (A) reacts with PhMgBr and is then hydrolysed.

(ii) (A) reacts with hydrazine and is then heated with KOH and ethylene glycol. 2

MARKING SCHEME OF
CHEMISTRY
SAMPLE PAPER-III

A.1 Negative deviation. 1

A.2 Fe3+ is a better coagulating ion due to greater positive charge on it 1

A.3 Octahedral crystal field. 1

A.4 Due to electron withdrawing effect of nitro group. 1

A.5 In preserving biological specimens and in making polymer like bakelite. ½ + ½

A.6 Due to the presence of lone pair of electrons on nitrogen of amines. 1

A.7 Because aluminium is a stronger reducing agent than carbon. 1

A.8 Amino acids. 1

A.9 $d = \frac{Z \times M}{N_a \times a_3}$ $\gamma = \frac{2}{2\sqrt{2}}$ ½

$a = 2 \times 0.144 \times 1.414\text{nm}$

$= .407\text{nm}.$ ½

$$d = \frac{4 \times 197 \text{g mol}^{-1}}{6.002 \times 10^{23} \text{ mol}^{-1} \times (0.407 \times 10^{-7}) \text{ cm}^3}$$

$d = 19.6\text{g / cm}^3$ 1

A.10 (a) p-type, because In has 3 Valence electrons. Holes are produced which can move through the crystal like a positive charge.

(b) n-type, because P-has 5 valence electrons. The fifth electron becomes delocalised and is free to contribute to electrical conduction 1+1

A.11 No. of moles of ethylene glycol = n_B

Molar mass of $C_2H_6O_2$ = (24+6+32)g mol^{-1}

$M_B = \frac{222\text{g}}{62 \text{ mol}^{-1}} = 3.58 \text{ mol}$ ½

mass of Solution = (250 + 222)g = 472g.

$$\text{Volume of Solution} = \frac{\text{mass of solution}}{\text{density of solution}}$$ ½

$$V = \frac{472g}{1.07g/ml} = 441.12ml$$ 1

$$M = \frac{n_B}{V} \times 1000$$

$$= \frac{3.58mol}{441.12L} \times 1000 = 8.12mol\,L^{-1}$$

A.12 The vapour pressure of the aqueous solution containing urea is less than the vapour pressure of pure water because urea is a nonvolatile solute. To boil this solution we have to heat it to the temperature higher than the normal boiling point of water. 1

To freeze the solution the temperature is lowered, the vapour pressure of solution also lowers. The vapour pressure of solution equalizes the vapour pressure of solid solvent at temperature lower than the normal freezing point of water. 1

A.13 (a) Rate = $k[H_2O_2]^1[I^-]^1$ ½

order w.r.t. $H_2O_2 = 1$ ½

(b) Molecularity -step I = 2 ½

step II = 2 ½

A.14 (a) Depressant is used in the froth floatation process for preventing the specific sulphide ore from forming froth in a mixture of sulphides. 1

(b) C is better reducing agent at higher temperature ½

CO is better reducing agent at lower temperature. ½

A.15 (a) $(NH_4)_2Cr_2O_7(s) \xrightarrow{\text{Heat}} N_2(g) + 4H_2O(l) + Cr_2O_3(s)$ 1

(b) $2I^-(aq) + O_3(g) + H_2O(l) \longrightarrow 2OH^-(aq) + I_2(s) + O_2(g)$ 1

A.16 $[NiCl_4]^{2-}$ = 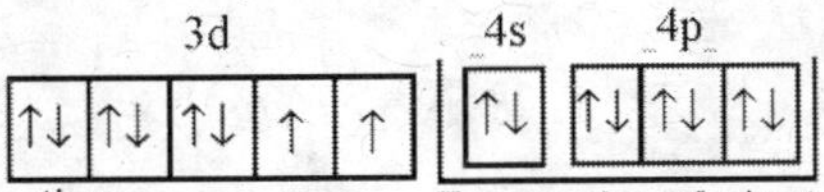

Sp3 hybridisation Four pairs of electrons from 4Cl⁻ ions

Geometry - Tetrahedral due to sp^3 hybrdisation

Magnetic character-Paramagnetic, due to the presence of 2 unpaired electrons in 3d orbitals. 1+1

A.17 (a) 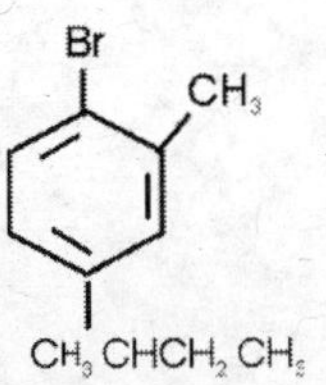

3

(b) $CH_3Br + NaI \xrightarrow{\text{dry acetone}} CH_3I + NaBr$ 1+1

Methylbromide Methyl Iodide

A.18 (a) As Grignard reagents react with water to give corresponding alkanes, therefore they are prepared under anhydrous conditions.

$RMgX + H_2O \longrightarrow R\text{-}H + Mg(OH)X$ 1

(b) $C_6H_5CHClCH_3$ is a 2° benzylic halide which can form a carbocation more easily in SN1 displacement reaction than $C_6H_5CH_2Cl$ which is a 1° benzylic halide. Therefore $C_6H_5CHClCH_3$ is more easily hydrolysed with KOH. 1

OR

(a) $C_2H_6I > C_2H_5Br > C_2H_5Cl$

C-I bond is weaker than the C-Br bond which in turn is weaker than C-Cl bond; the SN² displacement reaction becomes slower as the bond strength increases.

b) $CH_3CH_2CH_2CH_2Br > CH_3CH_2CHBrCH_2 > (CH_3)_3CBr$
As the steric hinderance on C which is attacked by nucleophile increases, the rate of SN² displacement reaction decreases.

A.19 (i)

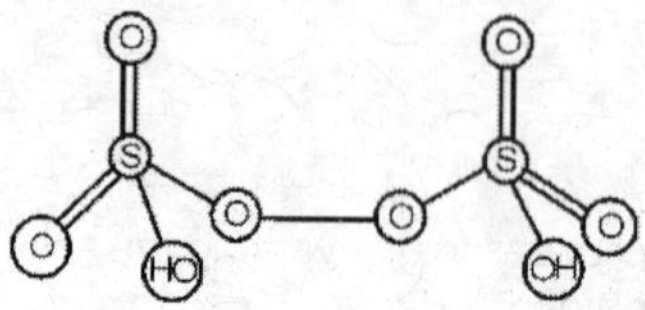

Peroxodisulphuric acid
(or Marshall's acid)
$H_2S_2O_8$

(ii)

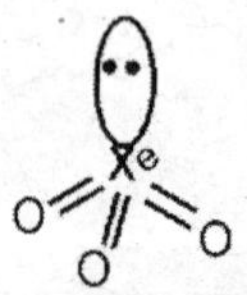

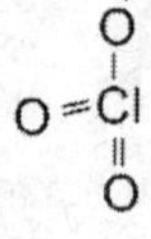

(iii) Chloric acid, $HOC1O_2$ 1x3=3

A.20 (a) a = 22g/L Initial Concertration a = 22 g/L ½

a – x = (22 – 5) = 17g/L Final Concertration

t = 300 min 1

$$K=\frac{2.303}{t}\log\frac{a}{a-x}$$ 1

$$= \frac{2.303}{300\ \text{min}} \log \frac{22gL^{-1}}{17gL^{-1}}$$

$= 7.6 \times 10^{-3} \log 1.29\ \text{min}^{-1}$

$= 7.6 \times 10^{-3} \times 0.11\ \text{min}^{-1}$ 1

$= 8.36 \times 10^{-4}\ \text{min}^{-1}$

A.21 (a) (i) In the cyclic structure of glucose - CHO group is not free as it forms a hemiacetal linkage with -OH group at C-5. 1

(ii) The amino acids have high melting points and solubility in water due to zwitter ion (polan) structure and strong intermolecular forces between them.

$$H_2N-\underset{\displaystyle R}{\overset{|}{C}}H-COOH \leftrightarrow \overset{+}{H_3N}-\underset{\displaystyle R}{\overset{|}{C}}H-COO^-$$

(b) Secondary structure of proteins refers to the shape in which a long polypeptide chain can exist. 1

A.22 (a) Buna-N

It is resistant to the action of petrol, lubricating oil and organic solvents. 1

(b) Monomers of Dacron are $HOCH_2CH_2OH$ and

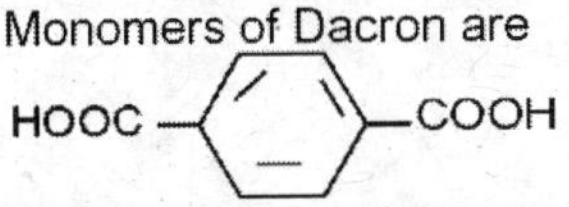

1

(c) Buna-S < Polythene < Nylon 1

A.23 (a) Aspartame 1

(b) Ester of stearic acid and poly ethylene glycol

$CH_3(CH_2)_{16}COO(CH_2CH_2O)nCH_2CH_2OH$ 1

(c) Morphine 1

A.24 (a) (i) Aniline and Ethylamine:-

Add benzenediazonium chloride to both the compounds in separate test tubes at low temperature. Aniline forms an orange dye. 1

(ii) Methylamine and Dimethylamine

Add chloroform and aqueous sodium hydroxide solution to both the compounds in separate test tubes. Methylamine gives foul smell of isocyanide. 1

(b)

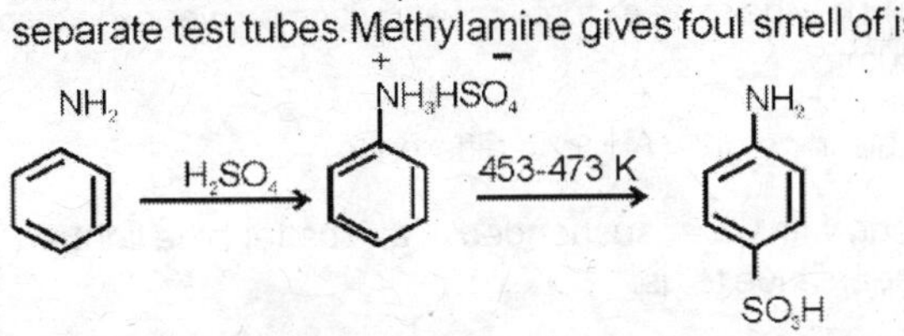

1

Anilinium hydrogensulphate

Sulphanilic acid

OR

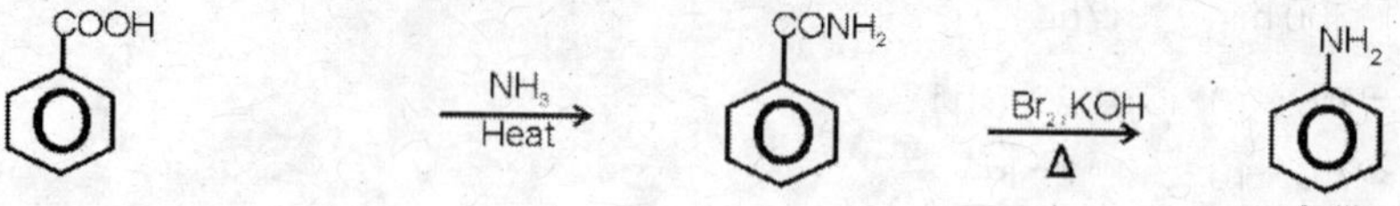

A B Aniline C (1,1,1)

A.25 (a) The formation of ether is a nucleophilic bimolecular reaction (SN^2) involving the attack of alcohol molecule on a protonated alcohol, as indicated below:

(i) $CH_3 - CH_2 - \ddot{O}-H + H^+ \longrightarrow CH_3 - CH_2 - \overset{+}{\ddot{O}}(H)-H$

(ii) $CH_3CH_2 - \ddot{O}(H): + CH_3 - CH_2 - \overset{+}{O}H_2 \longrightarrow CH_3CH_2 - \overset{+}{O}(H) - CH_2CH_3 + H_2O$

(ii) $CH_3CH_2 - \overset{+}{O}(H) - CH_2CH_3 \longrightarrow CH_3CH_2 - O - CH_2CH_3 + H^+$ 2

(b) Hydroboration oxidation reaction: 1

$R-CH=CH_2 + H-BH_2 \rightarrow \underset{\text{Alkyl borane}}{R-CH_2-CH_2-BH_2} \xrightarrow{R-CH=CH_2}$

$\underset{\text{Dialkyl borane}}{(R\,CH_2\,CH_2)_2\,BH} \xrightarrow{RCH_2=CH_2} \underset{\text{Trialkyl borane}}{(RCH_2CH_2)_3\,B}$

A.26 (a) Interhalogen compounds are more reactive than halogens because the X-X' bond present in interhalogens is weaker than the X-X bond present in halogens as the overlapping between orbitals of dissimilar atoms is less effective. 1

(b) PCl_5 exists because phosphorus can extend its covalency to five using empty 3d orbitals. Since d orbitals are not present in the valency shell of N, it can not form NCl_5. 1

(c) Xenon has bigger size and lower ionization enthalpy than the other noble gases As a result it is the only noble gas which is able to form compounds with oxygen and fluorine. 1

A.27 (a) Lyophillic colloids - (i) They have strong forces of attraction between the dispersed phase and dispersion medium. (ii) They are reversible in nature.

Lyobhobic colloids- (i) They have weak forces of attraction between the dispersed phase and dispersion medium.

(ii) They are irreversible in nature. (Any one difference) 1

(b) (i) Dust particles along with water suspended in air scatter blue light which reach our eyes and sky appears blue to us. 1

(ii) When we add a solution of $FeCl_3$ to freshly formed precipitate of $Fe(OH)_3$, peptisation occurs in which Fe^{3+} ions are adsorbed on the surface of precipitate which ultimately breaks down into smaller particles of the size of colloid. 1

A.28 (a) In the first cell silver is deposited at cathode according to the equation:-

(i) $Ag^{+}{}_{(aq)} + e^{-} \rightarrow Ag(s)$

$107.8 g Ag = 1F$ electricity 1

$1.078 g Ag = 0.01F$

$= 965C$ electricity

(ii) The oxygen gas is liberated at anode of first cell as well as second cell according to equation

$2H_2O(l) \rightarrow 4H^{+}{}_{(aq)} + 4e^{-} + O_2(g)$

4F electricity $= 1 mol\ O_2$ in each cell

$4F = 32g\ O_2$ in each cell

$0.01F = \frac{32g}{4g} \times 0.01g = 0.08g\ O_2$ in each cell

Total amount of oxygen liberated at anode of both cells

$= 2 \times 0.08g = 0.16g$ 2

(b) (i) Rusting of iron is prevented in the given case due to cathodic protection in which magnesium metal is oxidised in preference to iron and acts as anode. 1

(ii) When the concentration decreases the number of ions present in unit volume of solution decreases, as a result electrical conductivity decreases. 1

OR

(a) Galvanic cells, that are designed to convert the energy of combustion of fuels like [illegible]$_2$, CH_4, CH_3OH etc. directly into electrical energy are called fuel cells. They produce electricity with an efficiency of about 70% and are pollution free. 1

(b) Reactions taking place in Leclanche cell

[illegible] $^{2+}$(aq)+2e$^-$

Cathode : $2\,MnO_2(s) + 2NH_4^{+}(aq) + 2e^{-} \text{—} 2MnO(OH) + 2\,NH_3$ 1

(c) $Zn(s)/Zn^{2+}(aq)//Ag_2O(s)/Ag(s)/OH^{-}(aq)$

$E^0 == E^0{}_{Ag_2O/Ag} - E^0{}_{Zn^{2+}/Zn}$

Ag_2O== 0.344v – (– 0.76)v == 1.104 V 1

$Zn(s) + Ag_2O(s) + H_2O(l) \rightarrow Zn^{2+}(aq) + 2Ag(s) + 2OH^-(aq)$

$n = 2$

$$\log Kc = nFEo / 2.303RT = \frac{n\,E^\circ\,cell}{0.059} \text{ at } 25^\circ c$$

$$\log k_c = \frac{2 \times 1.104}{0.059}$$

$$= 37.42$$

$$K_c = anti\log(37.42)$$

$$= 2.34 \times 10^{37}$$

A..29 (a) Due to comparable energies of 5f, 6d and 7s subshells, all the electrons present in these subshells may participate in bonding, resulting in large number of oxidation states for actinoids. 1

(b) Transition metals form a large number of complexes because of small size and high charge of ions. They also have empty d orbitals to accept electron pairs from ligands. 1

(c) M-M interactions are strong in chromium due to the presence of six unpaired electrons in the 3d and 4s subshell , while in mercury all the electrons in the 5d and 6s subshell are paired and M-M interactions are weak. 1

(d) As the oxidation state of Mn in MnO is +2 while in Mn_2O_7 it is +7, MnO is basic while Mn_2O_7 is acidic. As the oxidation number of a metal increases, its acidic character increases due to decrease in size of the metal ion and increase in charge density. 1

(e) There are unpaired electrons in the ions formed by silver as silver can exhibit +2 oxidation state where it will have incompletaly filled - orbitats hence a transition element but zinc does not form any ion with incomplete d orbitals.

$_{47}Ag$ = 36 [Kr] $4d^{10}\,5S^1$

30 Zn = 18 [Ar] $3d^{10}4S^2$

OR

(a) (i) 4d and 5d transition series have almost same atomic radii.

(ii) It is difficult to separate lanthanoids from their mixture 1

(b) (i) $8MnO_4^- + 3S_2O_3^{2-} + H_2O — 8MnO_2 + 6SO_4^{2-} + 2OH^-$ 1

(ii) $Cr_2O_7^{2-} + 3Sn^{2+} + 14H^+ — 2Cr^{3+} + 3Sn^{4+} + 7H_2O$ 1

(c) Ion E.C. of ion No. of unpaired electrons

Mg^2 = [Ne]$3s^o$ 0

Ti^{3+} = [Ar]$3d^1 4s^o$ 1

$V^{3+} = [Ar]3d^2 4s^o$ 2

$Fe^{2+} = [Ar]3d^6 4s^o$ 4

Fe^{2+} has maximum number of unpaired electrons 1

(d) As the value of reduction potential increases, the stability of +2 oxidation state increases, therefore Cr^{2+} is less stable than Fe2+ which in turn is less stable than Mn^{2+}. 1

A.30 (a) A = CH_3CHO

B = $CH_3CHOHCH_2CHO$

C = $CH_3CH{=}CHCHO$ 1x3=3

(b) (i) $-NO_2$ group at p- position increases the positive charge at C-1 due to -I and -R effect, making the fission of O-H bond easier. 1

(ii) Acetone can make hydrogen bonds with water but benzophenone can not make hydrogen bonds due to steric hinderance of two phenyl groups. 1

OR

(a) (A) == $CH_3CH_2COCH_2CH_3$ 1

$$\underset{A}{CH_3CH_2COCH_2CH_3} \xrightarrow{\text{oxidation}} \underset{B}{CH_3CH_2COOH}$$ 1

$$CH_3CH_2COONa \xrightarrow{\text{Kolbe Electrolysis}} \underset{C}{CH_3CH_2CH_2CH_3}$$ 1

(b) (i) $CH_3CH_2C(Ph)(OH)CH_2CH_3$ 1

(ii) $CH_3CH_2CH_2CH_2CH_3$ 1

Series SOS | **Code No. 56/1**

Roll No. [| | | | | | |]

Candidates must write the Code on the title page of the answer-book.

- Please check that this question paper contains **12** printed pages.
- Code number given on the right hand side of the question paper should be written on the title page of the answer-book by the candidate.
- Please check that this question paper contains **30** questions.
- **Please write down the Serial Number of the question before attempting it.**
- 15 minutes time has been allotted to read this question paper. The question paper will be distributed at 10.15 a.m. From 10.15 a.m. to 10.30 a.m., the students will read the question paper only and will not write any answer on the answer script during this period.

CHEMISTRY (THEORY)

Time allowed : 3 hours | *Maximum Marks : 70*

General Instructions:

(*i*) *All questions are compulsory.*

(*ii*) *Marks for each question are indicated against it.*

(*iii*) *Questions number **1** to **8** are very short-answer questions and carry **1** mark each.*

(*iv*) *Questions number **9** to **18** are short-answer questions and carry **2** marks each.*

(*v*) *Questions number **19** to **27** are also short-answer questions and carry **3** marks each.*

(*vi*) *Questions number **28** to **30** are long-answer questions and carry **5** marks each.*

(*vii*) *Use Log Tables, if necessary. Use of calculators is **not** allowed.*

1. Define 'order of a reaction'. 1

2. What is meant by 'shape selective catalysis'? 1

3. Differentiate between a mineral and an ore. 1

4. What is meant by 'lanthanoid contraction'? 1

5. Write the IUPAC name of the following compound: 1

$$CH_2 = CHCH_2Br$$

6. Draw the structure of 4-chloropentan-2-one. 1

7. How would you convert ethanol to ethene? 1

8. Rearrange the following in an increasing order of their basic strengths: 1

$$C_6H_5NH_2,\ C_6H_5N(CH_3)_2,\ (C_6H_5)_2NH \text{ and } CH_3NH_2.$$

9. Explain how you can determine the atomic mass of an unknown metal if you know its mass density and the dimensions of unit cell of its crystal. 2

10. Calculate the packing efficiency of a metal crystal for a simple cubic lattice. 2

11. State the following: 2

(*i*) Raoult's law in its general form in reference to solutions.

(*ii*) Henry's law about partial pressure of a gas in a mixture.

12. What do you understand by the rate law and rate constant of a reaction? Identify the order of a reaction if the units of its rate constant are: 2

(*i*) $L^{-1}\ mol\ s^{-1}$

(*ii*) $L\ mol^{-1}\ s^{-1}$

13. The thermal decomposition of HCO_2H is a first order reaction with a rate constant of $2.4 \times 10^{-3}\ s^{-1}$ at a certain temperature. Calculate how long will it take for three-fourths of initial quantity of HCO_2H to decompose. (log 0.25 = –0.6021) 2

14. Describe the principle controlling each of the following processes: 2
    (*i*) Vapour phase refining of titanium metal.
    (*ii*) Froth flotation method of concentration of a sulphide ore.

15. How would you account for the following: 2
    (*i*) Cr^{2+} is reducing in nature while with the same d-orbital configuration (d^4) Mn^{3+} is an oxidising agent.
    (*ii*) In a transition series of metals, the metal which exhibits the greatest number of oxidation states occurs in the middle of the series.

16. Complete the following chemical equations: 2
    (*i*) $MnO_4^-(aq) + S_2O_3^{2-}(aq) + H_2O(l) \rightarrow$
    (*ii*) $Cr_2O_7^{2-}(aq) + Fe^{2+}(aq) + H^+(aq) \rightarrow$

OR

State reasons for the following: 2
    (*i*) Cu (I) ion is not stable in an aqueous solution
    (*ii*) Unlike Cr^{3+}, Mn^{2+}, Fe^{3+} and the subsequent other M^{2+} ions of the 3d series of elements, the 4d and the 5d series metals generally do not form stable cationic species

17. Explain what is meant by the following: 2
    (*i*) peptide linkage
    (*ii*) pyranose structure of glucose

18. Write the main structural difference between DNA and RNA. Of the four bases, name those which are common to both DNA and RNA. 2

19. A solution prepared by dissolving 8.95 mg of a gene fragment in 35.0 ml of water has an osmotic pressure of 0.335 torr at 25□°C. Assuming that the gene fragment is a non-electrolyte, calculate its molar mass. 3

20. Classify colloids where the dispersion medium is water. State their characteristics and write an example of each of these classes. 3

OR

Explain what is observed when 3
    (*i*) an electric current is passed through a sol
    (*ii*) a beam of light is passed through a sol
    (*iii*) an electrolyte (say NaCl) is added to ferric hydroxide sol

21. How would you account for the following: 3
    (*i*) H_2S is more acidic than H_2O.
    (*ii*) The N—O bond in NO^-_2 is shorter than the N—O bond in NO^-_3.
    (*iii*) Both O_2 and F_2 stabilize high oxidation states but the ability of oxygen to stabilize the higher oxidation state exceeds that of fluorine.

22. Explain the following terms giving a suitable example in each case: 3
    (*i*) Ambident ligand
    (*ii*) Denticity of a ligand
    (*iii*) Crystal field splitting in an octahedral field

23. Rearrange the compounds of each of the following sets in order of reactivity towards S_N2 displacement: 3
    (*i*) 2-Bromo-2-methylbutane, 1-Bromopentane, 2-Bromopentane
    (*ii*) 1-Bromo-3-methylbutane, 2-Bromo-2-methylbutane, 3-Bromo-2-methylbutane
    (*iii*) 1-Bromobutane, 1-Bromo-2, 2-dimethylpropane, 1-Bromo-2-methylbutane

24. How would you obtain the following: 3

(i) Benzoquinone from phenol

(ii) 2-Methylpropan-2-ol from methylmagnesium bromide

(iii) Propan-2-ol from propene

25. State reasons for the following: 3

(i) pK_b value for aniline is more than that for methylamine.

(ii) Ethylamine is soluble in water whereas aniline is not soluble in water.

(iii) Primary amines have higher boiling points than tertiary amines.

26. Draw the structures of the monomers of the following polymers: 3

(i) Polythene

(ii) PVC

(iii) Telfon

27. What are the following substances? Give one example of each. 3

(i) Food preservatives

(ii) Synthetic detergents

(iii) Antacids

28. (a) What type of a battery is lead storage battery? Write the anode and cathode reactions and the overall cell reaction occurring in the operation of a lead storage battery.

(b) Calculate the potential for half-cell containing

$0.10\ M\ K_2Cr_2O_7\ (aq)$, $0.20\ M\ Cr^{3+}\ (aq)$ and $1.0 \times 10^{-4}\ M\ H^+\ (aq)$

The half -cell reaction is

$Cr_2O^{2-}{}_7\ (aq) + 14\ H^+\ (aq) + 6e^- \rightarrow 2Cr^{3+}\ (aq) + 7H_2O\ (l)$,

and the standard electrode potential is given as E° = 1.33 V. 5

OR

(a) How many moles of mercury will be produced by electolysing 1.0 M $Hg(NO_3)_2$ solution with a current of 2.00 A for 3 hours? [$Hg(NO_3)_2 = 200.6\ g\ mol^{-1}$]

(b) A voltaic cell is set up at 25°C with the following half-cells Al^{3+}(0.001 M) and Ni^{2+}(0.50 M). Write an equation for the reaction that occurs when the cell generates an electric current and determine the cell potential.

(Given : $E^\circ_{Ni^{2}/Ni} = -0.25V$, $E^\circ_{Al^{3+}/Al} = -1.66\ V$) 5

29. (a) Draw the structures of the following molecules:

(i) $(HPO_3)_3$

(ii) BrF_3

(b) Complete the following chemical equations:

(i) $HgCl_2 + PH_3 \rightarrow$

(ii) $SO_3 + H_2SO_4 \rightarrow$

(iii) $XeF_4 + H_2O \rightarrow$ 5

OR

(a) What happen when

(i) chlorine gas is passed through a hot concentrated solution of NaOH?

(ii) sulphur dioxide gas is passed through an aqueous solution of a Fe (III) salt?

(b) Answer the following:

(i) What is the basicity of H_3PO_3 and why?

(ii) Why does fluorine not play the role of a central atom in interhalogen compounds?

(iii) Why do noble gases have very low boiling points? 5

30. (a) Illustrate the following name reactions:

(i) Cannizzaro's reaction

(*ii*) Clemmensen reduction

(b) How would you obtain the following:

(*i*) But-2-enal from ethanal

(*iv*) Butanoic acid from butanol

(*v*) Benzoic acid from ethylbenzene 5

OR

(a) Give chemical tests to distinguish between the following:

(*i*) Benzoic acid and ethyly benzoate

(*ii*) Benzaldehyde and acetophenone

(b) Complete each synthesis by giving missing reagents or products in the following:

(*i*) 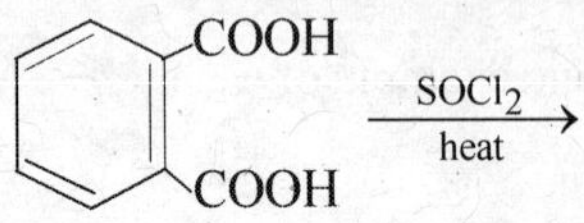

(*ii*) $C_6H_5CHO \xrightarrow{H_2NCONHNH_2}$

(*iii*) 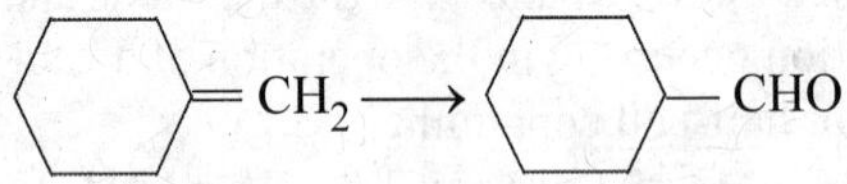

❑❑❑

Series SOS/1 | **Code No. 56/1/1**

Roll No. | | | | | | | |

Candidates must write the Code on the title page of the answer-book.

- Please check that this question paper contains **12** printed pages.
- Code number given on the right hand side of the question paper should be written on the title page of the answer-book by the candidate.
- Please check that this question paper contains **30** questions.
- **Please write down the Serial Number of the question before attempting it.**
- 15 minutes time has been allotted to read this question paper. The question paper will be distributed at 10.15 a.m. From 10.15 a.m. to 10.30 a.m., the students will read the question paper only and will not write any answer on the answer script during this period.

CHEMISTRY (THEORY)

Time allowed : 3 hours *Maximum Marks : 70*

General Instructions:

(*i*) *All questions are compulsory.*
(*ii*) *Marks for each question are indicated against it.*
(*iii*) *Questions number **1** to **8** are very short-answer questions and carry **1** mark each.*
(*iv*) *Questions number **9** to **18** are short-answer questions and carry **2** marks each.*
(*v*) *Questions number **19** to **27** are also short-answer questions and carry **3** marks each.*
(*vi*) *Questions number **28** to **30** are long-answer questions and carry **5** marks each.*
(*vii*) *Use Log Tables, if necessary. Use of calculators is **not** allowed.*

1. 'Crystalline solids are anisotropic in nature'. What does this statement mean? 1

2. Express the relation between conductivity and molar conductivity of a solution held in a cell. 1

3. Define 'electrophoresis'. 1

4. Draw the structure of XeF_2 molecule. 1

5. Write the IUPAC name of the following compound: 1

$$(CH_3)_3\,CCH_2Br$$

6. Draw the structure of 3-methylbutanal. 1

7. Arrange the following compounds in an increasing order of their solubility in water: 1

$$C_6H_5NH_2,\ (C_2H_5)_2NH,\ C_2H_5NH_2$$

8. What are biodegradable polymers? 1

9. The chemistry of corrosion of iron is essentially an electrochemical phenomenon. Explain the reactions occurring during the corrosion of iron in the atmosphere. 2

10. Determine the values of equilibrium constant (K_c) and $\Delta G°$ for the following reaction: 2

$$Ni(s) + 2Ag^+\,(aq) \rightarrow NI^{2+}(aq) + 2Ag(s),\ E° = 1.05\ V$$
$$(IF = 96500\ C\ mol^{-1})$$

11. Distinguish between 'rate expression' and 'rate constant' of a reaction. 2

12. State reasons for each of the following: 2

(*i*) The N—O bond in NO_2^- is shorter than the N—O bond in NO_3^-.
(*ii*) SF_6 is kinetically an inert substance.

OR

State reasons for each of the following: 2

(*i*) All the P–Cl bonds in PCl_5 molecule are not equivalent.

(*iv*) Sulphur has greater tendency for catenation than oxygen.

13. Assign reasons for the following: 2

(*i*) Copper (I) ion is not known in aqueous solution.

(*ii*) Actinoids exhibit greater range of oxidation states than lanthanoids.

14. Explain the following giving one example for each: 2

(*i*) Reimer-Tiemann reaction.

(*ii*) Friedel Craft's acetylation of anisole.

15. How would you obtain 2

(*i*) Picric acid (2, 4, 6-trinitrophenol) from phenol,

(*ii*) 2-Methylpropene from 2-methylpropanol?

16. What is essentially the difference between α-form of glucose and β-form of glucose Explain.

2

17. Describe what you understand by primary structure and secondary structure of proteins. 2

18. Mention two important uses of each of the following: 2

(*i*) Bakelite

(*ii*) Nylon 6

19. Silver crystallizes in face-centered cubic unit cell. Each side of this unit cell has a length of 400 pm. Calculate the radius of the silver atom. (Assume the atoms just touch each other on the diagonal across the face of the unit cell. That is each face atom is touching the four corner atoms.) 3

20. Nitrogen pentoxide decomposes according to equation: $2N_2O_5(g) \longrightarrow 4NO_2(g) + O_2(g)$. This first order reaction was allowed to proceed at 40°C and the data below were collected:

$[N_2O_5]$ (M)	Time (min)
0.400	0.00
0.289	20.0
0.209	40.0
0.151	60.0
0.109	80.0

(a) Calculate the rate constant. Include units with your answer.

(b) What will be the concentration of N_2O_5 after 100 minutes?

(c) Calculate the initial rate of reaction. 3

21. Explain how the phenomenon of adsorption finds application in each of the following processes: 3

(*i*) Production of vacuum

(*ii*) Heterogeneous catalysis

OR

Define each of the following terms: 3

(*i*) Micelles

(*ii*) Peptization

(*iii*) Desorption

22. Describe the principle behind each of the following processes: 3

(*i*) Vapour phase refining of a metal.

(*ii*) Electrolytic refining of a metal.

(*iii*) Recovery of silver after silver ore was leached with NaCN.

23. Complete the following chemical equations: 3

(*i*) $MnO_4^- + C_2O_4^{2-} + H^+ \longrightarrow$

(*ii*) $KMnO_4 \xrightarrow{\text{heated}}$

(*iii*) $Cr_2O_7^{2-} + H_2S + H^+ \square\longrightarrow$

24. Write the name, stereochemistry and magnetic behaviour of the following: 3

(At. nos. Mn = 25, Co = 27, Ni = 28)

(*i*) $K_4[Mn(CN)_6]$

(*ii*) $[Co(NH_3)_5Cl]Cl_2$

(*iii*) $K_2[Ni(CN)_4]$

25. Answer the following: 3

(*i*) Haloalkanes easily dissolve in organic solvents, why?

(*ii*) What is known as a racemic mixture? Give an example.

(*iii*) Of the two bromoderivatives, $C_6H_5CH(CH_3)Br$ and $C_6H_5CH(C_6H_5)Br$, which one is more reactive in S_N1 substitution reaction and why?

26. (a) Explain why an alkylamine is more basic than ammonia. 3

(b) How would you convert

(*i*) Aniline to nitrobenzene

(*ii*) Aniline to iodobenzene?

27. Describe the following giving one example for each: 3

(*i*) Detergents

(*ii*) Food preservatives

(*iii*) Antacids

28. (a) Differentiate between molarity and molality for a solution. How does a change in temperature influence their values?

(b) Calculate the freezing point of an aqueous solution containing 10.50 g of $MgBr_2$ in 200 g of water. (Molar mass of $MgBr_2$ = 184g)
(K_f for water = 1.86 K kg mol^{-1}) 5

OR

(a) Define the terms osmosis and osmotic pressure. Is the osmotic pressure of a solution a colligative property? Explain.

(b) Calculate the boiling point of a solution prepared by adding 15.00 g of NaCl to 250.0 g of water. (K_b for water = 0.512 K kg mol^{-1},
Molar mass of NaCl = 58.44 g) 5

29. (a) Give chemical tests to distinguish between

(*i*) Propanal and propanone,

(*ii*) Benzaldehyde and acetophenone.

(b) How would you obtain

(*i*) But-2-enal from ethanal,

(*ii*) Butanoic acid from butanol,

(*iii*) Benzoic acid from ethylbenzene? 5

OR

(a) Describe the following giving linked chemical equations:

(*i*) Cannizzaro reaction

(*ii*) Decarboxylation

(b) Complete the following chemical equations:

(*i*) 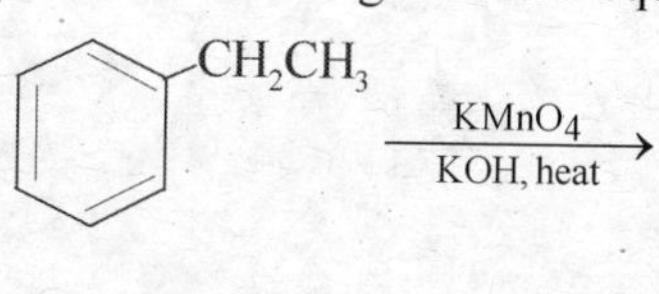

(*ii*) 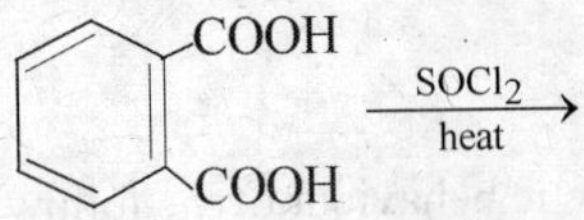

(*iii*) $C_6H_5CONH_2 \xrightarrow[\text{heat}]{H_3O^+}$

30. (a) Explain the following:

(*i*) NF_3 is an exothermic compound whereas NCl_3 is not.

(*ii*) F_2 is most reactive of all the four common halogens.

(b) Complete the following chemical equations:

(*i*) $C + H_2SO_4\,(\text{conc}) \longrightarrow$

(*ii*) $P_4 + NaOH + H_2O \longrightarrow$

(*i*) $\underset{(\text{excess})}{Cl_2 + F_2} \longrightarrow$ 5

OR

(a) Account for the following:

(*i*) The acidic strength decreases in the order $HCl > H_2S > PH_3$

(*ii*) Tendency to form pentahalides decreases down the group in group 15 of the periodic table.

(b) Complete the following chemical equations:

(*i*) $P_4 + SO_2Cl_2 \longrightarrow$

(*ii*) $XeF_2 + H_2O \longrightarrow$

(*iii*) $\underset{(\text{conc})}{I_2 + HNO_3} \longrightarrow$ 5

❑❑❑

Series SOS/2

Code No. 56/2/1

Roll No. | | | | | | | |

Candidates must write the Code on the title page of the answer-book.

- Please check that this question paper contains **12** printed pages.
- Code number given on the right hand side of the question paper should be written on the title page of the answer-book by the candidate.
- Please check that this question paper contains **30** questions.
- **Please write down the Serial Number of the question before attempting it.**
- 15 minutes time has been allotted to read this question paper. The question paper will be distributed at 10.15 a.m. From 10.15 a.m. to 10.30 a.m., the students will read the question paper only and will not write any answer on the answer script during this period.

CHEMISTRY (THEORY)

Time allowed : 3 hours *Maximum Marks : 70*

General Instructions:

(*i*) *All questions are compulsory.*
(*ii*) *Marks for each question are indicated against it.*
(*iii*) *Questions number* **1** *to* **8** *are very short-answer questions and carry* **1** *mark each.*
(*iv*) *Questions number* **9** *to* **18** *are short-answer questions and carry* **2** *marks each.*
(*v*) *Questions number* **19** *to* **27** *are also short-answer questions and carry* **3** *marks each.*
(*vi*) *Questions number* **28** *to* **30** *are long-answer questions and carry* **5** *marks each.*
(*vii*) *Use Log Tables, if necessary. Use of calculators is* **not** *allowed.*

1. What is meant by an 'intrinsic semiconductor'? 1

2. State Henry's law about partial pressure of a gas in a mixture. 1

3. What do you understand by 'denticity of a ligand'? 1

4. Which will react faster in S_N2 displacement, 1-bromopentane or 2-bromopentane, and why? 1

5. Give the IUPAC name of the following compound: 1

$$CH_3\text{—}\underset{\underset{CH_3}{|}}{C}=\underset{\underset{Br}{|}}{C}\text{—}CH_2CH$$

6. Write the structure of the following compound: 3-oxopentanal. 1

7. Why is an alkylamine more basic than ammonia? 1

8. What is meant by a 'broad spectrum antibiotic'? 1

9. Differentiate between molarity and molality of a solution. Explain how molarity value of a solution can be converted into its molality. 2

10. A 0.561 m solution of an unknown electrolyte depresses the freezing point of water by 2.93°C. What is Vant't Hoff factor for this electrolyte? The freezing point depression constant (K_f) for water is 1.86°C kg mol^{-1}. 2

11. Determine the values of equilibrium constant (K_c) and $\Delta G°$ for the following reaction: 2

$$Ni\ (s) + 2Ag^+\ (aq) \rightarrow Ni^{2+}\ (aq) + 2Ag\ (s),\ E° = 1.05\ V$$

12. Define the following terms giving an example of each: 2

(*i*) Emulsion
(*ii*) Hydrosol

13. Explain how the phenomenon of adsorption finds application in the following processes: 2

(*i*) Production of vacuum

(*ii*) Heterogeneous catalysis

14. How would you account for the following: 2

(*i*) The following order of increase in strength of acids:

$PH_3 < H_2S < HCl$.

(*ii*) The oxidising power of oxoacids of chlorine follows the order:

$HClO_4 < HClO_3 < HClO_2 < HClO$

15. Name the following coordination compounds and draw their structures: 2

(*i*) $[CoCl_2(en)_2]Cl$

(*ii*) $[Pt(NH_3)_2Cl(NO_2)]$

(At. no. Co = 27, Pt = 78)

16. Explain what is meant by the following: 2

(*i*) Peptide linkage

(*ii*) Pyranose structure of glucose

17. Name the products of hydrolysis of (i) sucrose and (ii) lactose. 2

OR

Mention three such properties of glucose which cannot be explained by its open chain structure. 2

18. State the reason in each of the following cases: 2

(*i*) Soaps do not work well in hard water.

(*ii*) Synthetic detergents are better than soaps.

19. Aluminium crystallises in a cubic close-packed structure. Radius of the atom in the metal is 125 pm.

(*i*) What is the length of the side of the unit cell?

(*ii*) How many unit cells are there in 1 cm^3 of aluminium? 3

20. A voltaic cell is set up at 25°C with the following half-cells, Al^{3+} (0.001 M) and Ni^{2+} (0.50 M). Write the cell reaction when the cell generates an electric current and determine the cell potential. 3

(Given: $E^\circ_{Ni^{2+}/Ni} = -0.25$ V, $E^\circ_{Al^{3+}/Al} = -1.66$ V)

21. State the principle on which each of the following processes operates: 3

(*i*) Recovery of silver after the silver ore has been leached with NaCN.

(*ii*) Electrolytic refining of a metal.

(*iii*) Vapour phase refining of a metal.

22. Complete the following chemical equations: 3

(*i*) $NaOH + Cl_2 \longrightarrow$
(hot and conc.)

(*ii*) $XeF_4 + O_2F_2 \xrightarrow{143\,K}$

(*iii*) $Br_2 + F_2 \longrightarrow$
(excess)

23. (a) Mention the optimum conditions for the industrial manufacture of ammonia by Haber's process.

(b) Explain the following giving appropriate reasons:

(*i*) Sulphur vapour exhibits paramagnetic behaviour.

(*ii*) Red phosphorus is less reactive than white phosphorus. 3

OR

Draw the structures of the following molecules:

(*i*) NF_3

(*ii*) $H_2S_2O_8$

(*iii*) H_3PO_3

24. Complete the following reaction equations:

(*i*) 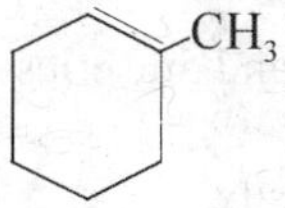 $+ HI \longrightarrow$

(*ii*) 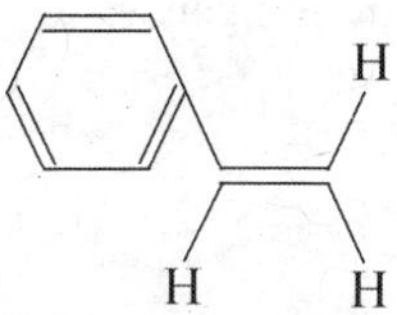 $+ HBR \longrightarrow$

(*iii*) $CH_3CH_2CH = CH_2 + HBr \longrightarrow$

25. Illustrate the following reactions giving a chemical equation in each case: 3

(*i*) Gabriel phthalimide synthesis

(*ii*) A coupling reaction

(*iii*) Hoffmann's bromamide reaction

26. How would you obtain 3

(*i*) Benzoquinone from phenol?

(*ii*) Propan-2-ol from propene?

(*iii*) 2-Methylpropan-2-ol from methyl magnesium bromide?

27. Mention two important uses of each of the following polymers: 3

(*i*) Bakelite

(*ii*) Nylon 6,6

(*iii*) PVC

28. (a) Express clearly what you understand by 'rate expression' and 'rate constant' of a reaction.

(b) Nitrogen pentoxide decomposes according to the equation

$$2N_2O_5(g) \longrightarrow 4NO_2\,(g) + O_2\,(g)$$

This first order reaction was allowed to proceed at 40°C and the data given below were collected:

$[N_2O_5]$(M)	Time (min)
0.400	0.00
0.289	20.00
0.209	40.00
0.151	60.00
0.109	80.00

(*i*) Calculate the rate constant for the reaction. Include units with your answer.

(*ii*) Calculate the initial rate of reaction.

(*iii*) After how many minutes will $[N_2O_5]$ be equal to 0.350 M? 5

OR

(a) Define:

(*i*) Order of a reaction

(*ii*) Elementary step in a reaction

(b) A first order reaction has a rate constant value of 0.00510 min^{-1}. If we begin with 0.10 M concentration of the reactant, how much of the reactant will remain after 3.0 hours? 5

29. (a) Complete the following reactions in an aqueous medium:

(*i*) $MnO_4^- + C_2O_4^{2-} + H^+ \longrightarrow$

(*ii*) $Cr_2O_7^{2-} + H_2S + H^+ \longrightarrow$

(b) How would you account for the following:

(*i*) Metal-metal bonding is more extensive in the 4d and 5d series of transition elements than the 3d series.

(*ii*) Mn (III) undergoes disproportionation reaction easily.

(*iii*) Co (II) is easily oxidised in the presence of strong ligands. 5

OR

(a) Complete the following chemical equations:

(*i*) $Fe^{3+} + I^- \longrightarrow$

(*ii*) $CrO_4^{2-} + H^+ \longrightarrow$

(b) Explain the following:

(*i*) Copper (I) ion is not stable in an aqueous solution.

(*i*) With same (d^4) configuration Cr (II) is reducing whereas Mn (III) is oxidising.

(*ii*) Transition metals in general act as good catalysts. 5

30. (a) Give simple chemical tests to distinguish between the following:

(*i*) Propanal and propanone

(*ii*) Benzaldehyde and acetophenone

(b) How would you obtain

(*i*) But-2-enal from ethanal

(*ii*) Butanoic acid from butanol

(*iii*) Benzoic acid from ethylbenzene 5

OR

(a) Describe the following reactions giving a chemical equation in each case: 5

(*i*) Cannizzaro's reaction

(*ii*) Decarboxylation reaction

(b) Complete the following chemical equations:

(*i*) 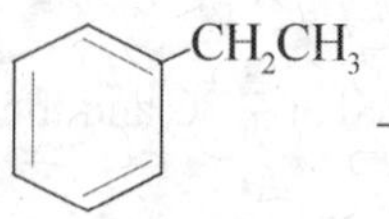 $\xrightarrow[\text{KOH, heat}]{KMnO_4}$

(*ii*) 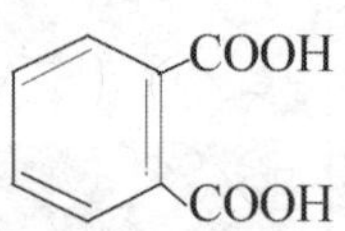 $\xrightarrow[\text{heat}]{SOCl_2}$

(*iii*) $C_6H_5CONH_2 \xrightarrow[\text{heat}]{H_3O^+}$

❑❑❑